INTERNATIONAL DEVELOPMENT IN FOCUS

Managing County Assets and Liabilities in Kenya

Postdevolution Challenges and Responses

MIHALY KOPANYI AND ABDU MUWONGE

Contents

Foreword   *xi*
Acknowledgments   *xiii*
About the Authors   *xv*
Abbreviations   *xvii*

Introduction   **1**

Note   4
References   4

PART I   ASSET MANAGEMENT IN TRANSITION   7

CHAPTER 1   Asset Management in National and County Contexts   9

Introduction   9
Why is good management of assets important?   10
National asset management framework   11
Asset management layers or dimensions   18
Establishing and running an asset management system   34
Devolution and asset management in transition: International
    experiences of relevance to current Kenyan challenges   39
Institutional frameworks and procedures for transfer and
    takeover of responsibilities and assets in CEE   42
References   45

**CHAPTER 2   Asset Management in Transition under Kenya's
Devolution   49**

Introduction   49
Legal and institutional framework for asset management and
    transfer during transition   50
Public financial management in transition   53
Asset-liability management and transfer during the initial
    transition period   54
Steps toward establishing an asset management governance
    framework, system, and asset registers   62
Progress at the national level   62
Progress at the county level   87
The COVID-19 pandemic impacts on cities and
    possible responses   90
Notes   104
References   105

CHAPTER 3   **Managing the Takeover of Disputed Assets and Liabilities: International Experiences and Options for Kenya   109**

Introduction   109
Options for institutional frameworks and procedures for workout of
    disputed assets and liabilities in Kenya   109
Managing financial assets and liabilities: Short assessment of NCC
    compared with a well-managed Australian local government   113
References   118

CHAPTER 4   **Challenges and the Way Forward: Policy Options   119**

Introduction   119
Incomplete tasks and unresolved issues   119
Policy options moving forward: Elements of a medium-term
    program   122
References   123

PART II   **COUNTY CASE STUDIES   125**

CHAPTER 5   **Asset Management Experiences in Seven Counties: Case Studies   127**

Introduction   127
Key features of sample counties   128
Notes   135
References   136

CHAPTER 6   **Nairobi City County   137**

Introduction   137
Revenue and expenditure analysis   138
Asset management   143
Managing financial assets and liabilities   159
Challenges NCC CALC faced during verification and validation of
    inherited assets and liabilities in 2017   164
NCCG achievements in developing a framework and instruments and
    managing county assets   164
Lessons learned   168
Notes   170
References   170

CHAPTER 7   **Kajiado County   173**

Introduction   173
Revenue and expenditure analysis   174
Asset management   177
Lessons learned   187
References   188

CHAPTER 8   **Kakamega County   191**

Introduction   191
Revenue and expenditure analysis   193
Asset management   197
Lessons learned   206
References   207

CHAPTER 9   **Kiambu County   209**

Introduction   209
Revenue and expenditure analysis   211
Asset management   216
Lessons learned   223
References   223

CHAPTER 10 **Machakos County**   **225**

    Introduction   225
    Revenue and expenditure analysis   226
    Asset management   231
    Lessons learned   239
    References   239

CHAPTER 11 **Makueni County**   **243**

    Introduction   243
    Revenue and expenditure analysis   244
    Asset management   249
    Lessons learned   258
    References   259

CHAPTER 12 **Nakuru County**   **261**

    Introduction   261
    Revenue and expenditure analysis   263
    Asset management   268
    Lessons learned   276
    References   276

Appendix A **County Asset Management Policy Model**   **279**

Appendix B **County Asset Management Strategy Model**   **303**

Appendix C **County Asset Management Plan Model**   **311**

Appendix D **County Asset and Liability Management Committee**   **319**

Appendix E **Checklist for Public Water Supply System Operation and Maintenance and Examples of Operation and Maintenance Tasks**   **325**

Appendix F **Key Legislation**   **329**

Boxes

1.1   *International Infrastructure Management Manual*   15
1.2   The Golden Gate Bridge   25
1.3   Information and communication technology asset management solutions   29
1.4   Reconciling legal rights to land and buildings and the balance sheet in the city of Varaždin, Croatia   35
1.5   Examples of asset classification frameworks   36
1.6   The objective of establishing a high-level asset management leadership committee in Nairobi City County, excerpts   38
2.1   Types of audit opinions   56
2.2   Nairobi City County audit report excerpts, 2013   57
2.3   Updated G20 action plan to support the global economy during COVID-19: Landmark commitments   103
6.1   The mandates and competence of the Transition Authority on asset transfer stipulated in the Transition Act   144
6.2   Nairobi City County audit report excerpts, 2013   145
7.1   Kajiado County audit report excerpts, 2013   179
7.2   Kajiado County Asset and Liability Committee methodology   183
8.1   Kakamega County audit report excerpts, 2013   199
8.2   Kakamega County assets and liabilities validation excerpts: Key actions   201

9.1   Kiambu County audit report excerpts, 2013   217
10.1   Machakos County audit report excerpts, 2013   233
10.2   Machakos County losses due to lack of land records,
       audit report excerpts   235
11.1   Makueni County audit report excerpts, 2013   251
11.2   Makueni County Asset and Liability Committee terms of reference and
       timeline, CALC report excerpts   254
12.1   Nakuru County audit report excerpts, 2013   269
12.2   Nakuru County Asset and Liability Committee work methodology   271

Figures

1.1   National asset and liability management governance framework   12
1.2   County asset management logical framework   13
1.3   Asset management plans with growing scope and deepening
       sophistication   16
1.4   Integrated asset management organizational framework in local
       governments   17
1.5   Functional dimensions of asset management in the Kenyan county
       context   18
1.6   Information letter to citizens on a bond issuance vote in Fairfax County,
       Virginia   20
1.7   Composition of 30-year life-cycle costs of the Gates Computer Building and
       a wastewater treatment plant   23
1.8   Comparison of reactive and preventive road maintenance   24
1.9   Concept of reliability-centered maintenance   26
1.10   Main functionality features of the REGIA system in Lithuania   30
1.11   REGIA layer for civil and fire safety   31
1.12   Possible asset hierarchy   33
1.13   Hierarchy and functions of asset registers   33
1.14   Institutional framework and work procedures in Hungary   43
1.15   Institutional framework and work procedures in Poland   44
2.1   Institutional framework for verification and transfer of assets in
       Kenya's devolution   51
2.2   Results of county audits, by audit qualification, fiscal
       years 2013/14–2016/17   56
2.3   Inherited current assets of 47 counties, March 27, 2013   61
2.4   Inherited current liabilities of 47 counties, March 27, 2013   61
2.5   National asset and liability management governance framework   63
2.6   Report on the assets and liabilities of the defunct local authorities,
       March 2013   72
2.7   Planned postponements of capital investments in an emergency   94
2.8   Effects of the COVID-19 pandemic crisis on subnational governments   95
2.9   Prioritized and deprioritized expenses during COVID-19 responses   97
2.10   Possible measures applied to mitigate the short- and medium-term
       negative effects of COVID-19 on subnational governments in OECD
       countries   99
3.1   Nairobi City County and 47 counties combined inherited current
       assets and liabilities, March 2013   110
3.2   Institutional framework and procedures to resolve asset and liability
       disputes and takeover   111
3.3   Composition of financial assets of Nairobi City County, 2017, and
       Australian Capital Territory, 2018   115
3.4   Composition of financial liabilities of Nairobi City County, 2017, and
       Australian Capital Territory, 2018   116
5.1   Main revenues and expenditures of the sample counties, fiscal years
       2013/14–2017/18   129
5.2   Share of labor in current expenditures against international benchmark,
       average, 2013–18   130

5.3   Share of development in total expenditures and share of maintenance in
        current expenditures, average, 2013–18   131
5.4   Development expenditures and debt service, totals, 2013–18   131
6.1   Nairobi City County OSR, fiscal years 2013/14–2017/18   141
6.2   Nairobi City County cumulative development expenditures, fiscal years
        2013/14–2015/16   143
6.3   Nairobi City County and 47 counties combined inherited current asset and
        liabilities, March 2013   148
6.4   Nairobi City County components of current assets and liabilities,
        March 2013   156
6.5   Composition of financial assets of Nairobi City County, 2017, and
        Australian Capital Territory, 2018   160
6.6   Composition of financial liabilities of Nairobi City County, 2017, and
        Australian Capital Territory, 2018   162
6.7   Nairobi City County logical framework for mass valuation of land   166
7.1   Kajiado County development expenditures, fiscal year 2016/17   178
8.1   Kakamega County OSR, fiscal years 2014/15–2017/18   195
8.2   Kakamega County cumulative development expenditures, fiscal years
        2013/14–2015/16   197
9.1   Kiambu County OSR, fiscal years 2014/15–2017/18   213
9.2   Kiambu County cumulative development expenditures, fiscal years
        2013/14–2015/16   215
10.1   Machakos County OSR, fiscal years 2014/15–2017/18   228
10.2   Machakos County cumulative development expenditures,
        fiscal years 2013/14–2016/17   231
11.1   Makueni County OSR, fiscal years 2014/15–2017/18   246
11.2   Makueni County Project Management System dashboard, 2019   248
11.3   Makueni County development expenditures, fiscal years
        2013/14–2017/18   249
12.1   Nakuru County OSR, fiscal years 2013/14–2017/18   265
12.2   Nakuru County cumulative development expenditures, fiscal years
        2013/14–2015/16   267
A.1   Asset and liability management reporting framework in Nairobi
        City County   299
B.1   Integrated asset management as a conduit across sectors and functions:
        Vision for the future   306
B.2   Initial asset management framework in Nairobi City County   307
C.1   Asset management plans with growing scope and deepening
        sophistication   312
C.2   Old asset management framework or practices in Nairobi City County   313
C.3   New asset management framework option in Nairobi City County   313
C.4   Asset management information system option   316
D.1   Governance framework for asset management   320

Maps

6.1   Nairobi City County   138
7.1   Kajiado County   174
8.1   Kakamega County   192
9.1   Kiambu County   210
10.1   Machakos County   226
11.1   Makueni County   244
12.1   Nakuru County   262

Photos

1.1   Gates Computer Building, where Google began   22
B1.2.1 The Golden Gate Bridge   25

Tables

1.1   Share of various fixed assets in local governments' balance sheets, various fiscal years   10

1.2   Summary of frameworks and procedures for transferring assets and liabilities in CEE countries   41

1.3   Comparison of frameworks and practices for transferring assets and liabilities, CEE countries and Kenya   45

2.1   The Kenya Transition Authority's asset management functions and responsibilities during transition   52

2.2   Public financial management during transition (excerpts from PFM Transition Act 2013)   53

2.3   Maintaining and transferring public records during transition   54

2.4   Inherited land parcels, Kenya counties total, March 27, 2013   74

2.5   Summary of inherited buildings, Kenya counties total, March 27, 2013   76

2.6   Summary of inherited motor vehicles, Kenya counties total, March 27, 2013   79

2.7   Summary of inherited current assets of Kenya's 47 counties, March 27, 2013   80

2.8   Inherited liabilities, Kenya counties total, 2013 and 2018   83

3.1   Nairobi City County current assets, March 2013   112

6.1   Nairobi City County revenues, fiscal years 2013/14–2017/18   139

6.2   Nairobi City County OSR, fiscal years 2013/14–2017/18   140

6.3   Nairobi City County expenditures, fiscal years 2013/14–2017/18   142

6.4   Nairobi City County asset management entities and their functions   147

6.5   Nairobi City County land and buildings from the identification, verification, and validation process   151

6.6   Nairobi City County fixed asset register summary, June 30, 2018   152

6.7   Nairobi City County inherited projects, 2013   153

6.8   Nairobi City County summary of inherited liabilities, 2013 and 2018   153

6.9   Nairobi City County net bank debts, November 2017, based on 2013 values   154

6.10   Nairobi City County current assets, March 2013   156

7.1   Kajiado County revenues, fiscal years 2013/14–2017/18   175

7.2   Kajiado County expenditures, fiscal years 2013/14–2017/18   176

7.3   Kajiado County asset management entities and their functions   182

7.4   Kajiado County land and buildings, by DLAs, after verification, 2017   184

7.5   Kajiado County fixed asset register summary, June 30, 2018   185

7.6   Kajiado County summary of inherited liabilities, 2013 and 2017   186

7.7   Kajiado County summary of inherited current assets, March 2013   186

8.1   Kakamega County revenues, fiscal years 2013/14–2017/18   193

8.2   Kakamega County OSR, fiscal years 2013/14–2017/18   194

8.3   Kakamega County expenditures, fiscal years 2013/14–2017/18   196

8.4   Kakamega County asset management entities and their functions   200

8.5   Kakamega County summary of inherited land and buildings   202

8.6   Kakamega County fixed asset register summary, June 30, 2018   204

8.7   Kakamega County summary of inherited current assets, by DLAs, 2013   204

8.8   Kakamega County summary of inherited liabilities, 2013 and 2017   205

9.1   Kiambu County revenues, fiscal years 2013/14–2017/18   212

9.2   Kiambu County OSR, fiscal years 2013/14–2017/18   213

9.3   Kiambu County expenditures, fiscal years 2013/14–2017/18   214

9.4   Kiambu County key financial ratios, fiscal years 2013/14–2017/18   215

9.5   Kiambu County asset management entities and their functions   218

9.6   Kiambu County summary of land and buildings from the identification, verification, and validation process, 2013   220

9.7   Kiambu County fixed asset register summary, June 30, 2018   221

9.8   Kiambu County summary of inherited current assets, March 2013   221

9.9   Kiambu County summary of inherited liabilities, 2013 and 2017   222

10.1   Machakos County revenues, fiscal years 2013/14–2017/18   227

10.2   Machakos County OSR, fiscal years 2013/14–2017/18   229
10.3   Machakos County expenditures, fiscal years 2013/14–2017/18   230
10.4   Machakos County asset management entities and their functions   236
10.5   Machakos County fixed asset register summary, June 30, 2018   237
10.6   Machakos County summary of inherited current assets,
        March 27, 2013   238
10.7   Machakos County summary of inherited liabilities, 2013 and 2017   238
11.1   Makueni County revenues, fiscal years 2013/14–2017/18   245
11.2   Makueni County OSR, fiscal years 2013/14–2017/18   246
11.3   Makueni County expenditures, fiscal years 2013/14–2017/18   247
11.4   Makueni County asset management entities and their functions   252
11.5   Makueni County land and buildings, March 2013   255
11.6   Makueni County fixed asset register summary, June 30, 2018   256
11.7   Makueni County summary of inherited current assets, March 2013   256
11.8   Makueni County summary of inherited liabilities, March 2013   256
12.1   Nakuru County revenues, fiscal years 2013/14–2017/18   263
12.2   Nakuru County OSR, fiscal years 2013/14–2017/18   264
12.3   Nakuru County expenditures, fiscal years 2013/14–2017/18   266
12.4   Nakuru County asset management entities and their functions   270
12.5   Nakuru County summary of verified land and buildings,
        by DLAs, 2017   272
12.6   Nakuru County fixed asset register summary, June 30, 2018   274
12.7   Nakuru County summary of inherited current assets, by DLAs,
        March 2013   274
12.8   Nakuru County summary of inherited liabilities, 2013 and 2017   275
B.1   Strategic actions and responsibilities in developing the asset management
        system for Nairobi City County   308
B.2   Development and rehabilitation plans by sectors: Long-term
        preliminary list form   309
C.1   Asset management action plan indicative template   315

Foreword

Managing County Assets and Liabilities in Kenya: Postdevolution Challenges and Responses provides a coherent and innovative summary of asset management issues in the context of local governments. It describes the pragmatic details of asset management frameworks, systems, and procedures, and it explains how they represent a sharp departure from a simplified accounting-oriented approach to asset management. It provides examples that clearly demonstrate that the ultimate objective of asset management is to deliver better services to citizens. This book also emphasizes the fact that assets and liabilities are transient forms of each other and thus should be managed together in a consistent manner. In line with this approach, it stresses that assets should be managed strategically and that local governments should focus particularly on those assets with the greatest strategic importance—land, buildings, plants, and infrastructure networks. Going beyond analysis, the book provides models of, and detailed guidance on, ways to establish asset management systems by the use of asset registers and by the verification and valuation of assets. Finally, it promotes the asset life-cycle principle and a recommended methodology for managing fixed assets.

The importance of good asset management cannot be overstated. Public entities around the world possess an enormous volume of assets and wealth: the land, buildings, historic sites, parks, forests, and networks of infrastructure that form the material base of public services and influence the quality of life for citizens. Public assets form the largest part of the national wealth in many countries; for local governments, they are often the single largest body of wealth in the jurisdiction.

International experience has shown that good management of assets and liabilities can be a vital catalyst for accelerating urban development, as well as for expanding assets and responding effectively to an increase in demand for public services from a rapidly growing population. *Managing County Assets and Liabilities in Kenya* emphasizes the importance of local governments approaching asset management in the broadest possible sense, by considering strategic issues along with financial and technical ones and avoiding the common mistake of seeing asset management as merely an accounting and reporting issue.

Kenya began a big-bang devolution in March 2013, when it dissolved more than 1,500 former local entities and formed 47 counties with newly elected local governments. This book provides a detailed institutional and financial analysis of the transition of assets and liabilities from the now defunct Kenyan entities to the new local government entities. Lessons drawn from this analysis can be valuable throughout Africa and the entire developing world.

Although much has been achieved in Kenya, the process of the transfer and takeover of assets and liabilities is incomplete nine years into devolution. The detailed analysis provided in *Managing County Assets and Liabilities in Kenya* underscores the urgency of moving this process forward, identifies the critical steps that need to be taken, and it explains the options available for doing so. This book demonstrates, through discussion of the concrete steps that can and should be taken, that modern asset and liability management is not only an urgent need but is also feasible in Kenya and in other low- and middle-income countries.

Managing County Assets and Liabilities in Kenya has grown out of the extensive analytic and advisory work that was completed under the Kenya Accountable Devolution Program of the World Bank. Many of the recommendations given in that process have been implemented, such as moving from a centralized to a decentralized asset transfer modality and managing assets and liabilities together. This advisory work has not only helped Kenyan stakeholders but also brought asset management into high policy priorities.

We are confident that this work will convey to Kenyan policy makers and stakeholders around the world the importance of sound asset management and the urgency of moving this agenda forward.

Keith H. Hansen
Country Director
Rwanda, Kenya, Somalia, and Uganda
The World Bank

Sameh Wahba
Regional Director,
Europe and Central Asia
and former Global Director,
Urban and Territorial Development,
Disaster Risk Management, and Resilience
The World Bank

Acknowledgments

The authors are extremely grateful for the support and cooperation of the partner entities of the Kenya national and county governments, including the Intergovernmental Relations Technical Committee, especially Professor Karega Mutahi, former Chairman, Dr. Billow Khalid, former Member, and Kithinji Kiragu, current Chairman; the Office of the Auditor General, especially Mr. Edward Ouko, former Auditor General; and the National Assets and Liabilities Management Department in the National Treasury, especially Ms. Beatrice Gathirwa, Director, and her team. This book also greatly benefitted from the dedication of the officers of Nairobi City County, especially Mr. Lawrence Mwangi, World Bank Coordinator; Mr. David Mwaura, Director; and Mr. George Mwariri, Deputy Director, Asset Management; Mr. Isaac Nyoike, Chief Valuer; and Ms. Martha Wambugu, Debt Management Office. The authors extend special thanks to the governors and staff of the surveyed counties, who have discussed the findings of this study with us and provided important updates and feedback: former Governor Kivutha Kibwana (Makueni County), former Governor Lee Kinyanjui (Nakuru County), late Governor Dr. Joyce Laboso (Bomet County), Governor Joseph Ole Lenku (Kajiado County), former Governor Alfred Mutua (Machakos County), former Governor James Nyoro (Kiambu County), and former Governor Wycliffe Oparanya (Kakamega County, and Chair, Council of Governors).

The authors are grateful for the financial support provided under the Kenya Accountable Devolution Program (KADP) multidonor trust fund and the Multidonor Trust Fund for Sustainable Urban Development that financed the technical assistance to county governments between 2016 and 2020. This book would not have been possible without the knowledge and committed works of Ms. Olga Kaganova, expert on managing public assets, who played an important role as a team member in the conceptualization and launch of this analytic and advisory work in Kenya in 2016.

The authors are grateful to the following peer reviewers of the original manuscript: Alessandra Campanaro, Operations Adviser, World Bank; Lourdes German, Assistant Professor, Boston College, US; Edward Ouko, former Auditor General, Government of Kenya; and Roland White, Lead Urban Specialist and Global Lead, World Bank. The team is grateful for the review and clearance of the original manuscript by Chorching Goh, Adviser, World Bank, and Albert G. Zeufack, former Chief Economist, Africa Western and Central Region, and Country Director for Angola, Burundi, the Democratic Republic of the Congo, and São Tomé and Príncipe, World Bank.

The authors are thankful for the guidance and support received from our colleagues at the World Bank: Meskerem Brhane, Practice Manager–Urban; Helene Carlsson Rex, Practice Manager–Social Sustainability and Inclusion; Peter D. Ellis, Practice Manager–Urban; Keith H. Hansen, Country Director for Kenya, Rwanda, Somalia, and Uganda; Sheila W. Kamunyori, Senior Urban Development Specialist; Muratha Kinuthia, Senior Social Development Specialist; Robin Mearns, Practice Manager–Social; Camille Lampart Nuamah, Operations Manager–Kenya Country Management Unit; Christine Anyango Owuor, Senior Public Sector Specialist and Task Manager of the KADP component of public financial management; Nicola Smithers, Practice Manager–Governance; Bernice K. Van Bronkhorst, Global Director–Urban; Sameh Wahba, Regional Director for Europe and Central Asia; and Timothy Stephen Williamson, Senior Governance and Public Sector Specialist. The authors extend profound appreciation to Pierre Laporte, Country Director for Ghana, Liberia, and Sierra Leone for supporting the successful completion of this project. Nicodemus Mbwika, Council of Governors; and Miriam Omolo, Consultant, played a major role in completing field interviews and data collection from the sample county governments. Elizabeth Wairimu Karuoya, Operations Analyst, and Angelina Darini Musera, Senior Program Assistant, provided immeasurable logistical support. The authors are grateful to Janice Tuten, who managed the production of this publication, the World Bank Cartography team, and the entire publisher's team for their patience, commitment, and exceptionally professional work.

About the Authors

Mihaly Kopanyi has more than 30 years of World Bank experience in hundreds of cities in 30 countries on four continents. His key areas of expertise include public financial management, asset management, own-revenues, and property taxation. Kopanyi led the World Bank's Municipal Finance Thematic Group for more than a decade until his retirement. He is a distinguished municipal finance adviser to project teams in urban lending projects and capacity-building programs, with a special focus on assessing the financial health of local governments and defining reform programs. He has written or edited numerous books and chapters, as well as dozens of papers, for the World Bank and the London School of Economics. Major volumes he has coauthored for the World Bank include *Better Cities, Better World: A Handbook on Local Governments Self-Assessments* (2019), *Municipal Finance Self-Assessment Toolkit* (2019), *Municipal Finances: A Learning Program for Local Governments* (2015), and *Municipal Finances: A Handbook for Local Governments* (2014). Kopanyi holds a PhD in economics from the Hungarian Academy of Sciences and a PhD in logistics and an MA in economics from Karl Marx University of Economic Sciences, Budapest (Hungary).

Abdu Muwonge, a Ugandan national, is the World Bank's Country Manager in Sierra Leone. He joined the World Bank in 2006 as a Young Professional. Muwonge served as a Senior Urban Specialist at the World Bank in Kenya, where he led and coordinated the urban and devolution work program. Earlier, he had served as Acting Program Leader for Sustainable Development, covering Kenya, Rwanda, Somalia, and Uganda. Before joining the World Bank's Africa Region, he served in the South Asia Region, where he led and supported programs on local government and water and sanitation in Bangladesh, India, Nepal, Pakistan, and Sri Lanka. He worked in the Eastern and Central Asia Region in the Human Development Economics Unit, where he contributed to the Moldova, Serbia, and Ukraine work program. Before joining the World Bank, Muwonge worked as a Research Fellow at the Economic Policy Research Centre in Uganda and taught undergraduate economics and statistics at Makerere University and Mbarara University of Science and Technology in Uganda. He is the coauthor of *Making Devolution Work for Service Delivery in Kenya* (2022) and "Chapter 1,

Intergovernmental Finances in a Decentralized World" in *Municipal Finances: A Handbook for Local Governments* (2014). Muwonge holds PhD and MA degrees in economics (public finance) from Georgia State University (US), an MA in economics from the University of Dar es Salaam (Tanzania), and a BSc in economics and statistics from Makerere University (Uganda).

Abbreviations

ACT	Australian Capital Territory
ALC	Asset and Liability Management Committee
ALM	asset and liability management
ALSC	Asset and Liability Supreme Committee
ALWC	Asset and Liability Workout Committee
AM	asset management
AMCF	Asset Movement Capture Form
AMDR	Asset Management Directorate
CALC	County Asset and Liability Committee
CBIRR	County Governments Budget Implementation Review Report
CCN	City Council of Nairobi
CECM	county executive committee member
CEE	Central and Eastern Europe
CFO	chief financial officer
CIDP	County Integrated Development Plan
CILOR	compensation in lieu of rates
CIP	capital improvement planning
CWC	County Workout Committee
DIR	departmental inventory register
DLA	defunct local authority
DMO	Debt Management Office
DoD	Department of Defense
GIS	geographic information system
GPS	global positioning system
IBEC	Intergovernmental Budget and Economic Council
ICT	information and communication technology
ICTAM	information technology representations of asset management
IFMIS	integrated financial management information system
IFRS	International Financial Reporting Standards
IGRTC	Intergovernmental Relations Technical Committee
IPSAS	International Public Sector Accounting Standards
ISO	International Organization for Standardization
K Sh	Kenya shilling

KADP	Kenya Accountable Devolution Program (World Bank)
KPA	key performance area
LAIFOMS	Local Authorities Integrated Financial Operations Management System
LAPFUND	Local Authorities Providence Fund
LAPTRUST	Local Authorities Pension Trust of National Social Security Fund
LCAM	life-cycle asset management
LCC	life-cycle costs
LR	land registration
MoF	Ministry of Finance
MTDF	medium-term development framework or planning
NALM	National Assets and Liabilities Management (Department in the National Treasury)
NCC	Nairobi City County
NCCG	Nairobi City County Government
NCWSC	Nairobi City Water and Sewerage Company
O&M	operation and maintenance
OAG	Office of the Auditor General
OECD	Organisation for Economic Co-operation and Development
OSR	own-source revenue
PDM	Public Debt Management (Directorate in the National Treasury)
PFM	public finance management
PPAD	Public Procurement and Asset Disposal (Act)
PPE	property, plant, and equipment
PPP	public-private partnership
PUC	public utility company
R&M	repair and maintenance
RBM	risk-based preventive maintenance
SGAM	strategic asset management
SP	Strategic Plan (of NCC)
TA	Transition Authority
TDG	Transition to Devolved Government (Act)
ToR	terms of reference
UAC	Urban Areas and Cities (Act)
WASREB	Water Services Regulatory Board

Introduction

Public entities possess an enormous volume of assets and wealth: land, buildings, historic sites, parks, forests, and infrastructure networks that form the material base of public services and influence citizens' quality of life. Public assets form the largest part of the national wealth in many countries (Bolva et al. 2013). Likewise, local governments often possess the single largest body of wealth in their jurisdiction. Mayors in developing countries are proud and happy to cut the ribbon when opening a community center, shopping center, road, or school, but they subsequently pay less attention to ensuring sustainable cost-efficient utilization of assets and systematic expansion of the city's wealth. Asset management is the process of making and applying decisions about operating, maintaining, refurbishing, acquiring, developing, or disposing of assets with the ultimate objective of providing public services adequately and sustainably.

This book is a result of a detailed analysis of the state of Kenya's asset management that underscores, with specific examples, the reality that modern asset and liability management is not only an urgent need but also possible in Kenya and in many developing countries. The book provides models and detailed guidance to establish asset management systems, policies, and procedures, including setting up asset registers and applying life-cycle-based asset operation and maintenance in Kenyan county governments (local governments) and likewise in cities across the developing world. The book further shows that good asset management is a vital catalyst for accelerating city development and expanding assets and services in response to the fast-growing populations' demand for public services (Detter and Fölster 2015, 2018). The book also emphasizes that cities should approach assets in the broadest possible sense, from strategy through financial to technical tasks, and avoid the common mistake of seeing asset management as a mere accounting issue.

Mayors in the developing world often follow developed cities and favor applying new instruments, such as geographic information system maps for spatial planning, modern websites, smart cities, metrorail systems, sports stadiums, or integrated financial management information systems. In the meantime, their cities often use obsolete asset management practices (Kaganova and Telgarsky 2018), such as using manual records or lacking asset registers altogether; lacking asset management systems, principles, and procedures; ignoring liabilities; and performing only fractions of due asset management. These shortcomings degrade assets and undermine accountability of city officers and political leaders, and they also allow corruption. Asset issues have been part of managerial, legal, and political debates during transitions of the intergovernmental systems in numerous countries since the 1990s (for example, in Eastern Europe) and recently in Kenya (Kaganova and Nayyar-Stone 2000; Peteri 2003).

There is a growing gap between the private and public sectors on asset management, since private enterprises increasingly use computerized asset management systems, some certified by the International Organization for Standardization, for their entire firm, with subsystems and off-the-shelf software tailored to their specific assets: fleet management, building operation and maintenance, water management, production management, and supply chain management. In contrast, some city leaders in the developing world have hesitated to pursue modern asset management practices, in part because of the large cultural shift entailed, the immense task of verifying each asset their cities possess, or because they simply lack both time and money. Nevertheless, substandard asset management generates enormous losses, some far greater than the resources required to finance the establishment of modern reliable asset management systems, policies, and procedures.

The COVID-19 global pandemic has had unprecedented negative impacts on cities and citizens' livelihood, as well as on economic performance, health, education, and all sorts of life factors, and challenged the management and financial capacities of national and local governments alike. Preliminary data show that local governments faced 10–25 percent revenue shortfalls, and meanwhile spent 10–15 percent more than planned on current expenses such as health, education, sanitation, and social assistance (Lall and Wahba 2020). In turn, many radically cut expenditures on development, repair, and maintenance. The negative financial impacts will require several years to correct, especially because the national governments also face shortages of finances, and thus will have moderate capacities to support financial recovery of local governments. The longer the crisis, the deeper the impacts that will occur on financial capacities, health, and investments of local governments. Therefore, the assets and recovery investments should be approached strategically (IMF 2020). Without recognizing and utilizing the strategic role of assets, Kenyan counties may accumulate debts, and some may be forced into quick sales or confiscation of their assets without supporting recovery. Experts predict a strong economic boom after the crisis ends, albeit when and how it will happen is still to be seen. Assets will undoubtedly play a strategic role in this process. First, the delayed developments and repairs need corrections; second, and more important, assets can be used strategically to fund financial and economic recovery of municipalities (Kaganova 2020).

Kenya started a big-bang devolution in March 2013 when it dissolved more than 1,500 former local entities and formed 47 counties with elected local governments. The legislative framework of the well-designed devolution provided a solid basis for enhanced and sustainable operation of the counties (TDG Act 2012; UAC Act 2011) with a clear and standard allocation of functions (expenditure assignment) and reliable revenue assignment with expanded financial transfers from national to local governments. The National Treasury has subsequently drafted national policy for asset and liability management and numerous guidelines for subnational entities. In contrast, the late and incomplete transfer of assets to the new counties from the defunct local entities and from national entities has become a drawback of Kenya's devolution and created substantial material losses. This book addresses the asset management issues that emerged during Kenya's devolution after 2013, with a special focus on postdevolution challenges and responses.

Kenya has achieved significant results on the bumpy road of devolution and the transfer of assets and liabilities to the devolved county governments (local governments). This challenging program, however, is still incomplete; counties are midway toward establishing systems and procedures, creating reliable asset and liability registers, verifying and valuing assets, and starting to use assets strategically to expand local services, especially water, road, and social infrastructure, and comply with the law (PFM 2012). The transfers of assets from defunct local entities have been completed, but transfers of assets and liabilities from national government entities has not even started after nine years in transition. This book addresses key issues, explores options for improvement, and advises specific corrective measures in short-, medium-, and long-term perspectives, since establishing asset and liability management systems from scratch requires long years to complete, and should be started urgently.

This book is a result of detailed analytic and advisory work that a World Bank team has provided for more than three years.[1] The government of Kenya requested this assistance in 2016 when slow progress and shortcomings on asset transfers and asset management at the national and county levels became apparent. The advisory team has worked intensively with national entities on streamlining the national legal and institutional framework and building capacity. Several achievements have emerged from this advisory work, for instance, the switch from centralized handover to a decentralized takeover of assets and the Legal Notice nos. 858 and 2701 (2017) that govern this change. This book complements the *Managing Infrastructure Assets for Sustainable Development* handbook (UN 2021) that provides rich technical details on managing fixed assets; this book expands knowledge by showing interlinks across various forms of assets and liabilities, emphasizes the financial aspects of asset management, and exposes the challenges that Kenyan entities face in institutionalizing asset management.

Main partner entities include the Intergovernmental Relations Technical Committee, the Office of the Auditor General, and the National Assets and Liabilities Management Department in the National Treasury. The team also occasionally consulted several ministries. It also worked intensively with the Nairobi City County Government to establish an asset management framework; draft policies, strategies, and plans; and assess the state of asset management, including addressing specific issues during the takeover of assets and liabilities. Results in Nairobi offer lessons and templates for the other 46 Kenyan counties. The team also consulted with and collected data and information from six other counties, advised corrective measures when requested, and held several training events for local government officers of Nairobi and a dozen counties.

The book consists of two parts. Part I is a synthesis report that summarizes high-level issues Kenya national and county governments face on asset management and compares Kenyan to international practices. We start with a detailed analysis of the legislative and institutional framework designed to facilitate devolution, asset transition, and establishment of an asset management system at the national and local levels. We then summarize challenges, achievements, and lessons in the three main phases of transition to devolved local governments. We synthetize lessons and detailed results in county case studies in part II, which consists of a comparative analysis of the seven counties' performance, followed by seven county case studies with detailed illustrative numbers and short explanations of events, progress, shortcomings, and advice moving forward. These case studies provide critical insights and ground reality of the county situation.

The book also includes six important appendixes that provide readers with examples of key asset and liability management documents without aiming to be prescriptive. Appendixes include A, "County Asset Management Policy Model," which presents a possible policy and uses lessons from a draft asset management policy of Nairobi City County (NCC) and a draft national asset and liability management policy, prepared under the National Assets and Liabilities Management Department in the National Treasury; B, "County Asset Management Strategy Model," which presents an asset management strategy drafted for NCC; C, "County Asset Management Plan," also Model drafted for NCC; D, "County Asset and Liability Management Advisory Committee," a model terms of reference; E, "Checklist for Public Water Supply System Operation and Maintenance and Examples of Operation and Maintenance Tasks," which follows a checklist from the United States Environmental Protection Agency; and F, "Key Legislation," a comprehensive list of Kenyan legislation discussed in this book. Counties may use these examples as guiding templates when drafting their respective county documents or regulations with changes to fit to local circumstances.

NOTE

1. Abdu Muwonge, task manager; Christine Ouwoyo, co–task team leader; Olga Kaganova and Mihaly Kopanyi, international consultants; and Miriam Omolo, local consultant.

REFERENCES

Bolva, Elva, Robert Dippelsman, Kara Rideout, and Andrea Schaechter. 2013. "Another Look at Governments' Balance Sheets: The Role of Nonfinancial Assets," IMF Working Paper WP/13/95. International Monetary Fund, Washington, DC.

Detter, D., and S. Fölster. 2015. *The Public Wealth of Nations—How Management of Public Assets Can Boost Economic Growth.* London: Palgrave Macmillan.

Detter, D., and S. Fölster. 2018. "Unlocking Public Wealth: Governments Could Do a Better Job Managing Their Assets." *Finance and Development*, International Monetary Fund: March 2018, pp 44–48. https://www.imf.org/Publications/fandd/issues/2018/03/detter.

IMF (International Monetary Fund). 2020. "Policies for the Recovery." *Fiscal Monitor*, October 2020. Washington, DC: IMF.

Kaganova, O. 2020. "How American Cities Can Benefit from 'Land Value Capture' Instruments in the Time of COVID-19 and Beyond." *Real Estate Issues* 44 (18). https://cre.org/real-estate-issues/how-american-cities-can-benefit-from-land-value-capture-instruments-in-the-time-of-covid-19-and-beyond/.

Kaganova, O., and R. Nayyar-Stone. 2000. "Municipal Real Property Asset Management: An Overview of World Experience, Trends and Financial Implications." *Journal of Real Estate Portfolio Management* 6 (4) 308–26. https://doi.org/10.1080/10835547.2000.12089624.

Kaganova, O., and J. Telgarsky. 2018. "Management of Capital Assets by Local Governments: An Assessment and Benchmarking Survey." *International Journal of Strategic Property Management* 22 (2): 143–156. doi:10.3846/ijspm.2018.445.

Lall, S., and S. Wahba. 2020. "No Urban Myth: Building Inclusive and Sustainable Cities in the Pandemic Recovery." World Bank, Washington, DC. https://www.worldbank.org/en/news /immersive-story/2020/06/18/no-urban-myth-building-inclusive-and-sustainable-cities -in-the-pandemic-recovery.

Notice 858. 2017. Gazette Notice no. 858, January 8, 2017: Intergovernmental Relations Act no. 2 of 2012. https://gazettes.africa/gazettes/ke-government-gazette-dated-2017-01-27-no-13.

Notice 2701. 2017. Gazette Notice no. 2701, March 24, 2017: Intergovernmental Relations Act no. 2 of 2012. https://gazettes.africa/archive/ke/2017/ke-government-gazette-dated-2017 -03-24-no-37.pdf.

Peteri, G. 2003. *From Usage to Ownership—Transfer of Public Property to Local Governments in Central Europe.* Budapest: Local Government and Public Service Initiative, Open Society Institute.

PFM. 2012. Public Finance Management Act, no. 18 of 2012. https://www.pcf.go.ke/index .php/public-financial-management-act.

TDG. 2012. Transition to Devolved Government Act, no. 1 of 2012, enacted March 9, 2012. http:// www.parliament.go.ke/sites/default/files/2017-05/TransitiontoDevolvedGovernmentAct No1of2012.pdf.

UAC. 2011. Urban Areas and Cities Act, no. 13 of 2011. http://www.parliament.go.ke/sites /default/files/2017-05/UrbanAreasandCitiesAct_No13of2011.pdf.

UN (United Nations). 2021. *Managing Infrastructure Assets for Sustainable Development: A Handbook for Local and National Governments.* New York, United Nations. https://www .un-ilibrary.org/content/books/9789210051880.

Asset Management in Transition

1 Asset Management in National and County Contexts

INTRODUCTION

Asset management (AM) is a process by which public entities make and apply decisions about acquiring, developing, operating, maintaining, refurbishing, or disposing of assets cost effectively. The ultimate objective is to provide public services adequately and sustainably. The *asset management framework* is a system of rules, procedures, and entities that informs and performs the tasks of AM. Among all public functions, AM has some of the most direct effects on citizens' quality of life, although the effects are more recognizable when it is done poorly. For instance, underfunded and mismanaged water supply systems—not uncommon in Asia and Africa—provide water intermittently and of poor quality. The latter results in waterborne diseases, which may create costs high above the amount that would be required to provide purified water sustainably.

Central governments bear general responsibility for the framework and management of public assets in their countries. This overall responsibility covers fixed (or nonfinancial) assets as well as current financial assets and liabilities. In addition, it may have responsibility for assets under the control of national, subnational, or local government entities. Financial and nonfinancial assets are transient forms of each other, and some assets are associated with liabilities that decrease their value. Thus, central government responsibility entails maintaining critical links among various forms of assets and adjacent liabilities and ensuring proper management of liabilities by using assets to serve them. Central governments also act as the responsible entity on public financial liabilities vis-à-vis foreign claimants, that is, they service due debts on behalf of national public entities that have failed debt service.

Central governments approach nationwide AM functions by allocating AM mandates and responsibilities to various public entities. The central government hosts and oversees the totality of public assets in portfolio modality; it does not deal with the specifics of assets. It decides to allocate central resources for development of assets here or there or decides to transfer assets across entities along policy priorities. Asset transfers to county governments under Kenya's devolution process is a prime example of the high-level mandate of the national government.

Good asset and liability management at the county level is important for both central and county governments (NALAS 2014; UN 2021). From a central government perspective, making county governments responsible for local services and transferring to them the fixed assets needed to provide those services is a cornerstone of successful devolution. From a county perspective, properly managing assets and corresponding liabilities is vital to maximize benefits, expand services, and maintain or increase the wealth of the county.

WHY IS GOOD MANAGEMENT OF ASSETS IMPORTANT?

Good AM is important for county governments for several interrelated reasons, including service delivery, urban development, wealth and income, budgeting, transparency and democracy, and management of liabilities.

Service delivery. Fixed assets are used for delivery of local services, so the scope, extent, and quality of public services often depend on the existence and physical condition of the related fixed assets. For example, if the road network is insufficient, local producers face difficulties and extra costs in delivering products to markets. If roads are in disrepair, travelers risk injuries. If water service drops to a few hours per day due to poor maintenance, public health and sanitation suffer. If a school building is overcrowded or in poor condition, students' ability to learn is reduced. The availability of fixed assets and the quality of their management define both the quality of life of citizens and the power of the local economy (Kaganova and Kopanyi 2016).

Urban development. Land owned or controlled by municipalities is a crucial resource for local governments for further urban development (Detter and Fölster 2015). County governments can leverage their land to provide space for new urban infrastructure and services (roads, solid waste facilities, and so forth) or social infrastructure (schools, health, cultural, sport facilities, and the like). Or they could sell surplus land to generate revenue for developing vital fixed assets (Detter and Fölster 2018; Kaganova 2020).

Wealth and income. Immovable properties (land, buildings, infrastructure facilities, and networks) are typically the most valuable assets owned by municipalities, cities, or counties (table 1.1). Anecdotal evidence suggests that

TABLE 1.1 Share of various fixed assets in local governments' balance sheets, various fiscal years

ASSET TYPE	WARSAW, POLAND, 2008	ASSET TYPE	LEEDS, UK, 2010/11	ASSET TYPE[a]	CAPE TOWN, SOUTH AFRICA, 2014/15
Asset total (fixed plus financial)	100%	Assets total (fixed plus financial)	100%	Assets total (fixed plus financial)	100%
Capital assets	94%	Capital assets	95%	Capital assets	78%
Land and easements	80%	Council dwellings	39%	Housing rental stock	3%
Building, improvements	8%	Land and other buildings	41%	Land, buildings, investments	5%
Infrastructure	8%	Infrastructure	19%	Infrastructure	38%
Equipment	—	Vehicles, plant, equipment	4%	Other	9%
	n.a.	Community assets	1%	Community assets	13%

Source: Kaganova and Kopanyi 2016.
Note: — = not available; n.a. = not applicable.
a. For Cape Town, some asset types from the balance sheet were grouped together for comparability with other examples.

some Kenyan counties may be rich in assets, particularly land (see Nairobi land assets in the Nairobi City County case study, chapter 6), but we could not include in this list a city or county from Kenya, because such value figures do not exist—counties have not yet assessed or accounted the value of their fixed assets, land, or buildings and thus we cannot estimate and measure the counties' wealth.

Budgeting. The quality of AM can have a strong impact on county governments' budgets. Prudent AM can reduce budget expenses on operation and maintenance of assets without jeopardizing their condition or the quality of related services. On the revenue side, good policies and practices can increase budget revenues from asset proceeds. For example, allocating public land for private use through auctions can produce substantial budget income, compared with nontransparent allocations of land at below-market prices and uncertain income. Charging an appropriate level of fees on leased or rented public assets (land, housing, or office spaces) can provide higher budget revenues to maintain the quality of assets and services and expanding assets (Detter and Fölster 2018).

Transparency and democracy. The experience of countries without a history of democratic governance and that went through devolution (for example, the Kyrgyz Republic) has demonstrated that AM serves as an important focal point for fostering local democracy and transparency (Kaganova, Akhmatov, and Undeland 2008).

Management of assets and liabilities. Assets are often associated with environmental, social, or financial liabilities; the latter can even be considered a negative form of assets. Proper asset and liability management is vital for sustainable development and the operation of assets and services. For example, a city may sell a solid waste disposal site to a private entity for 1 billon Kenya shillings (K Sh). However, the city may need to provide a guarantee of disposal of a certain minimum volume, say 2,300 tons per day (volumetric guarantee to pay the full tipping fee of the volume gap, if the volume falls below 2,300 tons a day), but also to provide the company with operating subsidies, say, K Sh 200 per metric tons disposed for 15 years to support financial viability. These are substantial financial contingent liabilities attached to the landfill assets.

In sum, the city turns landfill assets into cash (K Sh 1 billion) and saves future investment needs on the landfill, but in turn, it commits subsidies instead of investing them in assets. Such commitments are contingent financial liabilities, because, numbers suggest, the city has committed to pay a minimum of K Sh 160 million a year in tipping fee subsidies that may grow over the years as the volume of waste increases. It might also need to pay some volume guarantee charge in the beginning years of the contract. In short, discussing assets, valuing them, and managing them remain shortsighted and incomplete without considering the respective liabilities, especially financial liabilities if those exist, are measurable, and are attached to a particular group of assets.

NATIONAL ASSET MANAGEMENT FRAMEWORK

As noted, the *asset management framework* is a system of rules, procedures, and entities that informs and performs the tasks of AM. National legislation provides the legal and regulatory framework for the entire AM system and stipulates mandates and competencies for the various public entities responsible for managing assets in various forms and levels. The national government sets national AM policy, rules, and procedures and may provide templates for recording and reporting assets. The entities adopt internal AM policies, strategies, rules, and procedures to govern various AM aspects and management functions. Figure 1.1 depicts the functional structure of the Kenya national institutional framework for asset-liability management.

Figure 1.1 indicates that a network of entities fulfills the high-level asset-liability management functions over all public assets in Kenya. Let us walk through the organogram. There are three directorates in the National Treasury: (1) the Public Investment and Portfolio Management Directorate, which deals with AM on the highest level in portfolio modality; (2) the Public Debt Management Directorate, which oversees all public debts in the country; and (3) the Accounting Services Directorate, which regulates accounting for all public entities including AM. The Public Debt Management Directorate plays a critical role in managing liabilities on a large and strategic scale and vis-à-vis the international creditors on behalf of all national entities as a debtor of last resort. The National Assets and Liabilities Management (NALM) Department is supposed to play a pivotal role in managing all nonfinancial assets and the financial assets vis-à-vis the subnational entities such as county governments. The national AM entities play various AM and regulatory and oversight roles. The third row of boxes shows the main functions the departments fulfill. The last row of the chart shows entities (line ministries, county governments, and parastatal national government entities) that are the custodians of various financial and nonfinancial assets and therefore are responsible for the liabilities attached to the nonfinancial or fixed assets stipulated by law and regulations: for example, the Constitution of 2010; the Public Finance Management (PFM) Act of 2012, articles 12, 72, 104, and 153; the Public Procurement and Asset Disposal (PPAD) Act of 2015; and the Urban Areas and Cities (UAC) Acts of 2011 and 2019.

This framework exists and operates, albeit with some shortcomings in functionality, in various entities and functions (for example, county governments).

FIGURE 1.1

National asset and liability management governance framework

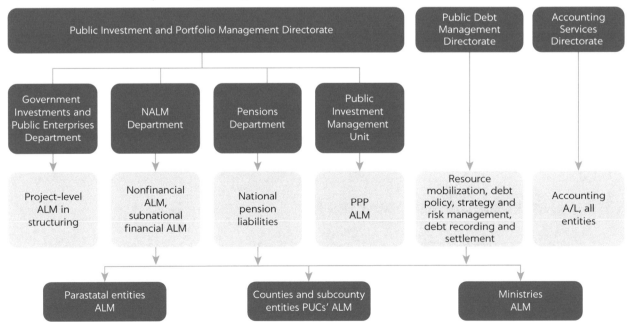

Source: World Bank.

Note: A/L = asset and liability; ALM = asset and liability management; NALM = National Assets and Liabilities Management Department in the National Treasury; PPP = public-private partnership; PUCs = public utility companies.

One remarkable shortcoming is that Kenyan national-level entities tend to focus on national policies and regulations more than on their functions in municipal, operation-level AM responsibilities at a national scale. The Public Debt Management Directorate in the National Treasury, however, has been managing national public debts vis-à-vis foreign creditors daily. In contrast, ministries or the NALM seem to be focused so far on policy setting and regulatory roles without a solid vision or plan to fulfill specific AM functions.

County asset management logical framework

The *asset management logical framework* (figure 1.2) is a hierarchical and perpetual cycle of AM that includes four quadrants: vision, strategy, planning, and operation: (1) The vision quadrant includes the county vision summarized in strategic plans, master plans, or detailed zoning or development plans; (2) the strategy quadrant contains the county AM policy, which regulates overall AM activities in harmony with national laws and regulations and the county vision, and the county AM strategy adopted for the long term (10 years or longer) in harmony with the county strategic plan, master plan, and other respective detailed plans; (3) the planning quadrant includes entities, systems, and activities such as demand management, life-cycle AM, capital improvement planning (CIP), and respective financial management; and (4) the operation quadrant includes the annual county AM plan,

FIGURE 1.2

County asset management logical framework

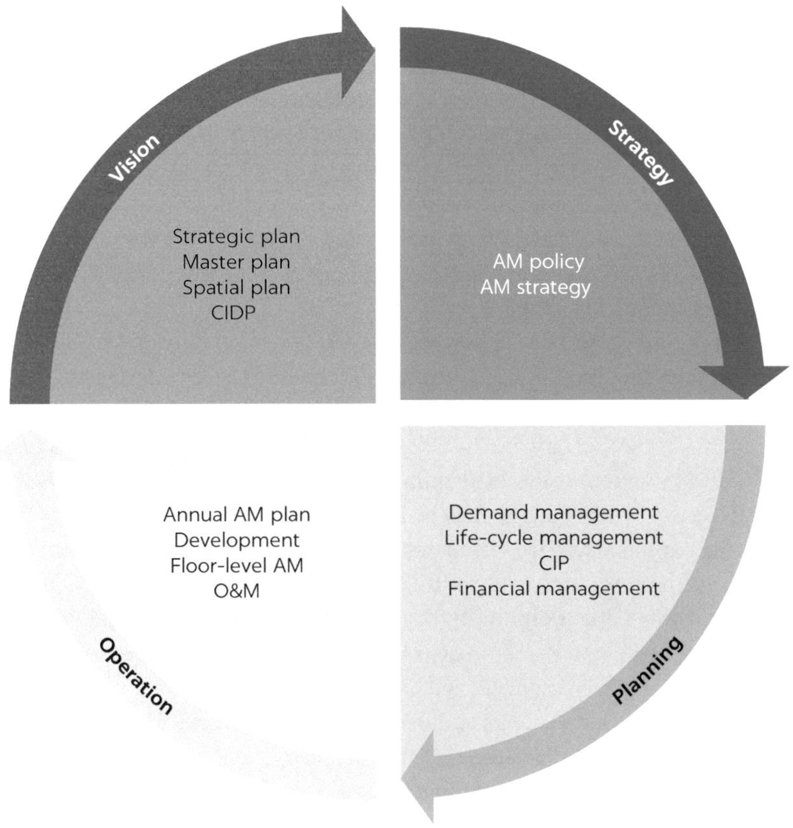

Source: World Bank.
Note: AM = asset management; CIDP = County Integrated Development Plan; CIP = capital improvement planning; O&M = operation and maintenance.

the floor-level AM entities, systems such as registers, logbooks, and procedures, and asset development and daily management of asset operation (Ottawa 2012; Cambridge 2013). In the following sections we discuss first the key building blocks of the county AM framework by following the quadrants of the circle of figure 1.2.

Vision quadrant. The county vision is the top layer of the county AM logical framework; the vision is summarized in the county strategy or strategic plan, the master plan, the County Integrated Development Plan (CIDP), or possibly in zoning or detailed development plans. Each building block of the AM framework should correspond to the vision, even though the vision often provides only distant and broad guidance to specific AM entities or procedures. The vision has the strongest effect on the substance, scope, and policy priorities of county *AM policy and AM strategy*. All subsequent quadrants of the AM framework are derived from or should correspond directly to the AM policy and strategy with more distant and indirect relation to the vision.

Strategy quadrant. Strategic-level AM consists of two important local *legislative documents* that summarize and rule AM policy and AM strategy, developed in correspondence with the national legislation (PFM Act 2012; UAC Act 2011; NALM 2020a, b, c). AM policy and strategy are local regulations or bylaws approved by higher governing bodies of the county (County Assembly or governor). They are published and made valid for long-term duration (10–20 years), with the possibility of revisions as changing local circumstances require (such as in response to the pandemic crisis). An AM policy stipulates rules and procedures and assigns mandates to entities and individuals to perform strategic functions or make strategic decisions (see templates for AM policy in appendix A and AM strategy in appendix B and DPLG 2006).

For example, a strategic function or decision could be to draft, discuss, and approve strategic-level AM actions such as acquisition or disposal of high-value assets or assets with strategic importance. Entities may include an AM directorate or team to complete the analysis and draft proposals for higher governing bodies such as the Finance Department, the Asset and Liability Management Advisory Committee that discusses and finalizes proposals, and the County Assembly and governor. The county AM strategy closely corresponds to the vision documents and stipulates specific strategic AM rules and planned actions in a long-term time frame, such as 10 years.

Planning quadrant. The medium-term level, in contrast, includes key medium-term planning building blocks: (1) *demand management* needs a dedicated analytic team and procedures to explore and quantify the demand for particular services (for example, a school or water); (2) *life-cycle AM* is an approach but also a role to be fulfilled by various teams in planning, finance, and service departments and in various phases of a life cycle, such as planning, selecting priority projects (medium-term planning such as CIP), comparing design-modalities, and managing repair, preventive maintenance, and refurbishment or disposition; and (3) *financial management* is a function fulfilled by the Finance Department and other AM teams in the various phases of the asset life cycle, which includes least cost analysis, financial analysis, funding plans, and liability analysis.

Demand management aims at enhancing the use and usefulness of assets by (1) analyzing trends and projecting future demand in key service areas, ideally in a consultative process; (2) defining adequate levels of services by comparing demand and current and future service options, scopes, and capacities; and (3) projecting demand, foreseen service levels, and projected capacities to support service enhancement programs by connecting priorities and funding capacities. (The life-cycle and financial AM will be discussed in more detail in later sections.)

Operation quadrant. The operational-level AM framework includes the *annual AM plan*, a guiding and ruling document, but also a framework for development and floor-level AM with dedicated entities—such as the public works department for development projects—or officers assigned responsibilities such as recording technical and financial actions or events regarding assets and attached liabilities, as well as operating and maintaining the fixed assets.

Many of these elements of a good AM framework do exist in various forms and quality in Kenyan counties (for example, see box 1.1). For instance, most counties have adopted a CIDP, which is a county strategy and/or master plan with a stated vision about development priorities in the county. Some counties have drafted an AM policy (for example, Bomet, Kiambu, and Nairobi) and some counties have drafted an AM strategy (Nairobi), but none of the counties have yet adopted or approved their AM policy or strategy. Many counties have formed some sort of AM annual work plan but without consistent interlinks to AM policy and/or strategy.

Finally, figure 1.2 strongly exemplifies two important aspects of AM: (1) the various building blocks and subsystems of the AM framework form a hierarchic order, and they are strongly and inherently intertwined, establishing that disconnected elements do not constitute an effective AM framework; and (2) good county AM has a much broader scope than just accounting (box 1.1), as some practitioners may assume in Kenya or some developing countries.

County asset management institutional and organizational framework

The organization framework of AM should be in harmony with the logical framework depicted in figure 1.2. However, the level of sophistication for an AM organization could be either quite simple or highly sophisticated and integrated depending on the local situation. To establish an AM system or AM functions from scratch, counties may start with a simple initial system in which departments work separately without a systematic, consistent, and complete set of interlinks that would constitute an *integrated asset management system* (figure 1.3 shows a gradual process). County governments can opt first for a simple system that may include the following actions: establishing an asset management *department, directorate,* or *team* that could support a gradually expanding AM organization

---

BOX 1.1

International Infrastructure Management Manual

The *International Infrastructure Management Manual* is among the most useful sources for senior asset management officers and senior practitioners. It focuses on infrastructure and is tailored to the corporate sector, but it is also adequate for local governments and is in harmony with the ISO 55000 guidelines. Thus, we can strongly recommend it for Kenyan officers. The most useful sections include developing a business case for asset management and key success factors; the strategic asset management plan and policy; risk management; operational strategies and planning; establishing and maintaining the asset management system; information management; asset management performance measurement and auditing; and assessing and managing infrastructure resilience.

Sources: IPWEA 2015; ISO 2014.
Note: ISO = International Organization for Standardization.

FIGURE 1.3
Asset management plans with growing scope and deepening sophistication

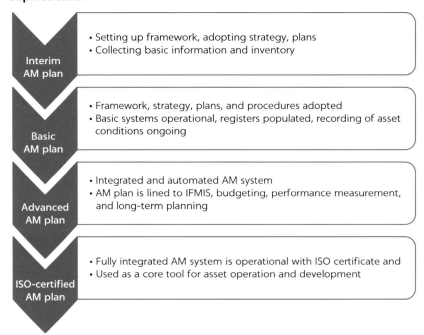

Source: Nairobi City County Government. For more detail, see appendix C.
Note: AM = asset management; IFMIS = integrated financial management information system; ISO = International Organization for Standardization.

framework and assignment of responsibilities, establishing *initial asset inventories* and later a reliable *central asset register* and technical registers in service entities, and then helping entities *populate the registers* with potential support from an external specialized consultancy firm. In short, developing an organizational framework for AM is a gradual process. However, it is useful to have a common vision and understanding about a more sophisticated AM system and organization as a final stage of an *integrated asset management system.*

An integrated AM framework (figure 1.4) shows a network of entities and allocation of AM functions in full harmony with the logical framework of AM (figure 1.2). The organizational framework in figure 1.4 is not an information and communication technology (ICT) realization scheme, but rather a functional division of mandates and responsibilities over the short term (for example, daily) and medium term across various entities. Large counties will be able to develop their AM system along the principle and logic of this scheme in the medium term. The figure shows that *most of the entities required to perform good AM already exist in Kenyan counties*, but mostly without consistent assignment of AM functions and communication lines.

Establishing a system pictured in figure 1.4 does not require establishing many new entities, since most of them do exist (for example, sectors and service departments or units). Instead, *a consistent set of functions, mandates, and responsibilities needs to be assigned.* A key takeaway is that establishing and empowering the AM system is one of the most demanding actions county governments need to undertake, but the payoff of doing so can be enormous. Figure 1.4 indicates that the Asset Management *Department* or *Directorate* (used interchangeably)—AMDR—is in a pivotal point in the AM system, and most of

FIGURE 1.4

Integrated asset management organizational framework in local governments

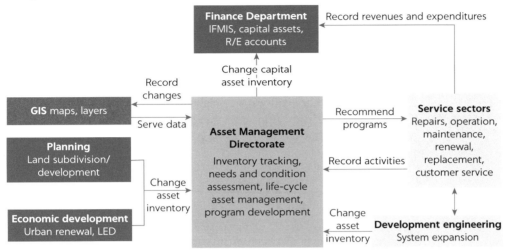

Source: World Bank based on Cambridge 2013.
Note: GIS = geographic information system; IFMIS = integrated financial management information system; LED = local economic development; R/E = revenue and expenditure.

the other entities responsible for specific AM functions are connected through the AMDR. This is only one possible modality of an integrated AM system that can be organized in various ICT realizations.

Note the following in figure 1.4:

- The AMDR is subordinate to the Finance Department and provides accounting asset information to the integrated financial management information system (IFMIS) and various accounts such as revenues and expenditures and the capital budget in an unintegrated management information system.
- The AMDR is also responsible for ensuring important analyses: inventory tracking, needs assessment, financial analyses for life-cycle management, and program development.
- Departments responsible for services should perform customer service, operation, repair, maintenance, and log activities in AM ledgers and the central asset register hosted by the AMDR.
- Sector-engineering units propose and complete renewals and replacements as well as log changes in the asset inventory or registers, while the AMDR may propose projects based on information obtained from other areas of the network and analyses completed accordingly.
- The AMDR may obtain information about a geographic information system (GIS) and provide asset information to log changes in GIS maps.
- A development engineering unit completes design and implementation of engineering projects based on approved programs and annual development plans and logs changes in asset inventory or registers in or via the AMDR at the completion of projects. The engineering units work in close cooperation with the service sectors to design and complete development projects and to hand assets over to services sectors.
- Urban planning and economic development units prepare medium- to long-term plans and inform other entities via the AMDR, which is responsible for drafting initial capital improvement plans.

Contrary to these principles and practices, Kenyan counties have been performing only parts of floor-level AM (for example, department of road or transport, housing, public works, solid waste management entities, park beautification team, stadium manager, and so on). The building blocks or subsystems of a good county AM framework are missing or not yet integrated and do not correspond to each other, and thus do not form a consistent and complete AM framework as depicted in figure 1.2 and figure 1.4. Developing an AM framework, culture, entities, and practices is a challenging task, but there are useful sources to help practitioners in the counties (see box 1.1); the Department of Provincial and Local Governments of South Africa issued very practical guidelines (DPLG 2006).

ASSET MANAGEMENT LAYERS OR DIMENSIONS

AM in all public and private sectors and entities and at each level of government consists of four fundamental and interrelated functional dimensions (figure 1.5):

- Strategic asset management (SGAM)
- Life-cycle asset management (LCAM)
- Accounting-oriented asset management (AAM)
- Information technology representations (ICTAM) of these dimensions that include networks, supporting procedures, templates, and various asset registers and ledgers (Ideally ICTAM is connected to the general IFMIS, although ICTAM often is developed as a separate business process.)

Figure 1.5 portrays the four functional dimensions and their overlapping relationships. It also indicates the specific entities responsible (or to be made responsible) for managing or fulfilling the specific functional layers of the county

FIGURE 1.5

Functional dimensions of asset management in the Kenyan county context

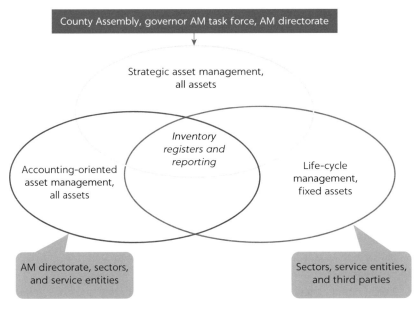

Source: Kaganova and Kopanyi 2016.
Note: AM = asset management.

AM system. However, the figure does not show that some aspects of these AM layers also are relevant at the national level, such as making key strategic AM decisions or regulating the other three layers.

National legislatures or government approach AM at the highest strategic level by adopting a legal and regulatory framework, making decisions on the highest strategic investments (a new hydropower plant, strategic highway, railway, port, and so forth), assigning competencies to entities, deciding on transfers of public assets across sectors or entities, and managing liabilities of strategic importance. But as previously discussed, the national government also shoulders the financial liabilities of all public entities as a last resort via the National Treasury. The rest of the asset groups are transferred, and functions are delegated to either subordinated entities of the national government or to state corporations (parastatal entities), or to counties (see figure 1.1). Let us take a closer look at the substance and nature of these AM layers in a county context, where a county executive committee, county treasury, or the chief accounting officer assigns mandates and responsibilities to specific county units or entities (PFM Act 2012, articles 105 (f), 148, and 153).

Strategic asset management in county context

Strategic asset management has three different and interrelated meanings that may be used interchangeably, but it is important to define them and clarify their differences. The first meaning of SGAM is managing strategic layers of AM, shown in figure 1.2, to adopt the highest strategic-level regulations for a county, AM policy and AM strategy. The second meaning is to manage assets at the highest strategic level, when the highest decision-making bodies make strategic decisions on the entire asset portfolio, including fixed or physical, intangible, and financial assets alike. Such decisions formally or informally consider the county vision, AM policy, and AM strategy. For instance, approving a capital investment plan with funding is a strategic-level county AM action. The third meaning of SGAM is to manage assets and attached liabilities with a strategic or large value (for example, a metrorail) or strategic importance by critical strategic decisions made by the highest governing bodies. Meanwhile, assigned sectors or officers perform the daily operative management of the important assets (buying or selling land, building a city hall, water plant, water reservoir, school, and so on).

SGAM is a higher-level management function that deals with all types of assets. It consists of high-level decisions on the overall asset portfolio, which takes into account all fixed, financial, or intangible assets, and decisions about transforming the wealth of the county from one form to another (for example, spending money to buy or sell land to generate money to fund construction of schools, roads, and so forth). It also entails decisions about obligating liabilities with strategic magnitude. Adopting or changing AM policy or AM strategy are also prime examples of high-level SGAM.

SGAM is therefore a domain of a county's highest decision-making bodies, which should discuss and approve asset decisions of a strategic nature or of large value (Kaganova 2015). Three specific bodies play important SGAM roles in Kenya: (1) the County Assembly, the governor and his or her executive members, (2) an AM leadership committee or task force, and (3) an AM department, directorate, or team. The AM committee or task force should discuss and present alternatives for the County Assembly's or executive's decisions by involving all the asset-related stakeholders. The AM directorate has multiple functions in strategic AM, including serving as the secretariat of the committee or task force, maintaining a central asset register, providing basic information for decisions from the central asset register or other sources, coordinating communication across stakeholders, and conducting or contracting out analytic work to support informed strategic decisions.

SGAM should also include establishing an *asset management strategy, policy, plan, guidelines, and rules,* and then adopting and publishing them as local bylaws that all sectoral entities with an AM mandate must follow. For example, rules may stipulate that leasing and sales of county property should be allowed only through open, competitive tender procedures (auctions), and perhaps requiring preapproval by county executives above a certain value threshold. Likewise, rules may stipulate that procuring debt above a certain threshold for financing asset acquisition or development requires a referendum to authorize the County Assembly and/or executive to approve debt financing.

Citizens also have a role in SGAM decisions. Figure 1.6 shows an example from Fairfax County, Virginia, USA, of a 10-page document sent to county residents to inform them about a county referendum to approve issuance of a US$182 million bond. (County voters approved the bond in November 2018.) This shows that citizens also have a role in the highest-level strategic AM decisions; in turn, the vote authorized the county to raise taxes if revenues appeared to be insufficient for serving the bond debt a few years later.

SGAM is related to and overlaps with both life-cycle management and accounting AM, since all strategic decisions should be properly accounted for

FIGURE 1.6

Information letter to citizens on a bond issuance vote in Fairfax County, Virginia

FAIRFAX COUNTY BOARD OF SUPERVISORS

2018 Public Safety Bond Referendum Information

Bond Issue on the Ballot on Nov. 6

In the Nov. 6 general election, Fairfax County voters will be asked to vote YES or NO on a public safety bond referendum question. The referendum question asks voters to allow the county to borrow up to $182 million to fund the cost of constructing, reconstructing, enlarging, renovating, equipping and acquiring land for public safety facilities.

If the majority of voters approves the question, the county currently plans to issue general obligation bonds to fund improvements to:

- Five fire stations
- Three police facilities
- Adult Detention Center
- Existing courtrooms as described below

The county may in the future alter these specific plans, but in such a case the county would have to use the funds for a purpose described in the ballot question.

Source: Fairfax County, Virginia, United States, 2018.

and fit well into the other parts of accounting and financial management (for example, planning; budgeting; asset-financing actions such as divestiture, refurbishment, or acquisition; and debt and liability management). Life-cycle AM (LCAM) and financial AM also support strategic decision-making by helping valuation and comparison of investment alternatives, but LCAM also follows strategy with effective life-cycle management of *strategic assets*.

Capital improvement planning. Development of a medium-term development framework (MTDF) or planning is mandated and is practiced in various forms and quality in most developing countries. However, most of MTDFs are static, adopted for five years and not revised despite changing circumstance. As a result, such plans increasingly lack reality and fail to provide guidance for strategic decisions. CIP (also known as capital *acquisition* planning) is a procedure for selection and prioritization of asset development projects systematically and with inherent connection between demand and technical and financial aspects of the projects. Despite donor promotion and available guidebooks (Kaganova et al. 2018; Kaganova 2011) many local governments in the developing world are reluctant to commence CIP; some argue that they prefer obeying the national regulation that stipulates a simple, less consistent, and less useful MTDF. Robust strategic AM requires rigorous selection of a priority investment process in harmony with life-cycle AM, that is, CIP. Substandard AM and poor service quality are often determined by the ill-managed selection of priority projects or technical or financial modalities. CIP helps avoid such common mistakes.

Life-cycle asset management and capital improvement planning

Life-cycle asset management is an integrated approach to maintain and optimize the useful life of a particular asset, from the conceptual design through daily operation, maintenance, and refurbishment to decommissioning or disposal. LCAM is a holistic approach that addresses an individual asset (a plant, an office building, and so forth) or an associated group of assets (public transport fleet) with a scope to cover, not only technical aspects, but also the required financial resources, business processes, data, and enabling technologies that are critical to best use, best service, or best functioning of an asset. The LCAM approach supports both strategic and short-term or daily operation and maintenance of assets but it is also relevant for the medium to long term and could include risk-based preventive maintenance.

LCAM plays vital roles at the strategic level. Most municipal fixed assets have a long useful life with proper repair and maintenance, depending on technology and asset specificity. Buildings can be used for 50 to 100 years or longer with proper refurbishments, roads can be used for decades or centuries, a metrorail system works for 50 to 100 years, and solid waste landfills are often designed for a 20- to 30-year useful life. Investments in such assets are not only long term but also immense in value; they are strategic because of their big size, long life, and importance in public services.

LCAM is vital in a medium-term investment planning CIP (or capital acquisition planning) and in supporting specific high-level investment decisions on asset acquisition, development, or refurbishment of assets with strategic importance (figure 1.2). However, LCAM is applicable to and important for all assets that have a medium- to long-term useful life (for example, compactor trucks).

The LCAM approach and especially the *life-cycle costing* of the strategic assets help in comparing the technical, operational, and financial alternatives. Strategic decisions should be based on comparisons of the *present value of life-cycle costs* of the various considered technical and financial alternatives. For instance, a water service system can be developed with overhead reservoirs that provide water with gravity; another alternative is permanent water pumping. The first requires higher initial investment costs, but the second costs much more to operate (electricity and maintenance). Experience suggests that a pumping system appears to be a lot more expensive than a gravity system in the medium to long term (if measured by life-cycle costs). Thus, higher decision-makers should discuss and select strategic projects based on life-cycle cost information about alternatives, and possibly with an analysis of various modalities instead of promoting project options with the least initial investment cost.

Life-cycle costs and cost structure

Life-cycle costs (LCCs) depend greatly on asset specificities; the size and structure of life-cycle cost for an office building are quite different from those of a wastewater plant or a compactor truck. For instance, the world-famous Gates Computer Building at Stanford University, Palo Alto, California, where the search engine Google began (photo 1.1), is an extravagant building with an initial project cost that represents a high 58 percent of the 30-year estimated life-cycle cost (figure 1.7); the utility costs represent another substantial 28 percent share of the estimated life-cycle cost (Stanford University 2005). Since it is unlikely that this building will be decommissioned after 30 years, we can assume that an LCC with a 60-year useful life would include a quarter of expenses for initial project cost, and a much greater share for operation and maintenance (O&M), while refurbishment may absorb a significant amount after 30 years.

PHOTO 1.1

Gates Computer Building, where Google began

FIGURE 1.7

Composition of 30-year life-cycle costs of the Gates Computer Building and a wastewater treatment plant

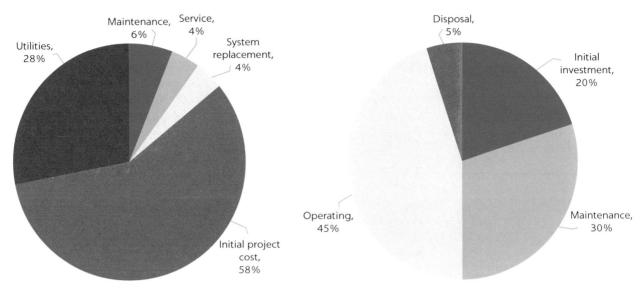

Sources: Panel a: Stanford University 2005; panel b: Koul and John 2015.

These numbers suggest that Stanford University is projected to spend in present-value terms about 2.4 percent of the initial investment cost for operation, maintenance, and replacements annually in a 30-year analyzed LCC. In contrast, a simple sewage plant in India had a small investment cost but in present-value terms spends over three times the initial investment cost annually for chemicals, labor, electricity, and maintenance in a 30-year useful life period (Koul and John 2015). The difference between the shares of cost of operation in these two cases is enormous, but it is not a measure of efficiency, since it is rooted in asset specificity, that is, the differing technical and operation natures of buildings and sewage plants. Kenyan counties should keep in mind this asset-specific nature of LCC when comparing various infrastructure investments and technical modalities. But also, that net present value analysis (the difference between the discounted present value of future revenues and future expenses) is one reliable way to compare projects and modalities in a life-cycle approach.

The case of India shows that a sewage treatment plant option would require in a 30-year useful life about 96 percent of LCC to cover chemicals, labor, and maintenance, and 1 percent spent on the initial investment in present-value terms in 30 years (Koul and John 2015). The case compares three different treatment technology options for Chandigarh City, India: anaerobic sludge blanket, sequencing batch reactor, and moving bed biofilm reactor. We used the numbers for the third technology to illustrate the cost structure from the Koul and John (2015) study.

These examples demonstrate the dangers and shortcomings of selecting infrastructure projects based purely on initial investment costs. An important lesson is that an asset donated in fully developed form as in-kind support may make the mayor or governor happy, and rightly so, because there would be no investment costs or bank debts. However, the mayor should be aware that such donations may incur substantial life-cycle costs that must be considered and

O&M expenditures budgeted annually to maintain the quality and service capacity of the received assets. Wrecked trucks, broken roads or water lines, or abandoned health equipment signal lack of LCC vision.

Performing LCAM in daily operation is the responsibility of the relevant service sectors or fixed-asset-holding entities or managers (such as a road department or a transport or water and sanitation company, or a manager of a stadium). Parts of LCAM functions have been performed in cities even in the developing world, albeit with different scopes and quality. Responsible entities must maintain *logbooks* to record daily operation and detailed *technical asset registers* that include all legal rights, maps, and technical records of networks, infra- and superstructures, age, time of acquisition, dates and scope of refurbishment, and periodically tested condition of assets or system elements. At the level of floor managers, LCAM primarily focuses on proper operation of assets and adequate preventive and reactive maintenance. The LCAM entities should ensure that all respective information is incorporated into the central asset register (if one exists) with costs and expenditures and is updated.

Reactive and preventive maintenance

Moving from reactive to preventive repair and maintenance. Preventive maintenance is an integral part of life-cycle AM. It is also an instrument for moving away from current dominant practices of reactive maintenance and toward proactive (preventive) maintenance. An example includes timely replacement of pumps, equipment, or sections of water networks based on the useful life defined by their manufacturers, or because of signs of malfunction, instead of waiting until a major breakdown causes physical and financial damage and service disruption.

Reactive maintenance practices are obvious on roads, where the delayed maintenance is visible as persistent problems, such as potholes, on the road surface. In contrast, the timely *preventive maintenance* results in permanently smoother surfaces and good road conditions. Furthermore, experience suggests that preventive maintenance eventually results in a lower life-cycle cost (AssetWorks 2014). In figure 1.8, the depiction of a 30-year life-span for a road indicates that it costs

FIGURE 1.8

Comparison of reactive and preventive road maintenance

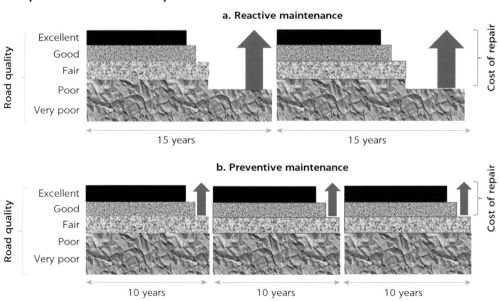

Source: Based on AssetWorks 2014.

less to do preventive or scheduled maintenance three times at, say, US$20 million per kilometer than to do reactive maintenance twice at, say, US$40 million. This effect is largely similar with many other assets, although measured by different parameters such as water losses or fuel or electricity usage.

The Golden Gate Bridge is not only a world-famous landmark that enables 110,000 vehicles to pass over daily but also a great example of the life-cycle AM and risk-based preventive maintenance (see box 1.2). The bridge operators cannot follow reactive maintenance practices and risk a major breakdown that requires closure for repairs; instead, they analyze the bridge daily, estimate risks, and perform preventive maintenance based on known technology parameters and analysis.

Risk-based preventive maintenance (RBM) is a sophisticated practice that boosts LCAM with risk assessment that assesses reliability in terms of safety, environmental risk, and financial risk to minimize the likelihood of system

---

BOX 1.2

The Golden Gate Bridge

The Golden Gate bridge was completed in 1937 and is operated under the Bridge Division of the Golden Gate Bridge, Highway and Transportation District (a form of special district and a local governing entity). About 200 employees operate and maintain the bridge under a manager. Since its completion, numerous rehabilitation and improvement projects have been undertaken to preserve, protect, and extend the life of this world-famous structure. Over 80 years of operation, most parts have been replaced and improvements have been made—for example, to reduce seismic risk exposure. Despite harsh weather conditions, the bridge is in excellent shape and quality due to the life-cycle asset management approach, preventive maintenance, timely repainting, and periodic improvements (photo B1.2.1).

PHOTO B1.2.1
The Golden Gate Bridge

Source: © ventdusud/iStock.com. Used with the permission of ventdusud/iStock.com; further permission required for reuse.

failure and its consequences. A good example is a risk-based asset management plan adopted by the Colorado Department of Transport (Colorado DOT 2019). RBM, which is often supported by software analytic applications, is useful for managing assets that carry a high risk of failure with substantial negative technical, social, environmental, or financial consequences (for example, bridges, water mains, treatment plants, or metrorail systems). RBM analysis signals the need to maintain such assets or specific parts that should have high priority over other assets that have a low risk of failure or low level of negative consequences.

Reliability-centered maintenance. Despite strong consequences of excessive reliance on reactive maintenance, it would be inappropriate to overemphasize preventive maintenance for several reasons: (1) reactive maintenance will remain a significant activity in addition to preventive maintenance, because the urban service systems are big and complex, and unexpected and unpredictable failures will happen time and again; (2) preventive maintenance requires sophisticated AM and analytic capacities, some expensive; and (3) the various components of a complex plant or network bear various levels of failure risk and various levels of consequences. The concept of reliability-centered maintenance aims to reduce the costs while providing a high level of system functionality and reliance by introducing four maintenance options based on asset specificities (figure 1.9).

Reliability-centered maintenance approaches maintenance in a spectrum of activities (figure 1.9). One of these is solely reactive maintenance, which, however, is advisable only for small, noncritical items or items unlikely to fail (Pride 2016). In the figure, the steps upward depict variants of preventive maintenance that increasingly require more sophisticated data and analysis. The simplest is interval-based preventive maintenance applied without detailed analysis of the assets, such as resurfacing a highway every 15 years. Equipment producers often advise using time-based replacement plans, too. Time-based maintenance works most of the time; but the manner of operation and unknown internal conditions could make an asset or equipment more reliable or less reliable than producers

FIGURE 1.9

Concept of reliability-centered maintenance

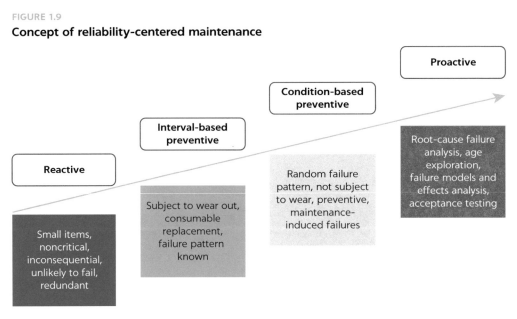

Source: Based on Pride 2016.

describe, so experts may rightly overwrite the time-based maintenance plan based on technical checks (for example, kilometer run of a truck).

Condition-based preventive maintenance requires an expert check of infrastructure systems, subsystems, or equipment without detailed and sophisticated analysis. Condition checking requires performance indicators, many provided by producers of the assets, and experts to inform decisions on time and nature of repair actions. Finally, root-cause failure analysis requires sophisticated data collection and complex evaluation methodology; local governments rarely own the expensive assets needed to use this method.

Operation and maintenance. There is no sharp dividing line between operation and maintenance since O&M actions are intertwined both in time and functionally. O&M is a popular acronym in reports of public entities. However, it has three different meanings or contexts. First, in financial terms, O&M is a budget line item that reflects the total amount of money spent in a year on all kinds of expenses that are parts of O&M. This figure, however, is too synthetic and shows only O&M expenses against administration, development, or transfers to subordinated entities; it fails to show the amount spent on repair and maintenance. Second, O&M can combine all expenditures spent for provision of a service, including details of labor, material, energy, and repair and maintenance. In this context, O&M helps cost accounting and cost control of services by forming cost centers, which help measure service performance in financial terms by comparing O&M expenditures with revenues collected from the same services.

Third, O&M also covers the combined technical activities of operating and managing assets; these include detailed procedures, rules, and decisions for corrective measures (repair or refurbishment). Appendix E includes excerpts from the O&M procedures that the US Environmental Protection Agency (EPA 2015) advises be performed in operating and maintaining water service systems to prevent environmental damage from improper O&M. This guidance, from an O&M manual (EPA 2012), advises sets of actions to be performed daily, monthly, quarterly, and annually. Similar O&M manuals exist for all main forms of assets such as buildings, water and sewage, or road O&M. Many of them are unknown or poorly followed in developing countries.

Annual repair and maintenance plans. Besides the medium-term capital acquisition plans, the departments and sectors that hold high-value assets and infrastructure should adopt annual repair and maintenance plans following the principles of preventive maintenance practices. These maintenance plans should be financed after approval with adequate funds appropriated in budgets for both planned and reactive maintenance. Unplanned reactive maintenance and repair of unexpected breakdowns are inevitable parts of regular AM, although those remain smaller expenses if preventive maintenance is well instituted and implemented. Departments and sectors also should set aside funds for unplanned reactive repair and maintenance in annual maintenance plans.

Annual plan and report for deferred maintenance. The annual maintenance plans should include a section that summarizes the plans for deferring maintenance due to a shortage of funds. But deferrals should not be kept secret. They should be well recorded in both the maintenance plans and the technical asset registers and reported to higher governing bodies such as the AM directorate, some even to the assembly, the county executive committee, the county secretary, and the deputy governor and governor.

Accounting-oriented asset management: Central asset register

Accounting-oriented AM, that is, accounting, registering, and reporting, is a specific aspect of AM that is largely the responsibility of the chief accounting officer and the AM department that maintains the *central asset register*, based partly on data received from service departments and technical asset registers. The accounting registers reflect historic values (also called book values) and depreciations and furnish balance sheets with aggregate figures of these value terms such as net value of fixed assets (historic value minus depreciation).

Income-generating and investment properties require special attention, some even a special account, and strategic management. The AMDR should establish specialized real estate expertise and supplementary registers especially for dealing with income-generating and investment properties. Investment properties, those in joint ventures, and/or those managed daily by legally independent entities do not fit into the fixed asset register since they are financial assets; still, managing them requires special attention to ensure adequate revenue generation.

To strategically manage these assets, the AMDR would need to undertake special targeted valuation of all income-generating and investment properties in the context of strategic management of the entire asset portfolio. Furthermore, any major strategic asset decisions such as planned divestiture, leasing, or moving assets to joint ventures should factor in updated market values of property. These valuations also are needed for annual assessment of the profitability of leased or other income-generating properties (for example, to estimate return on investment) and other periodic economic analyses to compare investment or divestiture alternatives (Detter and Fölster 2018).

The central asset register is the core accounting database for strategic AM, to be established and maintained by the AMDR or team. Strategic AM, as noted, has important links to the master plan, spatial development plans, and the capital investment plans, since SGAM decisions should be in harmony with those plans. There are good off-the-shelf ICT modules available to support various aspects of LCAM, from planning to risk analysis, many specialized to specific clusters of services or assets (water, transport, buildings, and so forth).

Income-generating properties. For income-generating or investment property operation, securing comparably adequate revenue flows from rental and lease income should be linked to LCAM to ensure the assets perform adequately, primarily in financial terms but also in technical terms. Analysis of financial performance of assets is a vital part of good AM (as figure 1.2 depicts). Market benchmarks of revenues should be set and verified annually or biannually to monitor financial performance. For instance, a department responsible for building management that rents and manages housing, office, or commercial buildings should properly calculate and report to the central register not only the collected revenues but also the foregone revenues when assets are leased out at below-market prices to support charitable or socially important activities, or for legal reasons that impede regular increase of the lease or rental fee.

ICT system and tools

ICT tools are underlying instruments that support most aspects of AM. There is a rich market of software applications that support the life-cycle, technical, or accounting AM with easy-to-use registers and analytic tools. The availability of costless GIS programs with digitalized maps and global positioning system (GPS) tools has greatly improved both ICT realization and verification and management of fixed assets. GIS-based systems can greatly improve operations, support business processes, and enable risk-based management of assets.

However, ICT tools are helpful only if reliable, consistent, and up-to-date asset information is uploaded. In other words, the best use of ICT and GIS tools still requires field verification of all technical, legal, and financial details of each fixed-asset item. These all, in turn, require a proper AM framework, standard operating procedures, and trained staff. Therefore, establishing a reliable AM system should start with establishing a framework and then acquiring adequate ICT that fits the framework and local circumstances. For instance, a large county like Nairobi City County (NCC) may opt for a large-capacity, sophisticated, and integrated ICT system; in contrast, most other Kenyan counties may run their small AM systems well with the support of a few simple ICT tools.

Today, adequate AM systems cannot be established without ICT support and solutions, not only because computerized systems provide faster and more reliable information and can be procured with affordable investments, but also because they can be and should be connected to other important ICT systems such as the IFMISs, which have been deployed in Kenyan counties. The market supply of off-the-shelf AM software solutions is abundant; although most of the systems are designed for private production or commercial companies, they have modules or modalities applicable to municipalities. A growing number of systems are designed specifically for municipalities and are increasingly supported with affordable GIS and GPS tools. Box 1.3 summarizes advanced solutions that are in harmony with the ISO (International Organization for Standardization) qualification.

ICT options should be considered carefully, but establishing AM systems should start with establishing a robust governance framework and an internal AM system with well-allocated functions across municipal units and clear standard operation procedures integrated into the business processes of the local administrations. Experience suggests that software-driven solutions eventually are either inadequate or too expensive (or both) and take a long time to become operational. The main reason is that the software modules are simply passive tools that remain useless without uploads of reliable, complete, and consistent information and updates daily.

BOX 1.3

Information and communication technology asset management solutions

Life-cycle asset management (LCAM) software solutions help ensure that all data regarding each major individual asset be housed in a single repository—from engineering through construction and operations to maintenance (sometimes called a *technical asset register*). This enables LCAM to comply with the requirements of the ISO 55000 quality control standard applied for municipal utilities.

Modules may include the following:

- Computerized maintenance management that includes cost management, operation and time management, vendor and inventory management, resource management, and safety and security management

- Plant engineering to capture operation costs and asset data

- Document management to capture changing asset specifications and unstructured data

- Project management for plant shutdowns, refits, and life-cycle extensions

- Contract management to capture the cost of external engineering, construction, and maintenance contractors

Note: ISO = International Organization for Standardization.

Some county and national government officers believe that a good module in IFMIS can well serve AM. They fail to realize that one of the biggest challenges Kenyan counties face is how to generate verified and reliable data to feed ICT systems and modules. Another lesson learned is that AM goes way beyond the accounting-oriented AM and an IFMIS module. Furthermore, it is questionable whether establishing good AM can at all start with an IFMIS module, because it cannot be populated with reliable information without fulfilling the functions other ICT tools and modules can perform (box 1.3).

The ideal solution would be establishing a complex integrated AM system with GIS platforms accessible by a diverse set of users, from county sectors or functional departments to the private sector and private citizens. Figure 1.10 and figure 1.11 reflect the main characteristics of such a system established and well operated in Lithuania, a small country in Eastern Europe with a total population of less than 3 million—by population it is smaller than NCC. Establishing such a high-tech system took over a year in Lithuania, which already had a reliable land cadaster, and the public utilities and other municipal assets were well documented on paper maps before the ICT solution was implemented.

Given the ground reality of AM in Kenya, NCC may opt for a high-tech ICT solution and build it gradually. But most of the other counties would be better off applying a small number of vitally important modules or ICT applications to automate some business processes for tracking and maintaining assets in county departments such as public works, building and facility maintenance, water, and sanitation. Important modules may include: the central asset register, life-cycle management, depreciation management, preventive maintenance, inventory control, incident and inspection management, or work-order management. The ultimate objective of installing ICT solutions for AM should be not only to fulfill narrow AM functions but also to eventually improve local public services. Such a system has proven to be extremely useful and effective in Lithuania (figure 1.10).

Lithuania's Regional Geoinformational Environment Service (REGIA) is a national registry service system operated by the State Enterprise Center for

FIGURE 1.10

Main functionality features of the REGIA system in Lithuania

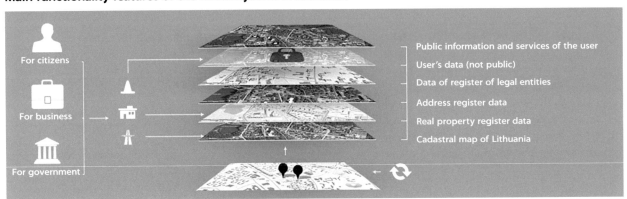

Working in the service environment, the REGIA users can
- Create and manage their own data layers
- Store and manage information or documents
- Decide whether this data layer is publicly visible and who is entitled to use it
- Ensure services in the review mode are publicly accessible

Source: Sabaliauskas 2013. Used with permission; further permission required for reuse.
Note: REGIA = Regional Geoinformational Environment Service.

FIGURE 1.11
REGIA layer for civil and fire safety

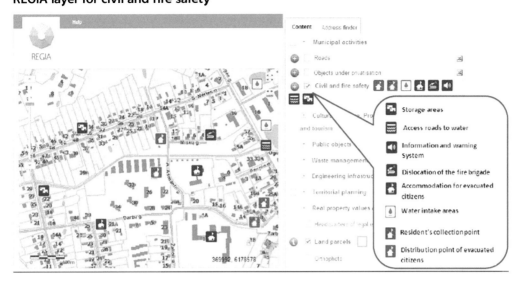

Source: Sabaliauskas 2013. Used with permission; further permission required for reuse.
Note: REGIA = Regional Geoinformational Environment Service.

Registers, which manages the national land register, among other things. All Lithuanian municipalities and a wide range of customers are now using the REGIA system (Sabaliauskas 2013), which is built on digitized GIS maps (by cities and regions) and includes multiple functional layers (figure 1.10). Each functional layer is managed by a dedicated service administrator (for example, a municipality or a road department of a municipality) which has rights to create or upload their own databases, store and manage information documents, and decide if information is for internal use only or is also accessible to the public.

The REGIA functionality serves, among others, as an AM system for specific users, but functionalities include much broader urban management fields such as planning, licensing, or property taxation. Government entities are the primary users of REGIA, most of which have administrator rights, while private businesses and citizens have *read-only* access to selected functions and information.

Figure 1.11 presents REGIA's functionality of a civil and fire safety department, with an interactive map that shows each important facility, access roads, warning systems, and so forth, and the public and private properties in a specific zone. Users can click on an icon of a specific safety unit and see the detailed underlying information to gain critical knowledge quickly in an emergency, such as water intakes, road access, and contours and floor maps of buildings.

Asset management methods and processes

There are two basic well-distinguished methods or approaches to address and manage assets: *portfolio asset management* and *technical asset management*. Portfolio asset management approaches assets as part of a large portfolio without considering their specific material forms. From this perspective assets are assumed to be transferable. Portfolio asset management supports changing or mixing assets over time to maximize the key strategic objectives of a county, such as to improve wealth or services.

Portfolio management, the dominant approach in strategic AM, refers to making decisions about investment mix and policies, matching investments to objectives, allocating assets to institutions, and balancing risk against performance at the highest overall county strategic level: for example, when a high-level committee discusses specific technical options for a major infrastructure investment. Portfolio management requires choices between debt and equity, domestic and international debts, growth, safety, financial or fixed assets, and many other trade-offs to maximize revenues or services with acceptable risk. Accounting AM also largely approaches assets in portfolio methods focused on the universal financial forms and value of assets while disregarding the material forms for accounting purposes. This is the way to account and manage all kinds of assets in a universal portfolio in the central asset register, and in balance sheets.

Bear in mind that technical AM supported with analytic asset registers and logbooks is the opposite of portfolio management, since it approaches, manages, registers, and keeps recording each asset with its material form, along with detailed technical and financial specificities. Life-cycle AM is the highest standard form of technical AM. Municipalities in the developing world often perform various parts and functions of technical AM when operating, repairing, refurbishing, or modifying specific service or infrastructure assets, but often without consistently utilizing life-cycle AM functions and strategic AM.

Asset hierarchy

The county assets appear either in a formal or a hidden structure of asset hierarchy that reflects the AM framework, the material form, and the technical specificities of assets. Modern ICT systems are naturally organized in a logical, technical, and governance hierarchy of assets and offer modules to manage specific assets (for example, tools for fleet management, road management, or building management).

Figure 1.12 illustrates asset hierarchy for managing fixed assets in NCC. SGAM, accounting AM, and a central asset register would be focused on the highest level (level 1) of asset hierarchy in portfolio modality. Level 1 includes the financial and current assets but also liabilities attached to the fixed assets. In short, the level 1 asset hierarchy is the domain for strategic and accounting AM. Level 2 is the domain of technical AM and LCAM and maintains the technical asset registers (called a departmental inventory register or DIR in NCC). However, the service units and departments also should play a substantial role in strategic AM by initiating and drafting proposals for strategic-level asset decisions based on their intimate knowledge of their mandated services and respective assets and liabilities and by managing assets in Level 2. The Level 2 and lower levels of asset hierarchy are subjects of the technical or service-level AM and in good systems using life-cycle AM for all and each substantial fixed asset.

Asset registers also have a practical and logical hierarchy with specific functions on each level. Figure 1.13 depicts the main functions and logical hierarchy of various asset registers. The general or main asset register has multiple functions, including accounting all assets, maintaining historic procurement values, recording repair and maintenance costs, and supporting SGAM decisions on portfolio modality. The accounting AM register also serves the balance sheet with book values, depreciation, and corresponding costs and liabilities in accrual accounting or it supplements cash-accounting with separate financial ledgers, as mandated in Kenya (PFM Act 2012).

FIGURE 1.12
Possible asset hierarchy

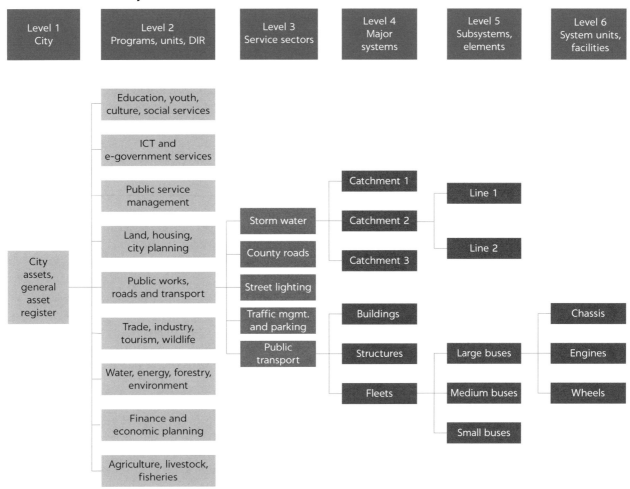

Source: World Bank.
Note: DIR = departmental inventory register; ICT = information and communication technology.

FIGURE 1.13
Hierarchy and functions of asset registers

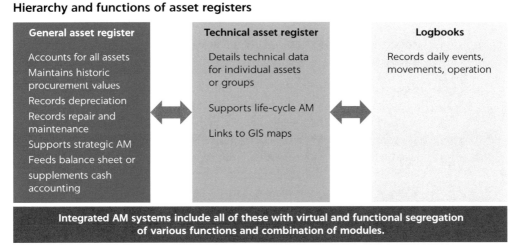

Source: World Bank.
Note: AM = asset management; GIS = geographic information system.

The technical asset register (also called the fixed asset register or the departmental inventory register) contains detailed technical specificities of fixed assets. It contains detailed technical data for each individual asset or groups, supports life-cycle AM, and often is linked to interactive GIS maps with legal, geographic, and key technical information, illustrated in figure 1.11. Logbooks are special supporting records to register daily events, movements, or operation of individual assets. Sophisticated integrated AM systems cover all the explained functions with internal or virtual segregation of the various functional areas and a structured access hierarchy of users depicted in figure 1.13.

ESTABLISHING AND RUNNING AN ASSET MANAGEMENT SYSTEM

Municipalities, even in emerging and developing countries, Kenya included, perform bits and pieces of good AM. They develop and then operate assets with repair and maintenance under public service units led by floor managers, albeit to various degrees and with various scopes and quality. Citizens and tourists walking in cities in the developing world, however, may well notice AM shortcomings in the poor quality of roads, public transport, buildings, air, or water. Cities in emerging and developing countries often fall short in SGAM (Bolva et al. 2013). They lack reliable, complete, and consistent asset registers, and many fall short in accounting AM. Instead, they have various inventories, financial reports, and balance sheet reports that cover assets and critical asset information often only partially (Kenyan examples are discussed in part II).

Therefore, cities in most emerging and developing countries are in desperate need to establish a reliable AM system from scratch (DPLG 2006): that is, to establish a completely new system and then transfer available data into the system while filling information gaps by uploading an enormous volume of new information derived from field verification of assets and liabilities. Kenya's devolution of the local government system with the amalgamation of 1,500 former local entities into 47 counties has amplified the need to establish basic AM frameworks, systems, and procedures and to urgently collect, verify, and register required information. In the following sections we summarize and explain the most critical issues in establishing AM, without aiming to be exhaustive.

Recognizing the dual nature of land, buildings, and infrastructure

Assets such as land, buildings, and infrastructure have a dual nature: they are *immovable property (real property)*, but at the same time they are *accounting assets*. Their dual nature should be recognized when they are transferred to counties and later when the counties manage them. In particular, the counties' legal rights to their parcels of real property should be properly verified, documented with title deeds, and protected. Furthermore, the fact that such property is "immovable" does not guarantee that it will not be lost or stolen. For example, in many countries (including Armenia, Bulgaria, Indonesia, Kosovo, the Kyrgyz Republic, and the Russian Federation), when local governments were introduced, some municipal land and buildings and the revenue streams they generated were grabbed by private actors, often through legally questionable transactions (Kaganova 2008). Reports completed by County Asset and Liability

Committees (CALCs) that were mandated to verify inherited assets in Kenyan counties often list a substantial number of assets verified as grabbed, encroached, or disputed and that need proper valuation and resolution. As a result, many such properties may have been lost in some Kenyan counties.

In Kenya, securing counties' property rights is urgent, given the uncertainty in this area. For example, the Nairobi City Council, according to a PricewaterhouseCoopers report, was able to produce title deeds only for about 30 percent of the land it claimed to own (PwC 2013). The identification of land parcels has improved substantially through the work of the CALCs under the guidance of the Intergovernmental Relations Technical Committee, whose 2018 report states that about 85 percent of land inherited from defunct entities has a registration number, but only 58 percent of counties' land parcels are surveyed nationwide, suggesting that 42 percent of land has no clear title and remained unsurveyed (IGRTC 2018).

Furthermore, recognizing the real estate nature of these immovable assets at the county level will establish a foundation for deploying specialized expertise and approaches to strategic management of building and land portfolios, an element universally acknowledged internationally as good practice (Deloitte 2011, 2012; Detter and Fölster 2015; Hentschel and Utter 2006).

Coordinating actions related to both aspects—legal ownership and accounting—requires sequencing steps depending on many factors. Approaches implemented in other countries that decentralized government and devolved assets often included an iterative process of clarifying legal rights and respectively revising lists of fixed assets included in the balance sheet (box 1.4).

Classifying assets specifically for good asset management

The dual nature of the assets discussed helps counties recognize that standard accounting classifications are not sufficient for the strategic and tactical decision-making and actions required for proper AM. Therefore, in managing their assets, virtually all governments proactively deploy other classifications as well. However, there are no universal types for such classifications; they often depend on the purpose of the classification, the focus of AM efforts (for example,

---

BOX 1.4

Reconciling legal rights to land and buildings and the balance sheet in the city of Varaždin, Croatia

The types of properties that had to be transferred to municipal governments in Croatia, after self-governments were reintroduced upon the disintegration of Yugoslavia, were defined by law. However, Croatia also embraced restitution of property (returning property or compensation to former private owners from whom property was expropriated and nationalized by socialist governments of Yugoslavia). This implied that some properties devolved to local governments were subject to restitution. Given this situation, the city government decided that it would not invest in valuation and maintenance of the properties that were going back to previous private owners. In addition, each year, a list of properties included on the municipal balance sheet was revised to exclude the properties restituted or otherwise disposed of and to include new acquisitions.

Source: USAID and UI 2006.

BOX 1.5

Examples of asset classification frameworks

Denver, Colorado, United States

- Mandatory: needed for the functions that are the responsibility of the local government by law (for example, police and fire stations)
- Discretionary: needed for the functions that the local government voluntarily supports and performs for social, political, or other reasons (for example, parks and social housing)
- Surplus or income-generating properties: properties not needed for any of the first two groups (for example, small cutoff land parcels or commercial rentals)

Cape Town, South Africa

More than 100 types of uses, clustered in eight main portfolios:

- Municipal use
- Infrastructure
- Social and community
- Investment: profit and land banking
- Economic development
- Housing
- Environmental
- Surplus

Sources: Utter 1989; Cape Town 2013.

land management or water system management), or the material form or function of the assets (Kaganova and Kopanyi 2014). The most common classifications consider the role of an asset in service delivery and other functions of local government. Examples of classifications used in Denver (Colorado, United States) and Cape Town (South Africa) are shown in box 1.5.

It is important to emphasize that the type of classification, recorded and/or declared often in *AM policy or strategy* is *a result of* a strategic approach to AM and not its prerequisite. It is advisable that the AM departments or teams in county governments consider introducing a relevant classification for AM purposes as one of its explicit AM tasks. However, developing such a classification can be left for later in the process of AM, given that a good classification would require contributions from the personnel involved in managing various assets, such as land, buildings, or infrastructure systems at floor level in service sectors and units. For instance, a large plot of land may host various water facilities for historic reasons; floor managers of water companies should be aware of and could help segregate such surplus land that can be made suitable for divestiture.

Focusing efforts on strategically important fixed assets—land, buildings, and infrastructure—and on strategic issues

Initial efforts in establishing an AM system, framework, and procedures should not focus on narrow accounting tasks, a common mistake in developing countries; just the opposite, the right approach should be based on all three dimensions and functions of AM explained in the preceding sections. All classifications used in AM need to recognize land and buildings explicitly, given that they often are the most valuable fixed assets. Inventory and verification of all sorts and forms of fixed assets are important tasks to complete, and the information will populate asset registers eventually, but the initial focus should be on the most valuable assets: land, buildings, infrastructure, vehicles, and high-value equipment.

Similarly, any prioritization needs to identify land and buildings, along with infrastructure facilities and networks, as the portfolios of the highest priority for AM throughout the county government. Finally, technical tasks, such as asset inventorying and related actions for asset recording such as verification and valuation, need to start with immovable property (for example, land, buildings, infrastructure networks), and not with small and costless movable property, as sometimes happens.

Adopting policy—establishing simple but binding principles of asset management

County governments would benefit from adopting a simple initial local document that creates rules for AM. This can be an initial asset management policy and strategy, adopted by the County Assembly and legally binding for the county government entities (appendixes A and B offer examples). An initial AM policy can cover issues such as the institutional setting and responsibilities for AM; the main principles of inventorying and auditing; transparency of rules, procedures, and mandates for assets; reporting rules; rules for disposition and allocation of assets for public and private uses; baseline principles of asset valuation; and overall priorities.

Setting up principles of asset valuation

County Assemblies should adopt the objectives and principles of asset valuation. The objectives and principles should include distinctions between historic values for accounting purposes and market values for decision-making and business purposes. These principles also should provide guidance about classification of assets that need to be valued (such as land, buildings, or other marketable assets) and asset clusters that have limited marketability, thus making precise market valuation difficult, impossible, or unnecessary (for example, roads, drainage, or school buildings). In such cases, simple value estimates may be allowed using the replacement cost and possibly comparable value estimates in a mass valuation modality (Detter and Fölster 2018).

A key rule (preferably defined in an initial asset management policy) should be that the current valuation is initial and approximate, serving for initial registering and accounting of assets, but it should not serve as valuation for acquisition or disposition. Therefore, no disposition of land or buildings can be approved and conducted without a specific target market valuation. Finally, given that valuation is an expensive and time-consuming process, priorities for initial valuation should be established. A good practice would be to start with initial valuation of the most valuable and marketable properties, such as land and buildings.

Establishing a robust organizational framework of intersectoral collaboration for introduction of comprehensive county asset management

Organizational settings can vary. However, a framework that proved to work well internationally in many cities includes (1) establishing a special AM department, directorate, or team; (2) appointing dedicated asset managers at specialized sectoral departments (land), enterprises (water, solid waste), or service units (stadium, community hall); and (3) creating a temporary or permanent AM taskforce or committee (for example, the AM and disposal committee in NCC).

International experiences show that such a task force or high committee can be an effective tool for overcoming fragmentation of AM within a local government and establishing a consistent, comprehensive countrywide AM system, approaches, and practices (Peteri 2003). The AM directorate should serve as a permanent secretariat of an AM committee, which should be led by a high-ranking county officer and include representatives of the main sectors and units that hold and are responsible for managing substantial volumes of fixed assets and/or have policy-making power. NCC government has adopted a plan and drafted terms of reference for setting up a high-level AM leadership committee (see box 1.6 and appendix D); other counties may emulate these terms of reference for forming AM committees.

Managing municipal enterprises or other subordinated entities

Municipal enterprises or other legally independent entities (public utility companies or PUCs) with full or majority county ownership (county corporations and county government–linked corporations) often play important roles in local services in both developed and developing countries, as in Kenya (for example, Nairobi or Kakamega Water Companies, Kajiado Waste Management Company). The critical mistakes local governments in developing countries make in this field include the following:

- Signing short and unclear contracts or failing to sign any specific agreement with PUCs
- Assuming that municipal delegates or chairpersons in PUCs' boards provide sufficient control over these PUCs and ensure proper management of these strategic assets
- Poorly measuring investments in PUCs or not measuring investment efficiency at all, or not considering investment alternatives or modalities, because the driving idea of the investment is to form an off-budget entity without considering best forms and modalities
- Providing huge capital and/or operating subsidies without measuring and conditioning performance

---

BOX 1.6

The objective of establishing a high-level asset management leadership committee in Nairobi City County, excerpts

To increase awareness of integrated asset management.

To discuss, approve, and propose for the County Assembly and the governor high-level strategic asset management decisions such as acquisition, disposal, divestiture, or restructuring of assets on strategic nature, size, and value.

To audit and report progress on a regular basis to the governor, the County Assembly, the audit committee, external auditors, and any other committee where necessary.

To fast-track the approval and implementation of the county's assets management documents such as asset management policy, strategy, plan, and information system, among others.

To establish and approve the performance reporting framework that communicates the status of asset management to all levels of the county.

Source: Excerpted from Nairobi City County draft terms of reference for a high-level asset management committee (see appendix D).

- Having low understanding and control over contingent liabilities granted to PUCs that often remain hidden, unmeasured, and unaccounted for until the demand for payment is called

In sum, counties in Kenya should put a high emphasis also on professionally managing PUCs in the course of strategic AM, not only because they are legally invested assets, but also because they have strong impacts on budgets (this is the case in all seven surveyed counties, discussed in part II), expenditure control, and services and AM practices. These responsibilities are well regulated in sections 183–185 of the PFM Act 2012 in Kenya. On the other hand, the counties inherited an overly complicated and somewhat dysfunctional governance framework for the water services that includes the following:

- Water service boards (WSBs) established to develop, own, and lease water assets to county governments (dissolved in 2016)
- The Water Services Regulatory Board (WASREB) as the regulator that provides licenses and approves water tariffs with lease fees payable to the WASREB
- Water works development agencies (WWDAs) with a mandate to develop cross-county public water works

As a result, the counties are unable to fully function as owners and regulators over their water companies; counties are constrained in developing assets, because WWDAs and WSBs often had undertaken most large developments without consulting with counties or water companies about the need, technical modalities, or financial feasibility. Consequently, counties and their water companies are not in full control of assets and expenditures. The Constitution and the Water Act 2016 require WASREB and WWDAs to hand over all assets and liabilities regarding the county water companies to the counties. However, this is a part of the tasks mandated by the Transition to Devolved Government Act of 2012 (TDG 2012) that has not been completed, that is, transferring assets from the national entities. This unclear and incomplete transition creates major losses and undermines the viability of the water companies, and in the longer term weakens viability of the counties' water services.

DEVOLUTION AND ASSET MANAGEMENT IN TRANSITION: INTERNATIONAL EXPERIENCES OF RELEVANCE TO CURRENT KENYAN CHALLENGES

The Kenyan devolution program was built on international experiences. It established a solid legal, regulatory, and institutional framework and assigned service delivery functions (expenditure assignments) adequate to the Kenyan situation and the characteristics of the new county governments. It also assigned largely adequate revenues with good own-source revenue mandates (revenue assignment) and a reliable system of transfers from the national government to counties. The equitable shares that are unconditional transfers provide a reliable and substantial source of revenue with apparent equalization effects, although NCC seems to be slightly underfinanced as measured by the per capita equitable shares, which are about half of the national average. This underfinancing might need closer scrutiny.

This section focuses on one critical aspect of devolution, namely, transferring assets and liabilities across government entities, especially from defunct to new local governments in Kenya, without aiming to analyze the Kenya devolution program or discuss and summarize the enormous literature of devolution or decentralization around the world (KADP 2018).

The Kenya devolution in 2013 has numerous similarities to the devolution programs in Central and Eastern Europe (CEE) that occurred in the early 1990s, but also significant differences. The lessons of CEE may offer helpful examples and solutions for several burning issues still unresolved nine years into Kenya's devolution. A most critical issue is the transfer of all assets related to the devolved functions, which has remained incomplete. The counties have received and partially taken over assets of the defunct local governments, but assets from national government entities have not yet been transferred. The other critical unresolved question is the counties' takeover of disputed fixed and financial assets and liabilities and resolution of disputes. This section summarizes related international experiences to highlight options for Kenya.

Several other developing countries have reorganized their intergovernmental systems in recent decades with frameworks like CEE countries. For instance, Pakistan took a centralized approach under a military regime that sought improved legitimacy; the National Reconstruction Bureau guided and implemented the devolution in Pakistan starting in 2001. The devolution program was focused on setting up a devolved system for provinces and local governments in parallel. The National Reconstruction Bureau had strong power to delegate functions and responsibilities that experienced Pakistani academics modeled after devolved federal systems (Paracha 2003; World Bank 2004). The devolution in Nepal that started in 2015 has emulated devolution models from Pakistan and even learned lessons from Kenya's devolution (Husain 2017).

Many Southeastern European countries also implemented decentralization or devolution programs by amalgamating small local governments into larger ones. Transferring inherited liabilities became a major problem in most of these countries, such as Albania, Bosnia and Herzegovina, and Montenegro, and most issues remained unresolved after three or four years or more in devolution (Merkaj, Zhllima, and Imami 2017). For instance, Montenegro's finance ministry settled liabilities with creditors and then accounted them as loans to the new municipalities, which became overburdened with huge debts that have paralyzed their development capacities for decades to come (Kopanyi et al. 2018). This was a questionable solution that saved creditors but left all burdens on the shoulders of the new municipalities. Municipal associations and the finance ministry keep fighting to find workable and pragmatic solutions for this debt burden on municipalities.

Kenya's devolution combined elements of both a *big bang* and a *gradual transition*. The devolution started as a big bang on March 27, 2013, with an immediate transfer of powers and responsibilities from defunct local entities to county governments as more than 1,500 entities were amalgamated into 47 counties. The transfer of assets and liabilities started a year before the local government elections, but it remained incomplete by the election. Instead, the transfer of assets and liabilities followed a gradual path and continued for over nine years. Unfortunately, this transition of assets has not been smooth, and it has generated substantial losses in both fixed and financial assets (see the Nairobi City County case study, chapter 6). Important actions are still needed and possible; these are the subject of this section.

Changing the intergovernmental administration system requires transferring assets from one tier of government to other tiers or entities with or without transfers of the attached liabilities. Local governments around the world often face great challenges in taking over assets and attached liabilities, whether because of financial, environmental, or social obligations.

Transfer actions often cause disputes between respective parties on takeover. Key issues include the following: (1) Is the takeover mandatory and unconditional, or voluntary? (2) Does the receiver have the right to reject the takeover entirely, for example, because the net value of a particular asset is negative due to high debts or large obligations attached (for example, environmental cleanup) that would cost more than the market value of the asset? (3) Is there an option to take over without obligations, which requires a third party (often the treasury) to cover liabilities? And finally, (4) who should be made responsible for the uninterrupted provision of services if assets are disputed, and the receiver (municipality) does not want to take them due to unmanageable obligations (for example, heavy debt)?

Table 1.2 summarizes the key characteristics of frameworks and procedures applied in transferring assets and liabilities in selected CEE countries. The general principles were to transfer service responsibilities, assets, and attached liabilities by law on a certain date, also known as big-bang devolution. But also, some laws mandated stakeholders (municipalities and ministries) to establish committees for dispute resolution (for example, in Hungary and Poland). An appeal framework supported not only fairness in the takeover system but also

TABLE 1.2 **Summary of frameworks and procedures for transferring assets and liabilities in CEE countries**

COUNTRIES	TRANSFER FRAMEWORK	ISSUES	DISPUTE RESOLUTION	COVERING OBLIGATIONS
Hungary	By virtue of law (LG Act, Transfer Act, Civil Code) or through PTCs and commissions	Land ownership, vacant land, and liabilities Disputes over value of public companies and their unused land	Right of refusal to accept, mandatory negotiations Ultimate authority through PTCs, court (civil code) in co-owned properties	Final owner of asset
Latvia	By virtue of law or through PTCs and commissions	Land ownership, vacant land, and liabilities Disputes over value of public companies and their unused land	Negotiations or court if unwillingness to accept assets	National government may transfer funds to cover cost of maintenance or clear debt Court decisions obeyed
Poland	By virtue of law, the *voivod* (chief of region) proposes transfers and approves takeover based on devolved functions	Appeals by municipalities or private individuals Disputes over land ownership, vacant land, and liabilities	Negotiation, if failed: National Enfranchisement Commission, Supreme Court, or Civil Court	Local governments' obligation to take over both assets and liabilities Treasury may pay legal and administrative costs to clear a property's legal status or provide earmarked grants to complete ongoing construction
Slovak Republic	By virtue of law via subdistrict or district offices of national government, municipalities, and Privatization Commission	Based on devolved functions Disputes over value of assets and liabilities of public enterprises	Negotiation and bottom-up order of decision power of following entities: national committees, district and regional offices of government, and municipalities	Liabilities transferred with properties up to the amount of value of transferred property No obligation to take over overdue suppliers' credits or overdue tax, welfare, and health insurance liabilities

Source: Peteri 2003.
Note: CEE = Central and Eastern Europe; LG = local governments; PTCs = property transfer committees.

incentivized stakeholders to seek mutually acceptable solutions out of court and without appeals. Many countries, however, issued more detailed regulations for asset and liability takeover within one year of the devolution after learning the initial experiences about disputed cases.

Asset data systems in CEE were also incomplete or imprecise, but legislators took pragmatic approaches to ensure uninterrupted use of assets and relatively fast takeover of the bulk of both assets and liabilities. Unclear ownership was quite common, with missing, overlapping, or conflicting ownership documents, but legislators built pragmatic and operational conflict resolution procedures. However, laws included rules to motivate stakeholders to seek mutually agreed-upon solutions. As a result, over 90 percent of transfers and takeovers (including both assets and liabilities) were completed within one year, although some complicated and problematic cases took several years to close.

Taking over assets together with liabilities was the common principle, but in turn governments (treasuries) often provided grants to ease the financial burdens posed by liabilities inherited by the new local governments (Poland) or the treasury took over and served most inherited liabilities (Slovak Republic). Major disputes related to the valuation of public enterprises if new local governments had to take them over with an unmanageable magnitude of liabilities, such as unpaid bills and debt service. These issues often overlapped with the national privatization programs in CEE, and some resolutions were reached by the national privatization entities' offsetting assets and liabilities (Croatia). Disputed private ownership and compensation obligations appeared in most of the countries (especially Poland); these resolutions often ended in court procedures, and many took several years to conclude, but these represented overall a small share of total asset value.

INSTITUTIONAL FRAMEWORKS AND PROCEDURES FOR TRANSFER AND TAKEOVER OF RESPONSIBILITIES AND ASSETS IN CEE

The most fundamental difference between Kenya and CEE is apparent in the institutional framework. The transfer in CEE countries was based on sets of designated entities such as committees in each key stakeholder and a higher-level entity for appeal and final decision power, but the new municipalities were in the driver's seat to initiate and effectively did initiate the processing of disputed cases. Legislators had anticipated conflicts and disputes, so they built in checks and balances, a framework, and rules for dispute resolution, whereas "mandatory" negotiations and compromises were the most fundamental instruments.

The basic idea was to clean up the ownership system after transition as quickly and simply as possible. This was successful overall, since 80 to 90 percent of properties had minor administrative issues, and the committees had to deal with only the remaining cases, mostly ownership and compensation issues with state enterprises and private owners. This way, the new municipalities became de jure and de facto owners of most assets within a few months or in the first year of devolution.

Hungary's and Poland's models represent the two basic institutional frameworks followed by other CEE countries with different modalities and are worth considering in Kenya.

The Hungarian model is an example of a *decentralized model of asset transfer*, in which a new local government takes over assets from national ownership and custody by various sectoral or functional ministries. As indicated previously, mandatory established committees in each key stakeholder and mandatory negotiations were the pivotal elements of the transfer/takeover framework and procedures in Hungary (figure 1.14).

In Hungary, the key attributes were (1) all assets and liabilities were transferred by the power of the law; (2) asset and liability transfer committees were established in all ministries and local governments; (3) local governments had to identify, list, and analyze disputed assets or liability cases and initiate dispute resolutions with respective ministries through the committees; and (4) local governments had to report and submit for verdicts failed resolution cases to the interior ministry, the governing body over the local governments.

Agreements were reached relatively easily, but appeals were also possible and happened in a noticeable number of cases, mostly regarding valuation, liability takeover, or compensation for the transfer of public companies. The interior ministry assessed appeals and issued verdicts to resolve disputes and close the cases. Court procedures were also possible but rarely used in Hungary.

In Poland, the asset transfer framework combined elements of both *centralized* and *decentralized models*. It was centralized for local entities in each region and decentralized at the national level. Regional offices of the central government and the chiefs of regions (*voivods*) played pivotal roles in asset transfer (figure 1.15). They approved the lists of assets to be transferred to the new municipalities and represented the state in appeals cases. When negotiations failed to reach mutually acceptable conditions and final agreement, the voivod forwarded the cases to the supreme court for final verdicts, which were mutually accepted. Many private citizens appealed, claiming private ownership of land or buildings since before World War II. These appeals often reached court, and some took years to conclude.

FIGURE 1.14

Institutional framework and work procedures in Hungary

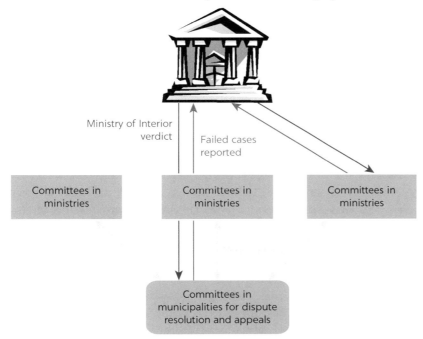

Source: Based on Peteri 2003.
Note: Green arrows indicate negotiations; orange arrows indicate submission of failed cases to the Ministry of Interior; red arrows indicate verdicts.

FIGURE 1.15
Institutional framework and work procedures in Poland

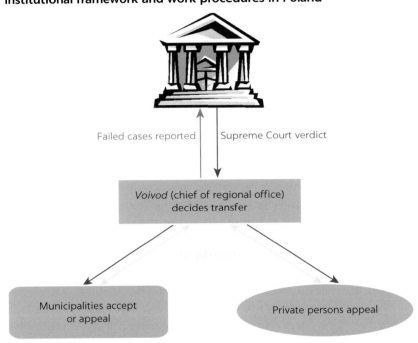

Source: Based on Peteri 2003.
Note: Green arrows indicate negotiations; orange arrows indicate submission of failed cases to the Supreme Court; red arrows indicate verdicts.

Table 1.3 summarizes the similarities and differences between Kenya and CEE countries on devolution, handover and takeover of assets and liabilities, and dispute resolution (details on CEE are in table 1.2). There are similarities in the fundamental characteristics of devolution, especially in the legal framework of devolution such as transfer of functions on the inauguration date of elected county governments (big-bang devolution) and the similar scope of devolved competencies. However, in Kenya under the Transition Authority (TDG 2012), the initial institutional framework and the procedures for asset handover/takeover were very centralized, thought to be largely completed in one year, and followed a different path than CEE.

The main differences between Kenya and CEE include the following: (1) there were no committees established for takeover of assets in Kenya; (2) the Transition Authority (TA) was entrusted to verify, validate, inventory, and transfer assets and liabilities to counties, but this modality had reached no transfers three years after devolution when the TA was dissolved; and (3) negotiations on disputed assets were not part of the accepted procedures, except as an option to report the case to the National and County Government Coordinating Summit (also known as the Summit), a coordination body established under the Intergovernmental Relations Act 2012, and an option for court procedures if the Summit advises, but this instrument has been used rarely in practice. NCC has tested the dispute resolution framework by appealing a case against national government entities to the Summit, which, however, ruled to take the case to the court. The court returned the case to the Summit ruling to hold out-of-court negotiations before the Summit, but those negotiations failed before the Summit due to the unwillingness of national entities to compromise and seek mutually acceptable solutions and the inability of the Summit to propose and enforce a final resolution.

TABLE 1.3 Comparison of frameworks and practices for transferring assets and liabilities, CEE countries and Kenya

CHARACTERISTICS AND ISSUES	CENTRAL AND EASTERN EUROPE	KENYA
Devolution	Big bang with one turnkey date of transfer of both responsibilities and assets and liabilities	Big bang with one turnkey date of transfer of responsibilities (devolved functions) but no immediate transfer of assets or liabilities
Scope of transfer of assets and liabilities	Transfer assets from national government or across local governments (Poland)	Transfer assets of defunct and amalgamated former local governments and foreseen transfer of service assets from national government entities
Legal-institutional framework to transfer assets and liabilities	By law, defined by devolved functions, the day of devolution Committees at national, regional, and local levels; higher national commission for appeal	Scope of assets defined by devolved functions, but Transition Authority (TA) was entrusted for verification, validation, inventory, and transfer In parallel, ministerial orders and audits ruled actions (some in conflict with TA law and TA's practice)
Transfer and takeover	Outgoing administration formal handover of documents	Takeover of service-related assets without formal de facto handover (and failed de jure handover)
Dispute resolution	Negotiation via committees; appeals to higher committees, national commission, or Supreme Court or civil court Higher commissions dealt only with disputed cases (tens of thousands of appeals in CEE)	Mediation by the Summit,[a] chaired by the deputy president (less operational than the CEE system) Assets transfer by virtue of law in February 2017 without specific framework for dispute resolution was adopted
National Treasury intervention	Financial support for workout of liabilities or to cover cost of procedures to solve legal issues	No framework at the time of devolution No financial support

Sources: Based on Peteri 2003 and Kenyan legal documents.
Note: CEE = Central and Eastern Europe.
a. The Summit = the National and County Government Coordinating Summit.

REFERENCES

AssetWorks. 2014. *Quick Guide: Asset Management 101, A Step by Step Asset Management Plan.* San Antonio, TX: AssetWorks. http://my.assetworks.com/rs/153-QDM-861/images /Quick%20Guide_EAM_Asset_Management_101_web.pdf.

Bolva, Elva, Robert Dippelsman, Kara Rideout, and Andrea Schaechter. 2013. "Another Look at Governments' Balance Sheets: The Role of Nonfinancial Assets," IMF Working Paper WP/13/95, International Monetary Fund, Washington, DC.

Cambridge (City of). 2013. *"Asset Management Plan—Core Service Sustainability"* Ontario, Canada: City of Cambridge.

Cape Town. 2013 "Asset Management Policy." City of Cape Town, South Africa. https://resource. capetown.gov.za/documentcentre/Documents/Bylaws%20and%20policies/Asset%20 Management%20-%20%28Policy%20number%2011724%29%20approved%20on%20 27%20February%202013.pdf.

Colorado DOT (Department of Transportation). 2019. *Risk-Based Asset Management Plan.* Denver: Colorado DOT). https://www.codot.gov/performance/assets/cdot_tamp_9-12-19 -website.pdf.

Deloitte. 2011. *Municipal Real Estate: Comparing Public Real Estate Management in European Cities.* London: Deloitte.

Deloitte. 2012. *Office Politics: Public Sector Property Management in New Zealand.* London: Deloitte.

Detter, D., and S. Fölster. 2015. *The Public Wealth of Nations—How Management of Public Assets Can Boost Economic Growth.* London: Palgrave Macmillan.

Detter, D. and S. Fölster. 2018. "Unlocking Public Wealth: Governments Could Do a Better Job Managing Their Assets." *Finance and Development,* International Monetary Fund: March 2018, pp 44–48. https://www.imf.org/Publications/fandd/issues/2018/03/detter.

DPLG (Department of Provincial and Local Government). 2006. *Guidelines for Infrastructure Asset Management in Local Government 2006–2009.* Pretoria: DPLG.

EPA (US Environmental Protection Agency). 2012. *Getting Started with CUPSS: A Workbook for Users.* Washington, DC: US EPA. https://www.epa.gov/sites/production/files/2015-10/documents/gettingstartedworkbook.pdf.

EPA (US Environmental Protection Agency). 2015. "Suggested Checklist for Public Water Supply System Operation & Maintenance Manual." Washington, DC: US EPA. https://www.epa.gov/sites/production/files/documents/om_checklisttasks.pdf.

Fairfax County (Virginia). 2018. "2018 Public Safety Bond Referendum." Fairfax, VA: Fairfax County Board of Supervisors.

Hentschel, J., and M. Utter. 2006. "U.S. Cities: An Entrepreneurial Approach to Municipal Real Estate Asset Management." In *Managing Government Property Assets: International Experiences,* edited by O. Kaganova and J. McKellar. Washington, DC: Urban Institute Press.

Husain, W. 2017. "Lessons for Nepal in Devolution Amendments: A View from Pakistan's 18th Amendment." *Nepal Journal of Legal Studies.* https://www.academia.edu/33176903.

IGRTC (Intergovernmental Relations Technical Committee). 2018. *Report on the Identification, Verification, Validation, and Transfer of Assets and Liabilities of the Defunct Local Authorities as at 27th March 2013.* Nairobi: IGRTC. https://igrtc.go.ke/download/consolidated-report-on-assets-and-liabilities-of-the-defunct-local-authorities-2018/.

IPWEA (Institute of Public Works Engineering Australia). 2015. *International Infrastructure Management Manual.* 5th ed. Perth, Australia: IPWEA. https://www.ipwea.org/western australia/publications/bookshop-old/ipweabookshop/iimm.

ISO (International Organization for Standardization). 2014. "ISO 55000:2014(en) Asset Management—Overview, Principles and Terminology." Geneva: ISO. https://www.iso.org/obp/ui/#iso:std:iso:55000:ed-1:v2:en.

KADP. 2018. *Kenya Accountable Devolution Program,* Annual Report 2018. Washington, DC: World Bank.

Kaganova, O. 2008. "Integrating Public Property in the Realm of Fiscal Transparency and Anti-Corruption Efforts." In *Finding the Money: Public Accountability and Service Efficiency through Fiscal Transparency,* edited by Gábor Péteri, 209–222. Budapest: Local Government and Public Service Reform Initiative/Open Society Institute.

Kaganova, O. 2011. "Guidebook on Capital Investment Planning for Local Governments." Urban Development Series Knowledge paper 13, October 2011, World Bank, Washington, DC.

Kaganova, O. 2015. "Strategic Management Models and Change Drivers in Government Real Estate." Paper presented at the Workplace Network 2015 Annual Conference, Mexico City, September 2015. https://www.researchgate.net/publication/282613360.

Kaganova, O. 2020. "How American Cities Can Benefit from 'Land Value Capture' Instruments in the Time of COVID-19 and Beyond." *Real Estate Issues* 44 (18).

Kaganova, O., A. Akhmatov, and C. Undeland. 2008. "Introducing More Transparent and Efficient Land Management in Post-Socialist Cities: Lessons from Kyrgyzstan." *International Journal on Strategic Property Management* 12 (3): 161–81.

Kaganova, O., B. Dash, K. Bat-Orig, and Y. Chen. 2018 *Guidebook on Capital Investment Planning for the Capital City of Ulaanbaatar.* Washington, DC: World Bank.

Kaganova, O., and M. Kopanyi. 2014. "Managing Local Assets." In *Municipal Finances: Handbook for Local Governments,* edited by C. Farvacque-Vitkovic and M. Kopanyi, ch. 6. Washington, DC: World Bank. https://openknowledge.worldbank.org/handle/10986/18725.

Kaganova, O., and M. Kopanyi. 2016. *Introducing County Asset Management in Kenya: Initial Guidelines and Draft Action Plan.* Washington, DC: World Bank.

Kopanyi, M., Merita Toska, Brankica Lenic, Goran Rakic, Anto Bajo, Marjan Nikolov, Natasa Obradovic, and Ljiljana Brdarevic. 2018. *Municipal Finance Self-Assessment (MFSA): Experiences in South-East Europe 2011–2015.* Washington, DC. World Bank.

Koul, A., and S. John. 2015. "A Life-Cycle Cost Approach for Evaluation of Sewage Treatment Plants." *International Journal of Innovative Research in Advanced Engineering.* 2 (7): 15–20. https://www.academia.edu/15445954/IJIRAE_A_Life_Cycle_Cost_Approach_for_Evaluation_of_Sewage_Treatment_Plants.

Merkaj, E., E. Zhllima, and D. Imami. 2017. "Fiscal Decentralization in Albania: Trends and Challenges at the Dawn of Territorial Reform." *Journal of Balkan and Near Eastern Studies* 19 (6): 684–699. https://doi.org/10.1080/19448953.2017.1328898.

NALAS (Network of Associations of Local Authorities of South-East Europe). 2014. *Municipal Asset Management Toolkit :Guidelines for Local Decision-Makers*. Skopje, North Macedonia. http://www.nalas.eu/Publications/Books/Municipal_Asset_Management_Toolkit.

NALM (National Assets and Liabilities Management Department). 2020a. "National Asset and Liability Management Policy 2020." https://www.treasury.go.ke/wp-content /uploads/2021/03/Asset-Liability-Mgt-Policy.-doc-Final.pdf.

NALM (National Assets and Liabilities Management Department). 2020b. "General Guidelines on Asset and Liability Management in the Public Sector." https://www.treasury.go.ke /wp-content/uploads/2021/03/GeneralGuidelines-on-asset-and-liability-management -2020-Final.pdf.

NALM (National Assets and Liabilities Management Department). 2020c. "Guidelines for Management of Specific Categories of Assets and Liabilities, 2020." https://www.treasury .go.ke/wp-content/uploads/2021/03/Specific-guidelines-2020-Final.pdf.

Ottawa (City of). 2012. "Comprehensive Asset Management Policy." Ottawa, Canada: City of Ottawa. http://documents.ottawa.ca/en/document/comprehensive-asset-management -policy.

Paracha, S. A. 2003. *Devolution Plan in Pakistan: Context, Implementation and Issues*. Budapest: Open Society Institute.

Peteri, G. 2003. *From Usage to Ownership—Transfer of Public Property to Local Governments in Central Europe*. Budapest: Open Society Institute.

PFM. 2012. Public Finance Management Act, no. 18 of 2012. https://www.pcf.go.ke/index.php /public-financial-management-act.

Pride, Alan. 2016. "Reliability-Centered Maintenance (RCM)." Washington, DC: National Institute of Building Sciences. https://www.wbdg.org/resources/reliability-centered -maintenance-rcm.

PwC (PricewaterhouseCoopers). 2013. "Consultancy Services for Development of Policies and Procedures for the Transfer of Assets and Liabilities, and Debt Resolution Systems Based on 15 KMP Beneficiary Local Authorities." Draft Final Report, July 2013. London: PricewaterhouseCoopers.

Sabaliauskas, Kestutis. 2013. "E-Governance in Lithuania." Presentation at "Collaboration for Secured Ownership" conference, Uppsala, Sweden, May 29–31, 2013. https://www .registrucentras.lt/en/.

Stanford University. 2005. *Guidelines for Lifecycle Cost Analysis: Building and Land*. Palo Alto, CA: Stanford University Press.

TDG. 2012. Transition to Devolved Government Act, no. 1 of 2012, enacted March 9, 2012. http:// www.parliament.go.ke/sites/default/files/2017-05/TransitiontoDevolvedGovernment ActNo1of2012.pdf.

UAC. 2011. Urban Areas and Cities Act, no. 13 of 2011. http://www.parliament.go.ke/sites /default/files/2017-05/UrbanAreasandCitiesAct_No13of2011.pdf.

UN (United Nations). 2021. *Managing Infrastructure Assets for Sustainable Development: A Handbook for Local and National Governments*. New York: UN. https://www.un-ilibrary .org/content/books/9789210051880.

USAID and UI (US Agency for International Development and Urban Institute). 2006. *Local Government Reform Project, 2000–2006*. Washington, DC: USAID and Urban Institute.

Utter, Marilee. 1989. "Public Asset Management." Economic Development Commentary, Denver, Vol. 13 (Fall): 4–11. https://journals.sagepub.com › doi › abs.

World Bank. 2004. *Devolution in Pakistan*. World Bank, Asian Development Bank, and DFID joint study. Washington, DC: World Bank.

2 Asset Management in Transition under Kenya's Devolution

INTRODUCTION

All countries transforming intergovernmental systems follow bumpy roads as they design and implement decentralization or devolution by amalgamating a large number of entities into a small number of new units. Whether developing, transitioning, or developed, all countries face numerous technical, legal, institutional, and political challenges.

Assets play a distinctive role in institutional reforms because they represent a bulky stock that remains in place, and most parts are literally immovable regardless of the direction or nature of the institutional changes. The government of Kenya recognized this way before the Kenya devolution program, and the Ministry of Finance (MoF) released a circular (MoF 2000) that outlined the procedure of public asset management (AM). The circular instructs accounting officers to establish government AM registries and committees in their respective ministries, departments, or local governments. Failure to comply with this circular for over a decade created one major impediment to the devolution and transition of assets to the new county governments.

Another peculiarity is that the assets are the material base of the local public services that need to be delivered uninterrupted during and regardless of the immense institutional or political changes. Thus, the assets should be kept operating regardless of institutional, legal, or financial uncertainties during transitions. The Transition to Devolved Government (TDG) Act clearly states these objectives: "The object and purpose of this Act is to provide a legal and institutional framework for a coordinated transition to the devolved system of government while ensuring continued delivery of services to citizens" (TDG Act 2012, preamble).

Finally, assets often are associated with environmental, social, or financial liabilities that should not be detached from assets and thus cannot be ignored; on the contrary, financial liabilities need close control and management during transition because they are growing unstoppably, some at high speed.

LEGAL AND INSTITUTIONAL FRAMEWORK FOR ASSET MANAGEMENT AND TRANSFER DURING TRANSITION

The formation of the legal and institutional framework for Kenya's devolution started with enactment of the new constitution in 2010, followed by numerous laws and regulations. The legal and institutional framework was by and large adopted, complete, and effective about one year before the devolution elections took place on March 27, 2013. The most important regulations include the following:

- Constitution of Kenya 2010
- County Governments Act, no. 17 of 2012
- County Public Finance Management (PFM) Act, Regulation 2015 (amended PFM Act 2012)
- Intergovernmental Relations (ITGR) Act, no. 2 of 2012
- Legal Notice no. 44: Regulation on Transition to Devolved Government (Mechanism for Closure and Transfer of Public Records and Information), Legislative Supplement no. 23, March 11, 2016
- Ministry of Finance (MoF), Circular no. 14 of 2000, October 13
- Ministry of Local Government (MLG), Circular ref. no. MLG/1333/TY/ (52) of February 18, 2013
- Public Finance Management (PFM) Act, no. 18 of 2012 (amended in 2015 by Legal Notice no. 34. Legislative Supplement no. 17, County PFM Act, March 20, 2015—see third bullet)
- Public Finance Management (PFM) Transition Act, no. 8 of 2013
- Transition to Devolved Government (TDG) Act, no. 1 of 2012
- Urban Areas and Cities (UAC) Act, no. 13 of 2011

Legislators were aware of the importance of regulation and facilitation of the transfer of assets from the defunct local entities to the new county governments. That's why they enacted the TDG Act 2012, which legislated establishment of the Transition Authority (TA) in March 2012, and with that action a centralized modality of transfer of assets and liabilities was stipulated and effectively established in Kenya a year before devolution. Figure 2.1 illustrates the institutional framework, characterized by clear assignments of functions and responsibilities, a strong chain of command, and clear checks and balances, with ultimate power of command by the president and the parliament. In the figure, red arrows indicate commands, and blue arrows indicate reporting duties.

The TA consisted of eight permanent secretaries from various state departments, the attorney general, and a TA secretary, an appointed person with no voting power. The TA directly reported to the Commission for the Implementation of the Constitution, the National and County Government Coordinating Summit (also known as the Summit), and the Council of Governors especially seeking guidance on the highest strategic decisions.

The TA was a powerful and knowledgeable body suitable for strong control, guidance, and high-level decision-making, but it was not equipped to perform daily operative tasks and fieldwork, which was performed by the the TA administration; the chair, who was the secretary of the TA; the staff of the TA administration; and a large fleet of consultants hired to complete field verification and validation. TA staff and hired specialists drafted work procedures, templates, rules, and regulations approved by the TA.

FIGURE 2.1

Institutional framework for verification and transfer of assets in Kenya's devolution

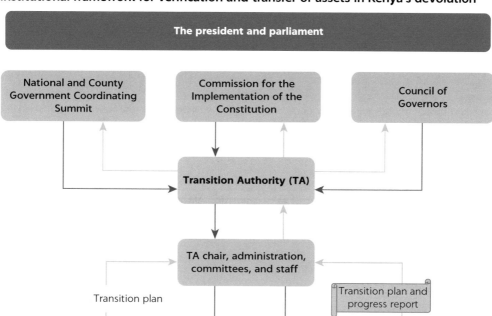

Source: Based on Transition to Devolved Government (TDG) Act 2012.
Note: Red arrows indicate command; blue arrows indicate reporting duties.

To support a smooth and controlled transition, the PFM laws (PFM Act 2012 and PFM Transition Act 2013) stipulated establishment of a transition county treasury in each county a year before elections, chaired by a transition principal officer who ought to report to the TA (table 2.1). This way, the TA was empowered to monitor, guide, and control all key aspects of PFM and asset and liability management in both the outgoing and incoming local entities a year before election.

The TA upon induction became the custodian of all national and county assets and liabilities—with a moratorium on asset transfers without TA approval (table 2.1)—still being held and used by various national government entities and 1,500 outgoing local entities from March 9, 2012, but also after induction of county governments until March 4, 2016. The well-justified logic behind this arrangement was that the TA was assumed to have (or was enabled to acquire) the professional and technical capacity to safeguard assets and liabilities during transition and prepare an initial inventory of assets and liabilities, because the outgoing local entities had neither asset registers nor even simple but reliable inventories.

The sectoral units (water, education, health, and so forth) of the outgoing entities had a substantial volume of asset information that was often incomplete and unverified but accessible to the TA one year before the election. There was an initial plan that all data on assets and liabilities of both the national government and the former local authorities would be stored in an Integrated National and County Asset Register Center housed initially at the Office of the Auditor General, but this plan has not materialized (TA-ICPAK 2013). The TA thus had

TABLE 2.1 The Kenya Transition Authority's asset management functions and responsibilities during transition

Transition period: Adoption of TDG Act 2012, three years after first election March 9, 2012–March 27, 2016 (texts from TA Law 2012)	
Transition Authority is custodial of county assets in transition period.	
Moratorium on transfer of assets. . . "local authority shall not transfer assets and liabilities during the transition period. But local authority shall—during *phase one*, transfer assets or liabilities with the approval of the Authority, during *phase two*, transfer assets or liabilities with the approval of the Authority; The Authority may, on its own motion or on a petition by any person, review or reverse any irregular transfer of assets."	
Phase one	**Phase two**
Enactment of TA Law until Induction of County Governments March 9, 2012–March 27, 2013	Induction of County Governments plus three years March 27, 2013–March 4, 2016
Transition Authority: (1) audit assets and liabilities of local authorities, to establish the asset, debts, and liabilities of each Local Authority; (2) audit local authority infrastructure in the counties, to establish the number and functionality of plant and equipment in Local Authorities; and (3) audit the government infrastructure in the counties, to establish the number and functionality of plant and equipment for the purpose of vesting them to either level of government.	**Transition Authority:** (1) complete any activity that may be outstanding from Phase One; (2) oversee the transfer of functions from the national government to the county government; (3) facilitate the county governments in the performance of their functions.

Source: Based on TDG Act 2012.
Note: TA = Transition Authority; TDG = Transition to Devolved Government.

an enormous task to establish and verify asset inventories from scratch before the election.

Legislators assumed that the TA would be efficient, effective, and fast, and thus it could complete most of the assigned tasks of facilitating asset transfers—that is, creating initial asset inventories and verifying and auditing all county assets and liabilities inherited from defunct local entities—within 12 months before the time of the local election and induction of new county governments on March 27, 2013. This period was called phase one of the four-year foreseen total transition period (see table 2.1). The initial vision suggested that in phase two, that is, within three years after induction of county governments, the TA would need only to focus on completing some outstanding activities, facilitate transfer of assets from national entities to counties, and help county governments perform their functions. However, in practice, the sequence of events and the groundwork appeared to be quite different from the initial optimistic visions.

The institutional framework of AM and transfer drastically changed further on March 4, 2016, when the TA was dissolved and the Intergovernmental Relations Technical Committee (IGRTC), a national government agency that supported the Summit and the Council of Governors with policy formation, was mandated to continue facilitating and completing the transfer of assets and liabilities to counties, both inherited from defunct local entities and transferred from various agencies of the national government. IGRTC also works with the Intergovernmental Budget and Economic Council (IBEC) on setting policies on management and transition of assets and liabilities.

This was a turning point since no asset or liability was transferred to counties by that date—the end of a four-year transition period and nearly three years into devolution. One serious shortcoming of this new institutional arrangement was that IGRTC received only a symbolic budget as compared with the former budgets of the TA, it received no staff, and it was short of expertise on AM and transfers. This arrangement eventually changed the Kenya asset transfer modality from a *centralized* to a *decentralized* model, in which IGRTC became a facilitator of asset and liability transition issues without continuing inventorying or verifying assets; in turn, counties had to facilitate and complete the takeover without formal handover of assets and liabilities (from the defunct local entities).

PUBLIC FINANCIAL MANAGEMENT IN TRANSITION

Legislators were aware of the importance of maintaining an effective public finance management system during transition despite landslide changes in governance framework, institutions, and staff. A public finance management framework and procedures were modernized in 2012, about a year before the devolution (per PFM Act 2012), but more specific PFM regulations and institutional arrangements were also legislated in January 2013 (PFM Transition Act). The laws were intended to ensure adequate control over public finances and assets during the last weeks before devolution. It mandated outgoing officers of local entities to properly close accounts and to transfer all accounts, reports, and other documentation to the incoming county officers under the guidance and monitoring of the transition principal officers, who were also considered as local representatives of the TA. The Ministry of Local Government issued a circular in February 2013 (MLG 2013) that further reconfirmed the importance of safekeeping and guided outgoing local officers to secure all accounts and documentation, close and consolidate bank accounts, and then transfer the latter to incoming county officers.

Table 2.2 summarizes key stipulations from the PFM Transition Act 2013, which assigned clear responsibilities to the outgoing local bodies and staff to prepare all PFM-related documents for handover and ensure uninterrupted functioning of PFM and in turn ensure the functioning of the incoming county governments. The two PFM laws and guidance from ministry were apparently assumed to be sufficient for proper PFM. But they set no implementation procedures and seem to have had weak enforcement power; thus, they appeared to be ineffective despite

TABLE 2.2 **Public financial management during transition (excerpts from PFM Transition Act 2013)**

Transition period: March 9, 2012–March 27, 2016

Establishment and Operation of Transition County Treasuries January 25–September 30, 2013

Objectives: Transition County Treasuries shall be established to monitor, evaluate, and oversee the management of county public finances and economic affairs of the county until such time that County Treasury is established.

Composition of Transition County Treasuries: Transition Principal Officer (head of Transition Treasury), Transition Head of the County Finance Department, Transition Head of the Economic Affairs Department, Transition Head of internal audit, Transition County Treasury.

Deployment of transition officer: No later than January 15, 2013, "the National Treasury, or any other relevant State Department shall, upon request by the Transition Authority, identify officers for deployment to the respective Transition County Treasuries. Upon the establishment of the county government, the Officers deployed under this section shall be deemed to be seconded to the county government."

Phase one: Until March 27, 2013	**Phase two: March 27–September 30, 2013**
Reporting: Transition principal officer reports to Transition Authority	**Reporting:** Transition principal officer reports to county executive member responsible for Finance

Responsibilities of Transition County Treasuries: "Arrange for the County Revenue Fund to be kept in the Central Bank of Kenya, authorize the opening and operating of bank accounts, facilitate and ensure operation of the establishment of Treasury Single Account at the Central Bank of Kenya, keep complete and current records of all bank accounts, ensure that all procurement of goods, works, services and disposal of assets required for the purposes of the county government or a county government entity is carried out in accordance with laws relating to procurement, and act as the custodian of an inventory of the respective county government assets except as may be provided [differently] by the Constitution or other legislation."

Source: Based on Public Finance Management (PFM) Transition Act 2013.

TABLE 2.3 Maintaining and transferring public records during transition

Legal Notice on Transition to Devolved Government Act:
Mechanism for Closure and Transfer of Public Records and Information (LN 44/2016)

Objective: To facilitate closure and transfer of records previously held by defunct Local Authorities, former provincial administration and County and National Government Ministries, Departments and Agencies and make all authorized and accounting officers at both the national and county governments responsible for ensuring closure and transfer of public records and information in their custody.

Implementation of regulations: (1) During the transition period, these Regulations shall be implemented by the relevant institutions under the guidance of the Transition Authority or the successor thereof and the Kenya National Archives and Documentation Service. (2) The Transition Authority shall establish a Committee known as the *Inter-Agency Technical Committee* to facilitate and co-ordinate closure and transfer of public records and information.

Records specified for transfer: shall include (1) financial statements; (2) payrolls and payment vouchers; (3) bank balances and certificate of closed bank accounts; (4) unused checkbooks and revenue receipts; (5) cashbooks and vote books; (6) receivable registers and credit registers; (7) copies of receipt and local purchase orders generated by the local authorities integrated financial office management system; (8) duplicate copies for local authorities integrated financial office management system; (9) unpaid local purchase orders and invoices; and (10) inventory of all assets and liabilities, among others. . . .

"All the former Clerks of the defunct Local Authorities and the Permanent Secretary responsible for Lands shall ensure that land and other related records are transferred to the respective County Government entities including but not limited to the following—
(1) drawings, plans and maps of town, trading or market centers; (2) files for allocation of parcels of land for plot allocation; (3) proof of payment of rates; and (4) bidders or plot record."

Source: Based on LN 44/2016 (Notice 44, 2016).
Note: LN = legal notice.

reconfirmation by the ministry, the deployment of trained PFM officers from national government entities to counties, and the general power of the TA.

Apparent shortcomings and gaps in either communication or oversight power across national and local bodies during transition led to passage of a regulation on maintaining and transferring public records during transition. It specified responsibilities and mandates but also listed specific records to be properly maintained and transferred. This regulation is clear, but it is still confusing, because it was issued days before the transition period ended and about three years after the dissolution of the defunct local government entities and their amalgamation into the new counties.

According to the legal mandates (table 2.2 and table 2.3), both the outgoing and incoming local government bodies and officers were undoubtedly responsible for proper safeguarding, handover, and takeover of public documentation since 2012. However, these regulations did not include implementation procedures and templates that would have provided guidance on proper actions. As a result, the laws and regulations (especially PFM Act 2012 and PFM Transition Act 2013) became apparently powerless, bypassed, or ignored in practice. Officers of the defunct entities left jobs or were transferred to other positions but had not been made responsible for proper safekeeping and handover of documents. Thousands of officers from defunct local entities continued working in the new county government administrations, many in the same or similar positions as before without being required to store and hand over critical information and all respective documents.

ASSET-LIABILITY MANAGEMENT AND TRANSFER DURING THE INITIAL TRANSITION PERIOD

Kenya had adopted a robust legal, institutional, and regulatory framework for the devolution, especially for managing and transferring assets and liabilities to the new county local governments. The framework was established in a timely manner; all key pillars of the legal and regulatory framework were enacted or commenced a year or even longer before the election and induction of new local governments. However, real life before and during transition seems to have followed a different development path on takeover and management of assets and liabilities, because many laws, rules, and regulations were not enforced, and some were in conflict with each other. The major shortcomings include the following:

- The TA was hardly able to start identifying and inventorying inherited assets, let alone complete an inventory by the time the new county governments were inducted, as was proposed in the TDG Act (see table 2.2).
- There were no procedures for handover of assets, liabilities, and documents that would have guided transition and handover immediately after the elected county governments' induction.
- The stipulation that the TA became custodian of assets, liabilities, and documents remained unenforceable because the TA had no capacity to quickly cover the entire country and the few thousand offices of the defunct local entities.
- Transition county treasuries or principal transition officers were either not appointed or remained silent and ineffective in preparing due accounts, safekeeping documents, and performing handovers. (Many field interviews suggested that such officers were not appointed.)
- Outgoing officers of defunct local entities left positions without preparing documents and information for handover, or sometimes without even having the authority to hand over documents to the incoming officers of the elected county governments. Interviews suggest that after the election day, officers of defunct entities were not allowed to return to their former offices. The lack of proper handover and takeover of documents was least understandable in Nairobi, where the takeover had to be done from one single defunct entity to one single new entity with many officers remaining in the same work positions.

Weak enforcement

The national entities responsible for oversight and guidance of local governments continued their regular duties and operations with some specific actions to support devolution and transfer of assets at the advent of new county governments. For example, the TA had issued guidelines on custody of documents and assets. The Office of the Auditor General report (OAG 2013) recommended that *the county governments coordinate with the TA on the asset and liability takeover,* but this recommendation induced no actions by the TA or the counties. The Ministry of Local Governments ruled preparation of closing accounts, safekeeping of public records, and handover of documents and reconfirmed stipulations of the TA Act 2012 and the PFM Transition Act 2013 weeks before closure of former local entities (MLG 2013). However, most of the guidance of this circular was neither obeyed nor enforced.

OAG conducted special audits in the second part of 2013 and assessed the status of registering, inventorying, and safekeeping of assets, preparation of closing accounts, and opening of new consolidated accounts in the National Bank of Kenya but found that the incoming county governments failed to establish asset registers. OAG failed to verify validity, completeness, and correctness of closing accounts, which often did not even exist (see county details in part II). It also found that financial accounts and reports were not standardized or complete and were generally of such low quality that OAG could not conduct audits (OAG 2013). As a result, OAG issued disclaimers in 39 counties, in addition to five adverse and three qualified audit opinions. (Box 2.1 explains the standard audit opinions an auditor may assert.)

OAG has continued annual audits in a timely manner and adequately, with clear and strong messages, but found only marginal improvements over the following years. No county government obtained clean (unqualified) audits in five years in transition, but in a remarkable sign of progress, the number of adverse audits and disclaimers of inability to audit was reduced by 2017 (figure 2.2). OAG audits were apparently timely and adequate based on current laws and regulations and standard audit procedures.

OAG audited the county government accounts rightly from the beginning and issued and published audit reports. Findings were adequate from an auditor's perspective, particularly regarding bank accounts, cash management, and

BOX 2.1

Types of audit opinions

An unqualified opinion is an auditor's declaration that the audited financial statements present a true and fair picture of the entity's financial position.

A qualified opinion is an audit declaration in which the auditor states that the information provided was limited in scope and/or the audited entity had not maintained generally accepted accounting principles.

An adverse opinion is an auditor's declaration that the audited financial statements do not present results fairly because of misstatements that are material and pervasive, and there are significant departures from generally accepted accounting principles.

A disclaimer of opinion is an auditor's declaration that no opinion was given regarding the financial statements of an entity because the information and documents provided restricted the scope of the examination to such an extent that the auditor was unable to form an opinion.

Source: Venkateswaran 2014.

FIGURE 2.2

Results of county audits, by audit qualification, fiscal years 2013/14–2016/17

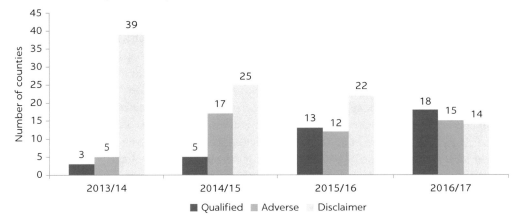

Source: OAG 2014–18.
Note: Qualified opinion is an audit declaration in which the auditor states that the information provided was limited in scope and/or the audited entity had not maintained generally accepted accounting principles.
Adverse opinion is an auditor's declaration that the audited financial statements do not present results fairly because of misstatements that are material and pervasive, and there are significant departures from generally accepted accounting principles.
Disclaimer of opinion is an auditor's declaration that no opinion was given regarding the financial statements of an entity because the information and documents provided restricted the scope of the examination to such an extent that the auditor was unable to form an opinion.

revenue collection. However, the requirement that incoming county governments establish asset registers overnight was unrealistic, at least in the first year of transition. The main reasons include the following:

- First, the outgoing local entities did not have asset registers and reliable asset records, so they were not able to provide them even if they were willing. However, they should have handed over all documentation they possessed regarding assets and liabilities. These would not have constituted asset registers but would have been useful for the incoming governments.
- Second, developing asset inventories with thousands of verified records from scratch takes a year or two, and it was unrealistic to expect the incoming governments to do them weeks or months after induction. However, the warnings in audit reports were right and timely. Box 2.2 shows excepts from the audit report of Nairobi City County (interpreting TA Law 2012).
- Third, the OAG interpreted the existence and operation of and communication by the TA to mean that the TA would inventory assets and would transfer assets and liabilities only after audits. Interviews suggest that county administrations believed that they were not authorized to take over assets and liabilities and inventory them after induction.

BOX 2.2

Nairobi City County audit report excerpts, 2013

Failure to take over by the county government

The County Government of Nairobi had not officially taken over the assets and liabilities of the former City Council of Nairobi (CCN). Overall, the audit found that Nairobi City County had 16 departments which were uncoordinated and operated as independent units. No [processes for] handing over notes were prepared and business continued as usual, and as a result it has not been possible to conclusively confirm the accuracy of the assets and liabilities taken over from the former CCN. A senior management committee to take over the role of the council during transition was not established as directed by the then Ministry of Local Government vide Circular no. MLG/1333/TY/52 of 18 February 2013.

Cash and bank balances

The defunct CCN historically operated 40 bank accounts out of which sixteen (16) bank accounts were dormant, while 12 accounts had credit balances totaling KES. 35,459,356.20. However, the County did not produce for audit all the cashbooks and bank reconciliation statements to confirm the accuracy of the cash and cash equivalents.

Failure to close bank accounts

The Ministry of Local Government had issued instructions via Circular no. MLG/1333/TY/52 of 18th February 2013 requiring all defunct local authorities accounts to be closed and the existing funds transferred to the General Rate Fund Account and as soon as practicable, a Single Account to be opened at the Central Bank of Kenya. However, the accounts were not closed as required and business continued as usual and instead four (4) new accounts were opened.

Failure by CCN bankers to confirm cash and bank balances

It was not possible to confirm whether the forty (40) bank accounts disclosed by the former CCN were the only accounts operated before the transition period as the CCN bankers, mainly, Equity Bank, Cooperative Bank of Kenya, Kenya Commercial Bank, and the National Bank of Kenya, did not respond to our requests for disclosure of all accounts previously held and also requiring them to confirm the balances in each account. The number of bank accounts varied

continued

Box 2.2, *continued*

from different lists presented for audit with some lists showing 40 [or] 41 and others 42.

Underbanking of revenue collected

Revenue records made available for audit revealed that during the period 1 January 2013 to 30 June 2013, a total of KES. 5,511,732,231 was collected from the various sources of revenue but only KES. 5,258,849,088 was banked resulting to under-banking of KES. 252,883,143.

The audit also revealed that out of the total under-banked revenue, KES. 29,021,813.00 was subsequently issued as IOU's to various officers while the balance of KES. 223,861,330.00 represented checks cashed in by County staff for various miscellaneous activities such as purchase of goods and services and other numerous consumable items.

It was also noted that during the period under review Cess Income totaling KES. 60,725,305.00 was collected in various divisions but only KES. 57,889,995.00 was receipted at the cash office and banked resulting in a difference of KES. 2,835,310.00 not accounted for and banked.

Source: OAG 2013.
Note: The audit uses the symbol KES. for the Kenya shilling.

These apparent legal, regulatory, and/or communication challenges hindered policy dialogue that would have clarified mandates and responsibilities and led to adoption of clear operation procedures for county governments on asset and liability takeover. Furthermore, the slow progress on asset verification was very apparent, since the TA did not complete, even in one single county, the verification and audit of assets inherited from defunct entities by the election day of March 27, 2013. Evidence of this severe delay was apparent already in 2013 but had not led to national policy dialogue or corrective measures that year or later until 2016, when the TA was closed.

By the same token, the counties failed in proper takeover and management of the bank accounts, cash, and inherited financial assets and liabilities that did not require an extensive workload to take over as compared with the requirements of fixed-asset registers. OAG had raised issues on bank and financial statements and repeatedly listed specific shortcomings in each county's audits. But these audit statements have not induced corrective measures in counties, nor have they opened a national policy dialogue to seek nationwide and strategic corrective options and stipulate immediate corrective measures months after induction of county governments.

The takeover of inherited assets was obviously problematic, but it is hard to justify the county administrations' inaction on starting simple but proper recording of the fixed assets acquired after March 27, 2013. The lack of handover of such assets did not constrain records, because those were new assets, although with many installed additions to old inherited assets (for example, new school rooms or a new ward of a health center). It is more worrisome that the financial transfers (equitable shares) from the national government had increased substantially at the course of devolution and the counties surveyed rightly invested about 30 percent or more of the local revenues and each acquired assets in billions of Kenya shillings in the years after devolution. (Nairobi City County [NCC] invested over K Sh 9 billion into fixed assets between 2013 and 2018.)

A small portion of the capital budgets would have been sufficient for the counties to hire a firm and develop a simple, pragmatic initial asset inventory or register. That would have been evidence of due diligence, although some would consider it a redundant action in parallel with the TA-planned asset inventory-ing and audits. Some experts had the view that the real reason behind avoiding formal takeover of assets was that counties did not want to take over stockpiles of inherited liabilities.

The World Bank supported Kenya's devolution process through, inter alia, the Kenya Devolution Support Program, a US$200 million Program for Results project, aimed at enhancing capacities and systems of county governments. Under this project, counties are taking steps to establish basic asset registers. However, there is generally no strong national policy dialogue and/or specific guidance to encourage counties to keep proper financial and asset records (in the form of quite simple registers or Excel tables), at least of the assets acquired from the current revenues after March 27, 2013. Overall, counties have achieved little progress toward establishing initial asset registers for both the inherited and the newly acquired assets in nine years of devolution.

Installation of the integrated financial management system (IFMIS) to coun-ties may have created another source of confusion. Gradually, the mainstream approach of counties became to wait for installation of an AM module in the IFMIS and use this need as a justification for lack of actions toward inventory and registration of county assets. This seems to be a misunderstanding or misin-terpretation of key aspects of both the IFMIS and AM. First, AM is not a mere accounting issue (as discussed in previous sections). Second, without verified field data, a reliable asset register cannot be established in a computer module due to lack of information. Third, such a module would remain a software appli-cation and while it would be a good start with possibilities would not yet consti-tute or turn automatically into an asset register.

Possession with partial takeover of inherited assets and liabilities

County governments jump-started operations right after induction and *managed to ensure uninterrupted provision of basic local services* (a key objective in TDG Act 2012) regardless of the noted issues on financial and bank accounts, assets, and liabilities. *This is a major achievement of the Kenya devolution that cannot be underestimated.* The incoming administrations assigned officers to manage key services and functions and operate services, plants, buildings, systems, and equipment. Thus, they had captured the flow of operation while overlooking the "stocks" of information and assets and stocktaking issues. In this sense, the devo-lution and transition to new county governments was smooth and pragmatic. One example is that county governments appointed or assigned officers to man-age the key services and fulfill key functions (less so though in financial and asset management), and the ministries provided seconded staff to fill gaps in human capacities, so the new county governments possessed assets and were fully func-tional from the beginning.

The county governments informally but effectively took over assets that were the material basis of local services and functions, such as offices, health centers, education buildings, markets, and roads. They even immediately started urgent repair and expansion of assets in areas of critical shortages: for example, building additions to health care and school facilities. With few exceptions, counties expanded development expenditures substantially as increased budgets permit-ted. The share of development expenditures between 2013 and 2018 increased from 10–15 percent to 20–30 percent or above in many counties, for example,

Kakamega and Makueni in our survey (see part II). In this sense, the devolution resulted in visible improvement of some assets and services and bettered the appearance of urban areas.

The counties' core fixed assets that serve key functions are under counties' possession and reasonable management, are operational, and fulfill required functions (schools, health facilities, offices, markets, stadiums, and water and sanitation facilities). However, the lack of a reliable inventory and register of land and buildings, especially those not attached to key services, is a major impediment to good AM. Thus, one can conclude that the partial takeover of assets was a pragmatic but unsatisfactory approach that may have resulted in substantial material loss of public wealth via encroachments or other forms of lost value.

Counties inherited a substantial volume of current assets and liabilities, K Sh 110.8 billion and K Sh 53.8 billion, respectively (figure 2.3 and figure 2.4). The numbers may suggest that the counties can easily pay off inherited liabilities from the inherited current assets, but this quick judgment is incorrect and needs closer scrutiny. NCC has inherited about two-thirds of the total local government sector in both current assets and current liabilities. These numbers are estimates as of March 2013, but the present value of current assets has since presumably changed substantially, because old and unverified claims and collectibles have little value (and the inherited claims are now nine years older). The stock of current assets also increased in the meantime, with uncollected new current assets due to a low level of collection efficiency. For example, the collection efficiency of property tax (property rate) is below 50 percent (see cases in part II), so collectibles are growing in nominal values.

In contrast, the present value of inherited current liabilities (claims against counties) has increased substantially since 2013, because of accumulating interests and penalties, even though some counties have made strong efforts to pay new liabilities. Estimates suggest that the volume of inherited current liabilities has doubled between 2013 and 2018 despite substantial repayments. The challenge is that the counties have limited capacities, expertise, and procedures to set policies and collect the inherited current assets, so the majority of the property rates have been uncollected for maybe over a decade. Thus, these face-value figures need careful interpretation and treatment, because a quick and simple conclusion that the counties can repay all inherited liabilities from the stock of inherited assets is unrealistic and misleading.

Counties made some efforts to work out inherited financial liabilities. For instance, the NCC government appeared to be ahead of other counties on these. Counties took over all the staff from the defunct local entities, and as a result, they faced severe redundancies and overstaffing in many areas. They started restructuring and streamlining the workforce, which often required substantial funds for severance payments. But counties were also more mindful of working out of inherited overdue staff emoluments, which they verified and largely paid in the first year of devolution. NCC also attempted to negotiate statutory deductions and aimed to annul penalties in exchange for paying inherited overdue deductions net of penalties. Most of these negotiations have failed, however, due to the reluctance of various fund administrators. Counties mostly continued servicing the inherited bank debt, except NCC has disputed some large inherited debts and has not started debt service to date.

FIGURE 2.3

Inherited current assets of 47 counties, March 27, 2013

Total K Sh 110.8 billion

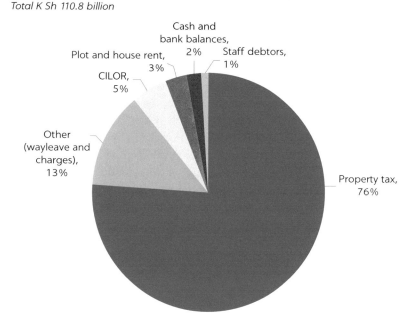

Source: IGRTC 2018.
Note: CILOR = compensation in lieu of rates; K Sh = Kenya shilling.

FIGURE 2.4

Inherited current liabilities of 47 counties, March 27, 2013

Total K Sh 53.8 billion

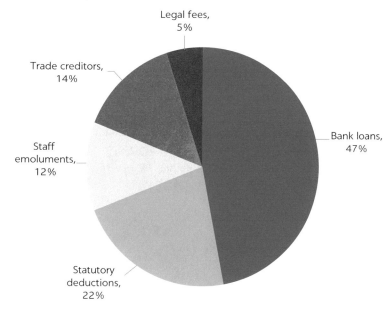

Source: IGRTC 2018.
Note: K Sh = Kenya shilling.

Counties have left unattended most inherited commercial liabilities and statutory deductions, some claiming that those have not been taken over. The inherited overdue statutory deductions require national-level policy setting, a resolution framework, and certainly involvement of the National Treasury and actions by IGRTC as facilitator of national policy and framework dialogue.

In contrast, counties should start working out inherited commercial debt (a good part of it is legal fees) through direct communication and settlement with private partners, and they should not wait for involvement of national entities (IGRTC or the National Treasury). Thorough analysis of the inherited current liabilities and estimation of the present value is an urgent and extremely important step that requires counties' action and a national program.

Counties made a few powerless attempts to work out inherited financial assets through verifying and collecting receivables (property taxes, water fees, and rental fees), many long overdue. A vital and urgent step would be to complete a thorough analysis of current assets, verify claims, write off nonverified claims, and then estimate a reasonable present value of the inherited current assets. These would serve as a basis for setting policies, adopting procedures, and starting a workout program with realistic and forceful collection to eliminate these huge stocks of current assets—that is, receivables. Rolling over such toxic assets and liabilities is unhealthful.

STEPS TOWARD ESTABLISHING AN ASSET MANAGEMENT GOVERNANCE FRAMEWORK, SYSTEM, AND ASSET REGISTERS

Significant progress was achieved at the national level and in several counties by 2019. There have been remarkable attempts and progress toward establishing governance, institutional, and organizational frameworks for modern AM at both the national and county levels, albeit in different scope and quality. The Kenya Devolution Support Program provides performance grants to counties for fostering good governance and establishing reliable organizational frameworks for AM and services. The main results are further discussed in the national and county sections that follow. One major achievement, as previously indicated, is that counties have been managing assets important for key services and functions, and services continued without major interruptions regardless of legal uncertainties and incomplete takeover of assets. Unfortunately, proper takeover of land assets, which represent the largest value in the counties' wealth, have not been treated seriously. Land has not been inventoried, verified, or registered under the names of the counties in the national land cadaster. Reports indicate that the lack of land data and management have caused substantial financial losses in many counties.

PROGRESS AT THE NATIONAL LEVEL

Kenya's legislators and the national government have taken significant steps toward establishing a consistent and complete national framework for management of public assets and liabilities at both the national and subnational levels in recent years following the devolution. The legal framework was largely developed in compliance with international standards by devolution in March 2013, but the AM framework has remained unintegrated, with gaps and/or silos of entities and disobeyed regulations and rules. The government has recognized the weaknesses and missing elements of the institutional framework and the lack of alignment of the division of responsibilities, even though most of the requisite actions for managing assets and liabilities had been legislated since the early 2000s: for example, the PFM Act 2012 and the Public Procurement and Asset Disposal (PPAD) Act 2015.

The government of Kenya has taken three formidable actions at the national level: (1) established the National Assets and Liabilities Management (NALM) Department in the National Treasury, (2) dissolved the TA when its legal mandate expired in 2016, and (3) assigned IGRTC to continue and complete asset transfers in a decentralized devolution modality.

Establishing NALM

Establishing NALM was one of the most significant institutional developments after devolution, which prompted the government to recognize the following: (1) assets and liabilities are transient forms of each other, so they should be managed jointly, consistently, and as one consolidated body of the national public assets; (2) there is a need for portfolio management of subnational public assets and liabilities with a dedicated entity; and (3) life-cycle AM principles and framework need to be institutionalized.

Before establishing NALM, the National Treasury had already consisted of five units that were dealing with various aspects of national AM (see figure 2.5). Two of these treasury entities have been performing largely regulatory functions (Pensions Department and Accounting Services Directorate), two have been performing largely specific AM tasks with minor regulatory roles for both national and subnational entities (Public Debt Management Directorate and the Public Investment and Portfolio Management Directorate), while the Public Investment Management Unit has been performing both management and regulation functions. However, none of these entities has a specific mandate, focus, roles,

FIGURE 2.5

National asset and liability management governance framework

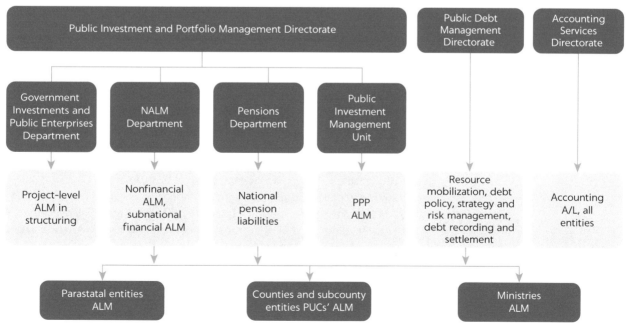

Source: World Bank.
Note: A/L = asset and liability; ALM = asset and liability management; NALM = National Assets and Liabilities Management Department in the National Treasury; PPP = public-private partnership; PUCs = public utility companies.

or responsibilities to either regulate or perform strategic AM for the subnational sector and entities. Establishing NALM seems to acknowledge and correct this institutional gap in the Public Investment and Portfolio Management Directorate.

Figure 2.5 indicates that NALM is mandated to oversee, regulate, and guide (1) the parastatal entities (state corporations and deconcentrated regional service entities); (2) counties and their subordinated independent legal entities (county-owned commercial or utility companies or units); and (3) AM functions of respective units in ministries. NALM therefore is mandated to play a pivotal role in establishing and guiding development of AM systems at subnational entities, *performing both regulator and portfolio asset manager functions.*

After its establishment, NALM had to define its position and faced two options: (1) define a narrow regulatory position or focus or (2) define a broad mandate and scope that comprised regulatory and portfolio asset manager functions. NALM's asset portfolio manager roles, by function, would be similar to the roles the Public Debt Management Directorate is performing—portfolio management and strategic management of national debt vis-à-vis foreign creditors, including (a) structuring and approval of large debts, all foreign debts, and debts with national guarantees; (b) completing daily transactions regarding international debt (disbursement, debt service); and (c) representing the country as a debtor or guarantor, and within that being "debtor of last resort" to continue serving debt to foreign creditors if subnational borrowers fail debt service. For example, the Public Debt Management Directorate services several water-sector debts on behalf of subnational borrowers. A similar portfolio management role would be important for NALM, that is, to become an entity that represents the highest national public ownership of assets, manage strategically the subnational public assets, and oversee, regulate, and guide management of subnational assets and domestic debt and other financial liabilities.

Draft asset and liability management (ALM) policy and guidelines

For review, approval, and enactment by the cabinet secretary of the National Treasury, NALM developed, with the help of the consulting firm (PricewaterhouseCoopers), a Government Asset and Liability Management Policy supplemented with dozens of guidelines in 2019 to exercise the power of the National Treasury based on PFM Act 2012 and Treasury Act 2012. The national ALM policy, scheduled to take effect in the 2020 fiscal year, represents a quantum leap toward approaching and managing assets and liabilities. It will bring uniformity and standardization to the management of assets and liabilities across the public sector in a manner consistent with government policies, priorities, and objectives and aligned with internationally recognized standards. The NALM issued the policy and guidelines in 2020 before final legislative approval (NALM 2020a, b, c). The COVID-19 pandemic crisis has slowed legislative processes and put the ALM policy on the back burner.

The overarching objective of the ALM policy is to promote accountability on management of assets and liabilities in the entire public sector, including national government and national government entities and county governments and their entities. To achieve this objective, the ALM policy aims to (1) make managing and safeguarding public assets effective; (2) standardize rules and procedures in all public sector entities around planning, identification, acquisition, maintenance, disposal, valuation or revaluation, and recording of assets; (3) regulate identification, disclosure, and reporting of assets and liabilities in the public sector; (4) regulate authorization of acquisition and disposal of assets; and (5) regulate record keeping and reporting to facilitate decision-making. The policy also aims at supporting the National Treasury to develop and maintain updated inventories of assets and liabilities at the national level.

The draft policy clarifies and regulates the institutional framework for ALM from the highest national entities down to local and county government entities. It defines the pivotal position of NALM in regulating and managing assets and adjacent liabilities for the entire public sector of Kenya. The institutional framework is adequate in international comparison, pragmatic, and feasible. One can say, however, that there is room for improvement, as discussed in following sections. The ALM policy sets the framework and specific policies for managing assets and liabilities. *Approaching joint management of assets and liabilities is one of the positive attributes of this policy that should not be underestimated.* Dozens of specific guidelines are appended to and support pragmatic and effective implementation of the ALM policy.

Governance and institutional framework

The ALM policy first summarizes the legal framework that underpins the national ALM policies well in line with the discussions in chapter 1 (figure 1.1). In defining the national governance framework, ALM policy defines the role of 16 specific entities that have some responsibilities and competencies in regulating and/or managing public assets and liabilities. The parliament, cabinet, and National Treasury top the ruling entities at the national level, while at the county level, the County Assembly, county executive committee, and county treasury are the top entities in ruling and managing ALM. We will discuss the role of only a few entities, such as NALM and IGRTC, which have specific and decisive roles in forming and implementing national ALM policy, and focus on issues that deserve attention and possibly further policy dialogue during the legislative discussion and approval of the ALM policy.

The ALM policy defines the role of the NALM Department in the following way:

"The NALM Department, which is headed by a Director, has the following functions:

(a) Development and management of complete assets and liabilities inventories.
(b) Continuous improvement and alignment of asset and liability policies and guidelines.
(c) Continuous support on optimal utilization of assets through development of an optimal utilization framework to guide public sector entities.
(d) Enhanced operational excellence for NALM Department."

This definition of functions apparently assigns both regulatory and portfolio management functions to NALM, but it needs refinement, improved consistency across articles, and better harmony with the detailed policies and guidelines that follow this definition but do not correspond to the four roles:

• Point (a) needs better clarity and a broader scope than, in essence, "managing assets and liabilities inventory." Instead, NALM should *perform as the highest-level portfolio administrator on subnational public assets.* This definition incorporates but is not limited to developing asset inventories, which, however, instead should be the function of various subnational entities. Besides, NALM is mandated to develop and maintain a national public asset register and liability register (article 30). The national asset register could be a virtual register organized as a network of subnational registers or a single consolidated register informed by the subnational registers. In contrast, the national public liability register is better organized as a single register hosted and managed by NALM and informed by the subnational liability registers. But most important, the portfolio administrator function, scope, and detailed mandates of NALM should be regulated in the national AM policy. Some details and options are discussed later.

- Point (b) needs better clarity since it suggests that the function of NALM is to align asset policies and liability policies and guidelines. Instead, NALM may need to develop, issue, update, and enforce national ALM policies and issue and update ALM guidelines, which NALM has been working on already. Besides, NALM shares regulatory or guiding roles with IGRTC, which temporarily is a focal entity for transferring assets and liabilities from defunct local entities and from national government entities.

- Defining national ALM policies needs substantial improvement in this document. NALM has subsequently segregated policy and guidelines in separate annexed documents, the national asset and liability management policy (NALM 2020a, b, c), and dozens of specific application guidelines, including a guide to help development and adoption of subnational ALM policies (a model is in appendix A). However, guidelines often merely quote long excerpts of laws (such as the PFM and PPAD Acts) instead of focusing on guiding principles and procedures.

- Point (c) needs a clearer mandate because it vaguely points toward NALM roles in daily ALM, which would be part of a well-defined portfolio management mandate. In addition, "optimal utilization framework" is a vague statement and hardly a measurable mandate of NALM. In short, point (c) needs clarity or can be omitted and incorporated as a specific set of tasks or actions under high-level national portfolio ALM functions of the NALM discussed in point (a).

In sum, limiting the role of NALM to a regulator would be insufficient, and as a result, key functions would be left undefined. Nevertheless, these and some related shortcomings can easily be corrected in the legislative process toward adoption of national ALM policy and guidelines.

Asset and liability management policy and framework

The national ALM policy may state that beyond and besides the national legislative bodies and the national government and cabinet, the National Treasury is the highest governing body for ALM of public assets. Six entities (figure 2.5) jointly perform the governance, regulatory, and advisory functions mandated to the National Treasury. A section can be dedicated to identifying specific policy and ALM portfolio management functions and explaining the scope and mandates of each of these six entities or departments. But it is vital to provide NALM with more detailed regulation as the focal entity for subnational sectors. Among these, one important point is clarification of the division of labor between NALM and IGRTC on national ALM and in completion of the asset transfers to or takeover by counties. As noted, the draft ALM policy is generally good, but there are issues that deserve further dialogue and elaboration.

The policy section also may summarize the main policy goals of the national ALM policy: (1) focus first on temporary, medium-term policy actions to establish reliable asset and liability registers, populate such registers at all levels of the

ALM framework and in each entity, and complete takeover by counties of inherited assets and liabilities; (2) complete handover of assets from national government entities and takeover by counties; (3) resolve disputes on inherited assets; and finally (4) launch a workout program for inherited liabilities. For these reasons, the national ALM policy should state specific policies regarding the deconcentrated regional entities of the national government and summarize functions and high-level policies of dissolving or repositioning them.

The policy may define how the national government plans to work out the inherited liabilities. But also, it may regulate all public entities to keep new overdue liabilities (those generated after 2013 and especially those generated annually) below some level of all liabilities (say, 5 percent of expenditures in any single year). The corresponding guidelines should provide clear guidance on how the entities should comply with this policy. Furthermore, a clear policy statement is required to clarify if and under what conditions the National Treasury would lead and financially contribute to reach agreements and resolution for disputed inherited liabilities (examples are summarized in chapter 3). It is vital that these high-level national policies be documented in the national ALM policy and then adopted, implemented, and enforced to complete transition of assets and liabilities in harmony with the devolution. This is by far the most important policy action, without which all the other policies and procedures will remain incomplete or unmanageable.

The draft already includes important policy objectives: (1) institutionalize the life-cycle AM principles and procedures; (2) institutionalize and enforce at all levels of the ALM framework medium-term capital acquisition planning (also known as capital improvement planning, or CIP) in close correspondence with capital budgeting; and (3) institutionalize a risk-based preventive maintenance framework and business procedures. These are all parts or instruments of good life-cycle AM. Many of these are already stated among guidelines and explained procedures, but now they are incorporated as key national ALM policy objectives and instruments. This is remarkable progress.

The national ALM policy should include detailed mandates and regulations for NALM for fulfilling high-level portfolio management functions over the subnational sector. Actions that would constitute NALM asset or liability management roles are necessary, because NALM has become an entity that functions as a last resort if the subnational sector or specific entities fail to fulfill required tasks in proper asset and liability management. This role of NALM is similar to the role of the Public Debt Management (PDM) Directorate, which is a focal point for managing public debt vis-à-vis international creditors and all international contexts. Furthermore, the PDM Directorate steps in as a "debtor of last resort" if any national or subnational entity fails to service debt to international debtors. One of the NALM roles similar to the PDM Directorate's is to take the lead on working out inherited liabilities, which may require the National Treasury to provide financial support that should be granted under tight and well-regulated rules and procedures. Such interventions should not be limited to the inherited liabilities, because interviews suggest that the subnational entities have been generating a substantial volume of new overdue liabilities since devolution.

But in many more areas of NALM's portfolio, ALM should be regulated in the policy. For example, what is the mandate or role of NALM in implementing the ALM policies in the subnational sector, and what is the NALM position vis-à-vis the subnational entities (listed in figure 2.5)? What are the NALM mandates in resolving conflicts between subnational entities; in resolving defaults in servicing liabilities, initiating, or guiding transfer of assets across national and subnational entities as it may deem necessary; and so on? These are all cases of national ALM policy implementation, and there are ample examples that show the damages made by a lack of such leadership in the takeover of county assets and working out of disputed inherited assets and liabilities, which have been left unresolved for over six years. Guidelines that define only roles and procedures for normal circumstances do not provide an effective framework and support for a challenging transition as in the case of Kenya.

The national ALM policy also should set policies and regulate divestiture of public assets. One option would be that NALM as the highest custodian of subnational public assets would be authorized to monitor fixed-asset divestitures, especially land, in the context of all assets. The counties would retain full power to plan and execute divestitures (including long-term leases), but only under national policy that states the following:

- Fixed assets and especially land should be divested in competitive procedures, and buyers should pay a market price.
- Counties and other subnational entities should report to NALM any plans of land divestiture above a certain value.
- Subnational entities should especially report allocations and/or divestitures of land planned with no financial compensation or below-market price that could be justified for social policy reasons, but such divestiture plans should be reported to NALM, which may have veto power on behalf of the nation.
- Free divestiture (granting entitlement) without reporting to and receiving no objection from NALM could be ruled as criminal offenses against respective officers of any public entity. One county officer pointed to the significance of a need for closer control on land divestitures by saying that "should we list pieces of land as excess/surplus property, it would soon vanish and be granted by some county officers to private persons as entitlements."

The national ALM policy should regulate and clarify whether (1) the national government would commit to supporting subnational entities' capacity building or leave it to the discretion of and funding by the entities and (2) NALM should be mandated to develop or arrange development of training materials, adopt curriculum, and implement trainings for subnational entities, because NALM has drafted and issued the national ALM policies and guidelines, and it issued dozens of sector- or asset-specific guidelines. Recent plans suggest that NALM indeed plans to roll out extensive training programs to help subnational entities understand and apply new ALM policies and guidelines.

Guidelines for managing public assets and liabilities

The draft guidelines for public ALM activities are long and well-drafted with detailed rules, regulations, and procedures. The guidelines rightly have specific sections for nonfinancial assets, for financial assets with sections following the asset life cycle, and for liabilities; with these they comply with the International Organization for Standardization (ISO) standards and provide comprehensive and complete guidance for the entire universe of public sector ALM (see NALM 2020b, c). Furthermore, the guidelines, as noted, support the principle of life-cycle AM with detailed guidance for managing assets and adjacent liabilities in key life-cycle phases: planning and project selection, construction, operation, and final disposal.

The guidelines include many international standard characteristics. However, the detailed regulations and guidance are often phrased in a way that seems to overemphasize and/or limit the scope of the guideline to the accounting aspect or accounting layer of AM. With that scope, it strongly undervalues, bypasses, or ignores the paramount tasks that are required for good ALM—as set in the ALM policy—that are in addition to the bookkeeping and accounting transactions. A good revision of the draft guidelines to reduce such imbalances in the scope would improve clarity. The guidelines seem to consider ALM as a universal instrument applicable for all kinds of assets regardless of who hosts them. This is adequate in most cases and is especially applicable to accounting layers of ALM. But this terminology and the size of this part of the guidelines may mislead readers that ALM is primarily an accounting issue.

Finally, national ALM guidelines should also specifically guide NALM and the main groups of subnational entities (state corporations, counties, and deconcentrated regional entities) to help establish local-level policies in harmony with the national regulations and guidelines, meanwhile taking into consideration the governance and operation specificities of these entities and the respective assets and ALM functions. For instance, counties with a limited number and moderate volume or value of fixed assets may not need very sophisticated local ALM policies and procedures. In fact, as noted, NALM plans to issue many more asset-specific guidelines that could fill a large part of these gaps.

Intergovernmental Relations Technical Committee

IGRTC was established in 2012 by article 11 of Intergovernmental Relations Act, no. 2 of 2012, with specific functions, including (1) day-to-day administration of the National and County Government Coordinating Summit (the Summit) and the Council of Governors, (2) coordination of implementation of resolutions of the Summit and the council (article 12 of Intergovernmental Relations Act, no. 2 of 2012), and (3) takeover of the residual functions of the TA after its dissolution. IGRTC received the mandate to wrap up unfinished tasks of the defunct TA when the government closed the TA on March 3, 2016, the expiration date of the TA's mandate (section 31(1) of the TDG Act 2012).

The major challenge facing IGRTC was not to wrap up residual tasks but instead to complete most of the work the TA was supposed to accomplish, because (1) the bulk of the work that had been assigned to the TA was left incomplete the day of closure; (2) against its mandates, the TA handed over nothing to counties by March 2016—an interesting approach to leave everything incomplete instead of complete and handing over the work county by county; (3) instead of verified, validated, and valued asset registers, the TA left IGRTC preliminary, unaudited, and incomplete asset and liability inventories for all 47 counties (IGRTC 2018); (4) the TA apparently failed to share fieldwork with counties or involve county staff, so counties were left uninformed about their assets and the TA's results for three years; and thus (5) IGRTC had to start everything from scratch in March 2016, with limited professional and financial capacity to fulfill the inherited paramount pile of tasks and responsibilities.

Detailed and quick situation analysis underscored IGRTC's main initial situation assessment and strategy, including the following: (1) IGRTC could not continue the TA's work on centralized identification, verification, inventory, and valuation of inherited county assets; (2) decentralized asset takeover would be a pragmatic solution that would emulate the Eastern European takeover framework and practices; and (3) IGRTC should become a regulator, facilitator, and guide in a decentralized takeover process with the help of international donors, including the World Bank. IBEC approved this strategy on September 28, 2016 (IGRTC 2018).

Based on the adopted strategy, IGRTC started a policy dialogue and began drafting a legal notice aimed at turning the centralized asset takeover to a decentralized process driven by County Asset and Liability Committees (CALCs). Drafting and facilitating enactment of the legal notice in a six-month period was the first and most significant achievement of IGRTC. The Gazette Notice no. 858 (January 2017) formally transferred the assets of the defunct local governments to the counties "by the Power of the Law" overnight. IGRTC supported the implementation by providing detailed training with templates and detailed guidance to hundreds of county and ministry officers in March and April 2017. Furthermore, IGRTC also shared with the counties the preliminary asset and liability inventories taken over from the TA; so, for the first time after three years in office, the county officers obtained their asset and liability inventories, but soon found a considerable number of errors and disputed items.

Notice no. 858 provided a clear framework for the systematic, quick, and full takeover of inherited assets and liabilities. However, it did not include enforcement regulations. Furthermore, many counties and governors appeared to be reluctant to take over assets, some because they did not want to take over unmeasured and presumably inflated liabilities generated by entities beyond the control of the current county governments. As a result, only about half of the counties established CALCs and assigned teams for fieldwork on asset identification, verification, and inventory by the May 2013 deadline, while valuation was left for a later stage. CALCs that were composed of officers from both central government entities (ministries) and counties were requested to complete all tasks and submit a detailed CALC report in three months' time.

CALCs started work by assigning teams of county officers to complete field verification based on the TA's preliminary inventories. These inventories were very helpful but did not negate the need for field verification. Teams used the inventories of respective asset groups (land, buildings, equipment, and so forth) and compared records with field findings and developed a revised CALC inventory in addition to the TA list; the discrepancies were numerous and substantial, especially in technical details. (Part II shows on-ground experiences of seven counties.) Shortages of funds, vehicles, and skilled staff strongly constrained the counties' abilities to fulfill the asset verification mandates. IGRTC responded to the apparent shortcomings and challenges by issuing a revised Notice no. 2701 in March 2017 to extend the deadline for submission of the CALC reports to June 2017. About two-thirds of the counties did submit the CALC reports by the extended deadline.

The county elections and incoming new leadership (governors, assemblies, administrations) that took place at the same time in 2017 created major hiccups in the asset takeover process and CALCs. First, the election campaigns disrupted the work of CALCs, most of which were suspended, closed, or abandoned. Second, the incoming county leadership (governors and assemblies) had even less ownership of the asset and liability takeover process than the first local leaders. Some argued that the work had been the task of the previous county governments and was not a responsibility of the county government or administration inaugurated in fall 2017. The ambiguous high-level political support had strongly also influenced the quality of the CALC reports. Third, most of the incoming governors and county governments were not willing to review and approve final versions of CALC reports inherited from the previous county administrations. Thus, most of the reports remained preliminary, incomplete, and at draft stage, because neither the outgoing nor the incoming county government was willing to approve them in 2017. This unfortunate timing weakened the results of the decentralized asset takeover.

These challenges also signaled that IGRTC had regulating and guiding power but lacked enforcing power and presumably also lacked high-level political support. To resolve the situation, IGRTC commenced intensive dialogue with counties, and eventually a new Gazette Notice was issued (no. 4370, May 11, 2018) that listed 16 counties that had not established CALCs to note violated regulation and extended the deadline for them to complete validation and submit CALC reports to IGRTC by August 31, 2018. The respective counties met the new deadline and IGRTC was in possession of 47 county CALC reports by September 2018.

IGRTC commenced detailed analysis of the CALC reports that revealed some shortcomings and challenges, including the following (IGRTC 2018): (1) most of the reports submitted to IGRTC were incomplete and many were marked as "draft"; (2) the draft reports did not indicate whether the requisite (outgoing or incoming) county governments (governors, assemblies) had discussed reports or instead the CALC secretaries submitted the unapproved reports to IGRTC; (3) many CALC field teams seem to have followed, accepted, and copied figures from unaudited preliminary TA reports without thorough verification; (4) some brave teams listed numerous discrepancies and parallel numbers and estimated differences against the TA report; (5) most CALC teams left disputed liabilities unattended; and (6) CALC teams were instructed to present the values "as of March 27, 2013" without trying to estimate the present values (as of 2017 or 2018) of financial assets and liabilities, which made financial results inadequate in 2018. IGRTC could have guided counties differently and could have requested both initial book values and present values, although estimating the initial book values was extremely difficult if not impossible.

After completion of the revision of CALC reports, IBEC clearance, and publication of the national summary report on county assets and liabilities, in November 2018 IGRTC shared the summary and county reports with the respective counties by submitting the reports to the governors for their information, consideration, and eventual adoption by county governing bodies. In parallel, IGRTC shared the summary report with the Summit, Council of Governors, National Treasury, IBEC, and auditor general, aiming to feed high-level policy dialogue on the main recommendations and, most important, eventual legislative measures toward final resolution of the transfer of inherited disputed assets and liabilities.

National summary of assets and liabilities of the defunct local authorities

IGRTC reviewed, commented on, cleared, and aggregated the 47 county CALC reports into one consolidated national report on asset takeover, which was

FIGURE 2.6

Report on the assets and liabilities of the defunct local authorities, March 2013

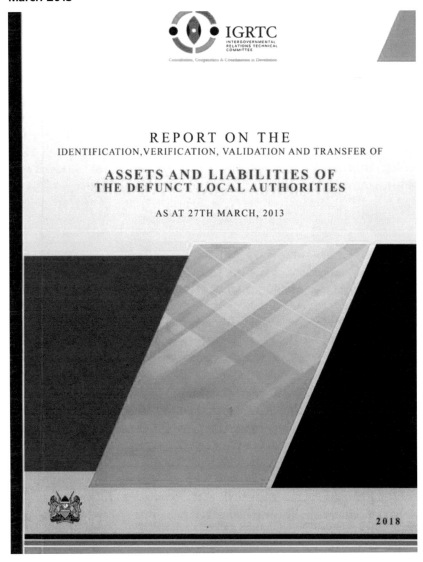

Source: IGRTC 2018.

published in November 2018 (IGRTC 2018) (see figure 2.6). This report is a significant achievement, despite noted shortcomings, because this is the first report that presents an aggregated picture of Kenya's county assets and liabilities. However, this does not include the assets acquired or liabilities committed (or generated or became overdue) after the induction of the county governments in 2013. And it remains unclear whether some verified assets were inherited or built after March 2013 (extension of schools, hospital wards, roads, and so on), because many of those were hardly separable from the inherited assets during field verification four to five years after induction of the new county governments. The report does not include references to such extended or new assets, and the CALC reports are brief about the technical details of assets (for example, school buildings recorded without specifying number and size of classrooms or amenities).

Furthermore, it is important to note that this report does not cover the assets and liabilities that various national government entities by law had been mandated to hand over to counties, because neither the TA nor IGRTC had yet commenced the verification and handover of these assets and liabilities. Instead, IGRTC stated, "The verified and validated inventory was expected to include not only the assets and liabilities of the defunct local authorities, but [also assets and liabilities from] ministries, departments, state corporations, and agencies." (IGRTC 2018, 1). In this section we briefly analyze and summarize the main results, challenges, and issues and draw lessons on transition based on the IGRTC 2018 report.

The report covers assets and liabilities the defunct local authorities (DLAs) possessed at closure on March 27, 2013. The main categories include (1) fixed assets, including land, buildings, motor vehicles, computers and accessories, furniture and fittings, plant and equipment, biological assets, and project works in progress; (2) financial assets, including investments (shareholdings and fixed deposits) and current assets; and (3) financial liabilities, including main groups such as loans or bank debts, emoluments, statutory deductions, commercial or trade creditors, and legal fees. The analysis aims to reflect the situation as of March 27, 2013, with a few exceptions, including noting that some liabilities were paid by August 31, 2018, and listing and noting projects in progress on March 27, 2013. Finally, the report does not provide an aggregated value of analyzed county assets and liabilities, because CALCs were not mandated to estimate the present value of assets and liabilities. We summarize main attributes and key findings from the report by asset groups in the following sections.

Land

Land is undoubtedly the most important asset of local governments because land holds or provides geographic space for buildings, plants, and infrastructure. It is also important because counties own undeveloped land parcels, some of which are surplus and ready for strategic divestiture, which has been a major source of funding infrastructure in most countries. Following this principle, the IGRTC report starts with and puts high emphasis on inherited land. The CALCs did a great job and identified 62,342 parcels of land, which is 50 percent more than the number of parcels in the TA list; moreover, of these parcels only 3,106 parcels (or 5 percent) are listed as disputed. A shortcoming of the survey, however, is that the committees have not verified the size of parcels. Due diligence at field verification would have required verifying, or if verification were not possible, at least estimating an approximate size of each parcel to secure ownership and constrain further grabbing or encroachment by such records. For instance, a 2.0-hectare land parcel (inventoried in 2018) may appear to be only 1.2 hectares as time goes by; the parcel remains there but land still can be lost by encroachment.

One important exception on land measurement is that the NCC government conducted a complete land identification and valuation exercise under the Nairobi Metropolitan Services Improvement Project of the World Bank in 2017–18 that identifies, locates in digital maps, and records the size of all land parcels in the NCC jurisdiction (details are discussed in the NCC case study in part II). This new land database identifies both private and public land, including land parcels owned by NCC and community land, but also other public land possessed by various national entities. Moreover, this mass valuation exercise also provides an estimated market value of land at a 2018 price. Two other counties (Bomet and Kiambu) have commenced land valuation for tax purposes, and they also capture county land, important for management of county land assets. These cases represent quantum leaps in a good direction.

Aggregate figures on land assets are summarized in table 2.4, which shows that 85.7 percent of land is registered in the national land registry, but not necessarily under the ownership of the respective counties. Only 58.3 percent of land was surveyed with survey data records, while 10.8 percent of parcels were identified as unsurveyed. Less than half of land parcels were planned with planning data, while over 20 percent were found as unplanned land. Unplanned land may be either developed or undeveloped or idle land. However, CALC teams have not noted or recorded whether a verified parcel was undeveloped or idle land or held some improvements registered under other asset categories such as a building, water or sanitation lines, road or other network infrastructure, pump stations, or other structures. This is a shortcoming, since the issue of idle land is buried under the pile of land and other asset reports. One reason behind this could be that the verification teams were segregated and worked without coordinating verifications of land and improvements.

Main observations regarding land properties and land verification. The following observations were gathered from IGRTC (2018) and interviews:

- *Lack of ownership document.* This is substantial, because CALC teams rightly identified land based on various sources (sometimes with the help of knowledgeable citizens) and listed land as owned without ownership documents, albeit most not disputed.
- *Lost documents.* During transition there was mishandling and lack of handover of titles, registry indexes, maps, index diagrams, sale or purchase agreements, council minutes, and survey certificates.
- *Inaccuracy of CALC reports.* This includes discrepancies in numbers found in tables and lists and supporting arguments.
- *Disputed land.* This represents only 5 percent of total parcels but over 3,000 cases and presumably K Sh billions of market value, including (1) public land held by private individuals due to illegal occupation, illegal obtainment of titles, or land encroachment; (2) irregular allotments or multiple allocations by DLAs; (3) land boundary issues between DLAs and private owners; and (4) land taken over by national government entities.

TABLE 2.4 **Inherited land parcels, Kenya counties total, March 27, 2013**

LAND CATEGORIES	NUMBER	% OF TOTAL
Disputed	3,106	5.0
Registered	53,453	85.7
Not registered	8,889	14.3
Surveyed	36,359	58.3
Not surveyed	6,755	10.8
Without survey data	19,228	30.8
Planned	27,640	44.3
Not planned	12,853	20.6
Without planning data	21,879	35.1
Parcels verified	62,342	100.0

Source: IGRTC 2018.

- *Shared easements and wayleaves.* This occurred when wayleaves were recorded as full ownership, instead of accounting wayleaves as intangible assets.
- *Unclear ownership of land.* This was due to lack of clear boundaries between DLAs, DLA ownership in other DLA territory (NCC water reservoirs and waterworks), for example, nontransfer of ownership in national land records, or contentious ownership of land (for example, temporary handover of land to a Chinese construction company without proper documentation).
- *Unclear records on land inherited but divested or allocated after transition.* County reports and interviews suggest that some counties have divested, allocated, or handed over parcels of land (with or without buildings) after transition (for example, Mombasa to statutory creditors); such land parcels are not reflected in the land inventory, an inconsistent approach when the list is supposed to reflect the status as of March 27, 2013.

Options for corrective measures at the county level include the following:

- *Register land under county ownership.* Since 85 percent of land is registered, the Ministry of Land and Physical Planning and the National Land Commission can support counties with fast-track registration to curb further encroachment and losses.
- *Survey unsurveyed parcels.* Demarcate boundaries and measure size (hectares) of each land parcel that has no survey documentation.
- *Launch a dispute resolution campaign.* These could include legal filings and out-of-court resolutions led by assigned teams of planners, valuers, and lawyers and maybe involvement of NALM to work out disputed cases.
- *Develop a reliable land asset register.* Support it with geographic information system (GIS) maps and global positioning system (GPS) and identification (the case of NCC is a good example).
- *Commence forensic investigation.* And create a list of land parcels the incoming county governments have divested, transferred, or allocated since March 2013.

Options for corrective measures at the national level include the following:

- *Develop a national public land register.* Do this in cooperation between the Ministry of Land and Physical Planning and the National Treasury NALM Department.
- *Mandate the National Land Commission and/or NALM to review and veto disposition of public land.* Do this especially with free allotments or when compensation is below market price.

Buildings

The Physical Planning Act Cap 286 2012 (PPA 2012) and the Land Act (LDA 2012) define "buildings" as any structure (superstructure) or erection, and any parts of any structure or erection of any kind whatsoever, whether permanent, temporary, or movable, and whether complete or uncompleted. It is worth noting that proper AM requires a much more differentiated approach to this group of assets with clear distinction of buildings, plants, networks, and other infra and super structures. Counties can do this without regulation, since creating asset subgroups would not violate the noted legislations. But CALC teams were satisfied with the template that clubbed all of these under the cluster name as buildings, thus we will adhere to the CALC terminology. The CALC teams have

TABLE 2.5 **Summary of inherited buildings, Kenya counties total, March 27, 2013**

BUILDING CATEGORIES	NUMBER	% OF TOTAL
Identified	4,938	58.4
Without identification	3,526	41.7
Additional by CALC	25	0.3
Disputed	160	1.9
Buildings verified	8,461	100.0

Source: IGRTC 2018.
Note: CALC = County Asset and Liability Committee.

verified 8,461 buildings, of which nearly 60 percent had clear identification with a registration number, parcel number, and allotment letter number (table 2.5). Less than 2 percent of buildings were found as disputed because of illegally or irregularly allocated ownership or location of a building in illegally or irregularly allocated public land. Some disputes are between national government entities and counties.

Main observations regarding building properties. The following observations were gathered from IGRTC (2018) and interviews:

- *Missing technical details and size of buildings.* One major shortcoming on building inventories is that CALC teams have registered building complexes with multiple units as single units without indicating technical details, such as number of rooms in office buildings, number of dwellings in a building or in a compound, and, more important, the size of each unit and the total floor area of a building in square meters is either missing or inaccurate.
- *Value of the buildings not established or registered.* Neither the historic book value nor present value net of amortization was established, while market value valuation was intentionally postponed for later stages due to the shortage of time.
- *Buildings listed without identification.* These were inventoried without corresponding to a land registry, land identification, and adjacent land size.
- *Lack of ownership proofs.* Some DLAs had constructed buildings on private land before completing the acquisition and left no proof of ownership.
- *Swap buildings for debt resolution.* Mombasa County aimed to work out inherited liabilities and handed over housing complexes to statutory bodies such as the National Social Security Fund, the National Health Insurance Fund, or the Local Authorities Pension Trust of the National Social Security Fund to eliminate debt. These were mainly housing estates (300 one-bedroom units, 144 one-bedroom units, and 144 two-bedroom units (IGRTC 2018, 27). These buildings are not included in the CALC lists (a sort of inconsistency, since the lists state that assets are verified as of March 27, 2013, while transfers or swaps have happened in subsequent years).
- *Valuable buildings are missing from lists.* IGRTC experts suspect that a considerable number of valuable buildings, such as leisure centers, mountain lodges, and so forth, are missing from these verified lists, whether intentionally or by human error.
- *Missing inventory of buildings from the projects or works in progress inventory.* Buildings that were planned with approved funding and/or were under construction at the time of transition (March 2013) are either not recorded in the

building inventory or are simply accounted as verified buildings or extensions without reference to projects inventory.

- *Missing inventory of posttransition buildings.* These would have been built after March 2013 and funded from development budgets of the new county governments, and they are not listed separately and some may be incorporated in the list of inherited buildings, especially when projects aimed to build extensions to existing schools, health centers, hospital wards, and so forth.

- *Missing inventory of divested buildings.* These include buildings the incoming county governments had inherited but divested, transferred, or allocated other ways between March 2013 and August 2018.

Options for corrective measures include the following:

- Revise building registers to include all due technical and financial details as regulated in PFM law.
- Segregate main groups of the building list: buildings, plants, network, and other infra- and superstructures.
- Obtain identification and registration numbers for all buildings.
- Conduct a forensic investigation of lodges in game reserves, natural parks, and mountain resort areas to find irregular allocation or illegal use or possession or appropriation of buildings.
- Do valuation of buildings starting with those rented, leased, or being managed as revenue-generating commercial assets with present market value established for such commercial properties. Buildings used for core urban services and assumed to be undivestible (schools, health centers, and so forth) can be evaluated in simplified methodology and at a later stage. (Detter and Fölster [2018] also suggest such a pragmatic approach.)
- Commence investigating existence and present status of buildings that are supposed to have been completed after March 2013 from the list of projects or works in progress.
- Develop a reliable inventory of buildings constructed from development funds of incoming county governments and cross-reference it with the building inventory of inherited assets (over K Sh 200 billion total value—see part II).
- Investigate to identify buildings and develop an inventory of buildings the incoming county governments have divested, transferred, or allotted after March 2013.

Projects: Works in progress

At the time of dissolution, DLAs were managing 4,308 projects in different phases of development. By the time of CALC verification, 55 percent were completed, 27 percent were in progress, and 745 (or 17 percent) had not yet started as of March 27, 2013 (and possibly not after). The estimated fair value of completed and ongoing projects as of March 2013 was about K Sh 16 billion, a substantial amount of development funding.

CALC teams approached verification of projects with nonchalance. As a result, the IGRTC report has several shortcomings. First, it does not provide a list of completed projects that should have been incorporated and cross-referenced in the respective fixed-asset reports (buildings, structures, infrastructure, or equipment). Second, it does not provide progress details and a breakdown as of August 2018 (completed, ongoing, stalled, canceled) on projects that were works in progress in 2013. Instead, the summary just states that "some projects were completed, others stalled or still to be completed" (five years after transition?).

Third, teams failed to trace the fate of projects that had not started by transition date, simply concluded that most of these never commenced, but more interestingly, no explanation is provided about the funds that were set aside to finance them. Possibly, the incoming county governments simply used the funds for other projects such as urgent repair of offices, schools, or health facilities.

Main observations regarding projects or works in progress. The following observations were gathered from IGRTC (2018):

- The list includes the "fair value" of projects as of March 2013 without reflecting the actual, final value at the date of completion.
- CALC teams found very unreliable data on projects, with lots of missing information.
- Verification of status in 2018 and segregation of buildings, structures, and equipment from respective inherited asset files did not happen.
- Completed projects represent over half of the projects or works in progress but were left in the project list because completion documents were missing, and some contractors did not hand over structures due to lack of payment or missing final administration.
- CALC teams found little evidence about funds allotted for projects that had not started by March 2013 but may or may not have started later under incoming county governments.
- Some of the projects could generate revenue from investments, but no segregated list has been generated, despite a risk of losing public revenues.

Options for corrective measures include the following:

- Commence investigation to clarify the status of each project and segregate results within regular inherited asset inventories.
- Estimate the final actual value of projects and the present value of the built assets.
- Commence forensic investigation to clarify the status of projects that did not start by transition and determine the disposition of allocated funds.
- Install project management information and communication technology modules for easy and consistent recording of all details of construction projects currently and in the future (Makueni County offers a good example for such a module in part II).
- Commence forensic investigation of projects that were aimed at revenue generation to clarify their status and reverse irregular transactions as necessary.

Motor vehicles

Motor vehicles are defined as self-propelled road or off-road vehicles, commonly wheeled and used for transportation: ambulances, cars, combine harvesters, ferries, fire trucks, lorries, motorbikes, motorboats, pickups, tractors, and vans.

CALC teams verified 2,617 motor vehicles (table 2.6) without book values. Two-thirds of vehicles were found in serviceable conditions, a quarter had no engine or chassis or registration number, and 60 were sold or stolen.

Incoming county governments took over motor vehicles since they desperately needed transportation or movement. Not quite understandably, some counties left old and used vehicles unattended ("due to lack of transfer"), most in open air, and many were dilapidated by the time of CALC verification. Numerous logbooks were lost during transition; verification teams found several logbooks but failed to verify corresponding vehicles. Thus, it is wise now to look to the

TABLE 2.6 **Summary of inherited motor vehicles, Kenya counties total, March 27, 2013**

VEHICLE CATEGORIES	NUMBER	% OF TOTAL
Grounded	838	32.0
No registration number	60	2.3
No engine or chassis number	570	21.8
Sold or stolen	60	2.3
Motor vehicles verified	2,617	100.0

Source: IGRTC 2018.

future and establish reliable registers and logbooks for vehicles. Also, to clean records (and the yards), counties should commence a final verification of grounded vehicles, and then divest them in open tenders or dispose of those that could not be sold.

Equipment, computer accessories, and furniture

We have summarized these three categories of assets together because of their low total value, low importance, and short useful life that was nearly ended by the time of verification for most of this equipment.

Equipment included in IGRTC report information technology distribution networks consisted of electronic appliances, household items, agricultural mechanization equipment, fishing and sport equipment, firefighting equipment, workshop items, and medical equipment. CALC teams verified 9,715 pieces of equipment, with a total estimated value of K Sh 319 million as of March 2013. CALC teams estimated no present value, but most likely most of the equipment was close to its end of useful life by the time of verification. Safekeeping, tagging, and annual inventory are the advised options.

Computers and accessories include desktops, laptops, personal data access devices, scanners, photocopiers, mouses, keyboards, projectors, and speakers. CALC teams have verified 5,276 computers and 5,100 accessories with no value estimates. General observations include poor handling and dilapidation, lack of serial number (of about 60 percent of computers), and lack of records on movement and handover of computers across departments, offices, and staff. Tagging, reliable inventories, and movement records should be institutionalized as standard practices.

Furniture and fittings verified include 36,761 items, less than half with value. The total value as of March 2013 was estimated at K Sh 211 million, but no present value was established. General observations included poor handling and dilapidation and lack of movement records. Tagging, reliable inventories, movement records, and safe handling should be institutionalized as standard practices.

Biological assets

Biological assets inherited from DLAs include domestic animals (cows, calves, donkeys), wild animals in farms (tortoises, snakes, lizards), tea and coffee plantations, and forests. Twelve counties reported biological assets with estimated value (as of 2013) of K Sh 293 million. Encroachment of land and losses of animals have happened during transition due to poor handling of biological assets. Several biological assets are disputed between DLAs and national government entities, churches, or private citizens who had supposedly grabbed plantations. One such case is under court procedure. Securing forests and plantations with demarcations and land records and general safe handling of biological assets are urgent follow-up steps counties should commence.

Current assets

CALC teams have reported three types of financial assets: current assets, shares, and term deposits in banks or other financial institutions. As indicated previously, estimating the face value of financial assets as of March 2013 is an accounting approach, but it is a questionable practice doing it many years later for financial analysis and AM. Table 2.7 summarizes the value and composition of inherited current assets. However, these inherited claims or collectibles were already over five years old at the time of verification, so the present values of many of these claims could be way below the listed nominal or face values as of 2013. IGRTC proposes that counties consider writing off uncollectable claims with reference to section 150 of PFM Act 2012, and sections 145–159 of County PFM Act Regulation 2015.

Furthermore, it would have been justified to provide some estimation of present values. For instance, interviews suggest that counties used up the inherited cash and bank deposits, and most likely the inherited inventories of materials, spare parts, or fuel. Thus, the real challenges relate to inherited collectibles, such as taxes as well as compensation in lieu of rates (CILOR), rents, and wayleave claims (rights of way fees). The IGRTC 2018 report is surprisingly brief on discussing the current assets; the section is limited to presenting aggregate figures and a few county-specific cases without qualification and guidance.

Property tax arrears. Inherited uncollected taxes (called "property rates" in Kenya) represent over three-quarters of inherited current assets, and NCC inherited most of them (table 2.7). The K Sh 84 billion value would be sufficient to pay out all inherited liabilities, but this is far from being real cash, and it is questionable if it is a current asset, due to its historic value and unverifiable source (Kelly 2002). At the time of the verification in 2018, these overdue tax claims were all over five years old, and some possibly were over 10 years old (Kelly, White, and Anand 2020). However, the claims estimated at K Sh 84 billion as of March 2013 could have substantially increased, because delinquent payers continued nonpayments and accumulated five more years of arrears above the initial amount. For instance, annual tax revenues in NCC have remained flat (K Sh 2.5 billion) between 2013 and 2018 (Kopanyi 2018). But also, applying regular penalties would have increased this amount further; in short, claims are likely to have exceeded K Sh 100 billion at the time of verification.

TABLE 2.7 **Summary of inherited current assets of Kenya's 47 counties, March 27, 2013**

ASSET CLASSES	K Sh (BILLIONS)	% OF TOTAL
Property tax	84.5	76.2
Plot and house rent	3.5	3.2
Cash and bank balances	2.3	2.1
Staff debtors	0.8	0.7
CILOR	5.2	4.7
Other (wayleave, charges)	14.2	12.8
Inventories	0.4	0.4
Total	**110.9**	**100.0**

Source: IGRTC 2018.
Note: CILOR = compensation in lieu of rates.

Nairobi City County's County Asset and Liability Committee (NCC CALC) verification team has attempted to verify the property tax arrears and learned that the records existed in financial department files but were only partially reflected in the Local Authorities Integrated Financial Operations Management System (LAIFOMS) or the fiscal cadaster. Thus, verification of many claims and identification of taxpayers appeared to be not only difficult but nearly impossible. The situation is presumably similar in other counties. Some countries' legislation permits tax forgiveness, and others do not. The accountant general may permit NCC to write off apparently uncollectable claims.

Options for corrective measures include the following:

- Commence a detailed analysis of available files and disaggregate tax claims by years.
- Adopt tax policy to annul tax claims older than five years (or more, up to 10 years) and annul claims older than 10 years with reference to PFM Act 2012 and County PFM Act Regulation 2015.
- Resume verification of claims that are supposed to be collected under the adopted tax policy.
- Announce a campaign to collect inherited tax arrears with rebates, say, 20 percent per year for those older than three years (at four years the owner pays 80 percent, five years 60 percent, six years 40 percent, seven years 20 percent) if owner pays within 12 months of the announcement.

The main objective is not only revenue maximization, but rather clearing files of financial assets and creating realistic and reliable databases. Some experts question tax rebates because they may incentivize owners to wait until their claims are annulled, but clever rules can eliminate such perverse incentives.

CILOR arrears. Payments dues by national government entities to counties in lieu of property taxes seem to be easier to collect because of the small number of payers as compared with private taxpayers (dozens compared with 150,000 in Nairobi). However, the power structure and the lack of political will combined with the shortage of money at the national level have made it difficult for counties to collect these unquestionable claims. For instance, the NCC government has attempted to swap CILOR claims for NCC liabilities—a logical and standard practice in the business and public sectors in many countries—but NCCG failed to reach a mutually acceptable agreement. This case underscores the need for high-level political support and national intervention (Summit, auditor general, and National Treasury via NALM, and maybe IGRTC as a policy facilitator).

Plot and house rent. Textbooks suggest that collecting house and plot rent is obviously much easier than collecting property taxes, because the benefit principle is more apparent, the number of payers is much lower than the total number of taxpayers, and the identification is easy and simple. Inherited uncollected property rents (K Sh 3.5 billion) are substantial and still mostly left unattended for five years into transition. Interviews suggest that most counties have improved collecting the annual house and plot rents after 2013, but few have solid plans for collecting rent arrears. It is also a fairness issue, because the rents are artificially low, so in fact implicitly subsidized and outdated, and when left unpaid, it is unfair to those who are willing to pay but unable to obtain a rental dwelling or shop.

Wayleave and other collectibles. Inherited claims on wayleaves that are uncollected fees from state corporations (national electricity company, telecom company) to compensate counties using their land based on right-of-way are very substantial (K Sh 14 billion as of March 2013) and make the bulk of inherited fee collectibles. Many of these claims are also disputed, and the state corporations are unwilling to pledge and pay these claims, and certainly the subsequent dues between 2013 and 2018. For instance, the NCC government has attempted to swap wayleave claims for unpaid electricity bills that are among inherited liabilities, but negotiations failed due to resistance of the electricity company. Furthermore, one large, disputed claim not reflected in the IGRTC summary is a claim by the defunct City Council of Nairobi (CCN) dated 1997 against the Department of Defense (DoD), which took over a 900-hectare parcel for a military garrison but never paid for that land. The defunct council commenced a court procedure that ended up with the High Court, but then an interministerial decision led to an out-of-court settlement that is still to be reached after over 20 years of dispute. These cases also underscore the need for high-level political support and national intervention (Summit, auditor general, and National Treasury via NALM, and maybe IGRTC as a policy facilitator).

Staff debtors. Staff debtors are minor items as compared to the other inherited collectibles or claims. The IGRTC report is silent on the present status of these claims, but anecdotal evidence suggests that most of them are being served by debtors, thus these are inherited but performing claims and loans. Or it is unclear if these are overdue payments by debtors or the face value of the loans. Counties should revisit these claims and clarify what part of this portfolio is performing and what part is nonperforming, and then counties may proceed with collection or write off nonperforming loans, while accounting the performing items as financial investments or loans instead of current assets.

Investments

Two types of investments are included in the IGRTC and CALC reports: shares or shareholdings and term deposits that counties inherited from the DLAs.

Shareholdings. Most shareholdings are in water and sewage companies that had been transferred to DLAs before transition. DLAs also invested in local commercial entities, presumably for revenue-generation purposes such as dairy farms, mining or manufacturing companies, and hotels or lodges. The list of such investments needs clarity about the number of shares or size (percentage) of shareholdings, and the book and present value of shareholdings. The CALC reports are brief and provide vague or only preliminary information about shareholdings.

Lacking information prevented IGRTC from establishing a national aggregate value of shareholdings; county estimates of present value show a wide variety, from unknown to inflated. Furthermore, the IGRTC report lists as investments those included in the TA unaudited inventory but excluded from CALC reports, which may reflect errors in the TA list or rather improper verification by CALC field teams. For instance, the NCC government listed a K Sh 56 million book value of 100 percent shareholding in the Nairobi City Water and Sewerage Company (NCWSC) but estimated present value as K Sh 25 billion (discussed in the NCC case study in part II). Finally, one can conclude that the list of shareholdings suggests that the counties manage these vital and valuable investments with insufficient care and are left underinformed and maybe underrepresented among shareholders.

Corrective measures may include the following:

- Commence investigation into each shareholding and clarify the number of shares, percent of shareholdings, voting rights, and power of the county in shareholder voting.

- Commence detailed analysis of financial performance of these investments, accounting for dividends and other financial gains, if any, and for financial supports the counties may have provided to these entities.
- Clarify and analyze the explicit and implicit contingent liabilities the counties inherited from DLAs in association with these shareholdings.
- Properly account for the book value and the fair market value of these investments.
- Make policy decisions about divestiture of seriously underperforming investments, especially those found to have negative net present value.
- There is a need for an urgent national program led by the National Treasury via NALM and the Ministry of Water and Sanitation to finalize outstanding issues and disputes regarding transfer of water companies' assets to full and unambiguous county ownership with pragmatic resolution of attached liabilities.

Fixed deposits. DLAs had deposited fixed deposits into commercial banks or various other financial entities (for example, building societies). The total amount of fixed deposits appears to be small, less than K Sh 90 million (as of March 2013). The CALC reports do not show the present value of fixed deposits but suggest that some entities had gone bankrupt and thus the investments are presumably lost. These cases suggest that DLAs and present counties manage fixed deposits without a strategy and keep anecdotal and unverified data. Corrective measures may include (1) revisiting the list of fixed deposits and segregating performing and nonperforming items; (2) verifying with partner entities the status and present value of each fixed deposit; (3) establishing clear records and a reliable inventory of fixed deposits; (4) adopting a strategy to hold, change, and manage these fixed deposits; and (5) writing off deposits accounted as held in entities that had moved out of business.

Inherited liabilities

Counties had inherited K Sh 53.8 billion in liabilities as of March 27, 2013, and NCC inherited over two-thirds of these (table 2.8). The broad categories of liabilities include domestic and foreign loans, unpaid staff emoluments, unremitted statutory deductions and insurance dues, unpaid trade creditors, and legal fees. CALC teams made little attempt to estimate the present value of inherited liabilities and failed to estimate the volume of nonperforming liabilities at the virtual

TABLE 2.8 **Inherited liabilities, Kenya counties total, 2013 and 2018**

	MARCH 27, 2013		NONPERFORMING, AUGUST 31, 2018	
LIABILITY CLASSES	K Sh (BILLIONS)	% OF TOTAL	K Sh (BILLIONS)	% OF TOTAL
Loans	25.4	47.3	19.4	45.6
of which overdrafts	2.1	3.9	0.0	0.0
of which foreign	15.3	28.5	15.3	35.9
Staff emoluments	6.3	11.7	2.2	5.2
Statutory deductions	11.6	21.7	11.2	26.3
Trade or commercial creditors	7.8	14.5	7.2	17.0
Legal fees	2.6	4.8	2.6	6.0
Total	**53.8**	**100.0**	**42.6**	**100.0**

Source: IGRTC 2018.

valuation date of August 31, 2018. Instead, they commented on some of the liabilities and challenges. CALC reports and interviews suggest that three major changes happened between 2013 and 2018: (1) counties have paid out some liabilities, such as short overdrafts and the bulk of staff emoluments; (2) counties continued performing several domestic loans, so those loans are inherited liabilities but performing; and finally, (3) counties failed to work out overdue statutory deductions and face increasing penalties, so the present value of statutory deductions with interest and penalties is estimated to have doubled by 2019.

In sum, despite repaying over K Sh 5.4 billion of liabilities and performing another K Sh 5 billion of debt, the present value of liabilities roughly remained the same amount (K Sh 53 billion) as the initial inherited volume in 2013. The IGRTC report indicates a K Sh 5.9 billion variation between TA and IGRTC/CALC inventories, but lower estimates by counties are presumably due to the inconsistent accounting of subsequent changes—repayment is reported to be about K Sh 5.4 billion (IGRTC 2018, 75). Counties should revise their inherited liabilities to precisely account the present value of inherited dues after several subsequent transactions and focus on the nonperforming liabilities for workout.

Loans. Counties inherited domestic commercial loans (K Sh 4 billion) and have been performing most repayments. NCC has inherited a foreign loan DLA borrowed for the NCWSC that is nonperforming, and Nairobi City County Government (NCCG) has failed verification of loan documents, even though the National Treasury keeps performing this loan from the foreign creditor and presumably has in its files the initial loan and on-lending agreement. NCCG simply accounts it in the balance sheet among liabilities regardless of unclear and nonperforming status. Furthermore, field interviews with managers suggest that NCWSC has no cash flow to serve this loan. Counties also inherited K Sh 2 billion bank overdrafts listed in the IGRTC report as nonperforming, although interviews suggest that many counties do repay and use overdrafts nowadays. Finally, there were some minor loans from the National Housing Corporation, and a K Sh 3.8 billion guaranteed loan from the Local Governments Loans Authority, which should have absorbed this loan based on the guarantee, but it is still accounted in the IGRTC inventory.

Unremitted deductions. Counties inherited K Sh 7.8 billion in unpaid statutory deductions and K Sh 2.4 billion in unpaid staff deductions. Unremitted deductions are not only the second largest item in the list of inherited liabilities, but they are disputed and the most poisonous liabilities, because this initial volume is growing fast daily with applied high penalties, some with over 30 percent annual interest. As a result, the present value of these dues is estimated to have doubled by 2019.

Many counties have attempted to work out inherited unremitted deductions. For example, Mombasa handed over 600 dwellings in three compounds to eliminate statutory health and social security insurance liabilities. (It is unclear if these unremitted deductions are still included in the IGRTC list of liabilities, because Mombasa's repaid deductions reflect a small number in the IGRTC list.) Nairobi has tried to negotiate repayment of the deductions' principals if creditors eliminate the high penalties, but negotiations failed. High-level national government actions are required to open this gridlock and seek pragmatic resolution on inherited deductions.

Staff emoluments. Counties paid out two-thirds of unpaid staff emoluments soon after the transition as part of the restructuring of staff and dues, and thus reduced the inherited K Sh 6.3 billion to K Sh 2.2 billion. Reports do not indicate the reason or plans toward further resolving issues on unpaid emoluments.

Trade and commercial creditors. The total volume of inherited liabilities vis-à-vis commercial creditors was estimated at K Sh 7.8 billion in 2013 value. Field interviews suggest that many counties had negotiated and revised commercial claims and compensated some trade creditors, sometimes by swapping assets and claims (maybe land). For instance, in 2018 NCC's commercial claims reached K Sh 11 billion, but the NCC government advertised that trade creditors should present supporting evidence of their claims and they would be paid after validation. As a result, the validated volume of claims after the K Sh 3 billion settlement dropped to K Sh 4.7 billion. These claims may coincide with the list of inherited projects or works in progress that had been completed and presumably paid subsequently. Thus, a double accounting may distort information on trade creditors. The IGRTC report is very brief about trade creditors and presents the estimated value as of March 27, 2013, without providing any update by 2018. A fair update of the trade creditor portfolio and a cross-check with the projects portfolio is an urgent corrective measure.

Legal fees. Both the IGRTC report and field information remain very brief about the nature, verified volume (K Sh 2.6 billion), and present value of legal fees, some of which also may have triggered penalty interest, and thus they may have expanded by 2019.

Corrective measures for inherited liabilities may include the following:

- Carefully (re)validate and update the portfolio of inherited liabilities to determine the legality of claims and the amount repaid or worked out in other ways.
- Segregate performing and nonperforming claims and loans and estimate the present values of the claims at the date of revision.
- Commence a national program to work out inherited unremitted deductions by drastically reducing penalties, seeking swap options, and encouraging parties to reach final solutions. Further rolling of these poisonous claims is unhealthy and should be avoided.
- High-level political support is needed, and intervention by the National Treasury, Summit, and other ministries is required to commence and implement a workout program aiming at full elimination of inherited nonperforming liabilities, because counties alone are unable to resolve these disputes and eliminate claims, either legally or financially.

IGRTC has elaborated these issues, defined options, and presented a list of proposals.

Liquidation options for inherited liabilities

IGRTC has analyzed and recommended liquidation options based on detailed consultations with key stakeholders in accordance with Section 2(2) of Gazette Notice no. 4370. The broad liquidation options include a combination of the following:

- Counties offset liabilities from their revenues (equitable shares and/or own-source revenues [OSR]).
- The national government sets up and populates a strategic intervention pool to allocate conditional grants for payment of some liabilities.

- National and county governments agree on joint payment of liabilities in agreed proportions.
- National government entities (OAG) rule to enable writing-off some liabilities and/or waiving penalties binding to both creditors and debtors.
- Use current assets to offset some liabilities, based on county-by-county analyses.
- Enable swapping third-party collectibles for liabilities to liquidate both debts and liabilities.

IGRTC has accomplished detailed negotiations with key stakeholders and listed resolution options for 17 liability categories with specific recommendations that reflect the options listed. IGRTC also lists entities that should play a role in resolving specific liability categories. The report is unclear, however, if the listed national or commercial entities (sometimes a dozen to participate in the workout of an item) have agreed and are able and willing to perform the expected roles, such as setting aside a substantial amount of money (for example, by the National Treasury) to support elimination of inherited liabilities.

Furthermore, the list of resolution options includes the face value of the inherited liabilities as of March 27, 2013. Instead, for a pragmatic resolution the portfolio of inherited liabilities should be restructured to reflect (1) the nonperforming liabilities that should be worked out and (2) the present value of nonperforming liabilities. This would indicate the magnitude of the problem and inform resolution seekers with realistic numbers and needs for restructuring. These can support a summary table of resolution options structured by key stakeholders to indicate the magnitude of their estimated willing contributions, without which no solid commitment can be considered, since without a specific contribution volume it would be a blank check for them to sign a list. The summary list with estimated specific contributions may include the following:

- Creditors with the magnitude of principal value and the penalties proposed to be written off
- Banks with interest to write off or capitalize, and the volume or principal of restructured loans
- National Treasury/NALM-projected magnitude of contribution on behalf of the national government
- Auditor General rule for writing off inherited overdue audit fees
- Statutory creditors with amount of forgiven penalties and a capitalized net volume of demands to be converted to long-term, 5- to 10-year maturity loans (The IGRTC report suggests giving a maximum 3 years for counties to pay out all dues, but counties simply have no free cash flow with a magnitude that would be required for fast repayment—for example, it would eat up over half of NCC's total annual budget for 3 years.)

This is a vicious circle because the amounts are imprecisely known before hard negotiations. Attaching amounts to options can be approached as an elaboration of options to inform hard negotiations, instead of being final results set by IGRTC or the national government. In short, there is a need to attach specific numbers to resolution options to provide solid ground to start an iterative process that would lead to final resolution and elimination of inherited nonperforming liabilities. Such elimination will include restructuring liabilities and converting immediate dues to long-term loans and moving nonperforming liabilities to performing ones, because, as noted, many counties cannot pay overnight or even in three years all nonperforming inherited liabilities accumulated over a decade or longer.

The recommendations at the start of this subsection are in full harmony with the final recommendations of the IGRTC (2018, 89) but present slightly revised proposals:

- Develop and implement liabilities workout implementation plans that should factor in county and national government budgets, supported by regulations if necessary.
- List specific national government interventions (with monetary numbers) such as waivers on interest and penalties and planned financial support by national government entities (mainly the National Treasury).
- The liquidation period should be three financial years. However, this statement needs clarification. The elimination of nonperforming liabilities should be done in one year with workout agreements that may include, among other things, cash transfers, asset swaps, and debt restructuring by turning current dues to long-term loans (instead of repaying all dues in three years).
- Agreements should be made with trustees of pension schemes on modalities to clear nonperforming inherited liabilities, which may include write-off of penalties, and converting net liabilities into long-term loans, and thus eliminating nonperforming statutory deduction liabilities.
- The national government should support an alternative out-of-court dispute resolution mechanism to avoid lengthy and expensive court procedures.

Considering these options, IGRTC should keep working on a liability resolution national framework and program with broad estimated aggregate figures that reflect specific options and modalities for a workout of inherited nonperforming liabilities. Developing such a program requires strong involvement of the National Treasury and especially NALM and continues negotiations with key stakeholders such as counties and national government entities.

PROGRESS AT THE COUNTY LEVEL

Most counties have reacted positively to the challenges of a troublesome asset takeover, many on a "learning by doing" modality because of a lack of clear and practical guidance, shortage of money, and issues regarding the TA centralized asset verification and transfer program discussed in chapter 1.

NCC achievements and plans in developing a framework and instruments for managing county assets

The NCC government has been working at the forefront of devolution reforms, including on establishing a framework, adopting instruments, and managing assets as a good bearer on a daily basis. The main actions and results include establishing an Asset Management Directorate (AMDR); drafting an AM policy, strategy, and initial plan; drafting terms of reference for an AM advisory committee to support strategic management of assets and the work of AMDR; and starting verification and workout of inherited liabilities years before the national legislation ruled establishing CALCs and commencing verification and workouts in 2018.

The NCC government established the first AMDR in Kenya in 2016; this is evidence of recognition of the importance of and the need for professional and high-level management of county assets. AMDR was established under the Finance and Planning Department with a squad of qualified staff. AMDR early on had started drafting programs for improving AM, including drafting an initial AM policy, strategy, and plan. It also organized a large workshop for leaders of all service and functional departments to sensitize top management about modern AM and lay out and discuss plans toward establishing a reliable and pragmatic framework for NCC. AMDR also started to position itself toward other departments and service sectors, albeit in a modality that leans toward accounting-oriented AM. AMDR also early on had approached international donors (including the World Bank) to seek technical assistance to boost AM knowledge and professional capacities on a fast-track mode. The main results to date include the following (some will be discussed in more detail in part II):

- A well-established AMDR exists with qualified staff.
- AMDR became the secretariat of the Nairobi CALC with the pivotal role of organizing and managing field verifications, despite the small budget assigned.
- A draft county AM policy was created, the first of its kind in Kenya (appendix A).
- A draft AM strategy was built on the key strategic documents, such as county vision, County Strategy 2015–25, master plan, detailed development plan (appendix B).
- A first AM plan focused on establishing an initial AM framework, entities, and instruments (appendix C).
- The Nairobi City County Government (NCCG) has become an informal leader and guide on AM; its results and documents have informed and inspired other counties to start working on AM more systematically.
- AMDR drafted a terms-of-reference statement for establishing a high-level strategic AM advisory committee to scrutinize, support, and propose strategic AM decisions for top county administration and governing bodies, and also to back AMDR in county administration (appendix D).
- AMDR completed several AM trainings for various county entities.
- NCCG has managed to appropriate a budget for and drafted a terms-of-reference statement for hiring a qualified firm for tagging and registering fixed assets.

AMDR has apparently made substantial, logical, and systematic efforts toward developing an internal legal and regulatory framework, system, and procedures for modern AM in NCC. However, most of these drafts failed to reach approval by the higher governing bodies (County Assembly, county cabinet, governor), in part due to the subsequent second county elections after devolution in 2017. The outgoing governing bodies and personnel were busy with elections and postponed dialogue and decisions on AM, and then the incoming county governments and governors initiated a substantial rotation of high-level staff and put AM reform among lower-priority actions. Despite a low level of support by higher governing bodies of the counties, NCCG and AMDR have achieved substantial progress on many key fronts, summarized below.

Land assets. In 2017, NCCG with AMDR, under the Nairobi Metropolitan Services Improvement Project of the World Bank, commenced a mass valuation of land parcels in NCC jurisdiction, aiming at revision of the property tax roll.

This comprehensive mass valuation uses GIS and GPS technology with geopositioning of each land parcel (about 230,000 parcels), measuring land sizes, and developing GIS map layers for clear identification and verification of parcels.

Mass valuation of land assets has three major implications on AM. First, besides private land for taxation, it has verified all public lands, including parcels owned by NCC and national government entities, thus providing a clear and precise register for NCC land assets that also helps subsequent verification of buildings, plants, and infrastructure assets. Second, it provides updated market values for NCC land parcels, making a separate land valuation for AM purposes unnecessary and making a quantum leap toward modern AM way ahead of other counties in Kenya. Third, the identification of private and national government properties helps detection of parcels and owners regarding inherited arrears on property tax, rents, and leases, including CILOR claims; this will help in the managing and workout of an enormous stock (K Sh 53.7 billion) of inherited current assets.

Liabilities. NCCG early on started the workout of inherited nonperforming liabilities, including (1) verification and payment of all verified inherited overdue staff emoluments; (2) announcement of a verification program for trade creditors who had to reconfirm their claims with supporting documents for NCC AMDR scrutiny and paid most verified inherited claims; (3) appointment by the Finance Department of a dedicated debt management team that has taken over verification of inherited bank liabilities and promotes uninterrupted servicing of verified domestic loans and proper accounting of financial liabilities, with annual reports to the National Assembly on the status of all NCC liabilities; and (4) an approach by NCCG to statutory creditors to settle claims if excessive penalties are annulled, but negotiations failed due to the rigidity of creditors.

Current assets. NCCG started a program for managing current assets well before the CALCs were established. Actions include (1) verification of property tax arrears that has reached only partial success due to lack of documents and unresolvable discrepancies between the files in the Finance Department and in the LAIFOMS accounting system and (2) approaching the national electricity and other companies to collect the wayleave (right-of-way) fees, but negotiations have failed due to noncooperative behavior by national entities. NCCG has also approached ministries and other national entities to collect overdue compensation in lieu of rates (CILOR), but negotiations again failed, so overdue CILOR collectibles still represent a large part of inherited current assets for Nairobi. These are significant items, because these claims are not only substantial but also suitable for working out NCC's liabilities vis-à-vis other national entities in a chain of swaps. This is a quite common approach in public and corporate practices and was well used in settling assets and liabilities at the transition of Eastern European municipalities.

Disputed assets. NCCG has approached DoD to settle a long-disputed case that the predecessor CCN had already taken to court without success. According to the claim, the CCN had purchased in free-market transaction a large parcel (900 hectares) of land for a housing development. However, DoD has taken over this land for defense and housing purposes without compensation. NCCG hired a valuer in 2018 to establish the present value of that land, and estimated it at about K Sh 33 billion, then approached DoD to negotiate fair compensation (not necessarily this estimated value if the parties reach agreement). However, DoD showed unwillingness to negotiate despite hard evidence on the claim. This case again underscores the need for a national policy on approaching asset transfers across national entities or national and county entities, and also the need for high-level political support to set fair compensation for the counties involved.

NCWSC is also a case of disputed assets or a case where several asset and liability claims need clarification, verification, and settlement. Parties involved include NCC, NCWSC, the Ahti Water Service Board (subsequently became defunct), the National Water Regulatory Board, and the Public Debt Management Directorate in the National Treasury. This is also part of the disputed and unfinished handover of assets from national entities that has not yet started and needs to be regulated, guided, and commenced in due course. NCWSC has been taken over by NCC, but there are lots of disputed assets and liabilities between NCC and the water board.

CALC verification and report. NCCG has been the forefront on asset verification and takeover and established the CALC early on and assigned numerous field verification teams to accomplish and support the work in accordance with the legal notices 858, 2701, and 4370. NCCG prepared a vast CALC report (over 600 pages) in a timely manner despite shortages of money, staff, vehicles, and sometimes even fuel for field verification. The field teams have identified large numbers of land parcels and buildings unidentified in the TA report, including capturing all land parcels that host the various water and sewer plants, lines, or other facilities that were missing from the TA report that presumably considered water assets as not under NCC ownership. In short, the NCC CALC report (2017) is a valuable document that supports establishing a reliable asset register in the medium term, even though the report also has remained in draft form, due to circumstances just noted.

Other progressive counties

The county case studies summarized in part II of this book exemplify remarkable progress and pragmatic approaches on county AM in counties much smaller than Nairobi in terms of population, budget, or economic power. Achievements include (1) all seven surveyed counties have appointed teams for AM under finance departments (albeit most with limited focus on accounting aspects); (2) counties ensured uninterrupted provision of key local services by assigning floor managers and also refurbishing and sometimes expanding important facilities such as schools, health facilities, and offices; (3) most surveyed counties have settled overdue staff emoluments in a course of reorganization of staff and human relations; (4) Laikipia and Bomet counties have drafted AM policy documents by emulating the example of Nairobi; and (5) Bomet and Kiambu counties hired qualified companies to verify and revaluate all land parcels in their jurisdictions, and this enables identification and market valuation of land owned by the county.

THE COVID-19 PANDEMIC IMPACTS ON CITIES AND POSSIBLE RESPONSES

The COVID-19 (coronavirus) global pandemic has had unprecedented negative impacts on cities' and citizens' livelihoods as well as on economic performance, health, education, and all sorts of life factors. It challenged the management and financial capacities of national and local governments alike (Blake and Wadhwa 2020). Preliminary data show that local governments faced 10–25 percent revenue shortfall, and meanwhile spent 10–15 percent more than planned on current expenses such as health, education, sanitation, and social assistances (Lall and Wahba 2020; Null, Rubnitz, and Smith 2020). In turn, many radically cut expenditures on development, repairs, and maintenance (EGI 2021; Maria et al. 2020; Kopanyi and Awan 2020).

The negative financial impacts will require several years to correct (Dzigbede, Gehl, Willoughby 2020), especially because the national governments also face shortage of finances, and thus will have moderate capacities to support financial recovery of local governments. The longer the crisis, the deeper the effects on financial capacities, health, and investments of local governments. Therefore, the assets and recovery investments should be approached strategically (IMF 2020). Without recognizing and utilizing the strategic role of assets, Kenyan counties and local governments may accumulate debts and some will be forced into quick sales or face confiscation of their assets without supporting recovery (Glasser and Wright 2020).

Experts predict a strong economic boom after the crisis ends (OECD 2020a), although when and how it will happen is still to be seen. Assets will undoubtedly play a strategic role in this process. First, the delayed developments and repairs need strategic corrections; second and more important, assets can be used strategically to fund financial and economic recovery of municipalities (Kaganova 2020). Furthermore, many envision that "The COVID-19 crisis entails an excellent opportunity for planners and policy makers to take transformative actions toward creating cities that are more just, resilient, and sustainable" (Sharifi and Khavarian-Garmsir 2020, 1).

Strategic use of assets is a challenge for developing countries. Local governments in developed countries have good experience in strategic use of assets for development financing, while most local authorities in developing countries lack expertise and management capacities for doing so. However, most municipalities in Kenya and the developing world do have a large stock of surplus assets suitable for strategic financing of postpandemic recovery. On the other hand, they lack reliable asset records, stable AM systems, strategies, and procedures that would be vital for using assets strategically to fund recovery. Said shortcomings can and should be corrected soon.

Governance, administration, and management shortcomings may prevent local entities from using assets in a timely manner and strategically. These underscore the importance of enhancing AM urgently in Kenya, to accelerate general development and pandemic recovery or avoid expensive mistakes. Fiscal and infrastructure deficits[1] of Kenyan counties are likely to grow substantially in the 2020/21 fiscal year and beyond (Kopanyi and Awan 2020; Maria et al. 2020). In turn, cities may waste an enormous volume of assets if they are divested rapidly and without a strategy to pay overdue bills. It is much better to account for and divest assets strategically and use some of the proceeds to pay the bills, instead of accumulating overdue bills and selling assets in a rush or letting creditors seize them to work out burning liabilities (likely the case of Mombasa asset swap).

Pandemic impacts on environmental, socioeconomic, urban design, and governance factors

Cities worldwide are on the front line of pandemic mitigations in all aspects, from education, health, and poverty to other social issues, while facing decreased revenues and stress on the local economy (Wahba et al. 2020; OECD 2020b).

The COVID-19 pandemic has encouraged the academic and practitioner communities to immediately analyze impacts in dozens of scientific areas. The Scopus abstract and citation database includes 140 articles on COVID-19 impacts on city planning, design, finance, and management, published in the first eight months of the crisis (Sharifi and Khavarian-Garmsir 2020).[2] The four major themes on cities include environmental impacts, socioeconomic impacts, management and governance, and transportation and urban design. Most papers covered environmental issues such as meteorology, temperature, humidity, wind, pollution levels, and air and water quality and their measurable or assumed impacts of spreading diseases, in part because of the importance of these issues but also because of data availability.

Socioeconomic issues such as measuring inequality, finance, or development required data that would be available only with a time lag. Many studies addressed long-standing structural inequalities and found that pandemics have hit minorities, migrants, and the bottom of social strata disproportionately (Blake and Wadhwa 2020; OECD 2020b; Wahba et al. 2020). The thinking about options for postpandemic recovery was based on initial findings and heuristic assumptions such as changing urban design, improving urban mobility and transport, housing for the poor, or green development (Ijjasz-Vasquez and Kaza 2020; Ortiz 2020; Tiverno and Lakovic 2020). Some emphasize that, not only change, but *transformational changes* are required, such as generating more actionable data, investing in cities as systems, building economic resilience by enlarging the safety net, and ensuring access to core services for all (Dasgupta 2020). During the first phase of the pandemic, interventions focused on mitigating immediate effects and curbing the spread of the virus—these required huge operating expenditures. In the second phase they could focus on long-term and sustainable recovery that requires investing in assets both public and private.

The pandemic has also had some positive impacts on cities and has resulted in some promising trends. The air quality has improved, telework options appear to be long-lasting and reduce the pressure on city transport, and digital technology has proven to be an available and powerful tool in managing pandemic and other city operations. Big data collection and analysis and smart city practices and options offer promising tools for managing pandemic and postpandemic recovery (Bhardwaj et al. 2020). Detailed analysis of the impact of city density showed that the density itself is not a concerning factor on spreading diseases. Rather, the overcrowded neighborhoods and living units and the poor municipal governance are the major challenges (Fang and Wahba 2020; Hamidi 2020; Hamidi, Sabouri, and Ewing 2020). Cities simply need to be better planned or reorganized (Lall and Wahba 2020). Finally, integrated urban governance has enabled some cities to successfully prevent the spread of the virus by being able to rapidly detect infected individuals through increased testing and improved surveillance (as in Singapore and Seoul) and timely lockdown and social distancing actions (Duggal 2020). However, for successful postpandemic recovery, a major concern is a city's economic geography: the interplay between its economic and physical setting (Lall 2020).

A major challenge, however, is that the most negative impacts of the pandemic crisis (revenue losses, extreme poverty, delays in addressing infrastructure gaps) seem to be growing. And positive effects, such as improved air quality and information technology, may hardly improve further. Meanwhile, some factors such as health care, poverty, and inequality may keep growing and will remain burdens on cities in the medium to long term. A quick assessment of

Nairobi and Mombasa has reconfirmed that such effects prevail and are substantial in Kenya too. This raises the question: How can strategic investments help to reduce the negative effects and boost the positive effects of the pandemic crisis and shorten the recovery period?

Pandemic impacts on national and local finances

The negative impacts on city finances struck with a dangerous "scissors effect" of rising expenditures and falling revenues. The S&P Global Ratings estimated that US local governments faced a scissors effect with 17 percent extra expenditures and a 21 percent revenue drop in 2020 (S&P 2021). Likewise, the US National League of Cities (NLC) reported a severe and long-lasting negative financial impact on US cities, with around a 21.6 percent loss of OSR in 2020 fiscal year (Yadavalli and McFarland 2020). NLC found that local governments face limited options for levying new taxes or raising existing ones. Increases in sales, income, or other types of tax rates are even less likely, and in the current economic climate, would prove fruitless. Studies on developing countries show similar scissors effects: over 20 percent revenue drop and over 10 percent increase of expenditures (Kopanyi and Awan 2020; Maria et al. 2020; Null, Rubnitz, and Smith 2020).

The strong negative impacts on cities' fiscal health (OECD 2020b; Beatty 2020) and stability leads to a question of how the projected, proposed, or foreseen transformative changes in the urban sphere would be financed when both national and local resources could face shortages in the medium term, especially in developing countries (IMF 2020; Kunzmann 2020). Findings are univocal on impacts: the tax base of many cities has declined and reduced their ability to implement urban development plans. "As cities are expected to experience significant financial deficits, they may need to prioritize investments and postpone or cancel some plans that they may deem less important, such as environmental and cultural investments" (Eltarabily and Elgheznawy 2020, 75). Figure 2.7 presents an Emergency Governance Initiative survey result that reflects the significant delay and cancellation of capital investment projects in nearly two-thirds of surveyed cities. But the unexpected further extension of the pandemic crisis is likely to move cities from a group of *unimpacted* to *delayed* and from *delayed* to *cancellation* of development projects. This effect is visible in Kenya. Nairobi and Mombasa reduced development expenses substantially in the 2019/20 fiscal year, while Makueni reduced investment expenses to one-tenth of previous average expenses.

Meanwhile the demand for investments is growing, and experts state that cities need to bring laser-sharp focus on investing in infrastructure and housing for better health, well-being, and resilience for the urban poor. "It means improving infrastructure in informal settlements across the developing world to bridge the urban services divide. And it means building infrastructure that is intentionally geared toward a low-carbon future" (Dasgupta 2020, 4). One can see, however, that most of these articles ignore or approach assets only as development targets rather than considering assets also as sources of postpandemic recovery.

Experts emphasize that the fiscal impacts of the pandemic on cities also depend on the degree of decentralization, particularly the assignment of spending responsibilities; the structure of own-source revenues; "fiscal flexibility" (that is, the ability to absorb stress and align expenditures and revenues); fiscal health or financial conditions (budget balance and debt, cash reserves); and support from higher

FIGURE 2.7

Planned postponements of capital investments in an emergency
Percent of surveyed cities/regions

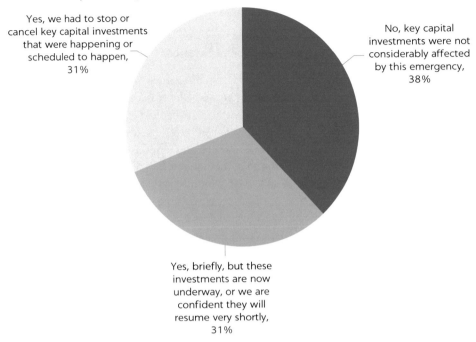

Source: EGI 2021, 4. © The Emergency Governance Initiative by Metropolis, United Cities and Local Governments and LSE Cities at the London School of Economics. Used with the permission of the consortium. Metropolis Secretariat General, Avinyó, 15. 08002 Barcelona, Spain; further permission required for reuse.

levels of government (OECD 2020b). Many countries, and the European Union, have reallocated public funding to crisis priorities, supporting health care, small and medium enterprises, vulnerable populations, and regions particularly hit by the crisis. And "financing constraints and competing spending priorities to save lives and livelihoods have caused many middle- and—especially—low-income countries to put domestically financed investment projects on hold" (IMF 2020, 1). The noted scissors effect on subnational public finances—that is, an increase in expenditures and a decline in revenue—could lead to increased deficits and accumulation of short- and long-term debt. This may lead to the need for fiscal consolidation plans in the medium term, as happened after 2010, leading to potential cuts in public investment and undermining recovery.

An Organisation for Economic Co-operation and Development (OECD) study put the impact assessment into a comprehensive picture (figure 2.8) of assets, liabilities, revenues, and expenditures that is conceptually universal but relevant more for developed countries (OECD 2020b). Let us see the situation of cities in developing countries that face somewhat different structures and status of assets, liabilities, revenues, and expenditures. They may have less capacity to align revenues and expenditures or mobilize extra resources for postpandemic development.

Assets and liabilities

In developing countries, cities have negligible volumes of liquid financial assets; they have negligible amounts of deposits or financial reserves and financial investments. Many do have shares in local public companies, but most of these shares are not tradeable and generate no dividend—instead cities

FIGURE 2.8

Effects of the COVID-19 pandemic crisis on subnational governments

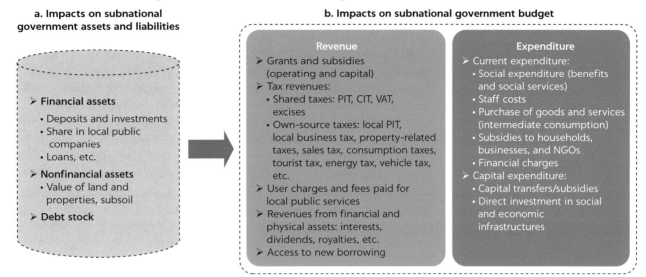

Source: OECD 2020b, 17.
Note: CIT = corporate income tax; NGO = nongovernmental organization; PIT = personal income tax; VAT = value added tax.

often subsidize the companies (Kopanyi and Awan 2020). Loans to public enterprises appear as forms of subsidies with no interest and unclear repayment terms. The OECD did not discuss a class of financial assets that are substantial in many developing countries, namely, uncollected overdue taxes and fees and other claims. Kenyan counties, especially Nairobi, inherited an enormous volume of such financial assets during devolution. And these will be hard to mobilize in the postpandemic recovery period.

Cities in developing countries, likewise Kenyan counties, own or possess a substantial volume of land, buildings, and other properties. However, they lack clear records, ownership titles, strategy, and policies that would support selection of marketable properties that can be used for supporting postpandemic recovery strategically if sold, swapped, or offered for public-private partnerships. They have vague ideas about the wealth they possess in the form of fixed assets.

Cities in developing countries show great variation in debt stocks and often have incomplete records of debt. Also, forced credits (unpaid liabilities, some long overdue for years) are often greater than the volume of formal debts (loans or bonds). Thus, debt restructuring may not appear as an option (common in developed countries), since only formal debts can be restructured in standard financial procedures. Moreover, many Kenyan counties, as discussed, are burdened with inherited overdue liabilities, some with unmanageable scale.

Revenues

Preliminary data suggest that grants from higher government tiers and shared taxes remained stable in the first three quarters of the pandemic crisis in developing countries, and many central governments even disbursed extra pandemic grants to cities. However, the capacity of some national governments to further provide extra funding to local governments in developing countries may decrease as the pandemic crisis endures and continues in 2021 and beyond. This is a critical issue since OSRs are low in most developing countries. Exacerbating the problem, in many countries, local budgets depend around 90 percent on transfers from higher government tiers. This is also the case in Kenya, where the counties' OSR are around 10 percent, except in Nairobi and Mombasa. In Africa, local governments could experience a drop in local finances of 30–65 percent, on average, depending on the severity of the crisis (Kochanov, Hong, and Mutambatsere 2020, 2). The national government in Kenya disbursed most of its equitable shares, albeit with delays, in the 2019/20 fiscal year, which was just partially impacted by the pandemic crisis. The pandemic may impact the disbursement or volume of equitable shares in the 2020/21 fiscal year and beyond.

As for tax revenues, studies found that the pandemic crisis had minor short-term effects on property tax revenues in developed countries, but this might change as the crisis is prolonged (Yadavalli and McFarland 2020). By contrast, tax revenues related to market factors (income, sales, business, consumption, and tourism taxes) have dropped harshly. Business and tourism taxes hit developing countries and hit Nairobi and Mombasa hard. Some user fee and charge revenues have been reduced on par with reduced consumptions in developed countries (OECD 2020b), but fee revenues have also dropped in developing countries when cities stopped collecting some user fees such as water charges during the crises (Kopanyi and Awan 2020). This deteriorated fee revenues that had already been below costs in part due to low collection rates.

Revenues from financial and physical assets have been low in developing countries, in great part because of poor asset records and management. But even in developed countries, income from physical and financial assets have been reduced and will suffer in the short term by drops in rental revenues, lost dividends from local public companies, less revenues from sales of land, lower royalty revenues resulting from decreased prices for raw material, and lower production. About two-thirds of subnational governments are anticipating a decline in revenues from assets in the United States (S&P 2020).

Experts envisage that access to loans will be a powerful tool for cities in developed countries to help ease debt limits and historic low interest rates in postpandemic recovery time (OECD 2020b). In contrast, in developing countries, cities have low capacity to access loans. Access is limited not only by regulatory debt limits that can be eased, but mainly by low creditworthiness and limited or no credit capacity. A major challenge is that some cities may turn to forced credits, that is, to accumulate further overdue bills, and in turn they may face legal actions or will be forced to sell or swap properties below market price. The case of swapping two housing estates to work out statutory debts in Mombasa resembles a forced sale case. Nevertheless, strategic use of assets to support postpandemic recovery is better than slipping into forced credit and quick sale.

Expenditures

Pandemic crisis interventions have induced substantial unplanned and unbudgeted expenditures all over the world, particularly in health care, social assistance, and sanitation. National governments and international donors have provided cities with substantial amounts of pandemic grants to cover actions and expenditures in these areas. Grants also supported information technology, smart city and big data gathering, and processing tools. Local governments in surveyed developing countries spent over 10 percent of operations expenditures above the amount budgeted from their own funds (Maria et al. 2020; Kopanyi and Awan 2020; Wahba et al. 2020). But even cities in the United States have taken on unprecedented increases in unbudgeted COVID-19-related expenditures; some have tapped into emergency relief funds, while others cut non-COVID-19 programming and services. Nearly 20 percent of cities indicate public works functions could be significantly affected by revenue shortfalls, and essential infrastructure spending dropped (Yadavalli and McFarland 2020, 11–15).

The reduced revenues forced the local governments to cut expenditures in nonessential areas, such as repair and maintenance, which was already low in developing countries at around 1 percent of current expenditures in Kenya against a 15 percent benchmark. Cities reduced subsidies to businesses (except processing national government grants) and nongovernmental organizations, some stopped paying for procured services (electricity, water), and most stopped capital transfers to affiliated entities, dropped capital projects, and widened infrastructure gaps (Kopanyi and Awan 2020). For example, in South Africa, many municipalities have historically failed to meet their obligations to Eskom, the country's power utility (Kochanov, Hong, and Mutambatsere 2020, 3). The IMF found that "about half of emerging market and developing economies for which data have been collected have had to cut investment spending, likely owing to financing constraints. The *World Economic Outlook* thus projects that public investment will be lower by 1 percent of GDP in 2020 than in 2019 in 72 out of 109 emerging markets and low-income developing countries." (IMF 2020, 31).

Figure 2.9 shows the gravity of pandemic responses measured by the number of cities and regions that responded to a survey by the Emergency Governance Initiative (EGI 2021). The columns do not represent the volume of money spent or saved, but it is most likely that the postponed infrastructure investments and public works would represent the highest volume of saved expenses. Furthermore, some operating expenses, such as in culture, sports, tourism, and travel, have been saved permanently without long-term consequences. By contrast, delayed

FIGURE 2.9

Prioritized and deprioritized expenses during COVID-19 responses

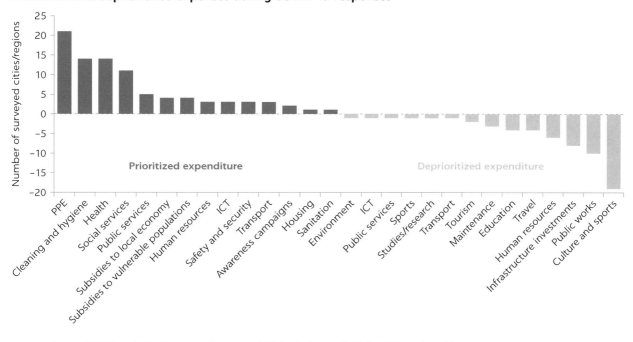

Note: ICT = information and communication technology; PPE = property, plant, and equipment.

or cancelled infrastructure investments and public works widened the infrastructure gaps and will need correction in the short to medium term. The IFC found similar effects in Africa, where central government transfers to support subnational government investment expenditures could decline by 26–63 percent (Kochanov, Hong, and Mutambatsere 2020).

Mitigating the pandemic effects

Many central governments in both developed and developing countries have implemented fiscal measures to help subnational governments cope with the fiscal shocks of the pandemic. State governments in federal countries have also announced measures to support local governments. Some aid directly helped municipal entities, such as public transport or utility companies. Two-thirds of OECD countries have adopted measures in support of subnational government finance. The OECD experts concluded, however, that increases in central or state government transfers are likely to be insufficient to fully offset decreased revenues from taxes, user charges and tariffs, and property income. Furthermore, in the longer term, central government transfers will probably be cut to rebalance national public budgets and restore national fiscal stability, which in turn will likely create negative medium- and long-term effects on fiscal health of local governments (OECD 2020a).

Figure 2.10 shows a great variety of tools and possible interventions available for governments in OECD countries, although they exist to varying degrees. Effective or planned interventions include revenue and expenditure side measures, fiscal and debt management rules, and financial management improvements. However, central governments in developing countries have more limited capacities than the OECD governments for supporting local governments, although most of the measures in figure 2.10 are legally or technically possible.

Central governments in developing countries face multiple challenges in implementing corrective measures to support local governments. Among revenue-side measures, increasing transfers, grants, or revenue shares are possible but unlikely since central governments need to generate resources for doing so. Grants and debt-relief programs have been implemented or announced, such as those by the World Bank, IMF, and many bilateral donors (IMF 2020; Wahba et al. 2020; G20 2020), that will help central governments by expanding the fiscal space for supporting local governments. But central governments may prefer centralized measures and leave small room for supporting postpandemic recovery by cities. Modifying tax arrangements may work by expanding tax shares, but assigning more taxing power to cities or creating new local taxes would take time to boost revenues and would be difficult to implement in developing countries.

Most of the expenditure-side measures listed in figure 2.10 appear to be of a temporary nature, and few are applicable in developing countries. Easing spending responsibilities or assigning back to central government may be an effective temporary measure, but it may raise the risk of permanent recentralization in developing countries. Exemption of the value added tax may help, but central governments will not make that permanent. Easing procurement rules is a two-edged sword, justified only in the most critical phase of the pandemic crisis. In short, expenditure-side measures initiated by central governments can be considered as moderate and temporary options. Central governments and donors may help instead by enhancing local capacities for controlling some critical operating and development expenditures by improving local financial management frameworks, systems, and procedures.

FIGURE 2.10

Possible measures applied to mitigate the short- and medium-term negative effects of COVID-19 on subnational governments in OECD countries

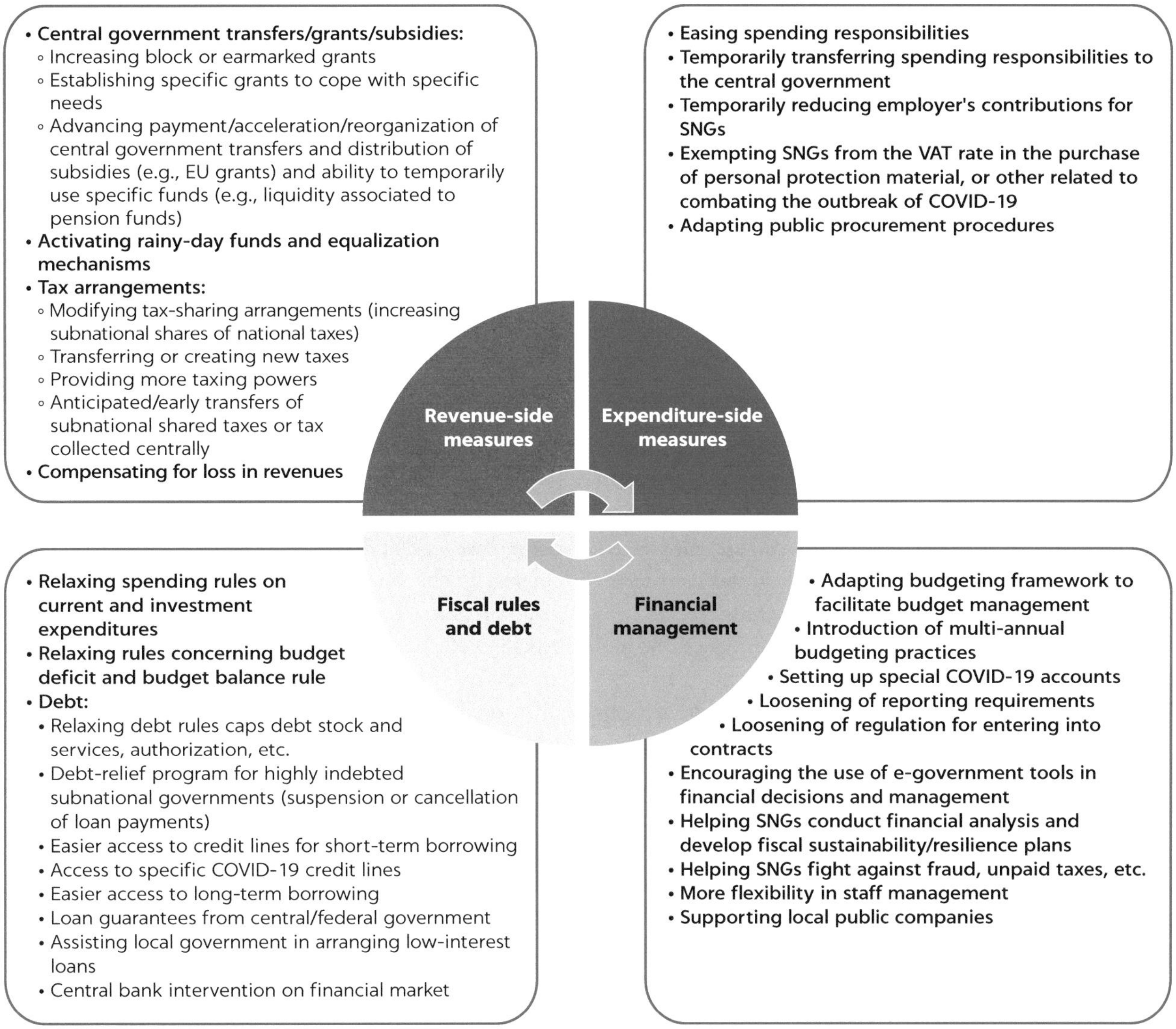

- Central government transfers/grants/subsidies:
  - Increasing block or earmarked grants
  - Establishing specific grants to cope with specific needs
  - Advancing payment/acceleration/reorganization of central government transfers and distribution of subsidies (e.g., EU grants) and ability to temporarily use specific funds (e.g., liquidity associated to pension funds)
- Activating rainy-day funds and equalization mechanisms
- Tax arrangements:
  - Modifying tax-sharing arrangements (increasing subnational shares of national taxes)
  - Transferring or creating new taxes
  - Providing more taxing powers
  - Anticipated/early transfers of subnational shared taxes or tax collected centrally
- Compensating for loss in revenues

- Easing spending responsibilities
- Temporarily transferring spending responsibilities to the central government
- Temporarily reducing employer's contributions for SNGs
- Exempting SNGs from the VAT rate in the purchase of personal protection material, or other related to combating the outbreak of COVID-19
- Adapting public procurement procedures

Revenue-side measures

Expenditure-side measures

Fiscal rules and debt

Financial management

- Relaxing spending rules on current and investment expenditures
- Relaxing rules concerning budget deficit and budget balance rule
- Debt:
  - Relaxing debt rules caps debt stock and services, authorization, etc.
  - Debt-relief program for highly indebted subnational governments (suspension or cancellation of loan payments)
  - Easier access to credit lines for short-term borrowing
  - Access to specific COVID-19 credit lines
  - Easier access to long-term borrowing
  - Loan guarantees from central/federal government
  - Assisting local government in arranging low-interest loans
  - Central bank intervention on financial market

- Adapting budgeting framework to facilitate budget management
- Introduction of multi-annual budgeting practices
- Setting up special COVID-19 accounts
- Loosening of reporting requirements
- Loosening of regulation for entering into contracts
- Encouraging the use of e-government tools in financial decisions and management
- Helping SNGs conduct financial analysis and develop fiscal sustainability/resilience plans
- Helping SNGs fight against fraud, unpaid taxes, etc.
- More flexibility in staff management
- Supporting local public companies

Source: OECD 2020b, 52.
Note: EU = European Union; SNGs = subnational governments; VAT = value added tax.

Fiscal-side and debt-management rules appear to be more relevant measures in developed than in developing countries. Relaxing spending rules on current and investment expenditures is meant to allow temporarily using capital revenues for covering operating expenditures. The challenges in developing countries are, first, that such rules are already applied quite readily; even clear classification of current and development revenues and expenditures are blurred in practice in many developing countries (Kopanyi and Awan 2020). Second, soft budget constraints are common in developing countries, budget deficits are often avoided in budget *plans*, but often appear substantial in actual budgets. So, offering to soften budget balances further may help but also sends dangerous policy signals. Debt relief and soft loans look like the most promising means to help cities' postpandemic recovery, in addition to targeted pandemic grants.

Financial management measures are vital means that can help postpandemic recovery. Most of the measures listed in figure 2.10 are applicable in developing countries. For example, improving budgeting has been a prime objective of donors with moderate success in developing countries for decades, yet it remains important as a medium-term measure. The use of e-government tools has started and shows promising results, and it should be further promoted. Setting up special COVID-19 accounts to ensure clear bookkeeping, spending, and measuring of results is a sensible tool. Helping cities to regularly conduct sound financial analysis to understand their fiscal health and plan informed actions is among the most powerful medium-term measures. Finally, enhancing financial management of municipal enterprises (like water utilities) and applying clear accounting of transactions between the municipalities and the enterprises are vital measures in the short to medium terms.

Postpandemic recovery

Experts predict a strong economic boom after the crisis ends (Buchoud et al. 2020; OECD 2020a), albeit when and how it will start and happen is still to be seen. Assets will play a special role in this process. First, delayed developments and repairs need corrections. Second and more important, assets can be used strategically to fund financial and economic recovery of municipalities. Third, well-selected investments can help cities transform the local sphere, improve resilience, and improve livability. The expectations are high. "The COVID-19 crisis entails an excellent opportunity for planners and policy makers to take transformative actions toward creating cities that are more just, resilient, and sustainable" (Sharifi and Khavarian-Garmsir 2020, 1).

Local governments are responsible for critical aspects of recovery measures in health care, social services, economic development, and public investments at the front line of crisis management in developed countries (OECD 2020b). In contrast, central governments in developing countries apparently prefer centralized measures, use units of national or regional governments, and request only logistic support by local governments. In doing so they might ignore local priorities. The recovery phase can help build prosperity and resilience by contributing to the long-term potential and sustainability of a country's development pathway, but recovery projects should be selected strategically. OECD experts warn avoiding against atomizing the allocation of the funding in a myriad of small infrastructure projects to spend the money rapidly at the expense of long-term priorities (OECD 2020b). Hammer and Hallegatte (2020) offer a checklist for selecting recovery projects that boost the economy and support sustainability and resilience.

Quality infrastructure investment is part of the answer to the COVID-19 crisis. National and subnational governments need to invest more—by better exploiting the existing and potential fiscal resources for investment and mobilizing private investment. The IMF *Fiscal Monitor* estimates that a 1 percent gross domestic product (GDP) increase in public investment in advanced economies and emerging markets has the potential to push GDP up by 2.7 percent and private investment by 10.0 percent, and to create between 20 million and 33 million jobs, directly and indirectly (IMF 2020, 41).

The fiscal impact of the COVID-19 crisis on subnational governments depends to a large extent on the support that central or federal governments provide them to maintain or boost subnational investment through capital grants (stimulus packages) and by building the borrowing capacity of subnational governments. Experts see both similarities and differences between the 2008 financial crisis and the COVID-19 pandemic crisis that will be vital to understand for investment recovery. "While watching the sustainability of public finances over the longer-term, it is important for countries to avoid replicating the scenario that took place after 2010, when drastic cuts in subnational public investments created a procyclical effect impeding the recovery. In some regions and cities, public investment projects are already cancelled or postponed" (OECD 2020b, 61).

Public investment recovery strategies

Before the COVID-19 crisis, the levels of public and private investments in the OECD countries were still below the 2008 precrisis level; a postpandemic investment boom seems inevitable. Many governments in developed countries have announced large investment recovery packages, and these are already much larger than those adopted in 2008. "The recovery packages prioritize three areas: strengthening health systems, digitalization, and accelerating the transition to a carbon neutral economy" (OECD 2020b). It is still to be seen how far developing countries would be able and willing to adopt, finance, and implement similar strategic priorities. Identifying sustainable financing instruments and modalities tailored to the circumstances of developing countries will play a critical role in postpandemic recovery.

Adopting adequate national and local strategies and policies for postpandemic investments is among the urgent next steps. IMF experts see four specific tasks for national governments: find out (1) how investments can be accelerated, (2) how investments can foster job creation, (3) how fiscal multipliers can have high positive effects, and (4) how investments can foster the society's resilience (IMF 2020). Lack of ready-made projects in developing countries may hinder recovery. Experts propose four critical steps to make investments effective: "focus on maintenance of existing infrastructure; review and reprioritize active projects; create and maintain a pipeline of projects that can be delivered within a couple of years; and start planning for the new development priorities stemming from the crisis" (IMF 2020, 34).

Maintaining current assets and operations. Maintenance works are underfunded and often deferred all over the world in crises, especially in developing countries; Kenyan counties spend a tiny fraction of required maintenance costs. Focusing first on maintenance in postpandemic recovery offers multiple benefits. Maintenance works are relatively small and simple and can be deployed quickly, and some create jobs for unskilled labor. Maintenance and renewal help advance technology, expand capacity, and reduce operation losses substantially in modalities cheaper than new projects.

The performance and impact of many infrastructure assets fall way behind projections because they are poorly managed. Cities invest in large-scale projects without proper calculation, planning, and budgeting for their operation phase (Lindfield and Teipelke 2019). Adequate and steady maintenance programs will be key for developing countries to achieve sustainable development goals. Adopting life-cycle AM policies and tools would also help enhancing maintenance programs. But these require reliable data on asset performance, clear accounting of capital and current expenditures, and assessing repair or replacement options in medium-term and life-cycle perspective. "For that to happen, budgets should report repair and maintenance spending exhaustively" (IMF 2020, 35).

Reviewing and reprioritizing projects. Many local governments had to cut investment spending and have suspended, delayed, or cancelled approved investment projects in 2020 (IMF 2020). Simply continuing all projects after the end of the pandemic crisis is inadequate or impossible. It is vital for governments to revisit development plans and reprioritize and restart budgeted projects that contribute the most to economic and service recovery. They may need to redo cost-benefit analyses based on new data and emerging situations (for example, changes in trade and tourism patterns), since the crises may have created uncertainties and risks resulting in the need to align or realign projects. Adopting postpandemic recovery action plans would be a powerful way to streamline investments and other interventions.

Establishing new development priorities. National and local governments alike may need to establish new development priorities in response to the global pandemic and economic crises. Correspondingly, they need to revisit project pipelines.[3] The problem is, however, that such pipelines hardly exist in either national or local governments in many developing countries. Thus, in responding to the pandemic crisis cities need to establish a medium-term project pipeline, for which a capital improvement planning procedure (CIP) and life-cycle AM approach would be instrumental. Accessing grants from donors or national government, or attracting private capital, requires a solid, convincing, realistic pipeline of projects, much more then vague ideas or enthusiastic visions. Furthermore, it is "important to ensure that investments from stimulus packages do not impose large, stranded asset costs on the economy in the coming decade: for example, because they bet on declining technologies or place projects in high-risk flood zones" (Wahba et al. 2020).

Funding and financing postpandemic recovery

Discussions on postpandemic recovery often ignore the challenges or assume optimistically the availability of funds and financing instruments. Instead, they focus on other aspects of recovery and let finance specialists bother with funding issues. (The other issues are equally important and include, for example, the environment, climate change, and social disparities.) Some tacitly assume that stimulus packages from donors and national governments will boost local investments but raise concerns about cities' motivation for quickly boosting development in ways that may ignore or undermine environmental sustainability (Bassi, Pallaske, and Guzzetti 2020).

International donors and other organizations led by the G20 have adopted a landmark global action plan to support developing countries (box 2.3), since inevitably national governments or national budgets will play a major role in financing recovery.[4] The main objective is to provide liquidity and enable developing countries to grow out from the crises over time with relative financial stability. However, the G20 action plan supports cities or local governments only indirectly (Blake and Wadhwa 2020). Undoubtedly international donors and national governments should provide stimulus grants eventually down to local governments too.

But a task force (T20) of the G20 pointed out that the international aids overwhelmingly target national governments, while most recovery measures can and should be implemented locally. Thus, T20 proposes including a specific *Urban Platform* in the G20 global action plan, revising the processes by which local priorities are incorporated into international financial institutions' development assistance programs, and adopting a G20 sustainable and resilient urbanization

BOX 2.3

Updated G20 action plan to support the global economy during COVID-19: Landmark commitments

- Extending the Debt Service Suspension Initiative to June 2021 to help developing countries finance their coronavirus response and recovery programs
- Commitment to consider a further six-month extension to the Debt Service Suspension Initiative at the International Monetary Fund and World Bank Group Spring Meetings in April 2021
- Agreement in principle to a historic Common Framework for Future Debt Treatments to provide debt restructuring to vulnerable countries on a case-by-case basis, bringing together G20 and Paris Club official creditors for the first time
- Supporting the World Bank Group's initiatives to make available US$16 billion of fast-track financing for developing countries' access to COVID-19 tools, with the aim of supporting equitable and affordable access for all
- Accelerating action to address longer-term global challenges, including harnessing new opportunities through the digital economy and supporting the potential for an environmentally sustainable and resilient recovery

Source: G20 2020.

investment plan. The fask force argues that "if cities and communities are ignored again [as they were after 2008] by markets and states, the multilateral system might collapse at the next global shock" (Buchoud et al. 2020, 13). Others emphasize that "top-down infrastructure projects may be tempting for COVID-19 recovery, but without community engagement many such efforts have failed in the past" (Null, Rubnitz, and Smith 2020).

Various measures are foreseen, and many are being activated worldwide to maintain, or even accelerate, public investment projects at the subnational level after the pandemic ends. Figure 2.10 summarizes measures applicable domestically, including grants and OSR, as well as relaxing budget rules, increasing capital transfers and subsidies, easing the access to long-term projects on both credit and financial markets, and supporting project preparation and implementation. However, it is important to note that asset-based financing may offer an option that can be mobilized in short-, medium-, and long-term efforts (Kaganova 2020). Other financing mechanisms—such as public-private partnership arrangements or other equity financing—may be activated in developing countries cautiously in the future.

Donors keep promoting and testing private investments in urban development and services with mixed results and slow progress. The postpandemic recovery underscores the great need for private resources to supplement the scarce aids and fiscal funds discussed. The private capital floating around the world seeking investment opportunities is estimated to be nearly US$100 trillion, while the estimated public infrastructure investment gap (national and subnational combined) is about US$6 trillion (UN-Habitat 2020). Supply well exceeds demand, but the two sides of the market appear to be disconnected. A great potential is there, but cities must not only attract but also *activate* private capital to make themselves more sustainable during postpandemic recovery. Electricity, water, sanitation, solid waste, or even some health care services are quasi-private goods; they can be and have been provided in part by private players not only in developed countries but in many developing ones. The pandemic crisis has underscored the need to develop services where the private sector can contribute.

Woetzel and Bouton (2020) discuss the main impediments and corrective measures needed to *activate* private capital: cities need a robust and transparent pipeline of well-prepared, bankable projects—even many national governments lack such pipelines (see IMF 2020); there is a need for stable and predictable policy and regulatory frameworks; cities need to adopt sustainable tariff policies and systems; cities need to apply market-conforming subsidization (for example, using vouchers instead of subsidized tariffs); and finally, smart city solutions can be profitable ventures for private companies. "Cities need to identify those areas where city agencies can step back and make room for other players to provide both capital and expertise" (Woetzel and Bouton 2020, 4).

Cities sometimes fail to understand and manage funding and financial structuring options, as explained in a C40 brief (Lindfield and Teipelke 2019).[5] Misconceptions blind many mayors when positioning pipeline projects; some say that if a project is good enough for the market, then the city should develop and profit from it, so they like to propose nonprofitable or problem projects to private investors. Furthermore, local governments in developing countries often lack the capacity to assess the relative benefits of financing and funding options and to select appropriate ways of funding the development and/or operation of infrastructure. Many rely on unsolicited offers of private agents who may aim only to sell technology rather than partnering with the city. Such risk could have substantial downsides as the postpandemic restructuring scales up.

Advanced financing and risk-mitigating instruments are quite complicated, and for this reason city leaders may not consider them among options. Local governments need to clearly understand the differences among financing instruments and funding options, that is, the sources of money required to pay back private financing and cover costs of operation. An IFC study (Kochanov, Hong, and Mutambatsere 2020) found that in emerging markets fewer than 100 of the largest 500 cities have local borrowing capacity. The other 400 have low ability to access debt through capital markets without credit enhancements. Furthermore, private financing requires a good reputation for transparency, that is, disclosing budget plans and financial statements in a market-conforming format and making these accessible online. Makueni County, Kenya, offers a great example that transparency is possible in developing countries (figure 11.2 and figure 11.3 in part II). Donors need to help local governments understand and operationalize advanced funding options—beyond user fees—including land-based financing such as land pooling, air rights, development charges, or value-capture tools (Lindfield and Teipelke 2019; Kaganova 2020).

NOTES

1. Infrastructure deficit due to the pandemic is defined as the volume of development project expenses that were planned and realistically expected to be completed but were delayed, postponed, or cancelled because of funding shortages or other restrictions in the pandemic.
2. This is a tiny fraction of the over 40,000 articles published on COVID-19 in eight months of the pandemic. One can say that cities have not yet attracted significant attention to related financial issues (Sharifi and Khavarian-Garmsir 2020).
3. Less than half of the 63 countries that have completed the Public Investment Management Assessment were found to have adopted investment project pipelines (IMF 2020).

4. The G20 is an international forum for the governments and central bank governors from 19 developed countries and the European Union.
5. The C40 Cities Climate Leadership Group is a group of 96 cities around the world that represents one-twelfth of the world's population and one-fourth of the global economy.

REFERENCES

Bassi, A. M., G. Pallaske, and M. Guzzetti. 2020. *Post-COVID-19* "Recovery: Harnessing the Power of Investment in Sustainable Infrastructure," ORF Issue Brief 426, Observer Research Foundation, New Delhi, India.

Beatty, Stephen C. 2020. "Uncovering the COVID-19-Related Risk Clusters That Could Impact Cities." New York: KPMG. https://home.kpmg/xx/en/home/insights/2020/06/most -interconnected-risks-clusters.html.

Bhardwaj, Gaura, Thomas Esch, Somik V. Lall, Mattia Marconcini, Maria Edisa Soppelsa, and Sameh Wahba. 2020. *Cities, Crowding, and the Coronavirus: Predicting Contagion Risk Hotspots.* Washington, DC: World Bank. http://documents.worldbank.org/curated /en/206541587590439082/Cities-Crowding-and-the-Coronavirus-Predicting-Contagion -Risk-Hotspots.

Blake, P., and D. Wadhwa. "2020 Year in Review: The Impact of COVID-19 in 12 Charts." *World Bank Blog*, December 14, 2020. https://blogs.worldbank.org/voices/2020-year-review -impact-covid-19-12-charts.

Buchoud, Nicolas J. A., Raja Al Marzoqi, Michael Cohen, Mitch Cook, Holger Kühle, Jörn Meyer, and Susan Parnell. 2020. 'Sustainable Urbanization and Infrastructure Response to the COVID19 Pandemic," G20 Task Force 11 COVID-19: Multidisciplinary Approaches to Complex Problems Policy Brief, Riyadh, Saudi Arabia, November 26, 2020. https://www .g20-insights.org/wp-content/uploads/2020/11/T20_TF11_PB15.pdf.

Dasgupta, A. 2020. "After the Crisis: How COVID-19 Can Drive Transformational Change in Cities." *City Fix*, April 28, 2020. https://thecityfix.com/blog/covid-19-can-drive -transformational-change-cities.

Detter, D. and S. Fölster. 2018. "Unlocking Public Wealth: Governments Could Do a Better Job Managing Their Assets. *Finance and Development*, International Monetary Fund: March 2018, pp 44–48. https://www.imf.org/Publications/fandd/issues/2018/03/detter.

Duggal, R. 2020. "Mumbai's Struggles with Public Health Crises from Plague to COVID-19." *Economic and Political Weekly* 55 (21): 17–20. https://www.epw.in/journal/2020/21 /commentary/mumbais-struggles-public-health-crises.html.

Dzigbede, K. D., S. B. Gehl, and K. Willoughby. 2020. "Disaster Resiliency of US Local Governments: Insights to Strengthen Local Response and Recovery from the COVID-19 Pandemic." *Public Administration Review* (May 30): 634–43.

EGI (Emergency Governance Initiative). 2021. "The Impact of the Covid-19 Pandemic on Subnational Finances." Emergency Governance Initiative Analytics Note 03, London School of Economics and Political Science. https://www.lse.ac.uk/Cities/publications/Policy -Briefs-and-Analytics-Notes/Analytics-Note-03-The-Impact-of-the-Covid-19-pandemic -on-Subnational-Finances?from_serp=1.

Eltarabily, S., and D. Elgheznawy. 2020. "Post-Pandemic Cities: The Impact of COVID-19 on Cities and Urban Design." *Architecture Research* 10 (3): 75–84. doi:10.5923/j.arch.20201003.02.

Fang, W., and S. Wahba. 2020. "Urban Density Is Not an Enemy in the Coronavirus Fight: Evidence from China." *World Bank Blog*, April 2020. https://blogs.worldbank.org/sustainablecities/urb an-density-not-enemy-coronavirus-fight-evidence-china https://blogs.worldbank.org /sustainablecities/urban-density-not-enemy-coronavirus-fight-evidence-china.

G20. 2020. "Updated G20 Action Plan to Support the Global Economy through Covid-19." G20 Secretariate. October 14, 2020. https://www.gov.uk/government/news/updated-g20-action -plan-to-support-the-global-economy-through-covid-19.

Glasser, M., and J. Wright. 2020. "South African Municipalities in Financial Distress: What Can Be Done?" *Law, Democracy and Development* 24 (December). doi:10.17159/2077-4907/2020 /ldd.v24.17.

Hamidi, S. 2020. "Urban Density Not Linked to Higher Coronavirus Infection Rates—And Is Linked to Lower COVID-19 Death Rates." *Journal of the American Planning Association.* https://www.jhsph.edu/news/news-releases/2020.

Hamidi, S., S. Sabouri, and R. Ewing. 2020. "Does Density Aggravate the COVID-19 Pandemic? Early Findings and Lessons for Planners." *Journal of the American Planning Association* 86 (4). doi:10.1080/01944363.2020.1777891.

Hammer, S., and S. Hallegatte. 2020. "Planning for the Economic Recovery from COVID-19: A Sustainability Checklist for Policy Makers." World Bank Blog, April 14, 2020. https://blogs .worldbank.org/climatechange/planning-economic-recovery-covid-19-coronavirus -sustainability-checklist-policymakers.

IGRTC (Intergovernmental Relations Technical Committee). 2018. *Report on the Identification, Verification, Validation, and Transfer of Assets and Liabilities of the Defunct Local Authorities as at 27th March 2013."* Nairobi: IGRTC. https://igrtc.go.ke/download/consolidated-report -on-assets-and-liabilities-of-the-defunct-local-authorities-2018/.

Ijjasz-Vasquez, E., and S. Kaza. 2020. "Better Trash Collection for a Stronger Recovery: Solid Waste Management as a Pillar of Urban Change." *City Fix*, December 21, 2020. https:// thecityfix.com/blog/better-trash-collection-for-a-stronger-recovery-solid-waste -management-as-a-pillar-of-urban-change.

IMF (International Monetary Fund). 2020. "Policies for the Recovery." *Fiscal Monitor*, October 2020. Washington, DC: IMF.

Kaganova, O. 2020. "How American Cities Can Benefit from 'Land Value Capture' Instruments in the Time of COVID-19 and Beyond." *Real Estate Issues* 44 (18). https://cre.org/real -estate-issues/how-american-cities-can-benefit-from-land-value-capture-instruments -in-the-time-of-covid-19-and-beyond/.

Kelly, R. 2002. "Property Taxation in Kenya." Washington, DC: World Bank.

Kelly, Roy, Roland White, and Aanchal Anand. 2020. "Property Tax Diagnostic Manual." Washington, DC: World Bank Group. https://openknowledge.worldbank.org/bitstream /handle/10986/34793/150373.pdf.

Kochanov, Pavel, Youngki Hong, and Emelly Mutambatsere. 2020. *COVID-19's Impact on Subnational Governments*. Washington, DC: International Finance Corporation.

Kopanyi, M. 2018. "Mass Valuation of Land in Nairobi City County," advisory note, World Bank, Washington, DC, November 2018.

Kopanyi, M., and A. W. Awan. 2020. "Impacts on and Responses by the Afghani Municipalities to the COVID-19 Pandemic Crisis." Kabul: Urban Programmatic ASA and Cities Investment Project—World Bank/IDLG Program.

Kunzmann, K. R. 2020. "Smart Cities after COVID-19: Ten Narratives." *disP–The Planning Review* 56 (2). https://www.tandfonline.com/doi/abs/10.1080/02513625.2020.1794120.

Lall, S. 2020. "Yes, Cities Will Survive COVID-19. But They Must Manage Their Economic Geography." *World Bank Blog*, June 18, 2020. https://blogs.worldbank.org/sustainablecities /yes-cities-will-survive-covid-19-they-must-manage-their-economic-geography.

Lall, S., and S. Wahba. 2020. "No Urban Myth: Building Inclusive and Sustainable Cities in the Pandemic Recovery." Washington, DC: World Bank. https://www.worldbank.org/en/news /immersive-story/2020/06/18/no-urban-myth-building-inclusive-and-sustainable-cities -in-the-pandemic-recovery.

Lindfield, M., and R. Teipelke. 2019. *How to Finance Urban Infrastructure?* London: C40 Cities Finance Facility, March 28, 2019. https://www.c40cff.org/knowledge-library/explainer-how -to-finance-urban-infrastructure.

Maria, Augustin, Herve Hocquard, Chaymae Belouali, Lamia Zaki, and Jean-Briac Ligot. 2020. "Impact and Response of the Moroccan Municipalities in the Context of the COVID-19 Crisis." World Bank Technical Note, April 8, 2020, Washington, DC.

MLG (Ministry of Local Government, Kenya). 2013. Ministry of Local Government Circular, ref. no. MLG/1333/TY/ (52) of 18 February 2013.

MoF (Ministry of Finance, Kenya). 2000. "Ministry of Finance Circular, no. 14 (October 13)." Nairobi: MoF.

NALM (National Assets and Liabilities Management Department). 2020a. "National Asset and Liability Management Policy, 2020." https://www.treasury.go.ke/wp-content/uploads/2021/03/Asset-Liability-Mgt-Policy.-doc-Final.pdf.

NALM (National Assets and Liabilities Management Department). 2020b. "General Guidelines on Asset and Liability Management in the Public Sector." https://www.treasury.go.ke/wp-content/uploads/2021/03/GeneralGuidelines-on-asset-and-liability-management-2020-Final.pdf.

NALM (National Assets and Liabilities Management Department). 2020c. "Guidelines for Management of Specific Categories of Assets and Liabilities, 2020." https://www.treasury.go.ke/wp-content/uploads/2021/03/Specific-guidelines-2020-Final.pdf.

NCC CALC (Nairobi City County, County Asset and Liability Committee). 2017. *Identification, Verification, and Validation of County Assets and Liabilities*. Nairobi City County Government.

Notice 44. 2016. Legal Notice no. 44: Regulation on Transition to Devolved Government (Mechanism for Closure and Transfer of Public Records and Information.) Legislative Supplement no. 23, March 11, 2016.

Null, S., T. Rubnitz, and H. Smith. 2020. "Cities, Battered by COVID-19, Remain Key to Recovery: How Can Investments Be Well Spent?" *City Fix*, May 4, 2020. https://thecityfix.com/blog/cities-battered-covid-19-remain-key-recovery-ensure-investments-well-spent-schuyler-null-talia-rubnitz-hillary-smith/.

OAG (Office of the Auditor General). 2013. "Special Audit of County Governments." Nairobi: OAG. https://www.cabri-sbo.org/uploads/bia/kenya_2013_oversight_external_audit_report_kenao_comesa_eac_igad_english1.pdf.

OAG (Office of the Auditor General). 2014–18 (annually). "Reports of the Auditor General for County Governments." 2014–18. Nairobi: OAG. https://www.oagkenya.go.ke/county-governments/.

OECD (Organisation for Economic Co-operation and Development). 2020a. *Cities Policy Responses*. Paris: OECD. https://www.oecd.org/coronavirus/policy-responses/cities-policy-responses-fd1053ff/.

OECD. (Organisation for Economic Co-operation and Development). 2020b. "The Territorial Impact of COVID-19: Managing the Crisis across Levels of Government." Paris: OECD. https://www.oecd.org/coronavirus/policy-responses/the-territorial-impact-of-covid-19-managing-the-crisis-across-levels-of-government-d3e314e1.

Ortiz, P. 2020. "Creating New Urban Centralities: The Way ahead for Mumbai in 2021." *Urban Futures* (Observer Research Foundation), December 22, 2020. https://www.orfonline.org/expert-speak/creating-new-urban-centralities-way-ahead-mumbai-2021.

S&P. 2020. "US Public Finance 2020 Year in Review: One Like No Other." S&P Global Ratings Webinar. December 10, 2020. https://www.spglobal.com/ratings/en/research/articles/201210-u-s-public-finance-2020-year-in-review-one-like-no-other-11773177.

S&P. 2021. "State and Local Government Outlook 2020." S&P Global Ratings Webinar, January 8, 2021. https://www.spglobal.com/ratings/en/events/webcast-replays.

Sharifi, A., and A. Khavarian-Garmsir. 2020. "The COVID-19 Pandemic: Impacts on Cities and Major Lessons for Urban Planning, Design, and Management." *Science of the Total Environment* 749. doi:10.1016/j.scitotenv.2020.142391.

TA-ICPAK (Transition Authority and Institute of Certified Public Accountants of Kenya). 2013. *Accountability and Transparency in County Governments*. Conference proceedings, "Financial Management and Reporting Conference for Counties," Nairobi: TA and ICPAK, April 24, 2013.

Tiverno, L., and K. Lakovic. 2020. "COVID-19 Has Revealed That 'Inclusive' Housing Policies Are Still Too *Exclusive*." *World Bank Blog*, November 6, 2020. https://blogs.worldbank.org/sustainablecities/covid-19-has-revealed-inclusive-housing-policies-are-still-too-exclusive.

UN-Habitat (United Nations Human Settlements Programme). 2020. *The New Urban Agenda*. Nairobi: UN-Habitat.

Venkateswaran, R. K. 2014. "Municipal Financial Management." In *Municipal Finances: A Handbook for Local Governments*, edited by C. Farvacque-Vitkovic and M. Kopanyi, ch. 3. Washington, DC: World Bank. https://openknowledge.worldbank.org/handle /10986/18725.

Wahba, Sameh, Maimunah Mohd Sharif, Mami Mizutori, and Lauren Sorkin 2020. "Cities are on the front lines of COVID-19." *World Bank Blog*, May 12, 2020. https://blogs.worldbank .org/sustainablecities/cities-are-front-lines-covid-19.

Woetzel, J., and S. Bouton. 2020. "Activating More Private Capital to Make Cities More Sustainable." *World Bank Blog*, September 17, 2020. https://blogs.worldbank.org /sustainablecities/activating-more-private-capital-Make-cities-more-sustainable.

Yadavalli, A., and C. K. McFarland. 2020. *What COVID-19 Means for City Finance*. Washington, DC: US National League of Cities. https://covid19.nlc.org/wp-content/uploads/2020/06 /What-Covid-19-Means-For-City-Finances_Report-Final.pdf.

3 Managing the Takeover of Disputed Assets and Liabilities

INTERNATIONAL EXPERIENCES AND OPTIONS FOR KENYA

INTRODUCTION

Transferring assets and liabilities across public entities on a mass scale naturally leads to disputes if receiver entities are hesitant to take over assets with doubtful value or unclear legal status and even less willing to take over liabilities. In private transactions, a buyer of assets calculates the fair market value by subtracting the estimated value of liabilities from the estimated value of assets and netting. In contrast, Kenyan counties as receivers of public assets are obliged to take them over without paying and netting, but some argue that the defunct entities were responsible for the excessive volume of liabilities accumulated over years or decades, so counties keep trying to avoid takeover of liabilities.

International experiences show examples of such takeovers, with various forms or resolutions explained in chapter 2. Takeovers of disputed assets and liabilities have remained unresolved in Kenya, where some counties have delayed formal takeover of financial assets to avoid taking over liabilities. This situation is not sustainable because some financial assets have deteriorated while some liabilities have grown fast since devolution.

OPTIONS FOR INSTITUTIONAL FRAMEWORKS AND PROCEDURES FOR WORKOUT OF DISPUTED ASSETS AND LIABILITIES IN KENYA

Gazette Notice no. 858 (2017) and Notice no. 2701 (2017) formally transferred the assets by the power of the law in March 2017. However, several challenges remained. First, a framework was needed for takeover of financial assets and liabilities not covered by the notices, according to expert opinions. Also, the disputed inherited assets and liabilities remained a major challenge in several counties, especially in Nairobi City County (NCC), which has inherited about two-thirds of the total national volume of counties' inherited financial assets and financial liabilities.

Disputed fixed assets are also substantial in many counties; these include grabbed or encroached land or buildings, unclear and disputed ownership, or missing compensation (part II provides details for a sample of counties). Establishing a workable framework and resolving these issues is urgent for at least three reasons. First, the assets represent substantial value and revenue potential. Second, some of the inherited liabilities are growing daily while inherited financial assets are eroding as time goes by. Third, the volume of these inherited assets and liabilities is enormous compared with the annual budget of NCC or some other impacted counties. Figure 3.1 indicates the 2013 value of financial assets and liabilities; there are no reliable data on the values at the end of 2019, but evidence suggests (part II) that the value of inherited liabilities has doubled.

The government of Kenya and the National Treasury could consider assessing options and seeking a suitable modality based on the Central and Eastern Europe asset and liability transfer framework. The supporting arguments include the following: (1) disputes can be resolved only by negotiations and reasonable compromises by all parties involved; (2) committees are well-tested forums for resolving such public disputes; and (3) County Asset and Liability Committees (CALCs) have played a reasonably effective role in facilitating the takeover of the fixed-assets verification and closed a four-year lapse. But the CALCs did not discuss or approve framework, rules, or options for workout of inherited disputed assets and liabilities. A reasonable framework would require appointing County Workout Committees (CWCs) with strong decision and negotiation power.

The composition of CWCs should be different from that of the CALCs; CWCs need finance, engineering, valuation, and legal specialists and high-level officers with decision-making power. The working arrangement for CWCs, however, should be similar to that of the CALCs: namely, supporting teams would need to analyze each case in detail and propose options with supporting documentation, then the CWC would discuss each case and take positions for resolutions and negotiations. Meanwhile, separate Asset and Liability Workout Committees (ALWCs) also should be established in each involved national government entity, not only in counties. Then the CWC should initiate negotiations with the respective national entity and the two committees would negotiate.

FIGURE 3.1

Nairobi City County and 47 counties combined inherited current assets and liabilities, March 2013

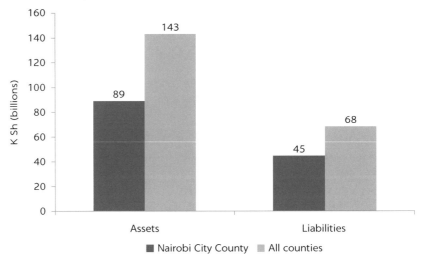

Source: IGRTC 2017.

Figure 3.2 depicts a modality for a framework. The National Treasury is the natural focal point to oversee issues on public assets; it may establish an inter-ministerial Asset and Liability Supreme Committee (ALSC), a higher supervisory and decision body for closing the disputed cases if negotiations between a county and a national entity fail to reach conclusion. The ALSC should include representatives of respective bodies of the national government entities—Office of the Auditor General (OAG), land and sectoral ministries, Intergovernmental Budget and Economic Council, and Intergovernmental Relations Technical Committee—and be chaired by a person with a distinguished high position.

ALSC or the National Treasury should issue rules, procedures, and policy guidance for dispute resolution and takeover of disputed financial assets and liabilities. The policy may include but not be limited to the following items:

- A strong instruction that the negotiating entities should seek solutions and the default result should be a mutually accepted and enforceable agreement, not court procedure.
- Failed cases should be submitted to ALSC (this is mandatory and not just an appeal option) for final assessment and verdict.
- The verdict of ALSC must be obeyed by all parties with corrective actions to be made in a timely fashion.
- Policy guidance may include a provision that the counties should use the proceeds from the negotiated and agreed workout of financial assets for funding the workout of inherited financial liabilities vis-à-vis public entities (for example, swap statutory deductions).

FIGURE 3.2

Institutional framework and procedures to resolve asset and liability disputes and takeover

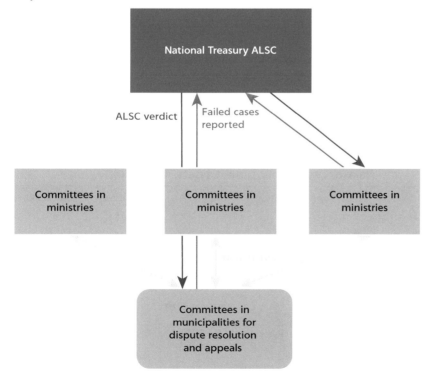

Source: World Bank.
Note: ALSC = Asset and Liability Supreme Committee. Green arrows indicate negotiations; orange arrows indicate submission of failed cases to ALSC; red arrows indicate verdicts.

- National government entities claiming debts with accrued interest and penalties should be open to compromise and reduce demand by annulling penalties or reducing interest to ease the financial burden of the counties. Alternatively, OAG or the National Treasury may set a one-time rule that the creditors in question must annul penalties on overdue statutory deductions.
- ALSC may rule that cases that have not started or have not concluded within six months after the start of the resolution program should be transferred to ALSC for assessment and a verdict without further negotiations between parties.
- A policy guidance may state if (1) claims vis-à-vis private persons or entities could be part of this resolution framework or (2) counties should work out private claims via direct negotiation or civil court procedures; the second option seems more rational.
- Each ministry and other entity involved in disputed assets or liabilities should establish an ALWC to analyze and negotiate the cases with the counties while following ALSC policy guidance, rules, and procedures.

The ALSC and the National Treasury may adopt another set of rules to guide full completion of asset and liability takeover in accordance with the Transition to Devolved Government Act 2012. The specific issues to regulate include but are not limited to the following:

- The ALSCs, the CWCs, and ALWCs of national government entities may continue working beyond the time frame of resolution of disputed inherited financial assets and liabilities to facilitate a pragmatic and quick transfer of assets from national government entities in accordance with the devolved functions, which may result in a new group of disputed assets and liabilities that need timely resolution under ALSC control.
- OAG and/or the National Treasury may assess the inherited tax and fee arrears that are paramount. Uncollected taxes and fees could be several times larger than the annual budget revenues of some counties (see NCC in table 3.1), but these are nominal numbers with presumably much lower present value. On the other hand, penalties and interest have been accumulating since devolution, which has increased the nominal value of inherited financial assets substantially. Including these inflated numbers in the municipal accounts (especially after adoption of accrual accounting standards) would make the

TABLE 3.1 **Nairobi City County current assets, March 2013**

	K Sh (MILLIONS)	% OF TOTAL
Rates (property tax)	53,643	44.1
Business permits	1,324	1.1
Kenya Power	583	0.5
Rents and others	607	0.5
Water company fee arrears	9,698	8.0
Water company others	773	0.6
Department of Defense land price	33,000	27.1
Water company shares	22,000	18.1
Total	**121,628**	**100.0**

Source: NCC CALC 2017.
Note: K Sh = Kenya shilling.

budgets unrealistic and unmanageable. Tax and fee arrears are hard to dispute, and thus could be taken over quickly, but policy guidance is required for rational and pragmatic treatment of these arrears. Also, programs are needed to build counties' capacities to collect tax and fee arrears, which have been accumulating since transition above and beyond the inherited arrears.

- The National Treasury might need to guide counties about how to address inherited bank debts, some of which are technically nonperforming, because counties have not served installments since devolution and predecessors stopped payments years before. Setting clear policy is vital, because the treasury is paying these debts on behalf of the counties without specific agreements on the counties' liabilities. Counties (especially NCC), on the other hand, cannot resume debt service and especially cannot start repaying the treasury for the new debt accumulated by the installment payments over the past several years. Should the treasury make counties liable for these payments, NCC would become deeply insolvent immediately.

International experiences suggest that the best resolution of such situations could be an *individualized debt restructuring program* between the National Treasury and the respective counties focused on capitalizing accrued interest and issuing a new long-term loan to counties. In short, a close analysis of the inherited financial assets and liabilities is an urgent task. The treasury faces great challenges, because rolling over these enormous volumes of debts and inflated receivables is like a rolling snowball that may grow out of control.

MANAGING FINANCIAL ASSETS AND LIABILITIES: SHORT ASSESSMENT OF NCC COMPARED WITH A WELL-MANAGED AUSTRALIAN LOCAL GOVERNMENT

Managing financial assets and liabilities is a natural part of strategic asset and liability management (ALM). The National Treasury via the National Assets and Liabilities Management Department has taken the lead in guiding counties toward enhancing practices and moving toward professional ALM. Financial and nonfinancial assets are transient forms of each other, so both are vital for healthy management of cities, but there are specific characteristics and challenges in financial ALM. At the strategic level, cities should establish two critical balances on financial assets and liabilities, regardless of the adopted accounting standards:

1. *Net debt*, the difference between the sum of *all financial assets* and the sum of *all debts and other direct financial liabilities*
2. *Net liabilities*, the difference between the sum of *all financial assets* and *debts and other direct and contingent liabilities* (Net liabilities often appear greater than net debt [ACT 2018] because they include contingent liabilities about uncertain outcomes.)

Assessing the quality of management of financial assets and liabilities in Kenyan counties is a difficult task, because counties apply only fragments of an adequate management framework and often lack staff and reliable data. NCC is far ahead of the other 46 counties, because it has a reasonable financial management system, qualified staff, an appointed debt and liquidity management team, and reasonable data. These offer a bold opportunity for comparison of Australian Capital Territory (ACT) and NCC—both are local governments with comparable characteristics (for example, population and economic position in the country). The major difference is that ACT is a historically well-run entity, despite that it also inherited a problematic portfolio when the pension funding system changed in Australia (as will be discussed). In contrast, NCC is still in transition because of issues discussed in this chapters and faces transitional challenges. We use the standard indicators of financial assets and liabilities to compare the two entities and draw lessons on managing financial assets and liabilities.

Liquidity management. Financial ALM also includes and plays a pivotal role in liquidity management, because the financial assets are more liquid than the fixed assets and thus can and should be used in liquidity management. Finance departments often include a team assigned to liquidity management that also includes risk management as part of ALM. NCC appointed such a team a few years ago. Cities may deposit surplus cash daily, not only because they cannot legally keep large sums of cash in vaults, but also to maximize overnight interest revenues. Likewise, financial assets are used to bridge gaps between revenue inflows and outflows to ensure stable liquidity and timely payments of due liabilities. Timely payment is not a well-obeyed principle in developing countries where ALM and liquidity management are poor and liquid financial assets (cash and financial investments) are miniscule, so invoices often land in drawers of mayors or chief financial officers to wait until cash inflow enables the city to pay the due liabilities. This might change when Kenya adopts accrual accounting for all public entities, but it will only help improve accounting and transparency without providing solutions for liquidity or solvency issues.

Financial assets. Financial assets broadly include investments in public entities, cash deposits, advances paid, financial investments and loans, and receivables (for example, uncollected fees and taxes). These values are found in cities' financial reports in both the developing and developed world, although cities in the developing world may keep and publish poor or no reports on financial assets. Books show great differences across these two groups of cities in composition and real present value of the financial assets, which impacts the quality of the ALM. Below we compare the composition of financial assets and liabilities of the ACT and NCC and show major differences in managing financial assets and liabilities.

Large differences in composition of financial assets. The situations of ACT and NCC are quite different. ACT financial assets are well recorded in books and are well performing (ACT 2018 report shows multiple evidence of good performance). In contrast, NCC has inherited its financial assets from the defunct local government as part of a devolution program, and the values of those assets have not been updated, which means they can be larger or smaller than the historical book value. For instance, a substantial volume of uncollected taxes and fees has accumulated since devolution, but this value is not yet reflected in NCC reports.

Figure 3.3 shows important differences in the composition of financial assets in NCC and ACT. ACT is heavy in financial and fixed investments, while NCC is heavy in tax and fee receivables. Other receivables are very substantial in NCC, while they are zero in ACT. Other receivables represent 20 percent of NCC revenues, including disputed revenues from various transactions between NCC and national government entities. Such disputes are common in developing countries, where national government entities are reluctant to pay fair compensation for assets they have taken over from cities.

Tax and fee receivables. Figure 3.3 shows that ACT has a healthy negligible volume of receivables in taxes and fees, while 60 percent of NCC's inherited financial assets are uncollected taxes and fees legally accounted as receivables,

FIGURE 3.3

Composition of financial assets of Nairobi City County, 2017, and Australian Capital Territory, 2018

Percent of total financial assets

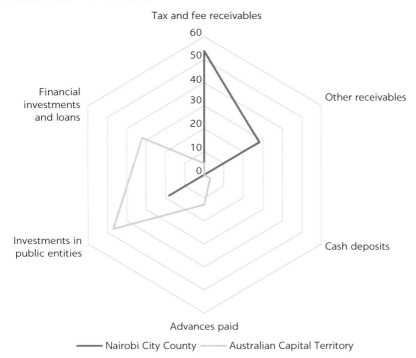

Sources: ACT 2018; NCC CALC 2017.

although they are not yet in NCC budgets. Receivables are enormous for NCC, twice as much as the volume of the total budget in the 2016/17 fiscal year. Such a situation is common in the developing world, since cities face large amounts of uncollected taxes and fees, often without good records or databases. This, again, is comparable to a huge rolling snowball growing beyond control. NCC needs to assess the real value of these receivables and develop a workout strategy, because a substantial part of these receivables is so old that it cannot be realistically collected, so it would be best to write them off from the NCC's balance sheet. Kampala city had a similar high volume of uncollected fees and taxes in the early 2000s but managed to collect or work out the bulk of them in a five-year concerted recovery program (Kopanyi and Franzsen 2018).

Investments in public entities. Investments in public entities are comparably realistic and active in both ACT and NCC. NCC has only one major investment in the legally independent Nairobi City Water and Sewerage Company, and this works well. NCC may co-own leisure compounds in forests: hotels that have been left unaccounted and unverified during CALC procedures. In contrast, ACT owns several public utilities, a common way to provide public services effectively, some in public-private partnerships (PPPs) with accounted contingent liabilities (ACT 2018).

Financial investments. NCC has no inherited financial investments, as opposed to the healthy 30 percent financial investments in the ACT financial assets portfolio. The latter underscores the vital role financial investments play in ALM in well-managed cities. For instance, ACT regularly issues bonds and immediately invests proceeds in secure financial investments (for example, treasury bills) to save the money received in bulk, while the use of the proceeds is gradual in line with the progress on infrastructure construction. Likewise, ACT is building a substantial reserve fund to be able to face the large inherited unfunded contingent liability on pension and termination benefits. For this reason, ACT regularly deposits money in a special fund to gradually extinguish the unfunded liability by 2030 (ACT 2018). Legal changes had created these huge contingent liabilities overnight, but the ACT took over these liabilities and adopted its own resolution program shortly afterward. This is a great example for a strategic way of thinking and strategic ALM. In addition, ACT accounts shareholdings in commercial entities or PPPs as financial investments, some with corresponding contingent liabilities.

Financial liabilities. Financial liabilities in a broad sense are composed of debts such as loans, bonds, due payables, advances received, and contingent liabilities such as guarantees, often labor- and pension-related contingent liabilities, and subsidy commitments. For instance, a city may commit to pay providers US$20 per each new water connection and add US$1.50 to each sold metro ticket and US$0.75 to each cubic meter of water billed and collected (Freire and Kopanyi 2018). Financial liabilities are moving targets, because they tend to change daily by payments of due amounts or enclosure of new liabilities. In short, managing the financial liabilities is part of prudent financial management, ALM, and liquidity management. Best ALM practices include provisioning of some specific contingent liabilities like guarantees provided or pension liabilities or even subsidies committed in contracts. To reiterate, comparing the financial liability portfolios of ACT and NCC again helps teach important lessons on financial liabilities in developed and developing countries (see figure 3.4).

Debts. These may include loans, bonds, or short-term instruments such as overdrafts. Debts are substantial in both NCC and ACT, and they are natural parts of the local government business. However, there are considerable differences in these two structures. Inherited NCC debt is quite large: 65 percent of the total inherited liabilities and about 150 percent of the volume of the total

FIGURE 3.4

Composition of financial liabilities of Nairobi City County, 2017, and Australian Capital Territory, 2018

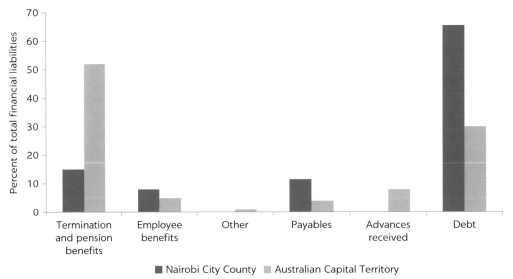

Sources: ACT 2018; NCC CALC 2017.

budget in the 2016/17 fiscal year. Furthermore, about three-quarters of the loans were borrowed, with a national government guarantee, from international donors, and most of them are nonperforming. This means that the National Treasury is paying the due service of the city debt, committed before devolution. However, the treasury (not yet the Nairobi City County Government, NCCG) accounts these guarantee payments as liabilities against NCC that are not reflected in the figure. This means that the present value of NCC's inherited debt liabilities is much greater than the nominal value reported in Transition Authority inventories. In contrast, ACT loans are well accounted, well managed, and served in a timely fashion. According to the 2018 budget report, ACT has obtained and retains a AAA long-term credit rating (ACT 2018), which would not be possible without good debt service records.

Termination and pension benefits. These are often regulated by national legislation and often lead cities into difficult situations, both in developed and developing countries (Grubišić, Nušinović, and Roje 2009; Holder 1998; Peskin 2001). Cities tend to address these labor liabilities as secondary to more urgent payments such as wages, electricity, or fuel. Another reason is that these liabilities are less visible and do not cause immediate harm if transferring the due amounts is delayed sometimes for years. This is particularly compelling when the cities manage the respective pension funds themselves (called a superannuation fund in Australia). In addition, cities may transfer portions of these off-budget funds back to the budget during liquidity crises, but some fail to return the money later.

Deferred payments to national pension funds. In other countries, cities must pay labor- and pension-related contributions into national or sectoral pension funds but suspend the payments if money is short, despite high-interest penalties and perpetual warnings. This was the case of the predecessor City Council of NCCG. There are often tacit agreements between the funds and the cities, in part because the fund managements are aware of how difficult it is to enforce these payments, but also, they may expect that the national government will eventually bail out the cities instead of letting them go bankrupt.

Pension liabilities. NCC, as noted, has inherited a sizable volume (about 15 percent of total inherited liabilities) of overdue liabilities on pension funds, because predecessors failed to transfer statutory deductions to national pension funds. The amount is not only sizable but is growing daily, some with a 15–35 percent annual rate of penalties since devolution in 2013. NCC's liability is overdue and thus no longer *contingent* but *direct* debt, and certainly today it has a much larger amount than the reported volume as of March 2013. In contrast, ACT has inherited a gigantic volume of contingent liabilities due to the regulatory changes that moved the pension benefit system from pay-as-you-go to a defined benefit scheme in 2005. But employees who were in the previous system should be paid according to the old scheme.

A lesson from this is that the ACT has clearly calculated this contingent liability based on the number of employees and employment profile and adopted a long-term plan to gradually extinguish this contingent liability by paying in a timely manner and fairly the due benefits at the day of retirement, but also gradually replenishing (provisioning) a special fund to back the contingent liability fully by 2030. Another lesson is that such big liabilities require both strategic decisions and time for full resolution. Thus, figure 3.4 reflects two vastly different situations regarding the termination and pension benefits. Finally, ACT liabilities are gigantic but under control, while the NCC liabilities are out of control and have become direct payables with no clear workout plans.

REFERENCES

ACT (Australian Capital Territory). 2018. "Asset and Liability Management." In *Budget 2017–18*, ch. 8. Canberra: Australian Capital Territory. https://apps.treasury.act.gov.au/_data/assets /pdf_file/0006/1069989/Budget-Paper-3.pdf.

Freire, M., and M. Kopanyi. 2018. *Asset and Debt Management for Cities*. London: International Growth Centre, London School of Economics. https://www.theigc.org/wp-content /uploads/2018/07/FINAL-Asset-and-Debt-Management-for-Cities_Working-Paper -062118.pdf.

Grubišić, M., M. Nušinović, and G. Roje. 2009. "Towards Efficient Public Sector Asset Management." *Financial Theory and Practice* 33 (3): 329–36. https://hrcak.srce.hr/file/74946.

Holder, A. 1998. "Developing the Public Sector Balance Sheet." *Economic Trends* 540 (November): 31–40. https://escoe-website.s3.amazonaws.com/wp-content /uploads/2020/01/01234506/ET-540-Developing-the-Public-Sector-Balance-Sheet -Andrew-Holder-Nov-1998.pdf.

IGRTC (Intergovernmental Relations Technical Committee). 2017. "Unaudited IGRTC Current Assets and Liability List as at 27 March 2013." IGRTC files from Transition Authority. IGRTC, Nairobi.

Kopanyi, M., and R. Franzsen. 2018. "Property Taxation in Kampala, Uganda: An Analytic Case Study on a Successful Reform," Africa Tax Institute Working Papers WP18-03, Pretoria. https://www.up.ac.za/media/shared/223/Working%20Papers/property-taxation-in -kampala-kopanyi-and-franzsen.zp146778.pdf.

NCC CALC (Nairobi City County, County Asset and Liability Committee). 2017. *Identification, Verification, and Validation of County Assets and Liabilities*. Nairobi City County Government.

Notice 858. 2017. Gazette Notice no. 858, January 8, 2017: Intergovernmental Relations Act no. 2 of 2012. https://gazettes.africa/gazettes/ke-government-gazette-dated-2017-01-27-no-13.

Notice 2701. 2017. Gazette Notice no. 2701, March 24, 2017: Intergovernmental Relations Act no. 2 of 2012. https://gazettes.africa/archive/ke/2017/ke-government-gazette-dated-2017 -03-24-no-37.pdf.

Peskin, M. 2001. "Asset/Liability Management in the Public Sector" In *Pensions in the Public Sector*, edited by O. S. Mitchell and E. C. Hustead, ch. 9. Philadelphia, PA: Pension Research Council of the Wharton School of the University of Pennsylvania.

4 Challenges and the Way Forward

POLICY OPTIONS

INTRODUCTION

Kenya has achieved remarkable progress on the road toward establishing modern and reliable asset management (AM) regulations, frameworks, and systems at both the national and county levels, as summarized in the three preceding chapters. However, numerous issues have remained unresolved. Substantial development challenges face Kenyan entities moving forward. Key challenges and options are briefly summarized in the following sections.

INCOMPLETE TASKS AND UNRESOLVED ISSUES

The main steps and issues include national and local- or county-level actions and challenges.

National-level issues

- The government established the National Assets and Liabilities Management (NALM) Department in the National Treasury to be a high-level regulator and custodian of public assets and liabilities, but delineation of the NALM mandates, responsibilities, and scope of work require further analysis and high-level decisions.
- NALM has developed a comprehensive asset and liability management policy and guidelines (NALM 2020a, b, c), but the policy is going through the legislative approval process and needs improvement (discussed in chapter 2 of this book). Likewise, the guidelines are under development and require approval.
- A national program is still to be adopted to facilitate the transfer of assets from national government entities and state corporations to counties in harmony with the Constitution 2010, the Urban Areas and Cities (UAC) Act 2011, and Transition to Devolved Government (TDG) Act 2012. Guiding this process is one of the most important incomplete tasks of the Intergovernmental Relations Technical Committee (IGRTC) and NALM.

- Resolution of inherited nonperforming current assets and liabilities has remained incomplete. IGRTC has analyzed the main groups of assets and liabilities and identified numerous workout options. There is still a need, however, for a framework and specific rules for pragmatic management of inherited assets and workout of inherited liabilities, with shared financial contributions by national entities, the treasury, counties, and all forced creditors. The large volume of unresolved claims and the complexity of possible resolutions require a national program and appointment of County Workout Committees (CWCs) and Asset and Liability Workout Committees. Presumably the National Treasury, represented by NALM, would need to take the lead.

- IGRTC has facilitated the transfer of assets and liabilities from defunct local authorities (DLAs) to counties "by the power of the law" per the enactment of Gazette Notices 858 (2017), 2701 (2017), and 4370 (2018). However, these notice regulations do not include enforcement rules, which may need to be developed for counties to complete asset takeover.

- County Asset and Liability Committees (CALCs) were established based on Gazette Notices 2701 and 4370 and have completed the validation and inventory of assets and liabilities and submitted detailed reports to IGRTC. But in most counties, CALC became inactive during and after local elections in 2018, so the completion of asset takeover falls on the shoulders of the county administrations and the AM directorates or teams.

- IGRTC has developed a consolidated report from CALC reports and submitted it to national and county entities and returned the specific revised county reports back to the newly elected governors and county administrations in 2019. This process, however, is incomplete, with no clear commitments for follow-up actions. There is a need to move away from the mere reporting function of CALC reports and instead use them as guiding documents for completion of asset takeover and resolution of liabilities.

- Counties need guidance and simple software solutions to install an information communication technology (ICT) system for simple but proper management of county assets. AM systems should be developed in the context of full life-cycle AM and from strategy to medium-term and annual planning to supporting daily AM functions along the asset hierarchy. Larger and well-developed counties such as Nairobi and Mombasa may acquire tailored, integrated AM ICT solutions. In contrast, the government/NALM may procure and provide a simplified and unified ICT solution to other counties that own relatively small asset portfolios. Providing counties with a simple accounting AM module in an integrated financial management information system is helpful for accounting AM, but it does not serve the purpose of modern and full-scope AM.

- A national program may be required to support counties to fast-track development of a verified asset register for land and buildings. This may require financial support to fund outsourcing the verification, surveying, and asset registering functions and maybe legal support for resolution of disputed asset cases.

- A national training program is required to fast-track development of human capacities needed for proper management of public assets. The asset and liability management guidelines NALM has developed or plans to develop could serve as the solid professional base for developing curricula and materials for AM training for various groups and levels of officers of national government entities and counties.

County-level issues

Most counties have placed AM on their priority lists and have managed assets important for service delivery or other social, political, or economic functions. Counties completed CALC reports with revisions, often substantially expanded the Transition Authority's unaudited inventory, and made progress on many fronts. However, counties have only just started to establish a reliable and modern AM framework, system, registers, and local procedures. The most important unresolved issues and tasks to be completed include the following:

- Complete a second revision of asset inventories captured in the CALC report and start developing reliable asset inventories and then registers in conformity with public financial management (PFM) regulations and NALM guidelines, such as including adequate technical details, tagging fixed assets, and establishing book value and/or market value, as necessary.
- Adopt a resolution or workout program for nonperforming liabilities with an assigned qualified team or committee (that is, CWC) of finance, planning, technical, and legal specialists to revisit each inherited liability focused on estimating present values and classifying nonperforming liabilities, proposing pragmatic resolutions, and performing or supporting higher-level county representatives in dialogue with creditors.
- Adopt a program for collecting and working out inherited nonperforming current assets after carefully analyzing and establishing present values and identifying options for pragmatic collection and partial write-offs that need rules and guidance from the Office of the Auditor General and/or the National Treasury.
- Appoint a qualified team (a CWC) of planning, finance, technical, and legal specialists to identify, analyze, and propose resolution options for disputed assets with a specific focus on land and buildings.
- Adopt a local AM policy with policy priorities and allocation of functions and responsibilities, and frame principles of strategic and life-cycle AM and joint management of assets and attached liabilities (appendix A and UN 2021).
- Institutionalize strategic asset and liability management, along with medium-term rolling capital improvement planning. Pandemic responses require revision of priority projects and adjustment of priorities to the postpandemic situation in a medium-term framework.
- Adopt an AM strategy in harmony with the AM policy, the county strategic plan, the county master plan, and other strategic decisions (appendix B).
- Adopt an initial AM plan that covers approximately two years, during which the fundamental framework documents are adopted, respective entities or job positions are appointed, and nonperforming assets and liabilities are worked out, with consideration of the postpandemic recovery (appendix C).
- Postpandemic recovery investments should be approached strategically. Without recognizing and utilizing the strategic role of assets, Kenyan counties and local governments may accumulate debts, and some may be forced into quick sales or confiscation of their assets in ways that don't support recovery.
- Improve human capacities by hiring a critical mass of skilled staff for AM positions and train all officers and staff involved in AM to ensure familiarity with and clarity on county AM policy, strategy, and plans. Send all respective staff to national training events organized by NALM and/or IGRTC or ministries.
- Procure a simple ICT system that would serve the full scope of AM functions beyond mere accounting and reporting assets.

POLICY OPTIONS MOVING FORWARD: ELEMENTS OF A MEDIUM-TERM PROGRAM

Discussion of issues, challenges, and possible responses in the previous chapters already covered options for moving forward and elements of a medium-term plan, but it is still useful to make a short list of priority options for further consideration. These include short-term or immediate actions and elements of a medium-term program.

Short-term or immediate actions at the national level

There are several national-level actions that deserve high priority and should be implemented urgently, including the following:

- Approve and implement a national asset and liability management policy with specific rules and regulations and adopt the principles of integrated asset and liability management and life-cycle AM.
- Commence a national program for resolution of the nonperforming current assets and liabilities that counties inherited from DLAs. It should include estimates of funds that the various stakeholders should contribute to ensure the fairness and viability of counties. Swapping assets or collectible claims with liabilities may also be one of the most powerful and pragmatic options.
- Commence extensive training on national asset and liability management policy and guidelines for all respective staff of national and county government entities.
- Provide a simple AM ICT solution for counties that own small asset portfolios and support counties with large portfolios in acquiring tailored and more complex integrated AM ICT solutions. Start by seeking a simple ICT solution that can be expanded later in conjunction with increasing human and management capacities and growing demand.

Short-term or immediate actions at the county level

Counties should prioritize and urgently implement several actions, including the following:

- Revisit and complete inventories of land and building assets and obtain clear ownership titles.
- Develop a program for collection of inherited collectibles.
- Develop a program for workout of inherited nonperforming liabilities in joint actions with resolution of inherited current assets.
- Appoint a team or committee (a CWC) with finance, planning, and legal teams to analyze and propose resolution of disputed land assets.
- Establish a small but adequate initial framework for county AM with an adequate number of skilled staff.
- Train all staff involved or planned to be involved in asset and liability management.

Medium-term actions at the national level

- Position and equip NALM to be the prime and last-resort custodian and regulator of all public assets and liabilities in Kenya.

- Transfer assets from national government entities and state corporations in accordance with the Constitution 2010, UAC Act, and TDG Act.
- Institutionalize strategic AM in all national- and county-level public entities.
- Develop a national register for public assets and another register for public direct financial and contingent liabilities.

Medium-term actions at the county level

- Institutionalize strategic and life-cycle AM from planning through procurement and development, operation and maintenance, and final disposal, with institutionalized proper preventive maintenance.
- Maintain up-to-date asset and liability registers along with asset hierarchy.
- Commence investigation of and register assets developed and overdue liabilities generated between March 2013 and the date of such investigation.
- Identify issues, estimate the magnitude of problematic or nonperforming financial assets and liabilities born between 2013 and the date of such investigation, and explore resolution options.
- Adopt policies and procedures to safeguard and drastically constrain the generation of uncollected receivables and accumulation of nonperforming or overdue liabilities. Develop reliable registers for both collectibles and payables (in accordance with PFM Law 2012). Prepare an annual report or include in the budget report a dedicated section that analyzes and reports on a portfolio of problematic, nonperforming collectibles and liabilities or payables.
- Revise the county AM policy and strategy to reflect the emerging situation and changing circumstances.

REFERENCES

NALM (National Assets and Liabilities Management Department). 2020a. "National Asset and Liability Management Policy, 2020." https://www.treasury.go.ke/wp-content/uploads/2021/03/Asset-Liability-Mgt-Policy.-doc-Final.pdf.

NALM (National Assets and Liabilities Management Department). 2020b. "General Guidelines on Asset and Liability Management in the Public Sector." https://www.treasury.go.ke/wp-content/uploads/2021/03/GeneralGuidelines-on-asset-and-liability-management-2020-Final.pdf.

NALM (National Assets and Liabilities Management Department). 2020c. "Guidelines for Management of Specific Categories of Assets and Liabilities, 2020." https://www.treasury.go.ke/wp-content/uploads/2021/03/Specific-guidelines-2020-Final.pdf.

NCC CALC (Nairobi City County, County Asset and Liability Committee). 2017. *Identification, Verification, and Validation of County Assets and Liabilities.* Nairobi City County Government.

UN (United Nations). 2021. *Managing Infrastructure Assets for Sustainable Development: A Handbook for Local and National Governments.* New York, United Nations. https://www.un.org/development/desa/financing/document/unhandbook-infrastructure-asset-management.

County Case Studies

5 Asset Management Experiences in Seven Counties

CASE STUDIES

INTRODUCTION

Part II of the book aims to provide a comprehensive picture of posttransition development and the present status of asset management at the county level, based on a sample of seven counties. The case studies exemplify the difficult situation faced by county governments following devolution. The analysis shows and appreciates the achievements and specific local responses to challenges, but also points out shortcomings that deserve attention and corrective measures. Part II presents more details on specificities, distinct progresses, and challenges that have been synthetized and included in assessing Kenya's nationwide situation in part I.

Kenya is one of the highly decentralized countries in Africa, and the state and evolution of asset management should be gauged in this context. The decentralized functions include agriculture, health, pollution control, cultural activities, transport, animal welfare, trade and development, county planning and development, preprimary education, village polytechnics, home craft centers and early childhood education, environmental conservation, public works, and local community public participation (fourth schedule of the Constitution 2010). The counties are mandated to provide the following services (Urban Areas and Cities Act 2011): water and sanitation, solid waste, public transport, street lighting, public housing, office and shop rental, hospitals, preschools, vocational schools, sport stadium, game-park, markets, and university campuses.

The Kenyan intergovernmental finance framework is conducive to locally driven development; the major transfer from central to local governments is called the *equitable share*, a formulae-based share of revenue provided from the central budget. It is an unconditional block grant that provides fiscal flexibility for counties to spend revenues against their highest priorities in both operational and capital budgets at their own discretion.[1] This is a major benefit of the Kenyan devolution. However, the counties are still under the pressure of inherited situations including legacy staffing, oversized administrations (for example, the share of labor expenditures is in the range of 60–70 percent of operating budget as opposed to the 35 percent international benchmark), and the unresolved asset takeover. These limit counties' abilities to adopt more ambitious development strategies and may constrain pandemic recovery measures.

The pandemic crisis has left Kenyan counties in an unfavorable situation, namely, already low levels of development and budgets for repair and maintenance are further stressed, as are high debt burdens in some counties. In funding development and debt repayment, counties rely on operating surpluses and moderate volumes of capital revenue from the sale or lease of assets. Only Kakamega County spent 40 percent of total expenditures on development in harmony with Kenya's national policy and international benchmarks, and this was in the first five years of devolution combined. The other six counties in the survey spent much less, around 25-30 percent, while Nairobi stands out with a bare 14 percent in the 2018/19 fiscal year and only 5 percent in the 2019/20 fiscal year. Such low rates of investment expenditures is a worrisome policy for a leading city of Kenya.

There are no development grants in the Kenyan intergovernmental finance system. This might change because a possible national pandemic recovery program could include targeted development grants to counties in the medium term. Unlike in most other developing countries, conditional grants are negligible, providing for about 5 percent of total revenues and supporting mostly operating expenditures. Development projects financed under donors' programs provide mostly loans to counties or affiliated entities. The Kenya Accountable Devolution Program (KADP) of the World Bank provides performance grants eligible for both operation and development expenses. There are no surveys on the quality of local public assets, but the extremely low level of repair and maintenance expenditures, around 1 percent of current expenses, suggests a substantial pile of dilapidated assets.

Nairobi City County (NCC) opens the case studies because NCC owns over half of the counties' assets and about two-thirds of inherited liabilities. Also, the NCC government (NCCG) has been moving ahead of other counties toward developing a reliable asset management framework, system, tools, and procedures;[2] many of NCCG's results could be emulated and replicated in other counties. The other county cases are presented in alphabetical order: Kajiado, Kakamega, Kiambu, Machakos, Makueni, and Nakuru. Some reform results achieved during the implementation of KADP in Bomet and Laikipia counties are also included in this study, without being presented as independent case studies.[3]

KEY FEATURES OF SAMPLE COUNTIES

The seven counties represent over half of Kenya's county assets and represent very substantial economic power in Kenya. They are a diverse group that well represents Kenya's 47 counties. While not considering them as a statistically selected representative sample, it is worthwhile to draw a consolidated picture of the financial and asset-related situation of this group of counties and assume that they exemplify the situation of the 47 counties. We will therefore refer to them as "sample counties" hereafter.

Financing operation and development

In 2013, the newly elected county governments received not only substantial mandates and devolved functions, but also benefitted from a substantial increase of financial transfers from the national government, largely in the form of unconditional equitable shares. Figure 5.1 depicts the situation of the sample counties. Equitable shares provide stable, predictable, and largely adequate funding for operations. In addition, conditional grants from ministries provide a minor (less than 5 percent) but helpful supplement to equitable shares and largely support financing operations of some services. One can conclude that the intergovernmental transfer system has provided solid ground to a smooth transition to devolved local governments and supported uninterrupted provision of devolved local services. This is a major achievement of the transition framework that should not be underestimated (Muwonge et al. 2022).

The situation is still challenging, however, because counties have repaid only a small fraction of their inherited financial liabilities, and some even accumulated new overdue bills from current operations between 2013 and 2018 (OAG 2013–18). The counties' real financial situations could be even worse than they appear in cash-based reports. However, figure 5.1 makes clear that counties' development capacity is largely dependent upon their own-source revenues (OSRs), which show a steady declining trend and eventually pulled down development expenditures after 2016.

The composition of current expenditures indicates another unfavorable characteristic, namely, that the counties spend an overwhelmingly high share on personal emoluments compared with a 35 percent international benchmark (Farvacque-Vitkovic and Kopanyi 2019). Figure 5.2 shows that counties (except Kajiado) spent around 60 percent or more of current expenditures on personal emoluments (including social insurance, albeit some left later unpaid). Hence, counties have limited room for proper operation and maintenance of assets and generate small operation surpluses that would be the source of development expenditures.

FIGURE 5.1

Main revenues and expenditures of the sample counties, fiscal years 2013/14–2017/18

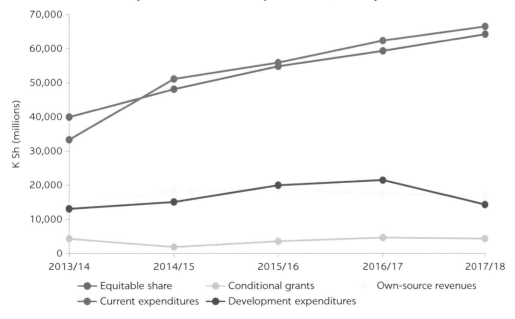

Source: OAG 2014–18.

FIGURE 5.2

Share of labor in current expenditures against international benchmark, average, 2013–18

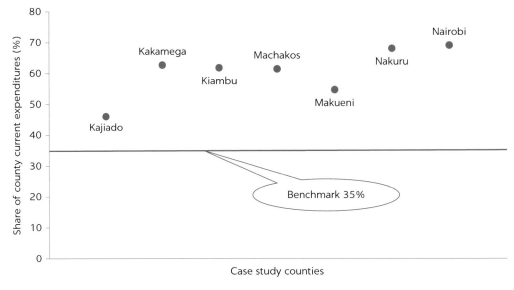

Source: OAG 2014–18.

Development, debt service, and repair and maintenance

Counties have managed to take over assets related to devolved functions and continue operations without major interruptions or breakdowns despite unclear legal and regulatory status (discussed in part I). This is a major achievement of smooth transition to new county governments. However, since the 2013 transition, development funds, financed basically by OSR, appeared to be insufficient to adequately develop, expand, and repair service infrastructure (figure 5.3).

Figure 5.3 shows that five years into devolution, the average share of development expenditures in total expenditures fell far below the 40 percent international benchmark (Farvacque-Vitkovic and Kopanyi 2019). Kiambu and NCC spent half or less than the benchmark. Only Kakamega County managed to maintain development expenditures on par with the international standard over the entire five-year period; this is a major achievement that signals sound development policy of Kakamega County government.

Figure 5.3 well exemplifies that the counties have overwhelmingly focused on developing assets, with minor and inadequate attention to and funding of repair and maintenance (R&M). The share of R&M expenditures in current expenditures is not only far from the 15 percent international benchmark, but is close to zero, fluctuating around 1 percent. The only exception is Kiambu, which spent remarkably more on R&M, yet only 3.4 percent.

Inherited financial liabilities appeared to be a major burden on some counties, and repayment of some debt (albeit only a small fraction in most cases) strongly constrained funds expendable for development. The financial reports remain unclear (and OAG commented on this) about whether debt repayment is aimed at resolution and workouts or continuation of debt-service dues borne from development, because financial reports often include large sums of "other payments."

FIGURE 5.3

Share of development in total expenditures and share of maintenance in current expenditures, average, 2013–18

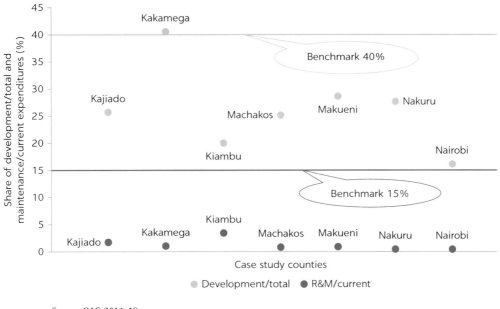

Source: OAG 2014–18.

Note: R&M = repair and maintenance.

FIGURE 5.4

Development expenditures and debt service, totals, 2013–18

Source: OAG 2014–18.

But workout of any inherited liabilities eventually absorbs money that could have been used to finance new development. Figure 5.4 shows that NCC and Makueni County have suffered the most on debt service. NCCG has spent more money on debt repayment than on infrastructure development in five years in devolution; debt repayment includes both amortization of loans and repayment of accumulated overdue liabilities.

Workout of inherited financial assets and liabilities

Asset management discussions often focus on or are limited to assessing fixed assets. In contrast, the Kenya devolution program rightly also has put the inherited financial assets and liabilities in the spotlight of asset management dialogues. There are three reasons: (1) the total inherited financial assets and liabilities are immense in some counties, such as NCC (IGRTC 2017); (2) the inherited financial assets have been losing value fast while the inherited financial liabilities are growing fast, some with excessive penalties, and in some cases representing the lion's share of the present value of inherited liabilities; and (3) against this significance, very little progress has been observed and achieved toward workout of inherited financial assets and liabilities over six years of devolution. These reasons underscore the conclusion and recommendation of this study (part I) that workout of the inherited financial assets and liabilities requires a national program with strong leadership of various national entities: National Treasury, Intergovernmental Budget and Economic Council (IBEC), Intergovernmental Relations Technical Committee (IGRTC), and the Council of Governors.

Sample county governments, especially NCCG, have made remarkable, albeit often powerless, efforts to manage and work out inherited financial liabilities. NCCG also has taken the lead in this area, including through the following actions: (1) NCCG established an Asset Management Directorate and a Debt Management Office (DMO) under the Finance Department; (2) DMO has developed a clear register of debts and other financial liabilities that covers both the inherited liabilities and those generated since the 2013 transition; (3) DMO prepares an annual report (NCCG DMO 2018) on the status of NCC's debts and workout efforts; (4) NCCG published Notice 2101 in the Kenya Gazette and established a Pending Bills Committee (NCC 2018) to advise on strategic decisions on workout of overdue debts; and (5) NCCG has initiated dialogue with creditors and even opened court cases but often failed to achieve resolution due to rigidity and the uncooperative nature of creditors.

NCCG's main debt management improvement efforts include the following: plans and negotiations with creditors, strengthening of commitment control to avoid generating overdue debt, debt-asset swaps, debt rescheduling, an increase in budget allocation for debt workout, and improved cash and debt management. In fact, NCCG spent more on servicing debts than on investing in infrastructure development between 2013 and 2018 (see figure 5.4). This is a signal of the determination of the NCCG to work out inherited liabilities and avoid systemic generation of overdue liabilities, but, as noted, some inherited liabilities seem to be growing out of control and beyond the capacity of NCCG to resolve. For example, penalties and interest on one nonperforming debt that NCC inherited were eight times greater than the principal amount in 2018 (NCCG 2018),[4] due to the extremely high penalties and the debtor's refusal to cut a portion of or all penalties and allow NCC to pay principal and interest under a debt-rescheduling program.

Inherited financial assets are also immense, and uncollected overdue taxes and fees represent the vast majority of financial assets. NCC inherited about two-thirds of counties' total inherited financial assets. However, as opposed to fast-growing inherited liabilities, the present value of the inherited financial assets (collectibles) is fast deteriorating. It is worth noting that a good portion of these collectibles were already several years old in 2013. Now they are nine years older and increasingly unlikely to be collected. Thus, the fact that the nominal value of inherited financial assets was greater than inherited liabilities in estimated 2013 nominal value (IGRTC 2018) is misleading and requires qualification with the estimated present values and a specific collection program.

Furthermore, counties in our sample and others alike have made unsuccessful efforts to (1) estimate the present value of the inherited financial assets and (2) adopt a strategy and specific program and procedures to collect a realistic share of inherited collectibles. But even the easiest and clearest collection cases have remained unsettled. This is a major shortcoming that disguises workout plans and dialogues. For instance, many counties have substantial collectibles on tax and fee payments from national government entities (per compensation in lieu of rates, or CILOR), and NCCG has proposed specific debt-asset swaps to clear both sides of its balance sheet, but it has achieved no results nine years into transition. The National Treasury should urgently step in to find a solution.

Most of the other counties have started to formally account overdue debt in liabilities accounts while implementing accrual accounting. Makueni and Kakamega counties also have spent substantial amounts on debt service over the past five years. Still, the magnitude and nature of inherited liabilities require urgent corrective measures. One can conclude that the counties gradually have started accounting of and managing inherited financial assets and liabilities, but most did not go beyond mere accounting. Real resolutions require detailed analysis of each claim and high-level policy decisions because counties have no power over the events and are weak in negotiations with creditors. Thus, a well-sorted national program is urgently required to close the long-pending transition. IGRTC and the National Assets and Liabilities Management (NALM) Department in the National Treasury have been working on identifying options and modalities for workout of assets and inherited liabilities, but plans are still incomplete, and implementation needs higher-level approval.

Institutionalizing asset management: First steps

Sample counties have made some steps toward establishing county asset management frameworks, systems, procedures, and databases. Progress by the end of 2019 includes the following achievements and shortcomings. Again, NCCG has been in the forefront of reforms. NCCG established an Asset Management Directorate in 2016 and the DMO in 2018, a signal of adoption of an approach to manage assets and liabilities jointly as part of a consolidated asset-liability management program that has preempted and is in line with the emerging national asset-liability management policy. NCCG drafted an asset management policy, strategy, and initial plan; commenced serious efforts for workout of inherited liabilities previously explained above; developed draft terms of reference (ToR) for hiring a firm to develop an initial but reliable, complete, and consistent asset inventory; and proposed a simple information and communication technology solution.

NCCG has just completed a geographic information system–based identification of land parcels in the NCC jurisdiction for property taxation purposes. This program also has provided NCC with a reliable land cadaster with updated market values for both national-government- and county-owned land, as well as private land. This is a very significant achievement that provides a solid technical ground for identification, verification, and eventual valuation of buildings and other improvements with which to populate a reliable asset register for land and buildings. Some land parcels and structures are outside the NCC jurisdiction and thus will require specific verification and valuation.

Several other counties, such as Bomet, Kakamega, and Kajiado, assigned small teams to deal with asset management, and have established draft asset management policies by hiring a consultant to draft a policy alone or under the KADP. But neither NCCG nor the other counties have formally approved and adopted the draft asset management policies. Counties' draft policies are in harmony with the national asset and liability management policy drafted subsequently by the National Treasury (per NALM), but this national policy still faces higher-level scrutiny and approval. Drafting county asset management policies are remarkable achievements as first steps. However, policies remain simply paper documents unless counties formally approve and adopt them, and particularly unless counties start using them effectively as regulations that guide all subordinated entities of counties in daily operation.

The public finance management regulations (PFM Act 2012) command establishment of asset registers, but none of the counties have complied with this regulation over nine years of devolution. NCCG stands out by having adopted a plan, drafted ToR, and allocated budget to hire a firm to develop and populate the asset register. But most counties have not yet adopted plans nor drafted ToR to develop an asset register.

County case studies and field interviews underscore that county officers or staff have no room in their regular workload to complete a very demanding field verification and registration of assets and to develop an asset register from scratch. Many expect that the national government will provide counties with a module in the integrated financial management information system (IFMIS), but NCCG has a more realistic understanding, spelled out in draft policy, that the accounting aspect of asset management is only one important but limited function in the broad scope of modern asset management. Besides, an IFMIS module would remain an empty shell, a software of limited use without field verification of assets, data collection, and development of a complete and consistent asset management system and various registers. While small counties with a moderate number of assets do not need a very sophisticated system, they still need much more than an accounting module.

It is also important to note that the national program that decentralized asset takeover by transferring all inherited assets by law under the IGRTC's leadership and regulation—per Notice 2701—has remained so far incomplete with no clear road map for full completion (discussed in part I). Field interviews at the end of 2019 suggest that the County Asset and Liability Committees (CALCs), which were aimed at guiding completion of asset verification, validation, and inventorying, had completed draft reports before the 2017 county election. However, many CALC reports remained in draft form and were incomplete, and committees remained dormant or inactive or they formally closed without being reinstated after the county elections in 2017. Thus, the development of the county asset management frameworks, systems, policies, procedures, and records of registered assets has fallen on the shoulders of the new county governments.

Most of the counties in this sample have made remarkable steps toward adopting accrual-based accounting and have started preparing financial reports following accrual-accounting principles in recent years. But good asset registers should reflect depreciation of assets regardless of whether or not a county follows cash-based accounting principles in bookkeeping and financial reports. Financial reports published by OAG with long lists of detailed comments reflect various stages, scopes, and quality of county financial reports that follow variations of modified accrual accounting. Many counties prepare income statements, some cash-flow statements, statements on financial assets and liabilities, and summaries of asset registers. These all are important steps in a good direction.

However, the summaries of fixed asset registers presented and published in OAG reports suffer from shortcomings, including the following: (1) they are limited to assets acquired after 2013; (2) the presented asset values do not match the total value spent on asset acquisition as reported in expenditure statements, and the latter are often much greater than the asset register reports; (3) the reports include annual additions but exclude amortization, so the stated book value of assets is inadequate; and (4) field visits suggest that the summary asset registers have been prepared outside the accounting system from data of nonexistent detailed asset registers. OAG reports note these discrepancies and shortcomings. These shortcomings underpin the fact that counties have not yet drafted balance sheets, neither full nor in limited scope (for example, without accounting fixed assets).

The lack of land asset inventories observed in all sample counties is among the most significant shortcomings. Most fixed-asset registers published in OAG reports include values for land that the counties acquired after 2013, but all counties failed to develop reliable land asset inventories that include inherited land assets. Preliminary inventories published in CALC reports are acknowledged as incomplete in scope (some without verifying even an approximate number of parcels), include unreliable land size records (suggesting poor and incomplete verification), and include numerous disputed land cases that may increase as further evidence of apparent or suspected land grabbing or encroachment unfolds during field verification.

Land grabbing and encroachment have occurred for decades and probably have continued since 2013. But proof and restoration of county ownership is getting more difficult as time goes by. The lack of a reliable national land register is among the difficulties counties face in identifying public land they own. Some counties (for example, Nakuru and Embu) have used community participation to identify land that was excluded from the preliminary asset registers drafted under the defunct Transition Authority. Developing reliable asset registers should start with drafting reliable land-asset inventories on an urgent basis.

NOTES

1. Earmarked grants are very substantial in many developing countries in Africa and beyond. For instance, Rwandan local governments receive a third or half of transfers from sectoral ministries and the Local Development Agency in the form of earmarked grants with 10 percent own-source revenues. This leaves little room for discretionary decisions on the share of operation and development and on priority development projects.
2. We use two separate terms and acronyms consistently. NCC refers to the county as the legal entity that owns assets, possesses liabilities, and is responsible for provision of local services according to the Constitution 2010 and federal laws, and can be sued and can commence court procedures. In contrast, NCCG is the governing body of NCC that manages but does not own NCC's assets; it issues local regulations and represents NCC vis-à-vis third parties.
3. The World Bank's KADP has funded the fieldwork to develop the county case studies. Miriam Omolo, Ph.D., local consultant, has played a substantial role in data collection and field interviews. The financial and asset-related data are largely derived from the annual county reports published by the Office of the Auditor General (OAG). The OAG reports contain numerous inconsistencies, reporting weaknesses, and data shortages, but despite

shortcomings, they provide single-source and consistent presentation of results. County internal reports from the Office of the Controller of Budget (OCB 2014–18) and CBIR reports have appeared to be less reliable and less consistent across years and across counties. Thus, for the most part OAG reports are used throughout the book.

4. The authors consider details of this internal report to the County Assembly as not for public release until OAG includes detailed numbers on liabilities in its next publication on county governments' financial audits. Thus, we aim to draw just key lessons and tendencies without publishing respective numbers.

REFERENCES

Farvacque-Vitkovic, C., and M. Kopanyi. 2019. *Better Cities Better World: A Handbook on Local Government Self-Assessments*. Washington, DC: World Bank. https://openknowledge .worldbank.org/handle/10986/32120.

IGRTC (Intergovernmental Relations Technical Committee). 2017. "Unaudited IGRTC Current Assets and Liability List as at 27 March 2013." Intergovernmental Relations Technical Committee from files of Transition Authority. Nairobi: IGRTC.

IGRTC (Intergovernmental Relations Technical Committee). 2018. *Report on the Identification, Verification, Validation, and Transfer of Assets and Liabilities of the Defunct Local Authorities as at 27th March 2013*. Nairobi: IGRTC. https://igrtc.go.ke/download/consolidated-report -on-assets-and-liabilities-of-the-defunct-local-authorities-2018/.

Kenya Constitution. 2010. http://kenyalaw.org/kl/index.php?id=398.

Muwonge, A., T. S. Williamson, C. Owuor, and M. Kinuthia. 2022. *Making Devolution Work for Service Delivery in Kenya*. Washington, DC: World Bank. https://openknowledge.worldbank .org/bitstream/handle/10986/37017/9781464817267.pdf?sequence=2&isAllowed=y.

NCC (Nairobi City County). 2018. NCC Gazette Notice no. 2101. "Committee on the Nairobi City County Government Pending Bills. Appointment." http://kenyalaw.org/kenya_gazette /gazette/volume/MTY4MQ--/Vol.CXX-No.33/.

NCCG DMO (Nairobi City County Government Debt Management Office). 2018. *Stock of NCC County Liabilities*. Debt Management Office 30th June 2018. Nairobi: NCCG DMO.

Notice 2701. 2017. Gazette Notice no. 2701, March 24, 2017: Intergovernmental Relations Act no. 2 of 2012. https://gazettes.africa/archive/ke/2017/ke-government-gazette-dated-2017 -03-24-no-37.pdf.

OAG (Office of the Auditor General). 2013–19 (annually). *Report of the Auditor General on Financial Statement of Counties*. Nairobi: OAG. http://www.oagkenya.go.ke/index.php /reports/cat_view/2-reports/11-county-governments/203-county-government-reports.

OCB (Office of the Controller of Budget). 2014–18 (annually). *Annual County Government Budget Implementation Review Report*. Nairobi: https://cob.go.ke/reports /consolidated-county-budget-implementation-review-reports/.

UAC. 2011. Urban Areas and Cities Act, no. 13 of 2011. http://www.parliament.go.ke/sites /default/files/2017-05/UrbanAreasandCitiesAct_No13of2011.pdf.

6 Nairobi City County

INTRODUCTION

Nairobi City County (NCC) is a small area in the south-central region of Kenya and hosts the country's capital. It has a total area of 696 square kilometers and sits 1,798 meters above sea level. NCC is bordered by Kajiado, Kiambu, and Machakos counties. Its administrative units include six subcounties—Embakasi Central, Embakasi North, Embakasi West, Kamukunji, Mathare, and Ruaraka—as well as 64 locations and 135 sublocations. The county's political units include 85 wards and 17 constituencies: Dagoretti, Embakasi Central, Embakasi East, Embakasi North, Embakasi South, Embakasi West, Kamukunji, Kasarani, Kibra, Kilimani, Langata, Makadara, Mathare, Roysambu, Ruaraka, Starehe, and Westlands (map 6.1).

Nairobi's population was estimated at about 4.4 million in 2019, with an estimated 4.05 percent annual growth rate fueled by both high natural growth and movement of people from rural to urban areas. Nairobi's population density was 6,247 per square kilometer as opposed to the country average of 82 per square kilometer (KNBS 2019). The dependency ratio of 31.4 percent is the lowest in Kenya, but the poverty rate is high at about 22 percent, albeit much lower than the national average of 36.1 percent (World Bank 2018; KNBS 2018). The city hosts the Kibera slum, which is the largest urban slum in Africa.

Nairobi is a major market and business center that hosts Kenya's key industries and financial and commercial entities; it is also the major transport hub for rural areas, other towns, and regional and international markets (NCCG 2018). The main products emanating from Nairobi include processed food, beer, vehicles, construction material, engineering industry, textiles, and chemicals. Areas around Nairobi are prime agricultural lands; food crops include maize, sorghum, cassava, beans, and fruit. Horticulture is a new growth sector, and flower exporting is a substantial revenue source. Tourism is a thriving business in NCC, served with a well-developed system of hotels, tourism companies, and game parks. Nairobi has an additional responsibility of providing infrastructure that sustains the seat of the national government, diplomatic missions, and businesses.

An aging infrastructure that fails to expand in line with fast population growth is the major urban issue (NCC 2018c). The annual development plan further states that road transport accounts for movement of over 80 percent of goods,

MAP 6.1

Nairobi City County

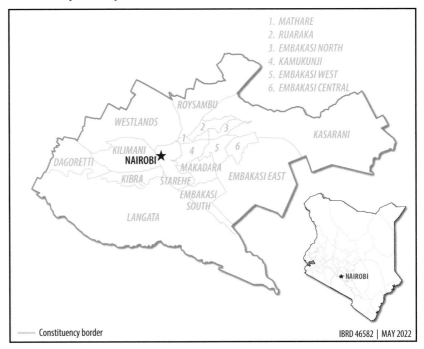

Source: World Bank.

services, and people within and across the city, but the road network has grown slowly and remained inadequate; of the network's 2,970 kilometers, only about 1,100 kilometers (38 percent) are tarmac, 600 kilometers (20 percent) are gravel, and 1,270 kilometers (42 percent) are earth. Due to the aging drainage infrastructure, flash floods remain persistent in some areas. Transport and especially public transport systems are ineffective. Traffic congestion is barely manageable and causes high carbon emissions, high costs for citizens and businesses, and poor quality of life. Solid waste management infrastructure is inadequate and causes poor sanitation, disease outbreaks, contamination of water, and air pollution. Inadequate housing and social amenities have led to mushrooming of informal settlements, increased crime, and poor quality of life. Increased investment in expansion and maintenance of infrastructure is the most important action the NCC government faces in the short to medium term.

REVENUE AND EXPENDITURE ANALYSIS

Analysis of revenues and expenditures[1] is an integral part of an assessment of asset management because it provides a solid background picture in which assets are positioned, developed, and managed. Revenues generate cash or cash-like instruments that are transient forms of assets, since land can be sold to generate cash revenue to develop schools, or cash can be saved for rainy days. Finally, the surplus remaining after current expenditures are covered with current revenues provides funds for development. Loans or other liabilities can also finance development. In short, revenue and expenditure analysis provides important insights and sheds light on the trends and capacities a county possesses in developing assets and expanding services.

Revenues

NCC's revenue base has grown steadily at an average rate of 8 percent per annum between the 2013/14 and 2017/18 fiscal years (table 6.1); this growth represents an approximate 2 percent real increase above the average inflation in the same period. The Government of Kenya has supported devolution by substantially and steadily increasing transfers to counties (CRAB 2015). *Equitable shares* grew by 12.8 percent and provide over half of revenues. It is worth noting that equitable shares amount to about 80–90 percent of revenues in most other Kenyan counties (CRAB 2015).

Conditional grants appeared to be small (less than 2 percent of revenues) and volatile. NCC obtained loans from development partners, the bulk from the World Bank to support various infrastructure projects. NCC obtained substantial loans and grants based on agreements between the county and the national government and donors such as the World Bank or the Danish International Development Agency, which funded mainly health care infrastructure and services.

The large volume of loans accounted in 2015/16 signals a classification error, since it is greater than the development expenditures (K Sh 6.2 billion in loans against K Sh 4.2 billion development expenditures). Presumably, the face value of loans was accounted rather than the amount disbursed in the same fiscal year. The enormous budget surplus (see table 6.3 in the next section) coincides with the accounted large loan disbursement in 2015/16 fiscal year (table 6.1); these classification and revenue entry transactions deserve scrutiny and corrections as may be required. The financial report also could reflect the cash reserves carried forward from previous years. The positive budget balances suggest the existence of such cash reserves, or as stated, the amount unspent for planned development.

TABLE 6.1 Nairobi City County revenues, fiscal years 2013/14–2017/18
K Sh (millions)

	2013/14	2014/15	2015/16	2016/17	2017/18	AVERAGE GROWTH (%)
Transfers from national government	**9,900**	**11,638**	**13,469**	**14,610**	**15,883**	**12.5**
Equitable share	9,510	11,340	12,997	14,020	15,402	12.8
Conditional grants	390	298.3	472	590	481	5.4
Own-source revenues	**9,206**	**11,417**	**11,238**	**10,933**	**10,158**	**2.5**
Taxes	4,880	6,497	5,117	5,730	5,319	2.2
Fees and charges	2,900	3,689	3,332	4,119	3,849	7.3
Asset proceeds	840	767.4	2,632.8	735.7	683.4	−5.0
Other revenues	586	465	156	349	307	−14.9
Financing	**0**	**298**	**862**	**0**	**0**	**n.a.**
Cash reserve from previous year	—	—	—	—	—	n.a.
Loans and grants	0	298	862	0	0	n.a.
Total revenue	**19,106**	**23,354**	**25,568**	**25,543**	**26,041**	**8.0**
Share of OSR (%)	48.2	48.9	44.0	42.8	39.0	−5.1
OSR actual/planned (%)	63.0	86.0	77.0	56.0	59.0	−1.6

Source: OAG 2014–18.
Note: — = not available; n.a. = not applicable; OSR = own-source revenue.

TABLE 6.2 Nairobi City County OSR, fiscal years 2013/14–2017/18

K Sh (millions)

	2013/14	2014/15	2015/16	2016/17	2017/18	AVERAGE GROWTH (%)
Taxes	**4,880**	**6,497**	**5,117**	**5,730**	**5,319**	**2.2**
Property rates (property tax)	2,580	2,595	3,110	2,250	2,093	−5.1
Business permits (business tax)	1,540	1,806	1,786	1,780	1,647	1.7
Other taxes and levies	760	2,096	221	1,700	1,579	20.1
Fees and charges	**2,900**	**3,689**	**3,332**	**4,119**	**3,849**	**7.3**
Parking fees	1,550	2,037	2,038	2,025	1,882	5.0
Urban services	557	552	513	552	513	−2.1
Social services	133	133	218	320	319	24.5
Licenses, permits, certificates	660	968	564	1,221	1,135	14.5
Asset proceeds	**840**	**767**	**2,633**	**736**	**683**	**−5.0**
Rents and leases	590	665	2,146	632	587	−0.1
Markets	250	102	487	104	96	−21.2
Other income	**586**	**465**	**156**	**349**	**307**	**−14.9**
Total OSR	**9,206**	**11,417**	**11,238**	**10,933**	**10,158**	**2.5**

Source: OAG 2014–18.

Note: OSR = own-source revenue.

NCC strongly relies on own-source revenue (OSR), high above other counties in Kenya. The share of own-source revenue fluctuated between 49 percent and 39 percent in the fiscal year 2013/14–2017/18 period (table 6.1). This share shrank by 5.5 percent per year and appeared to be particularly low when a substantial loan was accounted in 2015/16. The OSR grew by a mere 2.5 percent per year, way below the 6.7 average inflation rates (CBK 2020), while the transfers from the national government grew five times faster than OSR (12.5 percent per year) over the noted period. OSR collection appears to have been unsteady; it increased in 2014/15, and then collection shows a steady decline. The transition to the new county government is likely to have influenced OSR collection, but the increase was moderate and not sustainable. The actual/planned variation of OSR (last line in table 6.1) worsened by 1.6 percent per annum, increasing from 63 percent in 2013/14 to 86 percent in 2014/15, and then dropped back to 56 percent in 2016/17. This variation points to a need to substantially improve revenue management, planning, and collection.

Taxes represent the largest share of and generate over half of OSR (table 6.2), albeit showing low buoyancy; the trend indicates a slight overall increase (2.2 percent) in the 2013/14–2017/18 fiscal period. Property rates are the largest source of tax revenue but show a shrinking trend (−5.1 percent) in the same period that is hard to explain and accept in a fast-growing city. Business permits (internationally classified as business taxes) are the second-largest source of tax revenue; they increased overall by 1.7 percent per year. Other taxes that include a building permit fee (development tax)[2] are volatile and show strong 20 percent annual improvement over the surveyed period. Figure 6.1 depicts the volume, composition, and hints of trends of main OSR sources.

FIGURE 6.1

Nairobi City County OSR, fiscal years 2013/14–2017/18

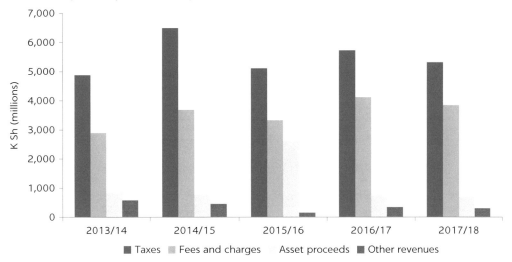

Source: OAG 2014–18.
Note: OSR = own-source revenue.

Fees have increased gradually; they show a dynamic 7.3 percent annual growth and generated nearly 40 percent of OSR by 2016/17, due to increases in main sources (table 6.1). Parking fees grew by 5 percent. Fees from licenses, permits, and certificates represent the second-largest fee revenue, increasing by 14.5 percent per annum over the same period. Revenues from social services (mainly health) increased by an unprecedented rate of 24.5 percent per annum, while revenues from urban services declined (or were accounted among other services and in part off budget under the Nairobi City Water and Sewerage Company).

Asset proceeds are almost negligible and decreased 5 percent per annum between 2013/14 and 2017/18, a signal of poor asset management. Revenues from markets, rents, and leases are insignificant and fast deteriorating. It is hard to justify how asset proceeds remain so small and are decreasing in a city with dynamic growth and a huge property asset portfolio. (NCC owns about two-thirds of total county assets of Kenya.) Revenues from "other sources" that may include asset-sale revenues were greater than asset proceeds and remained small and decreasing in the surveyed period. The low revenues from assets deserve scrutiny and may justify a change in asset policies and adoption of substantial corrective measures in the short and medium terms.

Expenditures

NCC's total expenditures show moderate growth of about 7.6 percent per annum, slightly below the growth rate of total revenues (8.0 percent) over the 2013/14–2017/18 fiscal period (table 6.1 and table 6.3). The current expenditures grew much faster (12.5 percent) than current revenues (8.0 percent) per annum. This is a combination of a 6.0 percent annual increase of labor costs and an unprecedented high 22.1 percent annual growth of cost of operation with negligible maintenance expenditures. The emphasis on operation and maintenance signals a move toward good governance if this includes substantial maintenance

TABLE 6.3 **Nairobi City County expenditures, fiscal years 2013/14–2017/18**
K Sh (millions)

	2013/14	2014/15	2015/16	2016/17	2017/18	AVERAGE GROWTH (%)
Current expenditures	**13,200**	**21,821**	**20,044**	**20,913**	**21,146**	**12.5**
Personal emoluments	10,300	13,104	12,478	12,739	12,987	6.0
Operation and maintenance	2,900	7,426	5,768	6,463	6,448	22.1
of which, repair and maintenance	0	209	48	99	14	n.a.
Transfers to other entities	0	1,291	1,799	1,711	1,711	n.a.
Noncurrent/development	**4,600**	**2,846**	**5,486**	**4,017**	**2,756**	**−12.0**
Acquisition of assets	1,900	2,110	2,428	1,763	1,436	−6.8
Debt repayment	2,700	735	1,235	30	868	−24.7
Other payments	0	0	1,822	2,224	452	n.a.
Total expenditures	**17,800**	**24,667**	**25,530**	**24,930**	**23,901**	**7.6**
Budget balance	**1,306**	**(1,313)**	**38**	**613**	**2,139**	**13.1**
Ratios (%)						
Operation and maintenance/current	22.0	26.0	32.0	36.0	30.5	0.1
Personal emoluments/current	78.0	74.0	68.0	64.0	61.4	−0.1
Current/total	74.0	89.0	83.0	85.0	88.5	0.0
Development/total	26.0	11.0	17.0	15.0	11.5	−0.2
Repair and maintenance/current	n.a.	1.0	0.2	0.5	0.1	n.a.

Source: OAG 2014–18.
Note: n.a. = not applicable.

expenditures, but Nairobi City County Government (NCCG) instead has strongly increased the cost of operation while maintenance expenditures have declined. However, this could also be a classification issue between accounting maintenance and development or accounting debt repayment (repayment of some overdue liabilities) as regular operating expenditures.

Labor costs (personal emoluments) remained high as a share of current expenditures, but they declined by 5.8 percent per annum, and dropped from a 78 percent peak to a 61 percent share in current expenditures in 2017/18. This share is, however, way above the international benchmark of 35 percent (Farvacque-Vitkovic and Kopanyi 2019). One reason is that NCC has inherited not only assets and liabilities but also an excessive volume of redundant labor, which NCC has failed to restructure or lay off six years in devolution.

NCC noncurrent expenditures totaled K Sh 19.7 billion over the five-year surveyed fiscal period, a substantial volume. But the volume of direct infrastructure investment was not only very volatile but amounted to only K Sh 9.6 billion, less than half of noncurrent expenditures (table 6.3). NCCG would have had funds to invest more but had to amortize K Sh 10.1 billion in debt instead, reflecting the reality that debt service is a vital part of local governments' responsibility. The share of investment expenditures remained dangerously low, and shrunk from 26 percent to 12 percent against the 40 percent international benchmark in the surveyed period.

Despite the challenges noted, NCCG completed major refurbishment work on assets that were vital for maintaining or reinforcing the value and service functionality of key inherited assets such as school buildings, offices, or other

FIGURE 6.2

Nairobi City County cumulative development expenditures, fiscal years 2013/14–2015/16

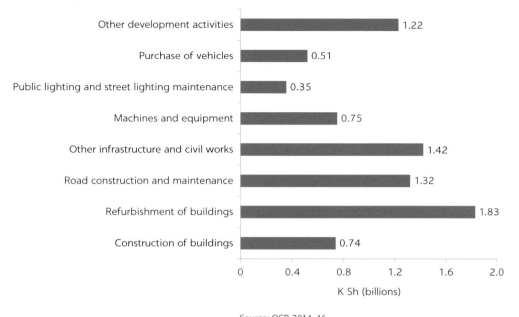

Source: OCB 2014–16.

structures. This spending signals that counties have approached asset management on the service level pragmatically and functionally despite the legal challenges they faced on asset handover and takeover matters.

Figure 6.2 provides a glimpse into the NCC development program in the first three years of devolution. It was rightly focused on building refurbishment, road and other infrastructure construction, building construction, and machine and equipment acquisition. This also signals that NCCG, like a diligent owner, has informally taken over the assets inherited from the defunct City Council of Nairobi (CCN) and invested substantial funds to enhance and expand the infrastructure regardless of the legal vacuum on asset transfers.

ASSET MANAGEMENT

The case studies focus on the transition period, before which Kenya's local governments did not have asset management systems, frameworks, and policies except for sporadic practices by officers of services to manage assets units daily. Despite legislated mandates—Public Finance Management Act 2012 (PFM 2012), Constitution 2010, Public Procurement and Asset Disposal Act 2015 (PPAD 2015), County Governments Act (CGA 2012), and circulars—local governments failed to establish asset registers, and even the accounting aspects of assets were poorly understood and followed before devolution. Local bodies failed to measure and aim for increasing the public wealth in the local government jurisdictions or manage the most important assets strategically. This case study illustrates the enormous challenges the incoming county government faced due to the inherited situation already noted (see also part I) and demonstrates its remarkable progress after devolution. But it also demonstrates that moving forward requires strong determination, vision, finances, and reformative actions toward modern and adequate management of assets that eventually determine the level and quality of mandated services and citizens' quality of life.

Asset ownership and transition to devolved government

The Transition to Devolved Government Act 2012 (TDG 2012), also known as the Transition Act, Article 7 and Fourth Schedule, regulated the takeover of the functions, assets, liabilities, and staff from the defunct local entities *after valida-tion and audit* by the Transition Authority (TA) (see box 6.1). The mandates, organization, budget, and operation of the TA suggested that the assets would be handed over to the incoming county governments by the TA after completion of the foreseen verification and validation in the short foreseeable future. This did not happen, however, and instead apparently paralyzed most incoming county governments; one can even say it also annulled the responsibility of the outgoing officers to hand over accounts, documents, and assets to the officers of incoming county governments.

Such a paralysis was less justified in Nairobi, where the handover was sup-posed to happen between one single outgoing body and one single incoming body and with numerous lower-level officers having uninterrupted work posi-tions—in contrast to other counties that had to amalgamate a handful of defunct entities. Part I offers detailed institutional analysis of the legal and governance framework of transition, but it is sensible to quote a few critical elements here.

In order to reinforce high-level legislative provisos—PFM Act 2012 (PFM 2012) and TDG Act 2012 (TDG 2012)—and despite the existence and operation of the TA, the Ministry of Local Government Circular MLG/1333/ in March 2013 directed the clerks as the chief executive officers of the outgoing local authorities to ensure the proper handover of documents and assets to the incoming county governments. The outgoing officers seem to have either not noticed or ignored this circular (issued days before an election that terminated their work positions).

But the circular apparently had no enforcement provision or effective enforce-ment power; the officers of the defunct CCN are reported to have just walked away. Some were suspended as of election day with no options to reenter their

---

BOX 6.1

The mandates and competence of the Transition Authority on asset transfer stipulated in the Transition Act

Article 7, subsection (2), stipulates that "Despite the generality of subsection (1), the [Transition] Authority shall . . . (e) prepare and validate an inventory of all the existing assets and liabilities of government, other public entities and local authorities; (f) make recommendations for the effective management of assets of the national and county governments; (g) provide mechanisms for the transfer of assets which may include vetting the transfer of assets during the transitional period."

The fourth schedule [Section 7(3)] stipulates that "(1) During Phase One of the transition period, the [Transition] Authority shall carry out the following activities—(2) audit assets and liabilities of local authorities, to establish the asset, debts and liabilities of each Local Authority; (3) audit local authority infra-structure in the counties, to establish the number and functionality of plant and equipment in Local Authorities. . . ."

Source: Transition to Devolved Government (TDG) Act 2012.

offices, and thus were no longer responsible for the accounts, documents, and assets they had been managing in years before. This legal uncertainty and poor governance resulted in very substantial losses, presumably in both fixed and financial assets. Audits performed on the transition year of 2013 found irregularities in bank accounts, but also, strangely, commercial banks of CCN were reluctant to furnish audits by providing reliable information to auditors on the defunct CCN's bank accounts, and thus presumably millions of shillings were lost (box 6.2).

BOX 6.2

Nairobi City County audit report excerpts, 2013

Failure to take over by the county government

The County Government of Nairobi had not officially taken over the assets and liabilities of the former City Council of Nairobi (CCN). Overall, the audit found that the NCC [Nairobi City County] had 16 departments whose work was not coordinated and which operated as independent units. No handing-over notes were prepared and business continued as usual and as a result; it has not been possible to conclusively confirm the accuracy of the assets and liabilities taken over from the former CCN. A senior management committee to take over the role of the CCN during transition was not established as directed by the then Ministry of Local Government vide Circular no. MLG/1333/TY/52 of 18 February 2013.

Cash and bank balances

The defunct CCN historically operated 40 bank accounts, of which 16 were dormant, while 12 had credit balances totaling K Sh 35,459,356.20. However, the county did not produce for audit all the cashbooks and bank reconciliation statements to confirm the accuracy of the cash and cash equivalents.

Failure to close bank accounts

The Ministry of Local Government had issued instructions vide Circular no. MLG/1333/TY/52 of February 18, 2013, requiring all defunct local authorities accounts to be closed and the existing funds transferred to the General Rate Fund Account and as soon as practicable, a Single Account to be opened at the Central Bank of Kenya. However, the accounts were not closed as required and business continued as usual and instead four new accounts were opened.

Failure by CCN bankers to confirm cash and bank balances

It was not possible to confirm whether the forty bank accounts disclosed by the former CCN were the only accounts operated before the transition period as the CCN bankers, mainly Equity Bank, Cooperative Bank of Kenya, Kenya Commercial Bank and the National Bank of Kenya, did not respond to our requests for disclosure of all accounts previously held and also requiring them to confirm the balances in each account. The number of bank accounts varied from different lists presented for audit with some lists showing 40 or 41 and others 42.

Under-banking of revenue collected

Revenue records made available for audit revealed that during the period January 1 to June 30, 2013, a total of K Sh 5,511,732,231 was collected from the various sources of revenue, but only K Sh 5,258,849,088 was banked that caused under-banking of K Sh 252,883,143.

The audit also revealed that out of the total under-banked revenue, K Sh 29,021,813 was subsequently issued as IOU's to various officers while the balance of K Sh 223,861,330 represented checks cashed by county staff for various miscellaneous activities, such as purchase of goods and services and numerous consumable items.

It was also noted that during the period under review, cess income totaling K Sh 60,725,305 was collected in various divisions but only K Sh 57,889,995 was receipted at the cash office and banked, resulting in a difference of K Sh 2,835,310 not accounted for and banked.

Source: OAG 2013.

The Office of the Auditor General (OAG) had performed annual audits on a business-as-usual basis despite the landslide of changes in devolution, governance, and personnel and against the background of the stipulation of the Transition Act. Following this approach, the OAG reports designated the incoming officers and governing entities to be responsible for the takeover of the documents, accounts, and assets, even though no officers or entities were in power for handovers months after elections. Also, reliable asset registers had not existed before transition, neither at the national nor the local level, and establishing such registers requires years not weeks to complete. The OAG audit specialists found that by September 2013, several directives had not been followed (see box 6.2). It is important to note that asset takeover in the form of inventorying was still technically possible by the incoming officers and county governments, so making them responsible was still sensible.

Informal takeover and use of assets, 2013–18

NCCG—without formal takeover, inventorying, and valuation—from its inauguration started to use and develop assets in a business-as-usual manner, especially those that formed the material basis of local services to ensure uninterrupted provision of services. Other assets unrelated to services (for example, land) remained unaccounted and unattended, so many may be lost or encroached. The OAG 2014 report recommended that "the County Government should coordinate with the Transition Authority on the asset and liability take over." However, the research team has found no evidence that the TA had provided NCCG or any other county government guidance, documents, or templates on takeover that could have been used before and beyond the TA planned-completion of asset validation, verification, and audit.

NCCG has been using and developing most of the assets of the defunct local government since March 2013. Despite the unresolved issues discussed in a later section, NCCG has taken a pragmatic approach in using and developing the assets. The magnitude of new investments is very significant; compared with the inherited K Sh 86 billion in current assets (table 6.6) plus the unmeasured value of fixed assets, the county invested nearly K Sh 10 billion in new assets, continued some debt service, and repaid over K Sh 10 billion in debt between 2013 and 2018 (table 6.3). Thus, the clear takeover and valuation of the inherited assets remained unresolved, but the asset management became increasingly important for adequate protection and management of both the old and new assets. NCCG moved ahead with establishing an Asset Management Directorate (AMDR) in 2016 (the first such entity in Kenya) with mandates to facilitate the establishment of a reliable asset management framework, systems, and procedures. AMDR had made reasonable progress by 2018, including drafting an asset management policy, a strategy, a short-term plan, a concept and terms of reference (ToR) for hiring a firm to establish and populate a reliable initial asset register, and a concept for a computerized integrated asset management system.

AMDR became later a secretariat for the County Asset and Liability Committee (CALC) and has played a vital role in organizing and supporting the asset verification fieldwork under CALC. The implementation of the asset verification and validation program and the new elections in 2017 had delayed progress toward the goals set by AMDR and left asset management policy, strategy, and plans in draft form without approval by higher governing bodies of the newly elected county government.

NCCG has clear arrangements for managing the assets by service or functional entities (table 6.4), but the service provisions are diverse and often poorly performed without county-level strategy. The mandated units have been working since the inauguration of NCCG in 2013 and fulfilling many asset-management functions. However, building a reliable asset register or even an initial inventory

TABLE 6.4 **Nairobi City County asset management entities and their functions**

SERVICES OR FUNCTIONS THAT REQUIRE SPECIFIC ASSETS OWNED BY OR USED BY THE COUNTY	ASSET MANAGEMENT ENTITIES		
	COUNTY DEPARTMENTS RESPONSIBLE FOR THE RESPECTIVE SERVICES	COMPANY OR OTHER INDEPENDENT ENTITY OWNED BY THE COUNTY	PRIVATE SERVICE PROVIDER OR PRIVATE MANAGING ENTITY UNDER PPP
General administration			
Office buildings	Public Works	n.a.	n.a.
Urban services			
Roads and drainage	Roads, Public Works, and Transport	n.a.	n.a.
Public transport	Roads, Public Works, and Transport	n.a.	Private business companies
Water and wastewater lines, plants, and equipment	Environment, Energy, Water, and Natural Resources	Nairobi City Water and Sewerage Company	n.a.
Solid waste	Environment, Energy, Water, and Natural Resources	NCC budget entities	Private collector companies
Street lighting	Roads, Public Works, and Transport	n.a.	n.a.
Fire protection	County Security, Compliance, Fire, and Disaster Management	n.a.	n.a.
Police, crime prevention	n.a.	n.a.	n.a.
Environmental protection	Environment, Energy, Water, and Natural resources	n.a.	n.a.
Vehicle fleet	Roads, Public Works, and Transport	n.a.	n.a.
Social services			
Health	Health Services	n.a.	n.a.
Education	Education, Youth, Gender, Sports, and Culture	n.a.	n.a.
Culture and religion	Education, Youth, Gender, Sports, and Culture	n.a.	n.a.
Housing	Land, Urban Renewal, and Housing	n.a.	n.a.
Recreation and sport	Education, Youth, Gender, Sports, and Culture	n.a.	n.a.
Parks	Education, Youth, Gender, Sports, and Culture	n.a.	n.a.
Social welfare	Education, Youth, Gender, Sports, and Culture	n.a.	n.a.
Commercial services			
Parking	Commerce, Tourism, and Cooperative Sector	n.a.	n.a.
Markets and livestock sale yards	Commerce, Tourism, and Cooperative Sector	n.a.	n.a.
Commercial assets, shops, office rented	Commerce, Tourism, and Cooperative Sector	n.a.	n.a.
Agriculture, forests, fisheries	Food, Agriculture, and Forestry	n.a.	n.a.
Slaughterhouse	Commerce, Tourism, and Cooperative Sector	n.a.	n.a.
Land development	Land, Urban Renewal, and Housing	n.a.	n.a.
Local economic development	Finance and Economic Planning	n.a.	n.a.

Source: Nairobi City County Government website and field survey.
Note: n.a. = not applicable; NCC = Nairobi City County; PPP = public-private partnership.

remained to be done. The water- and sanitation-related assets are managed by the ISO 9001–certified Nairobi City Water and Sewerage Company (NCWSC), a legally independent utility that the NCC fully owns and leases most of the fixed assets to, although it has no reliable asset inventory either. One reason behind this lack is a complicated governance framework established for the water sector that combines watershed management, irrigation, and rural and urban water development. Water-sector assets and liabilities are under unclear and often disputed control by the Water Services Regulatory Board (WASREB) despite legal ownership by NCC as mandated in the Kenya Constitution 2010.

WASREB is a public state corporation established in March 2003 as part of the comprehensive reforms in the water sector. The mandate of the institution is to oversee the implementation of policies and strategies relating to the provision of water and sewerage services; mandates were redefined by the Water Act 2016. WASREB also regulates water and sewer tariffs that are supposed to cover the full cost of services, including operation, development, and debt service (see WASREB 2020). In practice, tariffs hardly cover the cost of operation, which undermines the solvency, strategic development, and asset management of water companies, including NCWSC. This underscores the urgency to complete the asset handover-takeover process from national to county entities and devolve tariff setting.

Asset takeover by the power of law, 2017

Gazette Notice no. 858 (Notice 858) transferred the assets and stipulated workout of liabilities of the defunct local governments by law on January 27, 2017, and set a framework for validation, verification, and valuation of the assets and liabilities by the counties via CALCs under the guidance of and control by the Intergovernmental Relations Technical Committee (IGRTC). Notice no. 2701 of March 24, 2017 (Notice 2701), reconfirms and replaces Notice no. 858 and rules that the unaudited inventories of assets and liabilities developed by the TA, which was closed in March 2017, serve as the basis and reference for the verification, validation, and valuation of the assets under CALCs' management.

According to IGRTC and TA files handed over to counties in 2017, NCC inherited assets worth K Sh 89 billion accounted in current assets (figure 6.3),

FIGURE 6.3

Nairobi City County and 47 counties combined inherited current asset and liabilities, March 2013

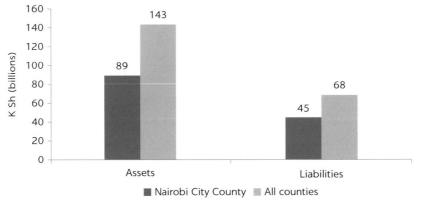

Source: IGRTC 2017.

K Sh 5.2 billion assets accounted under ongoing projects, and K Sh 45 billion in liabilities (measured by the TA as the 2013 estimated value, and therefore a symbolic number in 2017). The estimated values of inherited assets reflect largely the value of current assets as of 2013, since the TA did not estimate market values of the fixed assets such as land (about 653 parcels, of which 362 had an estimated area of 1,355 hectares), 831 buildings without an estimated book value, and 165 large machines, equipment, and plants. Infrastructure networks had not been even listed in the TA's preliminary asset inventory. Of these, the most problematic element is the missing land sizes and values, because of their presumed substantial wealth, which has substantially appreciated from 2013 to 2017. Thus, the verification and valuation of land is among the most urgent tasks the county faces.

NCC has a special status due to its size and share of assets; its current assets of K Sh 89 billion represented about 62 percent of the estimated combined current assets of the 47 counties. NCC total liabilities that amounted to K Sh 45 billion represented about 65 percent of total liabilities of 47 counties (figure 6.3). Therefore, good management of assets, timely completion of the asset takeover, resolution of disputed inherited assets and liabilities, and development of reliable asset registers with updated market valuation in NCC would substantially change the asset management picture of the entire country.

Progress by 2019

The NCC County Asset and Liability Committee (CALC) held its induction meeting on May 9, 2017. The committee had 14 steering members and eight appointed ("co-opted") members and assigned a secretariat (AMDR) to consolidate and submit report(s) as necessary. The committee adopted working principles and processes, and its early achievements included the following:

- Developed a work plan with milestones to be accomplished and set aside resources, both financial and nonfinancial, required for the asset verification and inventory
- Identified 80 team members within the county with relevant technical skills to help the committee identify, record, and verify assets and liabilities within their sectors
- Obtained the Transitional Authority's record of inventory from IGRTC for use as the basis for the verification exercise
- Developed data capture methodology at the sector level
- Developed templates for data collection with reference to IGRTC guidelines
- Embarked on compiling lists of the various assets and liabilities that existed as of March 27, 2013, and comparing them with inventory captured in the TA report

CALC was mandated to lead and undertake the verification exercise, but it delegated many tasks to AMDR, which worked in collaboration with the NCCG secretariat to form the asset identification and verification teams for seven work clusters: (1) land and buildings; (2) plant, machinery, and equipment; (3) vehicles; (4) projects or works in progress; (5) furniture and fittings; (6) computers, electronics, and electronic equipment; and (7) current assets, liabilities, and investments. CALC teams started fieldwork in May 2017 and completed the identification, verification, and validation work by early November; the CALC final report was drafted and sent to IGRTC at the end of November 2017. The results presented below are from the NCC CALC report 2017 and cross-checked with the IGRTC summary report (IGRTC 2018).

The report represents a great improvement in information compared with the TA preliminary inventories, but it remained incomplete; for instance, it states that "the land inventory is about 70 percent complete" (NCC CALC 2017, 13). Nevertheless, it provides a reasonable basis for further development of a reliable asset database and management system. The report not only identifies assets but points to numerous gaps, weaknesses, and a need for follow-up actions to be completed to resolve outstanding issues and eventually achieve a reasonably clear asset and liability inventory.

The CALC report sent to IGRTC in November 2017 was considered final even though the verification and validation was not fully completed due to time constraints. Some information in the report was based on desk review instead of field survey. There was still a need to verify that all assets that had documents, for example titles and logbooks, existed; such verification remained incomplete. Upon completion of the report, the CALC secretariat passed it on to the chairman of CALC, who signed it together with the two CALC secretaries: the internal auditor from NCCG and the external auditor from the National Treasury. The report was then submitted to IGRTC.

By the time the report was ready, CALC was inactive in the wake of the upcoming local government elections, after which a landslide replacement of local officers made CALC dysfunctional, because most former members left office. The 600-page CALC report included a statement dated November 2017 that reads: "The CALC committee has not reconvened since July 2017 to receive updates and deliberate on the way forward" (NCC CALC 2017, 11). The incoming NCC government has not reinstated CALC since November 2017.

IGRTC has collected, reviewed, and streamlined all CALC reports and prepared a consolidated national report on asset takeover and verification discussed in part I (IGRTC 2018). IGRTC returned the revised and reviewed report to each county and requested the governors' follow-up actions. NCCG had not formally discussed the CALC report received from IGRTC until late 2019; but important steps toward establishing a reliable asset management system can be considered adequate follow-up actions. Details will be discussed in the following sections. First, we summarize NCCG's specific findings and experiences in CALC procedures by main asset classes.

Land and buildings

Land. The teams assigned to verify land parcels and buildings did heroic fieldwork. They identified 993 land parcels (table 6.5), of which 97 percent had a land record or other identification numbers and 82 percent had estimated land areas. (Interestingly, neither the national landmark Uhuru Park nor City Stadium has a land record or other identification numbers.) The CALC team identified 50 percent more parcels and two-and-a-half times more estimated land area (3,364 hectares versus 1,355 hectares) than the TA inventory, in part, because the TA excluded an inventory of assets managed by NCWSC, while NCCG included the latter as a rightful owner.

About two-thirds of land is under NCWSC, but references suggest that the company leases from NCC instead of owning the land and buildings. These results strongly underscore the importance of the internal identification and verification of assets and also provide a good basis for future development of a reliable asset database, especially important for land and buildings. It also underscores the importance of valuation of land that could and should play a

TABLE 6.5 **Nairobi City County land and buildings from the identification, verification, and validation process**

	NCC NUMBER	NCWSC NUMBER	TOTAL	
			NUMBER	PORTION OF TOTAL (%)
Land				
Total parcels of land	347	646	993	100
With LR numbers	343	624	967	97
With estimated area	229	581	810	82
Estimated area (hectares)	1,192	2,172	3,364	n.a.
Buildings				
Total number of buildings	2,039	—	2,039	100
With LR numbers	1,273	—	1,273	62
With plinth areas	417	—	417	20

Source: NCC CALC 2017.
Note: — = not available; LR = land registration; n.a. = not applicable; NCC = Nairobi City County; NCWSC = Nairobi City Water and Sewerage Company.

vital role in forming and financing a long-term development strategy and medium-term development and asset management plans for the NCCG.

The CALC report does not include the surveyed size of land, which would have required much greater effort and longer time to obtain; both were unavailable for the CALC teams. The report also remained silent on the issue of encroachments or disputed lands, aside from flagging that the Department of Defense (DoD) had taken over 900 hectares of land decades ago without paying compensation to the defunct CCN. The CALC team included among current assets the size and (present market) value of this land in the report as one of the largest receivable items among current assets, with a disputed NCCG estimate of K Sh 33 billion.

Buildings. The CALC team identified 2,039 building as opposed to the 831 in the TA inventory (table 6.5). However, several of the building line items in the list include complexes with multiple buildings, so the effective number of buildings is much greater than the reported number. For instance, one line item includes 26 units of one-bedroom flats, 36 units of two-bedroom flats, and 16 units of three-bedroom flats (with a TA-registered size of *4.5 square feet total* [sic]).

The CALC report states that the team did not estimate the size of the buildings, but instead took the estimates from the TA inventory and with that presented size estimates of 20 percent of the identified buildings. Apparent huge numeric errors in estimated plinth areas exemplified by the line item just presented indicate the questionable quality of the TA reports; thus, it is hard to imagine how and why the CALC team simply borrowed the estimated plinth areas from TA files instead of using some simple measurement methodology.

The CALC team should have done a much better job. Even with very rough calculations made at the field visits by simply asking tenants or making simple measures of one one-bedroom model flat and projecting sizes for similar two- or three-bedroom units, the estimated total plinth area would have been much better. Interestingly, only 62 percent of the buildings have land identification or any other registration numbers as opposed to the 97 percent of land reported to be identified with such numbers. One might assume that the building has a land registry number based on the host land-plot, but this seems to be not a practice in Nairobi, or it could be a shortcoming of the verification process and possibly a lack of coordination across land and buildings teams.

For the first time, NCCG reported a summary fixed-asset register in 2018 in accounting modality that reflects book values on June 30, 2018 (table 6.6). This is a move in a good direction, but the table reflects some shortcomings: (1) gross book values are accounted without amortization, but good asset registers should reflect depreciation of assets regardless of whether or not the county follows cash-based accounting principles in bookkeeping and financial reports; (2) the total value of fixed assets reported is nearly twice the total value reported as the combined value of investments in fixed assets since devolution in financial reports (see table 6.3); and (3) no number of buildings or structures has been reported, so it is unclear how this group of assets relates to the assets verified and reported in the CALC report.

Furthermore, projects in progress in 2013 and subsequently finished presumably (and rightly) have been included in this financial report, but the reported values of inherited work-in-progress projects were much lower, and many were canceled (table 6.7). In short, consistency within and across financial reports should be revised and improved.

Projects. NCC inherited 989 projects with the value of K Sh 5.2 billion. These include infrastructure investments approved and/or ongoing as of March 2013. Table 6.7 summarizes the status of these projects retrospectively in late 2017. About 60 percent of these projects (K Sh 3.1 billion) had been completed by the time of CALC verification, and 15 percent (K Sh 0.8 billion) were still ongoing. It remains unclear but is likely that the respective assets, many of them buildings and structures, are accounted for also among the verified inherited assets, which could result in double accounting. About 24 percent of projects never started or were abandoned, suspended, or terminated

TABLE 6.6 Nairobi City County fixed asset register summary, June 30, 2018

K Sh (millions)

	HISTORICAL COST 6/30/2017	ADDITIONS IN FY 2017/18	DISPOSAL IN FY 2017/18	HISTORICAL COST 6/30/2018
Land not yet valued	—	—	—	—
Buildings and structures	4,474	633	0	5,107
Transport equipment	1,019	0	0	1,019
Office equipment, furniture, fittings	741	101	0	842
Information and communication technology equipment, software, others	111	0	0	111
Other machinery and equipment	453	0	0	453
Heritage and cultural assets	112	0	0	112
Intangible assets	66	0	0	66
Biological assets	30	5	0	35
Infrastructure	8,535	697	0	9,233
Work in progress	2,827	0	0	2,827
Total in register	**18,369**	**1,436**	**0**	**19,805**
Total fixed assets acquired after devolution	—	1,436	—	9,637

Source: OAG 2018.
Note: — = not available; FY = fiscal year.

TABLE 6.7 **Nairobi City County inherited projects, 2013**

STATUS	NUMBER	VALUE (K SH, MILLIONS)	SHARE OF TOTAL (%)
Complete	719	3,167	60.3
Not started	141	915	17.4
Ongoing	70	818	15.6
Unspecified	24	91	1.7
Stalled	22	99	1.9
Abandoned	7	34	0.6
Terminated	6	131	2.5
Total	**989**	**5,254**	**100.0**

Source: NCC CALC 2017.

TABLE 6.8 **Nairobi City County summary of inherited liabilities, 2013 and 2018**
K Sh (millions)

	BANK LOANS	EMOLUMENTS	STATUTORY DEDUCTIONS	OTHER CREDITORS	LEGAL FEES	TOTAL
As of 2013, TA report	28,440	3,454	6,500	3,815	1,191	43,400
As of 2013, CALC 2017	28,214	3,454	6,500	3,815	1,191	43,174
Value June 30, 2018	19,143	134.6	51,901	11,515	1,191	83,885
Total share in 2013 (%)	65.5	8.0	15.0	8.8	2.7	100.0
Total share in 2018 (%)	22.8	0.2	61.9	13.7	1.4	100.0

Sources: NCC CALC 2017; OAG 2018.
Note: CALC = County Asset and Liability Committee; TA = Transition Authority.

subsequently without records about what had happened to the incomplete structures and the funds set aside. It is also unclear how the CALC team, during verification, managed to segregate assets developed or acquired after 2013 (K Sh 10 billion) and the inherited assets without existing asset registers.

Inherited current liabilities and current assets

The CALC team faced major challenges verifying inherited liabilities, because some liabilities, such as the on-lent water loans and housing guaranties, are historical in nature and some date back to the 1970s and 1980s, pending and debated without resolution for decades (table 6.8). The CALC team had only capacities limited to listing liabilities, seeking and updating explanations, and suggesting or urging follow-up actions; effective workout of historical liabilities was far beyond the CALC competency and time frame. The CALC report stated that little information and supporting documents were available on debts inherited from the defunct CCN, especially on statutory creditors, on-lent water loans, and government guarantees that date back to the 1970s that were acquired to finance the water infrastructure and the Umoja II housing scheme.

NCC inherited K Sh 43.4 billion in liabilities (table 6.8) as of March 2013. These numbers are much higher today than TA estimates because of accumulated interest and penalties and the liabilities of NCWSC. The two big items—loans (22.8 percent of the total in 2018) and unpaid statutory deductions (61.9 percent of the total)—contain many long-disputed and unresolved items that will need workout with guidance and cooperation by the National Treasury and other national government entities. The disputed statutory deductions are burning issues; they represented 15 percent of total inherited liabilities in 2013 and nearly 62 percent in 2018. For instance, among statutory deductions, NCC inherited K Sh 3.6 billion deductions unpaid to the Local Authorities Pension Trust of the National Social Security Fund (LAPTRUST), which keeps accounting a 1.25 percent penalty compounded monthly that is a 16 percent penalty annually. The numbers suggest that this single claim grew from K Sh 3.6 billion in 2013 to K Sh 7.6 billion by 2018. NCCG settled emoluments and continued servicing one loan, thus reducing inherited emoluments liabilities by over K Sh 3 billion, down to K Sh 135 million.

Inherited loan portfolio. Inherited loans are largely problematic and the portfolio has not been served since 2013 or even before (table 6.9). These loans include a government-guaranteed housing loan (1985), an on-lent foreign water loan (2004), and a loan from the defunct Local Government Authority. The CALC team concluded that these loans were not being served and the team failed to substantiate them because, as the report reads, "Loan agreements were not available and NCCG requested the National Treasury to provide copies of respective loan agreements." (NCC CALC 2017, 43) The disputed loans amount to K Sh 22.1 billion, or 78.5 percent of total bank debts. Loan agreements of such sizable loans should have been found. The National Treasury or the Ministry of Finance do have copies of these loan agreements, especially those guaranteed and being served by the national government as guarantor. Further, the National Treasury accounts the paid debt service as a debt of CCN, so the current value of these debts is likely much greater than the historical 2013 values. A pragmatic resolution of these issues is urgent and extremely important, especially because the NCC financial capacity does not allow NCCG to resume this debt service while repaying the guarantee payments to the National Treasury.

Unpaid emoluments. Representing about 8 percent of total liabilities, unpaid emoluments largely have been worked out and paid to former staff and retirees of the defunct CCN. This is a substantial amount and part of the reason that NCC reported skyrocketed operation and maintenance costs in 2015; but also, this is an apparent misclassification of expenses because repayment of overdue emoluments was debt service, not cost of operation.

Unpaid statutory deductions. These include the Kenya Revenue Authority, National Social Security fund, LAPTRUST, and Local Authorities Providence Fund (LAPFUND) and represent the second-largest liability at K Sh 6.5 billion

TABLE 6.9 **Nairobi City County net bank debts, November 2017, based on 2013 values**

	K Sh (MILLIONS)	SHARE OF TOTAL (%)
Loan being served uninterrupted	3,666	13.0
Loan agreements not obtained, loan not served	22,144	78.5
Of which foreign loans	15,328	54.3
Loans fully repaid	2,181	7.7
Loans the water company borrowed	223	0.8
Total outstanding bank debts	28,214	100.0
Net bank debts, November 2017, based on 2013 values	26,032	92.3

Source: NCC CALC 2017.

(or 15 percent of total). They are a highly problematic group of liabilities because many of these are not only historical debts but also have triggered huge penalties. The CALC team stated, "Statutory creditors charge high interest and penalties in accordance with the Section 53 of the RBA Act Cap 197 with LAPTRUST charging interest at 1.25 percent per month (16 percent per annum compounded). Since the debt is historical in nature the debt has continued to grow even when the county remits statutory payments as at when the salary is paid. The county initiated discussions with some of the statutory creditors but little progress has been made because statutory creditors charge high interest rates and penalties" (NCC CALC 2017).

Other creditors. NCC inherited claims from suppliers of goods and services in the magnitude of K Sh 3.8 billion (or 8.8 percent of total) as of 2013. The NCC CALC (2017) report concludes that about a tenth of these claims have been paid subsequently. Nearly half the claims are verified and submitted to the Finance Department for further processing, and the rest need further verification. The report is silent about whether the creditors have demanded accrued interest, and thus if the actual amount of these debts is much larger than the verified 2013 amounts. But amounts paid out have inflated the current expenditure budget of NCC since 2015.

Progress in fiscal year 2018/19. In 2018, NCCG launched a campaign to review and settle liabilities of other creditors, asking them to submit their claims with supporting documentation, and continued workout discussions with statutory creditors. This campaign managed to reduce statutory deduction liabilities by K Sh 12 billion and commercial liabilities by K Sh 6 billion by June 2019 (NCCG 2019). The NCC continues debt service on a term loan from Equity Bank (now KCB Bank) with K Sh 3.7 billion in outstanding principal. NCCG has repaid the short-term liquidity (working capital) loans of K Sh 2.2 billion. Thus, the net debt from TA inventory is about K Sh 26 billion, but this amount excludes the principal and interest repaid by the National Treasury in the last 4 to 10 years.

Inherited current assets

The CALC team first verified the current assets listed in the TA inventory with the total value of K Sh 89 billion as of 2013. However, the team found that the TA report excluded the current assets of the NCWSC accounts with a value of K Sh 10.5 billion. In addition, the team found that the NCC inherited from the defunct CCN the shares of NCWSC with the estimated current value of the company of K Sh 22 billion as investments. This estimate may need further scrutiny (as will be discussed), and it is not a current asset. Table 6.10 summarizes the CALC list of current assets with the grand total value of K Sh 121.6 billion (of which K Sh 99.6 billion can consistently be considered as current assets). The total volume of current assets is about three times the value of total current liabilities (figure 6.4). However, most of these current assets were accounted with inflated value and thus will be hard to mobilize. Nonetheless, it is an achievement of the CALC team to account and list financial assets in a solid report that supports follow-up actions.

Property rates. These account for nearly half of the total current assets, and the team found an additional K Sh 3.2 billion in tax arrears in the accounting system (Local Authorities Integrated Financial Operations Management System) with no explanation or supporting documents. Staff members assume that these represent late payment penalties. One critical question the NCCG should address is the real present value of the property rate arrears. A vital piece of information would be the age distribution of these arrears; segregation of the historical

TABLE 6.10 **Nairobi City County current assets, March 2013**

	K Sh (MILLIONS)	SHARE OF TOTAL (%)
Rates (property tax)	53,643	44.1
Business permits	1,324	1.1
Kenya Power	583	0.5
Rents and others	607	0.5
NCWSC fee arrears	9,698	8.0
NCWSC others	773	0.6
DoD land price	33,000	27.1
NCWSC ownership shares	22,000	18.1
Total	**121,628**	**100.0**

Source: NCC CALC 2017.
Note: DoD = Department of Defense; NCWSC = Nairobi City Water and Sewerage Company.

FIGURE 6.4

Nairobi City County components of current assets and liabilities, March 2013

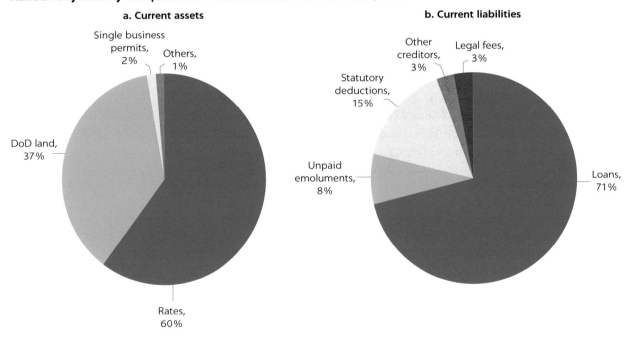

a. Current assets

b. Current liabilities

Source: IGRTC 2017.
Note: DoD = Department of Defense.

arrears that have been claimed over the previous five years and the short- to medium-term arrears would improve the reality of this picture.

The claims over five years might need to be written off (a practice in some countries) or accounted for with a high discount rate. Furthermore, the next step should be to adopt a pragmatic strategy for collecting these arrears in an exercise separate from the collection of the regular annual property rates. It is wise to explore legal possibilities to attach the properties of delinquent owners to motivate them to pay tax arrears. As part of the property revaluation and setting of new property tax rates, NCCG plans to write off old property tax arrears after 2020.

This is a good approach to improve the clarity and reality of receivables but will obviously not generate revenue.

Fee arrears. The same issues should be addressed regarding the arrears on business permits, rents, and other fee arrears. Financial reports show low and stagnant collection of rents and fees that suggest collecting arrears from these sources might be extremely difficult. A thorough revision of rental and lease contracts would be an urgent first step to verify and collect fee arrears on rented and leased NCC properties.

Kenya Power. There is an ongoing dispute with Kenya Power (KPLC) about the unpaid right-of-way charges (also known as "wayleave debt") of about K Sh 583 million. The CALC team concluded, "The wayleave debt has continued to grow over time. A case is currently pending in court since KPLC has not been willing to remit monies owed."

NCWSC receivables. The CALC team has included the fee receivables of K Sh 10.3 billion accumulated before March 2013 as a part of the inherited water company receivables. Accounting regulations would not require NCC to account expenditures, revenues, or receivables of an independent subordinated entity like NCWSC. In contrast, NCC has inherited land, buildings, and overdue liabilities and contingent liabilities as the current sole owner of the company. NCC leases out the lands, buildings, and some equipment to the company, but there is no agreement that would authorize NCC to secure the asset lease with stream of revenues or collectibles of the NCWSC. Nonetheless, estimating the present value of NCWSC's receivables (water bill arrears) in the manner noted earlier in the "property rates" paragraph and adopting and urgently implementing a pragmatic plan to help NCWSC collect these arrears would be steps in a good direction and good asset management practice. The CALC team stated that a substantial albeit unspecified part of water fee arrears is due from entities of the national government; these amounts can be settled against claims by national government entities.

DoD land price. The CALC team accounted K Sh 33 billion as current assets based on an estimated (2013) value as demanded compensation for the DoD-occupied land. The defunct CCN acquired through a market cash transaction a huge parcel of land in 1963 for housing schemes. DoD has occupied a roughly 900-hectare section of that land, and an agreement was reached in 1997 that the DoD would become rightful holder of the land if it pays compensation. DoD has never paid, and CCN initiated a court procedure in 2012, during which an interministerial meeting was held to craft an out-of-court agreement. Such an agreement has not been reached. The CALC report accounted the 2013 value estimated by a certified valuer and concluded, "The debt is still subject to dispute and an amicable solution with the national government needs to be sought" (NCC CALC 2017, 43). One can say this is a valid claim and a reasonable account of current assets, but realization requires concerted actions by NCCG and respective ministries, maybe guided by the National Treasury.

NCWSC ownership shares. The CALC team has included in the list of current assets as investments the inherited initial equity shares the CCN invested when it established the water company as a sole owner. This investment is undoubtedly an inherited asset of the NCC and should be accounted in the balance sheet and in an asset register as a long-term financial asset. In short, it is not a current asset, which typically includes categories such as marketable securities and short-term investments that can be easily liquidated, that is, turned to money. Another issue with this item in the CALC list is that the nominal value of the shares is K Sh 100,000, while the CALC team estimated "the depreciated book value of the company as of 2017 as K Sh 22 billion" (NCC CALC 2017, 55). These figures may or may not be in line with the company's balance sheet, since other references suggest that the company has been leasing the assets from CCN then NCC and may have only a small owner's equity share in the balance sheet. The balance sheet of NCWSC shows K Sh 7 billion total assets in 2019 (OAG 2019).

Rents and other receivables inherited. These represent a relatively small but still significant (K Sh 2.0 billion) amount. The CALC team found that most of these are unrecoverable, such as the single business permits, hospital debt, and loading-zone rent, because these are in the books of the Finance Department, but no evidence or documentation was found about the origin, timing, and possible subsequent payments. One way the county may address these receivables could be to auction the collection to the best offer and write down most of these receivables. But such an auction approach would also need a minimal amount of reasonable documentation and certainly approval by OAG.

Other assets

The CALC teams also verified other assets, albeit many with only symbolic value after six or more years of use. Nonetheless, clear inventorying is a best practice regardless of value. These include motor vehicles, plants and machinery, computers and accessories, and furniture and fittings.

Motor vehicles. The CALC team managed to verify the inventory of 329 motor vehicles with a K Sh 746 million book value in 2013. (About 80 percent of vehicles had book value, but the report is unclear if they were gross or net book values.) The team noted that about 40 percent of the details were missing in the TA inventory but successfully populated the template to about 90 percent accuracy with the details available from logbooks and institutional memory. The team also captured details of 32 vehicles that were leased out and handed over to NCWSC. These vehicles were missing from the IGRTC inventory. The information on the logbooks confirmed that all 32 vehicles used to be owned by the defunct CCN; these had no registered book value.

Logbooks for about 100 vehicles were not available; some had either been donated by the national government or donors or they were registered under projects. It is hard to understand why officers felt that logbooks were not needed for such donated vehicles. The CALC team noted that officers could not identify all the vehicles because the vehicles were in use for their normal operations the day of verification. Physical identification of engine and chassis numbers proved impossible as most of these had faded or their locations were unknown. This lack of documentation indicates poor cooperation between the CALC team and the field staff of service units.

Plants and machinery. The CALC report does not discuss plants and machinery. It simply presents a summary table that includes over 3,000 items, mostly machinery and equipment from road-grinders to tablespoons, without clusters. Plants and structures are listed among buildings without distinctions in the annex table on buildings. The list, however, includes most of the computers, electronic tools, and accessories found. The list does not include estimated or book value, since these have never been inventoried before nor listed in logbooks. Also, most of them have only symbolic value after six years of use or longer. Creating a structured inventory of high-value machinery and equipment would be an important step toward a consistent asset management.

Computers and accessories. The teams faced great difficulties in locating and inventorying computers and accessories. Among other challenges, there are 26 outpost stations comprising subcounty offices, hospitals, and other satellite offices where identification was not carried out due to dispersed geographical location and limited time. During data validation, inconsistencies occurred in TA data that constrained verification. The team reported that "80 percent of the records provided by TA did not match with data collected" (NCC CALC 2017, 62). An inability to determine fair values results from lack of valuation reports on computer electronics and accessories and an inability to match purchase records with specific assets. There probably were errors in data capture, especially missing device serial numbers, a critical unique asset identifier. Due to time constraints, the teams were unable to identify and review the asset disposal register and failed to comment or prove that such registers exist in service sectors.

Furniture and fittings. Verifying inherited furniture back from a distance of four and more years was a mission impossible, mainly because furniture has a relatively short span of useful life; thus, many represented a symbolic value. Since the inception of the county government, considerable modification and alterations of offices has happened where the furniture and fittings had been located; they were captured in the TA report. Some of these items had been moved while others had been damaged during movement and others had become obsolete over time. Since they did not have distinct markings, it was difficult to trace them for identification, verification, and validation. As a result, the team decided to accept the TA's report on these items. It is worth noting, however, that the accessories and furniture represent a minor value as compared with land, buildings, and equipment. NCCG could request a simple annual inventorying of furniture and accessories by the staff or respective departments and offices. In turn NCCG could focus more on verifying and safeguarding high-value items (land, buildings, and plants, for example a hectare of land worth more than K Sh 33 billion estimated in DoD claims).

MANAGING FINANCIAL ASSETS AND LIABILITIES

Managing financial assets and liabilities jointly is a natural part of strategic asset and liability management (ALM) as discussed in part I. Financial and nonfinancial assets are transient forms of each other, so both are vital for healthy management of cities (Freire and Kopanyi 2018). However, there are specific characteristics and challenges in managing financial assets and liabilities. Detailed data obtained from NCC and from a report of the Australian Capital Territory (ACT) offer a unique opportunity to analyze and demonstrate the fundamental differences between these two local government entities. ACT has a decent financial asset and liability portfolio while NCC has a transitional one, thus these two cases exemplify both good and poor management of assets and liabilities and show NCC direction for improvements. We have presented a short summary of these issues in chapter 3, but here we provide more detailed analysis for readers who are specifically interested in the NCC.

Strategic asset management. At a strategic level, cities should establish two critical balances on financial assets and liabilities: (1) net debt, the difference between the sum of all financial assets and the sum of debt plus other direct financial liabilities, and (2) net liabilities, the difference between the sum of all financial assets and debt plus other direct and quantified contingent liabilities. Net liabilities often appear much greater than net debt (ACT 2018) because they include contingent liabilities with uncertain outcomes. One major similarity between NCC and ACT is that both inherited immense direct and contingent liabilities, for which, however, ACT has reacted strategically while NCC still needs to find strategic responses.

Liquidity management. Financial ALM also includes and plays a pivotal role in liquidity management, because financial assets and liabilities are more liquid than fixed assets and thus can and should be used in liquidity management. Finance departments often have a team assigned to liquidity management that also handles risk management as part of ALM. These are common teams, and NCCG appointed such a team a few years ago. Cities may deposit the access cash daily, not only because they cannot legally keep large sums in vaults, but mainly to maximize overnight interest revenues via competitive bidding across banks. Likewise, financial assets are used to bridge gaps between revenue inflows and outflows to ensure timely payment of due liabilities. Timely payment is not a well-obeyed principle in developing countries where ALM and liquidity management are poor and liquid financial assets (cash and financial investments) are miniscule, so invoices often land in drawers of mayors or chief financial officers to wait until cash inflow enables the city to pay the due liabilities. This might change when Kenya adopts accrual-based accounting.

Financial assets. Financial assets broadly include investment in public entities, cash deposits, advances paid, financial investments and loans, and receivables (for example, uncollected fees and taxes). These values are found in cities' financial reports in both the developing and developed world, although cities in the developing world may keep and publish poor or no reports on financial assets. Books show great differences across these two groups of cities in terms of the composition and real present value of the financial assets, which impacts the quality of the ALM. Comparing the case of Australian Capital Territory (ACT 2018) and NCC (both are local governments) provides interesting lessons on financial assets and liabilities (figure 6.5).

FIGURE 6.5

Composition of financial assets of Nairobi City County, 2017, and Australian Capital Territory, 2018

Percent of total financial assets

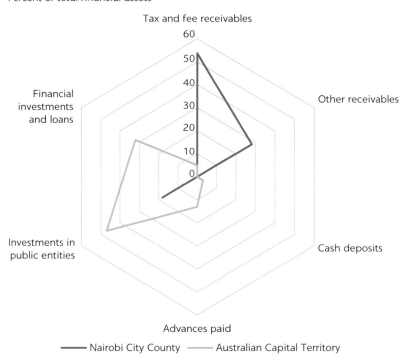

Sources: ACT 2018; NCC CALC 2017.

Large differences. Figure 6.5 shows important differences in the composition of financial assets in NCC and ACT. First, the most general difference is that ACT financial assets are well recorded in books and, although this is not visible in the figure, they are well performing. In contrast, NCC has inherited its financial assets from the defunct local government as part of a devolution program, and the value of those assets have not been updated, which means they can be larger or smaller than the historical book value. For instance, a substantial volume of uncollected taxes and fees has accumulated since devolution, but that value has not been included in this figure. Other receivables are zero in ACT but represent 20 percent of NCC revenues and include disputed revenues from various transactions between NCC and national government entities. This is common in developing countries, where national government entities are reluctant to pay fair compensation for assets they have taken over from cities. Finally, experiences suggest that the NCC's composition of financial assets is more common in the developing world.

Tax and fee receivables. Figure 6.5 also shows that ACT has a healthy 5 percent receivables in taxes and fees while about 60 percent of NCC's financial assets are uncollected taxes and fees that are legally accounted as receivables. They were enormous for NCC in the 2016/17 fiscal year, twice as much as the total budget. Such a situation is common in the developing world, since cities often have large amounts of uncollected taxes and fees, most without good records or databases. This is like a huge snowball that is rolling and growing beyond control. NCCG needs to assess the real value of these receivables and develop a workout strategy, because a substantial part of these collectibles is so old that it cannot be realistically collected, so it would be best to write them off the balance sheet. Kampala city had a similar high volume of uncollected fees and taxes in the early 2000s but managed to collect or work out the bulk of them in a five-year concerted recovery program (Kopanyi and Franzsen 2018).

Investments in public entities. Investments in public entities are comparably realistic and active in both ACT and NCC. NCC has only one major investment, in the legally independent NCWSC, which works well. In contrast, ACT owns several public utilities, a common way to manage public services effectively. Some utilities are in public-private partnerships (PPPs) with well-accounted contingent liabilities (ACT 2018).

Financial investments. NCC has no inherited financial investments, in contrast to the healthy 30 percent financial investments in the ACT financial assets portfolio. The latter underscores the vital role financial investments play in ALM in well-managed cities. For instance, ACT regularly issues bonds, and the proceeds are immediately invested in secure financial investments (for example, treasury bills) to save the money received in bulk. Proceeds are then used gradually, over two to three years, in line with the progress on the associated infrastructure development. Likewise, ACT is building a substantial reserve fund, to be able to face the large, inherited, unfunded contingent liability on pension and termination benefits (generated by regulatory changes). ACT deposits money in a special fund to gradually extinguish the unfunded liability by 2030 (ACT 2018). This is a great example of a strategic way of thinking and strategic ALM. Besides, ACT accounts shareholdings in commercial entities, utilities, or other PPPs as financial investments, some with corresponding well-accounted contingent liabilities.

Financial liabilities. Financial liabilities in a broad sense are composed of debts such as loans, bonds, due payables, advances received, and contingent liabilities such as guarantees, subsidy commitments (for example, a city pays providers US$20 per each new water connection and adds US$1.50 to each sold metro ticket and US$0.75 to each cubic meter of water billed and collected), and very often labor- and pension-related contingent liabilities. Financial liabilities are moving targets since they tend to change day to day by payments of due amounts, expiration of old accounts, or committing new liabilities.

Experience suggests that cities in developing and emerging economies should refrain from issuing bonds in or borrowing from international markets, especially in the long term (15–20 years), because they do not have revenues in foreign currencies, nor do they have the capacity to hedge against huge contingent liabilities of foreign exchange risks. This is a vital issue in managing financial liabilities.

In short, managing financial liabilities is part of prudent financial management, ALM, and liquidity management. Best ALM practices include provisioning of some specific contingent liabilities like guarantees provided or pension liabilities. Comparing the financial liabilities portfolios of ACT and NCC again helps draw important lessons on financial liabilities in developed and developing countries (see figure 6.6).

Debts. Debts include loans, bonds, or short-term instruments such as overdrafts. Debts are substantial in both NCC and ACT, and they are natural parts of the local government business. However, there are remarkable differences in these two structures. Inherited NCC debt is quite large (65 percent of the total inherited liabilities) and sizable (about 150 percent of the total budget of the 2016/17 fiscal year). Furthermore, about three-quarters of the loans were borrowed with national government guarantees from international donors and are nonperforming, some for over a decade. This means that the National Treasury services NCC's debt, committed before and after devolution. However, the treasury (not NCCG) accounts these guarantee payments as liabilities against NCC

FIGURE 6.6

Composition of financial liabilities of Nairobi City County, 2017, and Australian Capital Territory, 2018

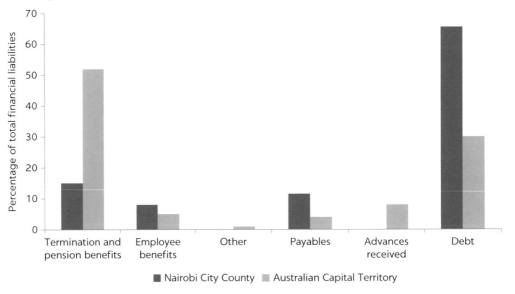

Sources: ACT 2018; NCC CALC 2017.

that are not reflected in the NCC figures. This means that the present value of debt liabilities is much greater than the reported nominal value. In contrast, ACT loans are well accounted, professionally managed, and served in a timely manner. This is evidenced by the fact that ACT maintains a AAA long-term credit rating (ACT 2018).

Termination and pension benefits. These often are regulated by national law and often lead cities into difficult situations both in developed and developing countries (Grubišić, Nušinović, and Roje 2009; Holder 1998; Peskin 2001). The reason is that cities tend to address these labor liabilities as secondary to more urgent payments, such as wages, electricity, or fuel. Another reason is that these liabilities are less visible and do not cause immediate harm if transfer of the due amounts is delayed sometimes for years. This is particularly compelling when the cities manage the respective pension funds themselves (called a "superannuation fund" in Australia). Another mistreatment of these funds, which are also off-budget, is that cities may transfer money back to the budget to prevent liquidity crises or even for fraudulent purposes and fail to return the money later. Such a case happened in Kampala in the early 2000s (Kopanyi and Franzsen 2018).

Deferred payments to national pension funds. In many countries, cities must pay labor- and pension-related contributions into national or sectoral pension funds but suspend such due payments if money falls short, despite high-interest penalties and perpetual warnings. This was the case of the CCN predecessor local government of NCC. There are often tacit agreements between the funds and the cities, in part because the fund managers are aware of how difficult it is to enforce these payments, but also they may expect that the national government will eventually bail out the cities instead of letting them go bankrupt.

Pension liabilities. NCC, as previously discussed, has inherited a sizable volume (about 15 percent of total inherited liabilities) of overdue liabilities on pension funds since predecessors failed to transfer statutory deductions to national pension funds (for example, LAPFUND and LAPTRUST). The amount is not only sizable but is growing daily at a 15–35 percent annual rate of penalties since devolution in 2013. The NCC's liability is overdue and thus no longer contingent but direct debt. In contrast, the ACT inherited a gigantic volume of contingent liabilities due to the regulatory changes that moved the pension benefit system from a pay-as-you-go system to a defined benefit scheme in Australia in 2005, although employees who were in the earlier system must be paid out from the old scheme.

The good aspect of this is that ACT clearly calculated this contingent liability based on the number of employees and their employment profiles and adopted a long-term plan to gradually extinguish this contingent liability by paying in a timely manner and fairly the due benefits at the day of retirement, but also gradually replenishing a special fund that would back the contingent liability fully by 2030. A lesson also worth noting is that such big liabilities require both strategic decisions and time to work out. Thus, figure 6.6 reflects two very different situations regarding termination and pension benefits. Finally, the ACT liabilities are gigantic but under control, while the NCC liabilities are out of control; they became direct payables with no clear work-out plan.

CHALLENGES NCC CALC FACED DURING VERIFICATION AND VALIDATION OF INHERITED ASSETS AND LIABILITIES IN 2017

In their report, the CALC teams highlighted major challenges they faced during the verification process. Many of these are mentioned in the previous sections, but following is a summary of some critical challenges and impediments that hampered and lowered the quality of the verification and the report.

- The field-team members were not trained properly on how to carry out the verification and validation exercise. As a result, their performance was lower than expected; some provided inconsistent information to the CALC secretariat and prepared likewise inconsistent reports with different length, scopes, and quality.
- Severe shortages of transport options and fuel hampered fieldwork. There was a transport hitch due to a grave shortage of vehicles for CALC. When they were available there was no fuel for days. (Some vehicles were made available only because there was no fuel for regular users.)
- The officers who worked in verification field-teams were not released from their normal duties, so they had limited energy and time for and attention to verification.
- Severe shortages of stationery and office equipment such as cameras, computers, laptops, printers, and scanners hampered the verification work during both the back-office and field stages.
- CALC did not reconvene after July 2017 and hence was not accessible to receive updates or advise on the way forward.
- Political uncertainty and demonstrations hampered fieldwork during the election campaign and postelection period in July–November 2017 (the peak of the asset verification period).

NCCG ACHIEVEMENTS IN DEVELOPING A FRAMEWORK AND INSTRUMENTS AND MANAGING COUNTY ASSETS

The NCC Integrated Development Plan 2013–17 states that NCC should implement an asset management system; create a plan and procedures to ensure assets are adequately maintained and used effectively, efficiently, and for intended purposes; and develop an integrated asset register and processes for regular updating (NCC 2014, 85). Also, the asset management (disposal, inventory, maintenance, repair, and so forth) and asset maintenance programs should be rolled out to the subcounty level. NCCG set up an AMDR in early 2016, under the Finance and Economic Planning division, with the objective of institutionalizing an integrated approach to the acquisition, monitoring, operation, maintenance, relocation, upgrading, and disposal of assets in a cost-effective manner. The following are the stated functions of the AMDR:

- Exercise stewardship over all assets.
- Maintain the county asset management system.
- Create and maintain the county master asset register.
- Develop and review an asset management policy and plans.
- Prepare annual financial statements data for capital assets.
- Schedule and perform physical asset verification of fixed assets.

- Approve and coordinate the final disposition of all surplus and obsolete assets.
- Facilitate the insurance of county movable and immovable assets.
- Revaluate assets.

NCCG has been working at the forefront of Kenya's devolution reforms, including establishing a framework, adopting instruments, and managing assets as a good bearer daily. NCCG established the first AMDR in Kenya in 2016; this is strong evidence of recognition of the importance of and the need for professional and high-level management of county assets. AMDR also started to position itself toward other departments and service sectors, albeit in a modality that leans toward accounting-oriented asset management. AMDR also early on approached international donors (including the World Bank and USAID) to seek technical assistance to boost asset management knowledge and professional capacities on a fast-track mode. The main results to date include the following:

- The county has a well-established AMDR with qualified staff.
- AMDR became the secretariat of the Nairobi CALC, with the pivotal role of organizing and managing field verifications.
- There is a draft county asset management policy (NCC 2017b), the first of its kind in Kenya. (It is used as one source of the asset management policy template presented in appendix A.)
- There is a draft asset management strategy (NCC 2017a) built on key strategic documents such as county vision, county strategy 2015–25 (NCC 2018c), master plan, detailed development plan, and so on presented in appendix B.
- The initial asset management plan (NCC 2017c) focused on establishing the asset management framework, entities, and instruments presented in appendix C.
- AMDR has become an informal leader and guide on asset management, and with shared documents has informed and inspired other smaller counties to work on asset management more systematically.
- AMDR has drafted ToR (presented in appendix D) for establishing a high-level strategic asset management advisory committee (the Asset and Liability Supreme Committee, or ALSC) to scrutinize, support, and propose strategic asset management decisions for top county administration and governing bodies, and more important, to back AMDR, which has achieved only a light-weight position in the county administration. But the ALSC is still to be established.
- AMDR has completed a number of asset-management trainings for various county entities.
- NCCG has appropriated a budget and drafted ToR for hiring a qualified firm for tagging and registering fixed assets (NCC 2018a).

AMDR has made heroic, substantial, logical, and systematic efforts toward developing a framework, a system, and procedures for modern asset management in NCC. However, the higher governing bodies (assembly, county cabinet, and governor) have not approved these drafts, in part because of the subsequent second county election after devolution in 2017. The outgoing governing bodies and personnel were busy with the election and postponed dialogue and decisions about asset management, and then the incoming new county government and governor initiated a substantial rotation of high-level staff and put asset management reform into a second group of priority actions. Despite a low level of support by higher governing bodies of the county, NCCG and AMDR have achieved very substantial progress on many key fronts.

Land asset verification. In 2017, NCCG with AMDR involvement began a mass valuation of land parcels in NCC jurisdiction under the Nairobi Metropolitan Services Improvement Project of the World Bank that aimed at revising the property tax roll (overdue for more than 30 years). This comprehensive mass valuation uses modern technology with geopositioning of each land parcel (about 230,000 parcels), measuring land sizes, and developing geographic information system (GIS) map layers for clear identification and verification of parcels. The land asset register with land values attached was developed in close cooperation between NCCG and the national land registry, which makes the results more powerful and consistent with national policy priorities. Figure 6.7 summarizes the mass valuation framework.

Mass valuation of land assets has three major implications for asset management.

1. First, in addition to private land for taxation, it has also verified all public lands, including parcels owned by NCC and by national government entities. The project identified 497 of 900 land parcels that have clear land records, thus providing a clear and precise register for most of NCC's land assets. This also helps with subsequent verification of buildings, plants, and infrastructure assets. Further work is required to complete

FIGURE 6.7

Nairobi City County logical framework for mass valuation of land

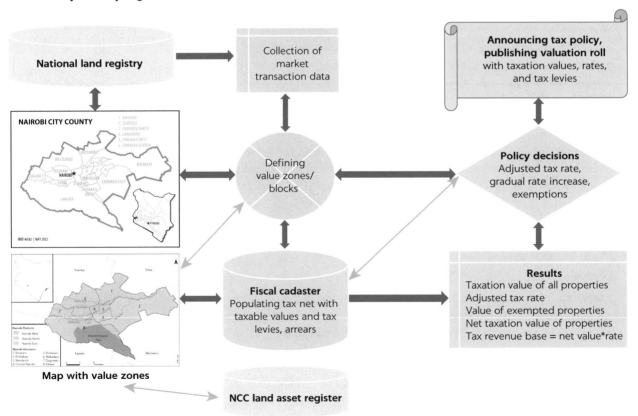

Source: Kopanyi 2018.
Note: NCC = Nairobi City County.

identification by obtaining a land registry record for all land parcels assumed to be owned by NCC.

2. Second, it provides updated market values for NCC's land parcels, making separate land valuation for asset management purposes unnecessary. With these, NCCG has made a quantum leap toward modern asset management ahead of other counties in Kenya.

3. Third, the precise verification of private and national government properties with GIS maps and global positioning system coordinates helps identify parcels and owners regarding inherited property tax and rent and lease arrears, including compensation in lieu of rates (CILOR) claims, to help management and workout of an enormous stock (K Sh 53.7 billion) of inherited current assets, that is, uncollected property tax from private and national government entities.

Liabilities. NCCG early on started workout of inherited nonperforming liabilities, including (1) verifying and paying all verified inherited overdue staff emoluments; (2) announcing a verification program (NCC 2018b) for trade creditors who had to reconfirm their claims with supporting documents for NCCG and AMDR scrutiny (NCC has paid most of these verified claims); (3) appointing via the Finance Department a dedicated debt management team that has taken over verification of inherited bank liabilities and promotes uninterrupted servicing of verified domestic loans and proper accounting and reporting of financial liabilities; and (4) approaching statutory creditors to settle claims if excessive penalties are annulled, although some negotiations failed due to rigidity of creditors. NCCG managed to work out K Sh 12 billion of disputed liabilities by June 30, 2019 (NCCG 2019).

Current assets. NCCG started a program for managing current assets way before the CALCs were established. Actions include (1) verifying property tax arrears, which has been only partially successful due to a lack of documents and unresolvable discrepancies between the files in the Finance Department and in the old accounting system; (2) approaching the national electricity company and other companies to collect the wayleave (right of way) fees, although negotiations have failed due to uncooperative behavior by national entities; (3) approaching ministries and other national entities to collect overdue CILOR, although negotiations again failed, so overdue CILOR collectibles represent a large part of inherited current assets for Nairobi. These are significant items, because these claims are not only substantial but also suitable for working out NCC's liabilities vis-à-vis other national entities in a modality that would work as a chain of swaps. This is a common approach in public and corporate practices alike and was well used in settling assets and liabilities at transition of Eastern European municipalities (Peteri 2003).

Disputed assets. NCCG has approached DoD to settle a long-disputed case the predecessor CCN had already taken to court without success. According to the claim, the CCN had purchased in a free-market transaction a large parcel of land (900 hectares) for a housing development. However, DoD took over this land for defense and housing purposes without compensation during the 1970s. NCCG hired a valuer in 2018 to establish the present value of that land and estimated that it had about a value of K Sh 33 billion. NCCG then approached DoD to negotiate fair compensation. However, DoD was unwilling to negotiate despite hard evidences on the claim. This case again underscores the need for a national policy on approaching asset transfers across national or county entities, but also high-level supports for a fair compensation of the counties involved.

NCWSC also faces disputed assets and presents a case in which several asset and liability claims need clarification, verification, and settlement. Parties involved include NCC, NCWSC, the Ahti Water Service Board (defunct in 2019), WASREB (taking over from said water board),[3] and the Public Debt Management Directorate in the National Treasury. This is also part of the disputed and unfinished handover of assets from national entities that has not even started and needs to be commenced, guided, and regulated in due course. NCC has taken over NCWSC from the defunct CCN, but there are many disputed assets and liabilities between NCC and the former Ahti Water Service Board, now the WASREB.

CALC verification and report. NCCG has been at the forefront of asset verification and takeover, established CALC early on, and assigned numerous field verification teams to accomplish and support the work in accordance with Notices 858, 2701, and 4370. NCCG prepared a vast CALC report (over 600 pages) in a timely manner, despite severe shortages of money, staff, and vehicles. The field teams have identified large numbers of land and buildings unidentified in the TA report, including capturing all land parcels that host the various water and sewer plants, lines, or other facilities that were missing from the TA report, which considered water assets as not under NCC ownership. In short, the NCC CALC report is a valuable document that supports establishing a reliable asset register in the medium term, even though the NCC CALC report also has remained in draft form due to circumstances already explained.

LESSONS LEARNED

This study has reviewed the revenues and expenditures of NCC and the status of asset management, preliminary results of the takeover of asset and liability ownership, and challenges going forward nine years in transition to devolved local governments.

NCCG has made important initial steps toward establishing a reliable framework, systems, and procedures for asset management. However, the road ahead is steep, bumpy, and long. AMDR has achieved substantial initial results in drafting key framework documents that set the stage for an integrated county-level asset management framework and systems. Draft documents include asset management strategy, policy, and a short-term plan, with a concept for a framework with the asset and liability management county committee (that is, the ALSC), AMDR under the Finance Department, and asset management units in each service sector or functional entity. But the new local government inaugurated in November 2017 has left these important documents in draft status without approval or plans toward implementation.

AMDR has raised the level of awareness across various NCC departments and functional units about the importance, scope, and structure of an integrated asset management system. AMDR held a one-day training for all department heads with the financial and professional help of the World Bank. AMDR also drafted the concept and ToR for hiring a professional firm to develop a detailed concept for a pragmatic asset register and to complete an initial asset inventory, because it is apparent that the staffs of the various county units are unable to populate an asset inventory in a consistent and timely fashion, especially in addition to their regular daily duties.

AMDR played a pivotal role in facilitating the work of CALC and the assigned field teams. The results of asset verification and validation are reasonable and represent a quantum leap toward establishing reliable asset inventories and eventually an integrated computerized asset register. The CALC teams made reasonable achievements, especially considering the impediments and the time constraints. However, the CALC report makes clear that the job has not been completed as planned; teams often stated that they had managed to verify 70–80 percent of assets with partial information. Therefore, the new county government needs to reopen the book and complete the takeover of assets and liabilities and continue work on planning, funding, and implementing important follow-up actions.

The most critical next steps follow, but it worth noting that several actions can be and should be commenced in parallel:

• Establish an asset management system that embraces the best practices globally, with links connecting assets with needs, funding, and budget plans and strategies.

• Establish a complete and consistent initial asset register based on the CALC results but with a capture of nearly 100 percent of assets.

• The register should structure the assets in a more detailed manner by sectors, services, functions, and form in the asset hierarchy by expanding on the level of initial main clusters used under CALC (land, building, equipment).

• Approve and implement an asset management strategy, plan, and policy that meet regulatory requirements and set clear and binding policies and plans for acquisition, operation, maintenance, and disposal and criteria for buy or lease decisions.

• Develop asset management information systems that include physical verification, auditing, tagging, and digitalized maps within an information and communication technology (ICT) platform. Provide asset management software for real-time asset management and monitoring. Complete documentation of the asset management system, including procedure manuals and both manual and electronic backup and control systems. Hire a firm to develop a pragmatic ICT framework and asset management system and train users.

• Complete the workout of disputed assets and liabilities and initiate urgent implementation. This requires actions by the highest governing bodies of the county, including the governor and the County Assembly.

• Resolve the disputed assets and liabilities, which requires a clear concept and framework by the national government and specific respective entities such as the IGRTC, National Treasury, Ministry of Finance, auditor general, and some sectoral ministries.

• Valuation of assets should start with a focus on land and buildings, because they represent the bulk of NCC's wealth and have huge financing capacity for future development if used strategically. An adequate structuring of the land and building inventory would be the first step toward focusing on valuating assets that have large revenue potential.

• Insource services of professional architects and professional valuers to lead valuation teams formed from NCC staff. The main challenge the CALC team faced was an inability to establish the value of land, buildings, plants, and high-value equipment, which would have required the services of architects and valuers. However, neither funding, logistics, human capacities or expertise, nor adequate time was available during CALC verification.

- Develop plans and procedures for advanced asset-based financing to accelerate development of key service infrastructure.
- Draft long-term county financial plans in harmony with asset management to determine the replacement values of inherited assets, likewise assets acquired after 2013, and at the same time explore long- and short-term financing options for maintenance and renewal based on needs assessment of service-level requirements in the context of life-cycle costing.
- Launch a comprehensive certificate asset management training program with both general and sector-specific modules and make it compulsory for all respective staff to attend, pass the final exams, and obtain a certificate. Divisions to be involved include Physical Planning, Public Health, Social Services and Housing, Primary Education Infrastructure, Inspectorate Services, Public Works, and Environment Management (with Agriculture, Livestock Development and Fisheries), Trade, Industrialization, Corporate Development, Tourism and Wildlife, and Public Service Management.

NOTES

1. The financial tables presented in this study reflect "actual" figures from the final accounts of the fiscal years, since "planned" figures are less reliable due to frequent and substantial changes during budget implementation. Meanwhile, comparing the actual and planned figures indicate the quality of budget planning and implementation.
2. To obtain a building permit, developers pay a one-time development fee of about 1.25 percent of the estimated cost of development. Therefore, this is not a small administrative fee for a permit but a tax.
3. From the WASREB website: "WASREB is a regulatory state corporation in Kenya established by the Water Act of 2016 operationalized in April 2017. Section 70 (1) of the Water Act of 2016 dissolved Water Boards and established WASREB with the main objective to protect the interests and rights of consumers in the provision of water services, while ensuring other stakeholders' interests are also safeguarded. WASREB sets, monitors, and reviews rules and regulations to ensure water services provision is affordable, efficient, effective, and equitable." "About Us," https://wasreb.go.ke.

REFERENCES

ACT (Australian Capital Territory). 2018. "Asset and Liability Management." Budget paper no. 3 (2017–18), chapter 8. Canberra: Australian Capital Territory. https://apps.treasury.act.gov .au/__data/assets/pdf_file/0006/1069989/Budget-Paper-3.pdf.

CBK (Central Bank of Kenya). 2020. Inflation rates 2013-2019, https://www.centralbank.go.ke /inflation-rates/.

CGA. 2012. County Governments Act no. 17 of 2012. http://www.parliament.go.ke/sites/default /files/2017-05/CountyGovernmentsAct_No17of2012_1.pdf.

CRAB. 2015. County Revenue Allocation Bill 2015–2017. http://kenyalaw.org/kl/fileadmin /pdfdownloads/bills/2017 /CountyAllocationofRevenueBill_2017.pdf.

Farvacque-Vitkovic, C., and M. Kopanyi. 2019. *Better Cities Better World: A Handbook on Local Government Self-Assessments.* Washington, DC: World Bank. https://openknowledge .worldbank.org/handle/10986/32120.

Freire, M., and M. Kopanyi. 2018. *Asset and Debt Management for Cities.* London: International Growth Centre, London School of Economics.

Grubišić, M., M. Nušinović, and G. Roje. 2009. "Towards Efficient Public Sector Asset Management." *Financial Theory and Practice* 33 (3): 329–36. https://hrcak.srce.hr/file/74946.

Holder, A. 1998. "*Developing the Public Sector Balance Sheet.*" Economic Trends 540 (November): 31–40. https://escoe-website.s3.amazonaws.com/wp-content/uploads/2020/01/01234506 /ET-540-Developing-the-Public-Sector-Balance-Sheet-Andrew-Holder-Nov-1998.pdf.

IGRTC (Intergovernmental Relations Technical Committee). 2017. "Unaudited IGRTC Current Assets and Liability List as at 27 March 2013." IGRTC files from Transition Authority. Nairobi: IGRTC.

IGRTC (Intergovernmental Relations Technical Committee). 2018. *Report on the Identification, Verification, Validation, and Transfer of Assets and Liabilities of the Defunct Local Authorities as at 27th March 2013.* Nairobi: IGRTC. https://igrtc.go.ke/download /consolidated-report-on-assets-and-liabilities-of-the-defunct-local-authorities-2018/.

KNBS (Kenya National Bureau of Statistics). 2018. *Basic Report on Well Being in Kenya* (based on Household Budget Survey 2015/16). https://www.knbs.or.ke/download/basic -report-well-kenya-based-201516-kenya-integrated-household-budget-survey-kihbs/#.

KNBS (Kenya National Bureau of Statistics). 2019. "Kenya Population and Housing Census." Nairobi: KNBS. https://www.knbs.or.ke/.

Kopanyi, M. 2018. "Mass Valuation of Land in Nairobi City County." Advisory note, World Bank, Washington, DC.

Kopanyi, M., and R. Franzsen. 2018. "Property Taxation in Kampala, Uganda: An Analytic Case Study on a Successful Reform," Africa Tax Institute Working Papers WP18-03, Pretoria. https://www.up.ac.za/media/shared/223/Working%20Papers/property-taxation-in -kampala-kopanyi-and-franzsen.zp146778.pdf.

MLG (Ministry of Local Government). 2013. Ministry of Local Government Circular ref. no. MLG/1333/TY/ (52) of 18 February 2013.

NCC (Nairobi City County). 2014. *Nairobi County Integrated Development Plan 2013–2017.* Nairobi City County Government. https://www.cog.go.ke/downloads/category /82-county-integrated-development-plans-2013-2017.

NCC (Nairobi City County). 2017a. "Draft Asset Management Strategy." Nairobi City County Government (2017).

NCC (Nairobi City County). 2017b. "Draft Asset Management Policy." Nairobi City County Government (2017).

NCC (Nairobi City County). 2017c. "Draft Asset Management Plan." Nairobi City County Government (2017).

NCC (Nairobi City County). 2018a. "Draft Term of Reference for Hiring a Firm to Complete an Asset Management Inventory." Nairobi City County Government. https://repository.kippra .or.ke/handle/123456789/2019.

NCC (Nairobi City County). 2018b. "Gazette Notice no. 2101 of 9th March 2018 on Establishment of a Pending Bills Committee." Nairobi City County Government.

NCC (Nairobi City County). 2018c. *Nairobi County Integrated Development Plan (CIDP) Covering the Period 2018–2022.* Nairobi City County Government. https://repository.kippra .or.ke/handle/123456789/2019.

NCC CALC (Nairobi City County, County Asset and Liability Committee). 2017. *Identification, Verification, and Validation of County Assets and Liabilities.* Nairobi City County Government.

NCCG (Nairobi City County Government). 2018. "Nairobi County Budget Review and Outlook Paper (CBROP) 2018." Nairobi: NCCG. https://nairobi.go.ke/download/nairobi -county-budget-and-review-paper-cbrop-2018/.

NCCG (Nairobi City County Government). 2019. *Stock of NCC County Liabilities.* Nairobi: Debt Management Office, NCCG.

Notice 4370. 2018. Gazette Notice no. 4370, May 11, 2018: Intergovernmental Relations Act no. 2 of 2012.

OAG (Office of the Auditor General). 2013–19 (annually). *Report of the Auditor General on Financial Statement of Counties.* Nairobi: OAG. http://www.oagkenya.go.ke /index.php/reports/cat_view/2-reports/11-county-governments/203-county -government-reports.

OAG (Office of the Auditor General). 2019. "Report of the Auditor General on Nairobi City Water and Sewerage Company Ltd." June 2019. http://www.parliament.go.ke/sites/default /files/2022-03/Report%20of%20the%20Auditor-General%20and%20Financial%20 Statements%20on%20Nairobi%20city%20water%20and%20sewerage%20company%20 limited%20for%20the%20year%20ended%2030%20June%2C%202019.pdf.

OCB (Office of the Controller of Budget). 2014–18 (annually). *Annual County Government Budget Implementation Review Report*. Nairobi: https://cob.go.ke/reports/consolidated -county-budget-implementation-review-reports/.

Peskin, M. 2001. "Asset/Liability Management in the Public Sector." In *Pensions in the Public Sector*, edited by O. S. Mitchell and E. C. Hustead, ch. 9. Philadelphia, PA: Pension Research Council of the Wharton School of the University of Pennsylvania.

Peteri, G. 2003. *From Usage to Ownership—Transfer of Public Property to Local Governments in Central Europe*. Budapest: Local Government and Public Service Initiative, Open Society Institute.

PFM. 2012. Public Finance Management Act, no. 18 of 2012. https://www.pcf.go.ke/index.php /public-financial-management-act.

PPAD. 2015. Public Procurement and Asset Disposal Act, no. 33 of 2015, December 18, 2015. http://kenyalaw.org:8181/exist/kenyalex/actview.xql?actid =No.%2033%20of%202015.

TDG. 2012. Transition to Devolved Government Act, no. 1 of 2012, enacted March 9, 2012. http:// www.parliament.go.ke/sites/default/files/2017-05/TransitiontoDevolvedGovernment ActNo1of2012.pdf.

WASREB (Water Services Regulatory Board). 2020. "Regulatory Rules." Nairobi: WASREB. https://wasreb.go.ke/regulatory-tools.

Water Act. 2016. Water Act no. 43 of 2016. https://wasreb.go.ke/downloads/Water%20Act%20 2016.pdf.

World Bank. 2018. *Kenya Economic Update*. 17th ed., April 2018. Washington, DC: World Bank. https://documents.worldbank.org/en/publication/documents-reports/documentdetail /327691523276540220/kenya-economic-update-policy-options-to-advance-the-big -4-unleashing-kenya-s-private-sector-to-drive-inclusive-growth-and-accelerate -poverty-reduction.

7 Kajiado County

INTRODUCTION

Kajiado County is in the southern region of Kenya and borders Kiambu, Machakos, Makueni, Nairobi, Nakuru, Narok, and Taita Taveta counties and the country of Tanzania (map 7.1). It covers an area of 21,900 square kilometers. Kajiado County has plains, valleys, and volcanic hills ranging from an altitude of 500 meters above sea level (Lake Magadi) to 2,500 meters above sea level in Ngong Hills (KNBS 2017). The county is divided into five political constituencies: Kajiado Central, Kajiado East, Kajiado North, Kajiado South, and Kajiado West and 25 wards. The county has five administrative units (subcounties)—Isinya, Kajiado Central, Kajiado North, Loitokitok, and Mashuuru—and 17 administrative divisions.

Kajiado County had an estimated population of 1.1 million in 2019 (KNBS 2018, 2019), with an average population density of 51 per square kilometer and a growth rate of 5.5 percent per annum. The most populated constituency was Kajiado North, which had 1,369 persons per square kilometer in 2014 and was expected to increase to 2,087 persons per square kilometer by 2017. The county has a low population dependency ratio of 43 percent as compared with the 78.3 percent national average.

In agriculture, production, livestock rearing, and horticulture are the main economic activities. Cash-crop production includes tomato, cabbage, kale, and banana. The county also produces the minerals soda ash and soda crushed raw. In the tourism sector, the county hosts Amboseli National Park, which receives over 100,000 visitors annually (Kajiado County 2018b). The trade and commerce sector consisted of 5,315 business entities, of which 3,115 were small and 520 were large scale. The mining and extraction sector had 13 businesses, and there were 27 industrial plants and manufacturing business entities (World Bank 2018). The county has 49 banks, most of them in Isinya (12) and Kajiado North subcounties. Kajiado County hosts one public university—Maasai Mara University—and five private universities: Africa Nazarene, Adventist University of Africa, East African University, KCA University, and the UMMA Islamic University.

Kajiado County's decentralized functions (Kenya Constitution 2010) include agriculture, health, cultural activities, animal welfare, trade and development,

MAP 7.1
Kajiado County

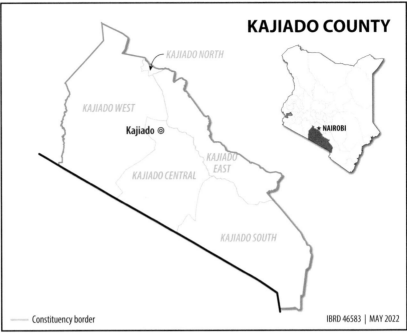

Source: World Bank.

county planning and development, preprimary education, village polytechnics, home craft centers and early childhood education, environmental conservation, public works, and local community public participation. The county is mandated to provide the following services: solid waste dumpsites, street lighting, public housing, office and shop rental, hospitals, preschools, vocational schools, sport stadium, game-park, and markets, per the Urban Areas and Cities Act 2019 (UAC 2019) and County Governments Act (CGA 2012).

Kajiado County has a 2,344-kilometer road network, of which only 300 kilometers are tarmac. During rainy seasons, most roads become impassable, which increases the cost of doing business. The county's rapid growth rate (5.5 percent against the national average of 2.9 percent) combined with rapid urbanization stimulates strong and growing demand for urban services (Kajiado County 2018a). There is a growing gap between demand and the poor and inadequate infrastructure, especially in water supply, electricity, and telecommunication services. Health care facilities in Kajiado include Kajiado District Hospital, Loitokitok District Hospital, Nairobi Women's Hospital (Kitengela), Namanga Hospital, and Ngong Sub-District Hospital. However, there is a severe shortage of health facilities; the average distance to a health facility is 14 kilometers, so access to health care remains low.

REVENUE AND EXPENDITURE ANALYSIS

Analysis of revenues and expenditures is an integral part of an assessment of asset management because it provides a solid background picture in which assets are positioned, developed, and managed. Revenues generate cash or cash-like instruments that are transient forms of assets, since land can be sold to generate cash revenue to develop schools, or cash can be saved for rainy days. Finally, the surplus remaining after current expenditures are covered with current revenues provides funds for development. Loans or other liabilities can also finance development. In short, revenue and expenditure analysis provides important insights and sheds light on the trends and capacities a county possesses in developing assets and expanding services.

Revenues

Kajiado County's revenue base grew steadily at an average rate of 13.9 percent per annum between the 2013/14 and 2017/18 fiscal years (table 7.1). This represents about a 6 percent increase above the average inflation in the same period (CBK 2020). The Government of Kenya has supported devolution by substantially and steadily increasing transfers to counties (CRAB 2015). *Equitable shares* form the bulk of revenues (almost 90 percent of total) and grew by 15.6 percent per annum.

The conditional grants are negligible and show a flat trend. Conditional grants support level 5 hospitals, free maternal health care, compensation of foregone user fees, grant leasing of medical equipment, and a road maintenance levy. However, not all of these services are supported each year. The loans and grants were from the Danish International Development Agency, which supported health care service provision. The county government noted persistent delays in the disbursement of the equitable shares from the national government.

The own-source revenues (OSR) have remained low and volatile, and their share shrank from 12.7 percent to 9–10 percent of total revenues in the

TABLE 7.1 Kajiado County revenues, fiscal years 2013/14–2017/18
K Sh (millions)

	2013/14	2014/15	2015/16	2016/17	2017/18	AVERAGE GROWTH (%)
Transfers from national government	**3,511**	**4,064**	**4,631**	**5,119**	**6,092**	**14.8**
Equitable share	3,227	3,850	4,413	4,761	5,768	15.6
Conditional grants: national government	284	214	218	358.2	324	3.4
Own-source revenues	**511**	**773**	**651**	**557**	**680**	**7.4**
Taxes	—	—	—	—	239	n.a.
Fees and charges	—	—	—	—	162	n.a.
Asset proceeds	—	—	—	—	70	n.a.
Other revenues	511	773	651	557	209	−20.0
Financing	**0**	**0**	**90**	**150**	**0**	**n.a.**
Cash reserve from previous year	—	—	—	—	—	n.a.
Loans and grants	0	0	90	150	0	n.a.
Total revenue	**4,022**	**4,837**	**5,372**	**5,826**	**6,773**	**13.9**
Share of OSR (%)	12.7	16.0	12.1	9.6	10.0	−5.7
OSR actual/planned (%)	72.0	81.9	52.8	44.6	65.0	−2.5

Source: OAG 2014–18.
Note: — = not available; n.a. = not applicable; OSR (own-source revenues) is displayed in the "other revenues" line because of lack of detailed revenue figures until 2017/18.

2013/14–2017/18 fiscal period. OSR grew on average by 7 percent per annum; as a result, the county is increasingly dependent on national government transfers. The county collected a high share of planned OSR in 2013/14 and 2014/15 when OSR collection was 81 percent of the targets. However, collection dropped by more than one-third in volume with a corresponding drop of actual and planned performance to 45 percent in 2016/17, then improved to 65 percent in the 2017/18 fiscal year. At the same time, Office of the Auditor General reports (OAG 2013–15) further noted that the formats for the approved budget and financial statements were different, which made it impossible to analyze the county's OSR performance in detail.

Expenditures

Kajiado County's total expenditures show very dynamic growth at over 23 percent per annum over the 2013/14–2017/18 fiscal period (table 7.2). It is worrisome that expenditures grew nearly twice as fast as revenues (table 7.1); this reduced the budget surplus but has not caused a budget deficit so far. The current expenditures grew by 19 percent per annum, a slower pace than the total expenditures, but the share of current expenditures remained high, about 75 percent in the same period. Labor costs (wages and salaries) absorbed an increasing share and nearly half of current expenditures (48 percent in 2018), high by international comparison (Farvacque-Vitkovic and Kopanyi 2019).

Operation and maintenance (O&M) expenditures show a declining trend (1.9 percent per annum); further, in fiscal year 2016/17 the main expenditure

TABLE 7.2 **Kajiado County expenditures, fiscal years 2013/14–2017/18**
K Sh (millions)

	2013/14	2014/15	2015/16	2016/17	2017/18	AVERAGE GROWTH (%)
Current expenditures	**2,249**	**3,508**	**3,599**	**3,961**	**4,506**	**19.0**
Personal emoluments	1,009	1,467	1,798	1,809	2,158	20.9
Operation and maintenance	1,240	2,041	1,801	1,103	1,150	−1.9
Of which, repair and maintenance	0	64	52	81	73	n.a.
Transfers to other entities	0	0	0	1,048	1,198	n.a.
Noncurrent/development	**577**	**1,303**	**1,250**	**1,225**	**2,082**	**37.8**
Acquisition of assets	577	1,026	1,250	1,225	2,082	37.8
Debt repayment	0	0	0	0	0	n.a.
Other payments	—	—	—	—	—	n.a.
Total expenditures	**2,826**	**4,811**	**4,849**	**5,185**	**6,588**	**23.6**
Budget balance	**1,196**	**26**	**523**	**641**	**185**	**−37.3**
Ratios (%)						
Operation and maintenance/current	55.1	58.2	50.0	27.9	25.5	−4.5
Personal emoluments/current	44.9	41.8	50.0	45.7	47.9	5.0
Current/total	79.6	72.9	74.2	76.4	68.4	−1.8
Development/total	20.4	27.1	25.8	23.6	31.6	6.5
Repair and maintenance/current	n.a.	1.8	1.4	2.0	1.6	n.a.

Source: OAG 2014–18.
Note: — = not available; n.a. = not applicable.

under O&M was domestic and foreign travel (K Sh 433 million or 11.4 percent), and operating expenses ranked second (K Sh 179 million or 4.7 percent).

This is worrisome and suggests shortcomings in asset management and maintenance, since the county invested over K Sh 6 billion in fixed assets in the same period, which undoubtedly has increased the need for O&M expenditures. The share of repair and maintenance remained steadily low (1.4–2.0 percent of current expenditures); this is somewhat better than other surveyed counties, but it is way below the 15 percent international benchmark. Maintenance expenditures are important components of asset management and are meant to ensure sustainable services. Routine maintenance of both old and new assets installed after 2013 would have required increasing rather than shrinking the share of maintenance expenditures.

Kajiado County had a stronger emphasis on development expenditures than other counties surveyed and spent 32 percent of the total expenditures in 2017/18 for development. This is high above most Kenyan counties but still below the 40 percent national policy and international benchmark. A comparison of the 2013/14 and 2017/18 fiscal years indicates that development expenditures quadrupled; the average growth of development spending was over 37 percent per annum over this fiscal period. Furthermore, the share of development spending in total expenditures increased by 6.5 percent annually and moved from a 20 percent to 32 percent share of the total expenditures by 2018.

A review of development spending from the commencement of devolution listed in the successive reports (OCB 2014–18) indicates that Kajiado County began construction of key assets: roads, health centers, and dams. During this same year (2016/17), the county spent K Sh 228.8 million on markets and sheds; hospital wings were the second largest plans, but Kajiado County completed only a third of planned hospital wings.

In 2015/16, the county spent its development funds for construction of classrooms, health centers, and bus parks; refurbishing of buildings; and fencing of dumpsites, among other projects. The county also spent K Sh 44 million of its development budget to establish valuation rolls for land parcels (OCB 2017). Figure 7.1 shows the latest development spending by Kajiado County. In sum, one can state that Kajiado County has well utilized the transfers from the national government, and compared to other surveyed counties it used a relatively high share for financing infrastructure development for improving local services in the surveyed five years.

The development budgets show persistently high variation between plans and actual development spending. The Office of the Controller of Budget (OCB 2017) recommended "the need to increase absorption of development expenditure." OCB does not state the main causes of low absorption rates, but field experience suggests that poor design, poor planning, poor contract management, and eventual delays of construction could be among the key underlying reasons.

ASSET MANAGEMENT

The case studies of this book focus on the transition period, before which Kenyan local governments did not have asset management systems, frameworks, and policies except some sporadic practices to manage assets daily by officers of service units. Despite legislated mandates—Public Finance Management Act 2012

FIGURE 7.1

Kajiado County development expenditures, fiscal year 2016/17

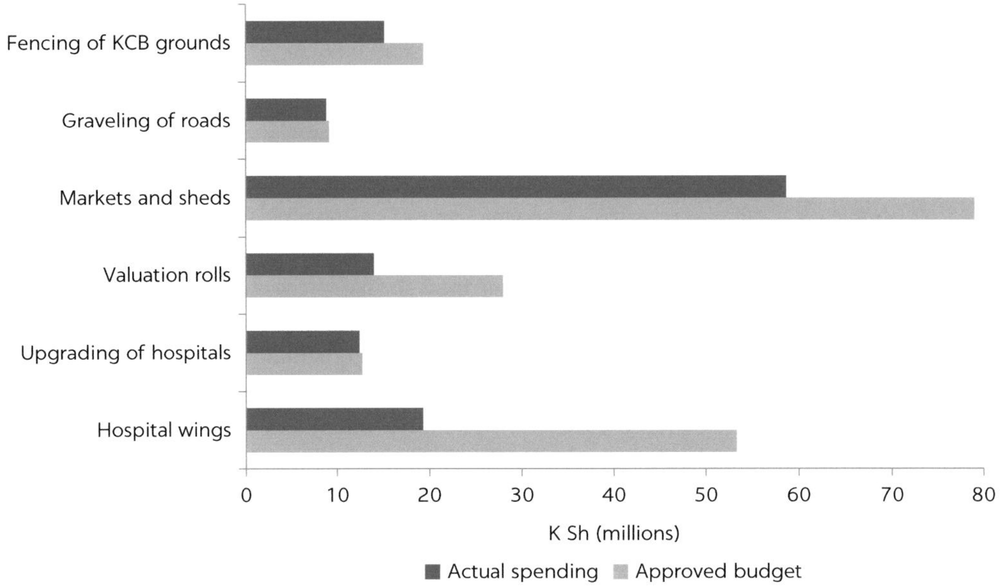

Source: OCB 2017.
Note: KCB = Kajiado Central Bus Terminal.

(PFM 2012), Constitution 2010, Public Procurement and Asset Disposal Act 2015 (PPAD 2015), and government circulars—local governments failed to establish asset registers, and even the accounting aspects of assets were poorly understood and obeyed before devolution. Local bodies failed to measure the wealth of public assets in the possession of local entities and did not aim for increasing it or manage the most important assets strategically (IGRTC 2017, 2018). This case study illustrates both the enormous challenges the incoming county governments faced due to the inherited situation and the remarkable progress achieved after devolution. It also demonstrates that moving forward requires strong determination, vision, finances, and reformative actions toward modern and adequate management of assets that eventually determine the level and quality of local public services.

Asset ownership and transition to devolved government

Article 23 of the Transition to Devolved Government Act (TDG 2012) (also referred to as the Transition Act) regulated the takeover of the functions, assets, liabilities, and staff of the former local authorities of Olkejuado County Council and Kajiado Town Council by the county government of Kajiado, which was assumed to take over assets and liabilities after validation and audit by the Transition Authority (TA) (TDG 2012). The Ministry of Local Government Circular MLG/1333 directed the clerks as the chief executive officers of the outgoing local authorities to ensure proper handing over to the incoming county government. This was a timely and important directive, but it had no enforcement power over the outgoing officers. It also conflicted with the TDG Act, which seems to have paralyzed the local actions for years, since counties were waiting for the TA to hand over its report. OAG found that by

September 2013, the following MLG/1333 directives were disobeyed in Kajiado (see also box 7.1):

- The fixed assets register for audit verification was not updated. It contained neither the assets taken over from the defunct local authority nor new assets acquired during the period under review.
- The fixed asset register provided for audit did not have asset values. Consultancies suggest that such asset registers did not exist at all, so auditors may have seen fragments of asset lists instead of a register.
- The defunct local authority had 54 parcels of land that had no ownership documents. The source of information about the land sizes and values was unclear.
- Under biological assets, 26 cattle were accounted, despite being subsequently disposed of from the demonstration farm.
- Several buildings were refurbished for use by the governor and his deputy as residences, as well as an office block for the county public services board. However, the main risk was that over K Sh 45 million was used for refurbishments without establishing the ownership status of those buildings, and without their being formally transferred to the county.

BOX 7.1

Kajiado County audit report excerpts, 2013

5.1 *Failure to hand over by the County Council to the Kajiado County Government*

Ministry of Local Government Circular Ref. no. MLG/1333/TY/52 of 18 February 2013 directed the Clerks as the Chief Executive Officers of the Local Authorities to ensure there is proper handing over to the incoming County Government. As part of the handing over, [outgoing] Clerks were expected to ensure that statements of Assets and Liabilities were prepared by 28 February 2013. However, handing over of resources to the new County Government by the former Olkejuado County Council was to be done with the coordination of the Transition Authority. No reason was provided why the handing over was not done contrary to the above circular. Therefore, it is not possible to determine the amount of assets and liabilities taken over by the County Government of Kajiado.

Recommendation

A handing over report should be prepared by the Transition Authority so that what was transferred from the defunct Local Authority to the County Government can be determined and properly accounted for.

5.2 *Bank Accounts*

(a) Closure of Bank Accounts

The Transition Authority issued letters reference no. TA/7/5/ (20) dated 12 February 2013 (TA 2013b) and MOF/IFMIS/41 dated 7 March 2013 (TA 2013a), which instructed all local authorities to freeze all their bank accounts except for the receiving bank account. However, the defunct Olkejuado County Council did not close its bank accounts by 28 February 2013 but continued operating them up to 26 August 2013. The date of accounts closure and amounts transferred from three (3) accounts held by defunct local authority to County Revenue Collection Account was not provided.

Recommendation

Explanation on failure to adhere to requirements of the directive by Transitional Authority and details on

continued

Box 7.1, *continued*

closure and transfer of money on three (3) accounts should be provided.

5.3 Debtors

Section 149 (2) (b) of the Public Finance Management Act, 2012 requires that an accounting officer shall, in respect of the entity concerned ensure that the entity keeps financial and accounting records that comply with the Act. The statement of assets and liabilities by the defunct Olkejuado County Council showed that debtors amounted to K Sh 319,886,135. However, no analysis [or] schedule was provided to show the composition of the above figure and also the age of the debts.

Recommendation

The County Government should provide a proper debtor analysis [or] schedule to indicate the composition of the debtors.

5.4 Creditors [and/or] Suppliers and Other Liabilities Balances

Section 149 (2) (b) of the Public Finance Management Act, 2012 requires that an accounting officer shall, in respect of the entity concerned, ensure that the entity keeps financial and accounting records that comply with the Act. The statement of assets and liabilities by the defunct Olkejuado County Council showed that creditors amounted to K Sh 238,254,956.

Source: OAG 2013.

However, the council did not maintain creditors ledgers.

Recommendation

The County Government should ensure that proper creditors' ledgers are maintained to enable production of reliable creditors schedule and balances.

5.5 Motor Vehicles, Office Equipment, and Other Assets

Section 149(2) (b) of the Public Finance Management Act, 2012 requires that an accounting officer shall, in respect of the entity concerned, ensure that the entity keeps financial and accounting records that Comply with the Act. The respective County Government entity should have adequate systems and processes in place including an asset register that is current and accurate. Ownership documents for 169 parcels of land out of 171 belonging to the defunct Olkejuado County Council were not made available for audit verification. Further, ownership documents to authenticate that the assets listed existed and were properly owned by the council were not provided.

Recommendation

The County Government should initiate the process of obtaining title deeds to secure the properties within its jurisdiction in order to safeguard the County assets.

Informal takeover and use of assets

The county government, without formal takeover, accounts, and valuation, from its inauguration started to use and develop assets, especially those that formed the basis of local services to ensure uninterrupted provision of services. This was a very pragmatic and important approach. Other assets unrelated to services (for example, land) remained unaccounted, some unattended, and therefore, many may be lost or encroached. The OAG (2014) report further recommended that the Kajiado County government should coordinate with the TA on the asset and liability takeover. However, the county government apparently was not in a position to commence takeover in a unilateral action. Furthermore, the TA did not coordinate or guide counties for formal takeover of assets and liabilities; the TA rather aimed to list, verify, validate, and valuate assets before handover.

Kajiado county has been using and developing most of the inherited assets since March 2013. Despite the unresolved issues just discussed and the lack of handover and takeover, the county government has taken a pragmatic approach in using and developing the assets. The Kenya Constitution 2010 and the Urban Areas and Cities Act 2011 (UAC 2011) assign local service functions to counties and assets that can be assumed to be possessed and managed under the respective county departments (such as the Asset Management Directorate in NCC, explained in chapter 6).

Under this governance framework, the Kajiado County government has created four companies to provide water in the different regions of the county: (1) Notresh Water and Sewerage Company is co-owned by Makueni and Machakos counties and serves the south region of Kajiado County; (2) Oldonyorok Water Sewerage Company (WSC) serves the Namanga region; (3) Olkejuado WSC serves the Central region; and (4) Ololeisa WSC serves the northern region. For solid waste management, the county has taken over dumpsites in the towns of Kitengela, Loitokitok, and Manga, while Kiserian, Ngong, and Rongai share a dumpsite in Ngong. Each town has a lorry that transports garbage to the dumpsite. Table 7.3 summarizes specific service provision arrangements.

Asset takeover by the power of law, 2017

Gazette Notice no. 858 (Notice 858, 2017) transferred the assets and liabilities of the defunct local governments by the power of the law on January 27, 2017, and set a framework for validation, verification, and valuation of the assets by the counties via County Asset and Liability Committees (CALCs) under guidance and control by the Intergovernmental Relations Technical Committee (IGRTC). Notice no. 2701 (Notice 2701, 2017) of March 24, 2017, reconfirms and revokes the Notice 858 rules that the unaudited inventories of assets and liabilities developed by the TA, which closed in March 2016, serve as a basis and reference for the verification, validation, and valuation of the assets under CALC's management. The results presented below are from the Kajiado CALC report 2017 and cross-checked with the IGRTC summary report (IGRTC 2018).

According to IGRTC and TA files, handed over to counties in 2017, Kajiado County inherited assets worth K Sh 200 million and liabilities worth K Sh 310 million from the Olkejuado County Council and the Kajiado Town Council in fiscal 2013/14 (measured by TA as a 2013 estimated value—a quite symbolic number in 2017). Due to poor recordkeeping, the auditor general was unable to establish the true verified value of the inherited assets and liabilities of Kajiado County as of the end of 2013. Therefore, proper recordkeeping of assets and liabilities remained a key recommendation (box 7.1). The estimated values of inherited assets reflect largely the value of current assets as of 2013, since the TA did not estimate the value of the most valuable fixed assets such as land, buildings, and infrastructure networks. Of these, the most problematic element is the value of land because of presumed high volume, but also because this value has substantially appreciated between 2013 and 2017. Thus, the verification and valuation of land has remained among the most urgent tasks the county faces even to date.

Progress by the end of 2019

Given the numerous reports from OAG on lack of proper handover of assets and liabilities from the defunct local authorities, Kajiado County government

TABLE 7.3 **Kajiado County asset management entities and their functions**

SERVICES OR FUNCTIONS THAT REQUIRE SPECIFIC ASSETS OWNED BY OR USED BY THE COUNTY	ASSET MANAGEMENT ENTITIES		
	COUNTY DEPARTMENT RESPONSIBLE FOR THE RESPECTIVE SERVICES	COMPANY OR OTHER INDEPENDENT ENTITY OWNED BY THE COUNTY	PRIVATE SERVICE PROVIDER OR PRIVATE MANAGING ENTITY UNDER PPP
General administration			
Office buildings	n.a.	n.a.	Outsourced competitively as per PPA Act 2012
Urban services			
Roads and drainage	n.a.	n.a.	Outsourced competitively as per PPA Act 2012 for completion of specific projects
Water and wastewater lines	n.a.	Four water companies operate, but owned by the county	n.a.
Solid waste	In other towns, dumpsites and waste transport are served under the Lands, Physical Planning, Environment, Wildlife, and Natural Resources Department	Kajiado town has a company managing waste	n.a.
Vehicle fleet	Transport and Communication Department	n.a.	Private providers of public transport
Social services			
Health	Health Services Department	Health centers and hospitals owned by county or national governments	n.a.
Education	Education, Youth, Sports, and Social Services Department	Schools owned by county or national governments	n.a.
Commercial services			
Slaughterhouse	Inspected by Agriculture, Livestock, and Fisheries Department	Hide and skin processing plant in Isinya	Agriculture, Livestock, and Fisheries Department provides staff to private entities to monitor and inspect the meat for quality control
Local economic development	Agriculture, Livestock, and Fisheries Department	n.a.	n.a.

Source: Kajiado County government website and field survey.
Note: n.a. = not applicable; PPA = Physical Planning Act; PPP = public-private partnership.

undertook a program to enhance asset management. The county procured the services of a private firm for tagging its assets and further establishing an asset register with a global positioning system survey of main assets (land and buildings). When this program is completed, the county will have an initial asset register. Second, following Notice no. 858 of January 8, 2017, on asset and liability identification, verification, and validation, the county government of Kajiado appointed a team for managing assets and duly set up a CALC to oversee the verification exercise. The Kajiado County CALC team was trained by the IGRTC on the procedures for asset and liability identification, verification, and validation. IGRTC also provided the team with a manual to assist them in data collection. Box 7.2 exhibits the terms of reference and methodology used by the Kajiado CALC team in assets and liability data collection.

The CALC team strongly focused on land assets, collecting information on public and community land. It did an exemplary job in identification, registration, and size estimation of land parcels (table 7.4). The TA report included 836 parcels of land; in contrast, the team verified 685 parcels, because the TA list included much repetition of parcels and only a few reference numbers. The CALC team also identified 70 additional parcels that were not in the TA list, while public consultations helped identify another 29 parcels. Finally, the CALC team managed to identify a total 784 parcels of land. The team further made efforts to retrieve land reference numbers from the national land registry and other land reference documents and managed to verify 749 parcels in land registries. Consequently, the number of parcels without reference numbers dropped to 35.

The TA report included 476 parcels with estimated sizes. The CALC increased this to 595 after the exercise. However, these sizes remained only estimated and not surveyed, and most of the parcels did not have ownership documents. Public consultations revealed that 10 parcels of land set aside for public utilities had been encroached; for example, the 10-acre land for Loitokitok District Stadium was occupied by the prisons department, while the Loitokitok and Masimba bus parks had been encroached by private individuals. The county has commenced procedures to restore ownership, but this lengthy process is still underway.

The buildings with adjacent structures that the CALC team captured in the inventory included schools, markets, government offices, water points, cattle dips, housing estates, safari club, and others. A total of 98 buildings was captured,

BOX 7.2

Kajiado County Asset and Liability Committee methodology

The process was guided by the guidelines and tools developed by the Interagency Technical Committee (IATT) per the classes of the assets and liabilities. The following data collection strategies to collect both primary and secondary data were also used:

Interviews. These were conducted with key informants and officers at the county headquarters, subcounties, and those who previously worked in the defunct local authorities, including treasurers and clerks.

Document review. The team examined primary supporting documents such as title deeds, logbooks, asset registers, valuation reports, certificates, and other related records. Secondary data were collected through valuation reports, auditor-general reports, handover and takeover reports, land registry records,

adjudication registers, preliminary index maps, registry index maps, bank statements, financial statements, and review of Local Authorities Integrated Financial Operations Management System (LAIFOMS) reports.

Physical inspection and verification of assets through site visits.

Public participation. Additional data were collected from the public, members of which submitted written memoranda following public notices in both print and electronic media sent to churches and public gatherings requesting information on assets and liabilities of defunct local authorities.

Data were analyzed using the narrative method and presented using thematic analysis.

Source: Kajiado CALC 2017.

TABLE 7.4 **Kajiado County land and buildings, by DLAs, after verification, 2017**

	OLKEJUADO	KAJIADO	TOTAL
Land			
Total parcels of land	766	18	784
With LR or other reference numbers	731	18	749
Without LR or other reference numbers	35	0	35
Buildings			
Total number of buildings	79	19	98
With LR or other reference numbers	76	19	95
Without LR or other reference numbers	3	0	3
Buildings with plinth areas	18	15	33

Source: Kajiado CALC 2017.
Note: DLAs = defunct local authorities; LR = land registration.

and most of the land registration (LR) numbers for these buildings were retrieved; only three buildings remained without LR numbers. In contrast, most of the buildings did not have LR numbers in the TA report. The CALC team failed to establish the plinth areas for most of the buildings, so it recorded the 33 plinth areas based on the TA report. Table 7.4 provides a summary of the land and buildings from the CALC report.

The movable assets the CALC team identified were as follows:

- *Motor vehicles.* The CALC team reconfirmed the 48 vehicles in the TA report, identified 34 motor vehicles, 4 motorcycles, and 10 trailers. These included cars, refuse-collection trucks, exhausters and trailers, fire engines, and road construction equipment such as graders, tippers, and rollers.
- *Furniture.* This included tables, chairs, stools, sofas, lockers, beds, cupboards, cabinets, bookshelves, benches, and kitchen equipment. The team captured a total of 392 pieces of furniture for Olkejuado County Council and 53 for Kajiado County Council.
- *Equipment.* This included such items as typewriters, telephone headsets, fire extinguishers, TVs, water engines, water dispensers, and calculators, among others. The team collected 93 items for the Olkejuado County Council and 23 items for the Kajiado Town Council.
- *Computers.* There were 87 computers and 92 computer accessories consisting of printers, UPS, fax-machines, photocopiers, and LCD projectors.
- *Biological assets.* These included cows, bulls, heifers, and calves totaling 150 and estimated at a value of K Sh 5.2 million as indicated in the valuation report dated February 28, 2013. However, 88 animals were sold in May 2014 and the balance left was 62; verification found 127 animals in 2017 due to subsequent calving.

Following national government guidance, Kajiado County government prepared a fixed-asset register summary for the 2017/18 fiscal year (table 7.5). This is an important step despite shortcomings. First, financial reports suggest K Sh 6 billion asset acquisition since devolution (table 7.2). Against that, this summary reflects only K Sh 3 billion, and for fiscal year 2017/18 only K Sh 1 billion acquisition against the K Sh 2 billion in the financial report. Second, the report

TABLE 7.5 Kajiado County fixed asset register summary, June 30, 2018

K Sh (millions)

	HISTORICAL COST, JUNE 30, 2017	ADDITIONS IN FY 2017/18	HISTORICAL COST, JUNE 30, 2018
Land	0	0	0
Buildings and structures	1,338	630	1,967
Transport equipment	136	40	176
Office equipment	155	4	159
ICT equipment and software	0	202	202
Other machinery	479	146	625
Heritage, cultural assets	0	0	0
Intangible assets	0	0	0
Total in register	**2,108**	**1,020**	**3,128**
Total asset acquisition/development after devolution	0	2,082	6,160

Source: OAG 2018.

Note: FY = fiscal year; ICT = information and communication technology.

seems to reflect gross value, since no amortization is accounted in this report, despite rules set in PFM Act 2012. Good asset registers should reflect depreciation of assets, regardless of whether the county follows cash-based accounting principles in bookkeeping and financial reports. Thus, it is important to improve accuracy of reports and consistency across financial reports.

Table 7.6 provides a glimpse into the inherited liabilities identified by the CALC team; these are substantially greater than the TA estimates (K Sh 448 million against K Sh 310 million). The difference is largely due to inclusion of accrued interests. More than half of inherited liabilities (54 percent) were due to commercial creditors—construction companies and suppliers of goods and services.

The county managed the inherited bank loans and emoluments well and thus reduced inherited liabilities by nearly K Sh 100 million; the outstanding bank loans are performing. In contrast, the county failed to work out inherited statutory deductions, and even the nominal value in 2017 may exclude interest and penalties accrued after 2013 (report states as of 2013). Likewise, no resolution has occurred on commercial creditors, the largest volume of inherited liabilities, and the claims keep increasing with accrued interest. This is an unhealthy situation that deserves attention and pragmatic measures. One good measure is that the county has appointed a pending bills committee to take closer control of liabilities and manage workouts. The summary of liabilities as of March 27, 2013, verified in 2017 for both the Olkejuado County Council and the Kajiado Town Council include the following:

- *Loans.* The Olkejuado City Council had a loan of K Sh 89 million from Co-operative Bank of Kenya to finance the purchase of eight motor vehicles. This loan was continuously serviced and was settled during FY 2016/17. The Kajiado Town Council had an outstanding loan of K Sh 4.2 million.
- *Unpaid emoluments.* The Kajiado Town Council had unpaid staff emoluments amounting to K Sh 7.4 million. This balance was cleared soon after the county government took over. In addition, the Olkejuado City Council and the

TABLE 7.6 **Kajiado County summary of inherited liabilities, 2013 and 2017**
K Sh (millions)

	BANK LOANS	EMOLUMENTS	STATUTORY DEDUCTIONS	OTHER CREDITORS	TOTAL
Olkejuado	89.0	0.0	99.9	239.2	428.1
Kajiado	4.2	7.4	3.6	4.7	19.9
Total as of 2013	93.2	7.4	103.5	243.9	448.0
Share of total liabilities (%)	20.8	1.7	23.1	54.4	100.0
Net value total in 2017	4.2	0.0	103.5	239.2	346.9

Source: Kajiado CALC 2017.

TABLE 7.7 **Kajiado County summary of inherited current assets, March 2013**
K Sh (millions)

	CASH AND BANK DEPOSITS	PROPERTY RATES	HOUSE AND PLOT RENTS	OTHER CURRENT ASSETS	TOTAL
Olkejuado	42.0	278.0	0.0	1.0	321.0
Kajiado	1.4	61.4	0.0	181.8	244.6
Current assets	43.4	339.4	0.0	182.8	565.5
Share in total %	7.7	60.0	0.0	32.3	100.0

Source: Kajiado CALC 2017.

Kajiado Town Council had unremitted statutory deductions amounting to K Sh 99.9 million and K Sh 3.6 million, respectively. These payments are yet to be settled.

- *Other creditors.* The Olkejuado City Council and the Kajiado Town Council had other creditors totaling K Sh 239.2 million and K Sh 4.7 million, respectively. These included suppliers of goods and services, contractors, and legal fees, left unsettled as of 2017.

Table 7.7 provides a summary of the current assets collected by the Kajiado CALC team. These figures suggest a substantially larger amount of current assets identified by the CALC team (K Sh 565 million) against the amount in the IGRTC/TA report (K Sh 200 million). The inherited current assets are concentrated in rents, property rates, and commercial debtors, while inherited bank deposits represent only 7.7 percent of the current assets. It is not clear from the CALC report if the bank values reflect 2013 deposits or accrued values as of 2017.

The comparison of tables 7.6 and 7.7 shows that the inherited current assets were about 26 percent greater than the current liabilities, so the liabilities could be settled if the current collectibles were recovered. However, the bulk of inherited current assets are uncollected overdue property rates that will be difficult if not impossible to collect, because those are already overdue six years or longer, and many are poorly documented. Other current assets include claims against national government entities, and a minor portion is staff loans, which the CALC team had not specified whether they were performing. Subsequently, the county hired a debt collector to accelerate collection of inherited current assets in the 2019/20 fiscal year. The current assets for Kajiado County were estimated as of March 27, 2013, to be as follows:

- *Cash and bank.* The Olkejuado City Council operated seven bank accounts in three different banks with balances totaling K Sh 42 million. The Kajiado Town Council operated six bank accounts in three different banks with a cumulative balance of K Sh 1.4 million. All these inherited accounts were closed in November 2014 and the balances transferred to the Kajiado County single revenue account.
- *Property rates.* The Olkejuado City Council and the Kajiado Town Council had outstanding property rates of K Sh 278 million and K Sh 61 million, respectively.
- *House and plot rents.* The Kajiado Town Council had outstanding house and plot rents worth K Sh 361,300. This balance has since been recovered.
- *Other current assets.* Kajiado County inherited K Sh 181.8 million other current assets from the Olkejuado City Council (including uncollected contributions in lieu of rates [CILOR], Magadi royalties, and housing compensations) and K Sh 960,000 from the Kajiado Town Council, which consisted of staff debt.

The CALC team recommended that the county government should pursue and recover the outstanding plot rates and house rents and ensure financial data are reconciled in LAIFOMS. The team further recommended carrying out an audit to verify and determine the authenticity and accuracy of all liabilities.

Challenges Kajiado CALC faced during verification and validation of inherited assets and liabilities in 2017

According to the CALC report, the major challenges faced by the CALC identification and verification teams included the following:

- Identification of land encroachment, particularly for land set aside for bus parks and markets, was left in disputed status.
- Verification of land parcels was left incomplete due to inadequate supporting evidence, such as title deeds for the identified pieces of land.
- There was a limited time frame to produce the CALC report.
- Poor recordkeeping and inadequate information in the existing files made verification time-consuming and slow.
- Asset verification remained incomplete due to the vastness of the county and the time constraints.
- Public participation was important, but the veracity of information obtained from the public forums was difficult to ascertain, as some information provided was conflicting and not supported by documents or other solid evidence.
- The data from LAIFOMS was unreliable and inconsistent with financial statements.
- Some of the key staff of defunct authorities had been transferred subsequently and therefore were not available to provide clarifications for the CALC team.

LESSONS LEARNED

The institutionalization of asset management is an important component of any financial management system. The Kajiado County government has taken up several initiatives that are important for asset management, including asset tagging and registering, with values and specifics of the property. The main challenge is that asset management functions are performed in silos; a small assessment management team is assigned, but no department is designated to strategically manage the assets and maintain reliable information related to assets centrally. The most critical lessons include the following:

- The Supply Chain (procurement) Department is responsible for procuring the assets. This is in line with the PPAD Act 2015, which includes both procurement and disposal. The department has nine permanent staff and two staff on contract management. The Finance Department is the custodian of asset registers in the county, but the information on land is with the Lands Department, thus a consistent asset management framework and system is still to be established.

- The county has no policy, strategy, or asset management plan. There is an opportunity to further engage with the county government to establish a pragmatic and reliable framework for asset management.

- Even though functions such as agriculture have been devolved, the national government Ministry of Agriculture has been hesitant to provide land titles for agricultural land to the county government. Under education, the only devolved functions are the county vocational training institutions and early childhood education. However, the land on which primary and secondary schools are built was donated by the county government. It is not clear how or if the county will hand over such assets to the national government.

- The verification and valuation of assets are incomplete and need more time and concerted efforts. It is vital for the county government to understand the gravity of the next steps and assign adequate resources and personnel. Adopting a short- to medium-term action plan for establishing an asset management framework, working out disputed cases, and completing valuation is a logical and vital next step.

- The CALC and teams had no responsibility to identify assets, lands, and buildings or current assets in custody of various national government entities who are supposed to hand over assets to the county based on the devolved functions. Takeover assets from national government entities is a very substantial next step for full takeover of county assets and further movement toward a balanced devolution.

REFERENCES

CBK (Central Bank of Kenya). 2020. Inflation rates 2013-2019, https://www.centralbank.go.ke/inflation-rates/.

CGA. 2012. County Governments Act No. 17 of 2012. http://www.parliament.go.ke/sites/default/files/2017-05/CountyGovernmentsAct_No17of2012_1.pdf.

CRAB. 2015. County Revenue Allocation Bill 2015–2017. http://kenyalaw.org/kl/fileadmin/pdfdownloads/bills/2017/CountyAllocationofRevenueBill_2017.pdf.

Farvacque-Vitkovic, C., and M. Kopanyi. 2019. *Better Cities Better World: A Handbook on Local Government Self-Assessments.* Washington, DC: World Bank. https://openknowledge.worldbank.org/handle/10986/32120.

IGRTC (Intergovernmental Relations Technical Committee). 2017. "Unaudited IGRTC Current Assets and Liability List as at 27 March 2013." Intergovernmental Relations Technical Committee from files of Transition Authority. Nairobi: IGRTC.

IGRTC (Intergovernmental Relations Technical Committee). 2018. *Report on the Identification, Verification, Validation, and Transfer of Assets and Liabilities of the Defunct Local Authorities as at 27ᵗʰ March 2013*. Nairobi: IGRTC. https://igrtc.go.ke/download/consolidated-report-on-assets-and-liabilities-of-the-defunct-local-authorities-2018/.

Kajiado CALC (County Asset and Liability Committee). 2017. *Kajiado CALC Report*. Kajiado County CALC, August 2017.

Kajiado County 2018a. "County Budget Review and Outlook Paper 2018." Kajiado, Kenya: County Government of Kajiado. https://devolutionhub.or.ke/resource/county-government-of-kajiado-budget-review-and-outlook-paper-2018.

Kajiado County. 2018b. *County Integrated Development Plan 2018–2022*. Kajiado, Kenya: County Government of Kajiado. https://cog.go.ke/cog-reports/category/106-county-integrated-development-plans-2018-2022?download=362:kajiado-county-integrated-development-plan-2018-2022.

Kenya Constitution. 2010. http://kenyalaw.org/kl/index.php?id=398.

KNBS (Kenya National Bureau of Statistics). 2017. *Kajiado County Statistical Abstract*. Nairobi: KNBS. https://www.knbs.or.ke/download/kajiado/#.

KNBS (Kenya National Bureau of Statistics). 2018. *Basic Report on Well Being in Kenya* (based on Household Budget Survey 2015/16). Nairobi: KNBS. https://www.knbs.or.ke/download/basic-report-well-kenya-based-201516-kenya-integrated-household-budget-survey-kihbs/#.

KNBS (Kenya National Bureau of Statistics). 2019. "Kenya Population and Housing Census." Nairobi: https://housingfinanceafrica.org/documents/2019-kenya-population-and-housing-census-reports/.

Ministry of Local Government (MLG) Circular, ref. no. MLG/1333/TY/ (52) of February 18, 2013.

Notice 858. 2017. Gazette Notice no. 858, January 8, 2017: Intergovernmental Relations Act no. 2 of 2012. https://gazettes.africa/gazettes/ke-government-gazette-dated-2017-01-27-no-13.

Notice 2701. 2017. Gazette Notice no. 2701, March 24, 2017: Intergovernmental Relations Act no. 2 of 2012. https://gazettes.africa/archive/ke/2017/ke-government-gazette-dated-2017-03-24-no-37.pdf.

OAG (Office of the Auditor General). 2013–19 (annually). *Report of the Auditor General on Financial Statement of Counties*. Nairobi: OAG. http://www.oagkenya.go.ke/index.php/reports/cat_view/2-reports/11-county-governments/203-county-government-reports.

OCB (Office of the Controller of Budget). 2014–18 (annually). *Annual County Government Budget Implementation Review Report*. Nairobi: https://cob.go.ke/reports/consolidated-county-budget-implementation-review-reports/.

PFM. 2012. Public Finance Management Act, no. 18 of 2012. https://www.pcf.go.ke/index.php/public-financial-management-act.

PPAD. 2015. Public Procurement and Asset Disposal Act, no. 33 of 2015, December 18, 2015. http://kenyalaw.org:8181/exist/kenyalex/actview.xql?actid =No.%2033%20of%202015.

TA (Transition Authority). 2013a. "Transition Authority Guidelines," Ref. MOF/IFMIS/1/41 dated 7 March 2013.

TA (Transition Authority). 2013b. "Inventory of Assets and Liabilities Debts and Human Resource Profile in Public Organizations." Circular Ref. no. TA/2/5 dated 9 January 2013.

TDG. 2012. Transition to Devolved Government Act, no. 1 of 2012, enacted March 9, 2012. http://www.parliament.go.ke/sites/default/files/2017-05 /TransitiontoDevolvedGovernmentActNo1of2012.pdf.

UAC. 2011. Urban Areas and Cities Act, no. 13 of 2011. http://www.parliament.go.ke/sites/default/files/2017-05/UrbanAreasandCitiesAct_No13of2011.pdf.

UAC. 2019. Urban Areas and Cities (Amendment) Act 2019. http://kenyalaw.org/kl/fileadmin/ pdfdownloads/AmendmentActs/2019/Urban AreasandCities_Amendment_Act_2019.pdf.

World Bank. 2018. *Kenya Economic Update*. 17th ed., April 2018. Washington, DC: World Bank. https://documents.worldbank.org/en/publication/documents-reports/documentdetail/327691523276540220/kenya-economic-update-policy-options-to-advance-the-big-4-unleashing-kenya-s-private-sector-to-drive-inclusive-growth-and-accelerate-poverty-reduction.

8 Kakamega County

INTRODUCTION

Kakamega County is in western Kenya and borders Bungoma, Nandi, Siaya, Trans-Nzoia, Uasin Gishu, and Vihiga counties. The county covers approximately 3,051 square kilometers. It has 12 administrative units: Butere, Ikolomani, Khwisero, Likuyani, Lugari, Lurambi, Malava, Matungu, Mumias East, Mumias West, Navakholo, and Shinyalu. There are 60 wards and 187 village units. The political units also match the administrative units (map 8.1). Hence, there are 12 constituencies and 60 electoral wards with 60 elected members of the County Assembly.

Kakamega County had a population of 2.1 million in 2019 (KNBS 2019), with an average annual population growth rate of 2.5 percent. In 2019, the average population density was 618 people per square kilometer. Kakamega County has a population dependency ratio of 50 percent as compared to the 78.3 percent national average.

Of the county's total area, about 2,209 square kilometers are arable, of which 1,071 square kilometers are high-potential land (World Bank 2018). The main food crops include cereals (maize, sorghum, finger millet, and rice), pulses (beans, peas, and grams), or roots and tubers (cassava, sweet potato, and arrowroot). The county has three sugar factories that process sugarcane, including one in Mumias, one of the biggest sugar factories in the country.

Kakamega County hosts 11,083 retail traders, 1,180 hotel operators, and 8,733 other businesses (Kakamega County 2018b). It has one national park, and two campsites, which are managed by the national government. Kakamega Forest is a major tourist attraction, with numerous species of birds, butterflies, and other animals. Over 50,000 tourists visit the county annually. There is one public university, six university campuses (five public and one private), and three technical training institutes. The county has one county general hospital, nine subcounty hospitals, nine mission-hospitals, 27 public health centers, and 66 public dispensaries. Private health service provision includes one private hospital, eight nursing homes, and 107 private clinics.

The decentralized functions (Kenya Constitution 2010 and CGA 2012) of the county government include agriculture, health, control of pollution, cultural

MAP 8.1
Kakamega County

Source: World Bank.

activities, transport, animal welfare, trade and development, county planning and development, preprimary education, village polytechnics, home craft centers and early childhood education, environmental conservation, public works, and local community public participation. The services the county is mandated to provide—per Urban Areas and Cities Acts 2011 and 2019 (UAC 2011, 2019)—include services in solid waste, street lighting, public housing, office and shop rental, hospitals, preschools, vocational schools, a sports stadium, a game park, markets, and constituency university campuses, among others.

Kakamega County has 4,451 kilometers of roads, of which 308 kilometers are tarmacked, the rest being made of gravel or earth. There is an urgent need to increase the length of tarmac road to ease access to markets and mobility of factors of production (OCB 2018). The railway infrastructure remains underutilized; there are two railway stations in Lugari and Butere and a total of 35 kilometers of rail line crossing the county. Housing development remains a priority in Kakamega County. Of the total 392,000 households, 78.3 percent live in bungalows, and 87 percent of the residents own these dwellings. However, approximately 77 percent of the households do not have improved sanitation, so development of sanitation is important.

The county currently generates about 2,400 tons of solid waste per day, 68 percent in Kakamega town. However, the daily collection rate ranges between only 1,100 and 1,500 tons (Kakamega County 2018a). Less than 1 percent of the waste from households is collected by the county government, the rest by private entities and communities. The county still faces the challenge of negligible waste recycling due to a lack of technology and procedures for recycling and energy recovery. Consequently, illegal dumping of solid waste is increasing. Approximately 90 percent of the county's households have access to improved drinking water (KNBS 2018). However, the common source of improved water is protected springs, which are the main source of water for half of the households. Only 11 percent of households have access to piped water. Kakamega County acknowledges that despite significant investments in water supply and resource management, water service levels and management of water sources are challenges.

REVENUE AND EXPENDITURE ANALYSIS

Analysis of revenues and expenditures is an integral part of an assessment of asset management because it provides a solid background picture in which assets are positioned, developed, and managed. Revenues generate cash or cash-like instruments that are transient forms of assets, since land can be sold to generate cash revenue to develop schools, or cash can be saved for rainy days. Finally, the surplus remaining after current expenditures are covered with current revenues provides funds for development. Loans or other liabilities can also finance development. In short, revenue and expenditure analysis provides important insights and sheds light on the trends and capacities a county possesses in developing assets and expanding services.

Revenues

Kakamega County's total revenue base grew steadily at an average of 9.7 percent, slightly above the inflation rate (CBK 2020) between the 2013/14 and 2017/18 fiscal years (FY) (table 8.1). Like most counties, Kakamega County largely relies

TABLE 8.1 **Kakamega County revenues, fiscal years 2013/14–2017/18**
K Sh (millions)

	2013/14	2014/15	2015/16	2016/17	2017/18	AVERAGE GROWTH (%)
Transfers from national government	**7,356**	**8,729**	**9,713**	**10,596**	**10,781**	**10.0**
Equitable share	6,515	7,773	8,908	9,612	9,936	11.1
Conditional grants: National government	841	956	805	984	845	0.1
Own-source revenues	**251**	**533**	**502**	**449**	**505**	**19.1**
Taxes	0	138	134	101	96	n.a.
Fees and charges	—	276	235	235	295	n.a.
Asset proceeds	—	119	56	73	74	n.a.
Other revenues	251	0	78	40	39	−37.2
Financing	**311**	**206**	**279**	**12**	**177**	**−13.1**
Cash reserve from previous year	—	—	—	—	—	n.a.
Loans and grants	311	206	279	12	177	−13.1
Total revenue	**7,918**	**9,468**	**10,494**	**11,056**	**11,463**	**9.7**
Share of OSR (%)	3.2	5.6	4.8	4.1	4.4	8.5
OSR actual/planned (%)	12.0	57.0	50.0	50.0	66.0	53.1

Source: OAG 2014–18.
Note: — = not available; n.a. = not applicable; OSR = own-source revenue.

on national government transfers, which account for more than 95 percent of total revenues, while own-source revenue (OSR) has remained below 5 percent of total revenues in the surveyed period. The national government has supported devolution by substantially and steadily increasing transfers to counties (CRAB 2015). Transfers from the national government grew at an average rate of 10 percent. OSR is small, as noted, but it has grown twice as fast as national transfers (19 percent per year) and doubled from 2013 to 2018. The equitable share grew by 11 percent, while the conditional grants remained small and flat, growing by 0.1 percent annually. However, funding from development partners was substantial in the first three years, then dropped, so that overall it declined by 13 percent per annum. In FY 2013/14 and 2014/15, loans and grants supported Kakamega Provincial General Hospital (Danish International Development Agency [DANIDA] and World Bank), but in 2016/17 DANIDA provided only small supplementary grants for financing health facilities. OSR collection remained not only low but also poorly predicted and volatile; collection efficiency exceeded 50 percent in the 2014/15 fiscal year, then dropped back, and then improved in 2017/18 to 66 percent.

The share of OSR is one of the two lowest among the surveyed counties (only Makueni has collected less OSR). Table 8.2 presents detailed OSR figures for Kakamega County for the past five fiscal years that shows that the OSR has fast increased (by 19 percent per year) albeit from a very low basis. Tax revenues were extremely low, below 1 percent of total revenues, and property taxes were particularly low. They were insignificant in 2014/15, but the volume increased slightly in the 2015/16 fiscal year, and then strangely they were left unreported in the past two years of the surveyed period, with a corresponding drop in total tax revenues (that suggests an entry error or policy changes or revenue classification mistakes—maybe they were accounted among "other revenues").

TABLE 8.2 **Kakamega County OSR, fiscal years 2013/14–2017/18**

K Sh (millions)

	2013/14	2014/15	2015/16	2016/17	2017/18	AVERAGE GROWTH (%)
Taxes	—	138	134	101	96	**−11.5**
Property rates (property tax)	—	5	19	0	0	n.a.
Business permits (business tax)	—	91	71	59	69	−9.1
Other taxes and levies	—	42	43	42	27	−13.6
Fees and charges	—	276	235	235	295	**2.3**
Parking fees	—	2	57	59	56	215.1
Urban services	—	1	1	8	12	136.0
Social services	—	260	176	154	188	−10.3
Licenses, permits, certificates	—	13	0	14	40	44.8
Asset proceeds	—	119	56	73	74	**−14.4**
Rents and leases	—	2	24	27	38	149.3
Markets	—	116	32	46	37	−31.8
Other income	251	0	78	40	39	**n.a.**
Total OSR	251	533	502	449	505	**19.1**

Source: OAG 2014–18.

Note: — = not available; n.a. = not applicable; OSR = own-source revenue.

FIGURE 8.1
Kakamega County OSR, fiscal years 2014/15–2017/18

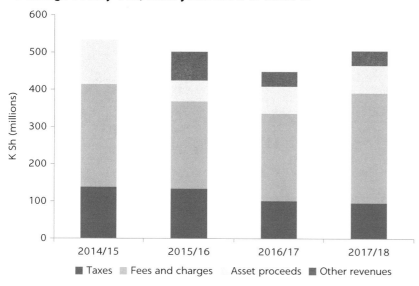

Source: OAG 2014–18.
Note: OSR = own-source revenue.

The actual/planned variation of OSR is extremely high, 50 percent or more (table 8.1) and suggests that OSRs are planned with ease or high optimism.

Fees and charges represent over half of OSR (figure 8.1). It is strange that charges in health facilities provided the bulk of fee revenues, while fees from commercial services like parking or use of the slaughterhouse remained negligible. This is not a healthy composition of fee and charge revenues. Fees and charges from health facilities were the main source of OSR in 2015/16, but they declined by 32 percent in 2017.

Tax revenues show a steady declining trend in both absolute terms and in share of OSR. This is a very worrisome trend that deserves attention and corrective measures. According to county officers, the main reasons behind the overall low own revenues include a lack of automation (that is, manual collection continues as the norm) and ineffective enforcement of revenue collection (Kakamega County 2018b). Asset proceeds were substantial but volatile, fluctuating around 15–20 percent of total OSR. OSR doubled from fiscal year 2013/14 to 2014/15 but remained flat for the rest of the surveyed time. In sum, there is no measurable improvement in OSR sources or in collection efficiency in five years in devolution.

Expenditures

Total expenditures for Kakamega County grew on average by 15 percent annually (table 8.3). That is, expenditures grew at a substantially higher rate than revenues, which grew only by an average of 10 percent annually if the 2013 transition year is omitted (table 8.3). This growing revenue-expenditure gap has eaten up budget surpluses and caused budget deficits in the last two years of the surveyed period.

Current expenditures grew on average nearly 22 percent per year, over twice as high as revenues and high above total expenditures. The two main factors

TABLE 8.3 **Kakamega County expenditures, fiscal years 2013/14–2017/18**

K Sh (millions)

	2013/14	2014/15	2015/16	2016/17	2017/18	AVERAGE GROWTH (%)
Current expenditures	**3,680**	**4,380**	**5,817**	**7,334**	**8,050**	**21.6**
Personal emoluments	2,610	2,940	3,951	3,714	4,571	15.0
Operation and maintenance	1,070	1,440	1,866	1,396	1,651	11.5
Of which, repair and maintenance	—	81	57	45	63	n.a.
Transfers to other entities	0	0	0	2,224	1,828	n.a.
Noncurrent/development	**2,930**	**3,613**	**4,247**	**5,033**	**3,514**	**4.6**
Acquisition of assets	1,520	3,107	4,247	4,972	3,062	19.1
Debt repayment	1,350	0	0	0	0	n.a.
Other payments	60	506	0	60.4	452	65.7
Total expenditures	**6,610**	**7,993**	**10,064**	**12,366**	**11,564**	**15.0**
Budget balance	1,308	1,475	430	−1,310	−101	n.a.
Ratios (%)						
Operation and maintenance/current	29.1	32.9	32.1	19.0	20.5	−8.4
Personal emoluments/current	70.9	67.1	67.9	50.6	56.8	−5.4
Current/total	55.7	54.8	57.8	59.3	69.6	5.7
Development/total	44.3	45.2	42.2	40.7	30.4	−9.0
Repair and maintenance/current	n.a.	1.9	1.0	0.6	0.8	n.a.

Source: OAG 2014–18.

Note: — = not available; n.a. = not applicable.

include fast-growing labor expenditures (15 percent per year) and a jump in current transfers to subordinate entities, which have been important to sustain services but are indicative of an apparently unsustainable revenue-expenditure mismatch.

Infrastructure investments have driven the growth of total expenditures; they grew by 19 percent per year on average. Kakamega County well utilized the fast-growing transfers from the national government, and spent over K Sh 16 billion and over 40 percent of total revenues to infrastructure investments. These results are truly outstanding among Kenyan counties and are comparable to the best international practices (Farvacque-Vitkovic and Kopanyi 2019). However, the share of development expenditures dropped to 30 percent of the total, apparently because the county had to provide large current subsidies to other entities in 2017 and 2018. Kakamega County stands out among Kenyan counties and the group of sample local governments with these high shares of development expenditures. Expenditure figures underscore a need for tight control over operation subsidies, such as through performance contracts.

There are also concerning trends; for example, personnel costs grew faster than operation and maintenance expenditures (15 percent and 11.5 percent, respectively), and the current expenditures also grew much faster than revenues. Among the main current expenditures, domestic and foreign travel is the single largest item (very uncommon in international comparison). Finally, it is a matter of concern that expenditures on repair and maintenance remained negligible, below 1 percent of current expenditures as opposed to the 15 percent

FIGURE 8.2

Kakamega County cumulative development expenditures, fiscal years 2013/14–2015/16

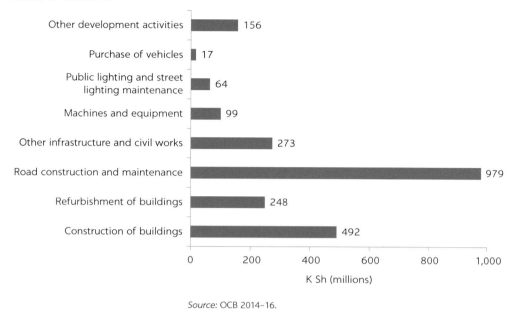

Source: OCB 2014–16.

international benchmark; they even show a declining trend. This is a major shortcoming that deserves attention, policy changes, and corrective measures since it undermines the sustainability of assets and services.

Figure 8.2 provides a glimpse into the composition of cumulative development spending from the sample in the first three years of devolution. Road construction and maintenance was by far the largest investment program, construction and refurbishment of buildings was the second and rather substantive investment program, while other construction and civil works were reported to have received the most substantial funds. In 2016/17, besides the noted investment areas, nonrecurrent expenditures also included preparations for digital topographical mapping (in preparation for a spatial plan) and the preparation of a draft valuation roll. Development of spatial plans have positive implications for the development of a county asset base; the spatial plans provide vision, direction, and opportunity for coordinated actions for investment in county assets and help avoid duplication of actions by various county departments. The updating of the valuation roll with geographic information system maps and global positioning system identification of properties is expected to boost tax revenues and OSR and also provide a solid basis for establishing an initial land asset register with precise location, size, and market value of land owned by Kakamega County. This further opens the gate toward land-based financing of infrastructure.

ASSET MANAGEMENT

The case studies of this book focus on the transition period, before which Kenyan local governments did not have asset management systems, frameworks, and policies except some sporadic practices to manage assets daily by officers of service units. Despite legislated mandates—Public Finance Management Act (PFM 2012),

Kenya Constitution 2010, Public Procurement and Asset Disposal Act (PPAD 2015), County Governments Act (CGA 2012), and government circulars—local governments failed to establish asset registers, and even the accounting aspects of assets were poorly understood and obeyed before devolution. Local bodies failed to measure the wealth of public assets in the possession of local entities and did not aim for increasing it or manage the most important assets strategically. This case study illustrates both the enormous challenges the Kakamega government faced due to the inherited situation and the remarkable progress achieved after devolution. It also demonstrates that moving forward requires strong determination, vision, finances, and reformative actions toward modern and adequate management of assets that eventually determine the level and quality of local public services.

Asset ownership and transition to devolved government

Article 23 of TDG Act 2012 (TDG 2012) regulated handover of the functions to the County Government of Kakamega the assets, liabilities, and staff of the defunct county councils of Butere-Mumias, Kakamega, and Lugari; municipal councils of Kakamega and Mumias; and town council of Malava. Furthermore, the Office of the Auditor General (OAG) conducted a special audit for the period of March 5 to June 30, 2013, to assess and ensure a seamless transition process and proper systems for accountability of public resources before, during, and after transition to county governments (OAG 2013). In its 2013 report, OAG expressed constraints and delays in obtaining requisite information and supporting documentation that hampered completion of the OAG audit. It also noted that key staff of former local authorities had left and were no longer available to provide adequate information.

The audit report makes clear that there was no handover or takeover of assets and liabilities by June 30, 2013 (box 8.1). There were no creditors' ledgers in defunct local authorities, and debtors' records were not updated, even though PFM Act 2012 mandates such requirements. Likewise, debtors' registers lacked relevant supporting documents to authenticate the amounts that Kakamega County claimed. Furthermore, limited financial reports provided for the auditor indicated the balance of creditors as K Sh 297 million and debtors as K Sh 498 million at the end of the 2013/14 fiscal year.

It was not possible to establish the cash and bank balances, because in some cases, such as Kakamega Municipal Council and the county councils of Butere-Mumias and Lugari, the bank statements and reconciliations were not available for audit verification for the period of January to June 2013 and there were no certificates of bank balances as of March 27, 2013. Furthermore, the defunct local authorities did not close bank accounts on March 26, 2013, as directed by the Transition Authority (TA) and Ministry of Local Government's Circular MLG/1333/TY; instead, the audit found irregular cash withdrawals from bank accounts that were unaccounted for in financial reports. The outgoing local entities did not comply with accounting and financial rules and principles mandated in PFM Act 2012 regardless of transition, since historically those had not been enforced.

As for fixed assets, such as motor vehicles, even though there was handover of vehicles it was not possible to determine on what basis the book values were established since there were no asset registers and no valuation was done. Moreover, Kakamega County Council was the only defunct local authority that handed over motor vehicles; it is not clear whether other defunct local authorities did not own motor vehicles or if all vehicles were managed centrally within

BOX 8.1

Kakamega County audit report excerpts, 2013

Municipal Council of Mumias

Debtors. The debtors records were not updated. There was no evidence including, among others, invoices, and demand notices to confirm recovery efforts for Debtors amounting to K Sh 10,242,367 as of April 1, 2013.

Recommendation: The county government should authenticate debtor's balances and maintain proper accounting records.

Creditors and suppliers. The total creditors handed over to the county amounted to K Sh 18,018,491 some of which were not supported with original documents.

Recommendation: The county government should authenticate creditor's balances before they are paid, and such determination should be supported by valid contract agreements and evidence of service [and/or] goods delivery.

County Council of Butere

Debtors. Debtors' files handed over to the county government amounted to K Sh 6,472,381. However, debtors' ledgers and registers were not maintained.

Recommendation: Debtors' records should be updated before they are handed over to the county government.

Creditors. Creditors' files handed over to the county government amounted to K Sh 17,319,926. However, there were various expenditures that had not been supported by the required relevant supporting documents. These included payment vouchers for K Sh 2,892,152, insurance payments of K Sh 3,498,905 and payments to contractors amounting to K Sh 37,000,176.

Recommendation: Creditors' ledger should be updated, and balances validated before any payments are made.

County Council of Lugari

Debtors. Debtors files handed over to the county government amounted to K Sh 222,082,368. It was

established that debtors' ledger and register were not maintained to confirm the same.

Recommendation: Records should be updated and handed over to the county government.

Creditors. Creditors' files handed over to the county government amounted to K Sh 11,780,967. However, electronic funds transfer payments to a consulting firm amounting to K Sh 2,192,000 and paid on March 1, 2013, were not supported by a payment voucher, contract agreement, or goods received notes.

Recommendation: The county government should authenticate creditor's balances before they are paid, and they should be supported by valid contract agreements and evidence of services or goods delivery and an updated record for suppliers and ledger should also be maintained.

Town Council of Malava

Creditors. The creditors' files handed over to the county government amounted to K Sh 8,437,921, but they were not supported by verifiable documents.

Recommendation: The county government should authenticate creditors' balances before they are paid. Payments should be supported by valid contract agreements and evidence of services and goods delivery.

County Council of Kakamega

Debtors. There was no documentation in support of debtors' balances handed over to the county of K Sh 148,720,043.

Recommendation: Debtors' records should be updated and handed over to the county government.

Creditors. There were no records in place in support of creditors' balances handed over to the county amounting to K Sh 43,402,385. The county government should authenticate creditors' balances before they are paid.

Recommendation: Further action should be taken against those who failed to maintain updated records for suppliers and approved or authorized payments with neither supportive documents nor evidence of goods or services received.

Source: OAG 2013.

Kakamega County Council. An audit of the operations of Kakamega County during this time also shows that even though nine vehicles had been procured at a cost of K Sh 49.4 million, the vehicles could not be physically verified at the time of the OAG audit. The OAG 2014 audit report states that Kakamega County failed to present a fixed asset register even though records available showed that K Sh 200 million was spent on procurement of noncurrent assets.

Informal takeover and use of assets, 2013–17

Kakamega County informally took over the assets from the defunct local authorities pragmatically and has continued to operate, develop, refurbish, maintain, and manage assets directly needed for sustaining services through various departments of the county government (table 8.4). There was a reasonable collaboration in management of assets by the various departments in provision of urban services. For example, the Finance and Planning Department usually collects the fees on behalf of the entities, such as user charges under health services, market fees, or parking fees collected under the transport infrastructure, public works, and energy docket. Kakamega County is responsible by law to manage all assets, and conceptually the respective departments are in charge of managing devolved assets according to Constitution 2010 and UAC 2011. Table 8.4 reflects

TABLE 8.4 **Kakamega County asset management entities and their functions**

SERVICES OR FUNCTIONS THAT REQUIRE SPECIFIC ASSETS OWNED BY OR USED BY THE COUNTY	ASSET MANAGEMENT ENTITIES		
	COUNTY DEPARTMENT RESPONSIBLE FOR THE RESPECTIVE SERVICES	COMPANY OR OTHER INDEPENDENT ENTITY OWNED BY THE COUNTY	PRIVATE SERVICE PROVIDER OR PRIVATE MANAGING ENTITY UNDER PPP
General administration			
Office buildings	Transport Infrastructure, Public Works, and Energy	n.a.	n.a.
Urban services			
Roads and drainage	Transport Infrastructure, Public Works, and Energy	n.a.	Outsourcing construction of large infrastructure projects
Public transport	Transport Infrastructure, Public Works, and Energy	County provides for no public transport	Some private providers: taxi, rickshaw, minibus
Water and wastewater lines	Environment, Water, and Natural Resources	Kakamega Water and Sanitation Company; Community water projects run by counties	Water resource users' associations manage small water entities
Solid waste	Environment, Water, and Natural Resources	n.a.	Outsourced to private sector to support Kazi mashenani initiative[a]
Social services			
Health	Health Services	Chief staff of health facilities	n.a.
Education	Education, Science, and Technology	Chief staff of schools	n.a.

Source: Kakamega County Government website and field survey.
Note: n.a. = not applicable; PPP = public-private partnership.
a. Public works jobs for unemployed youth.

a special arrangement for managing specific county assets either by county entities like Kakamega Water and Sanitation Company or by private entities like private minibuses serving public transport.

Construction of all buildings is done by the public works, transportation, or energy departments. However, entities of ministries kept managing many assets that ought to have been handed over to devolved local governments. The county staff and entities did not pay much attention to assets unrelated to devolved service functions such as land; this has caused substantial financial and material damages, still unmeasured to date.

Asset takeover by the power of law, 2017

Gazette Notice no. 858 (Notice 858, 2017) transferred the assets and liabilities of the defunct local authorities by the power of the law and set a framework for validation, verification, and valuation of the assets by the counties. The gazette notice also ruled to create County Asset and Liability Committees (CALCs) whose function was the identification, verification, and validation of the assets and liabilities of the defunct local authorities as of March 27, 2013. The work was conducted under the policy and leadership direction of the Intergovernmental Relations Technical Committee (IGRTC). CALC appointed field verification teams by main asset classes such as land, buildings, equipment, vehicles, furniture, and accessories and used the unaudited list of assets from the TA (IGRTC 2017).

Further, Notice no. 2701 (Notice 2701, 2017) extended the deadline for completion of the exercise from March 31, 2017, to July 31, 2017. Box 8.2 explains key actions conducted to verify and validate assets and liabilities in Kakamega County under CALC. IGRTC and the TA records handed over to counties in 2017

BOX 8.2

Kakamega County assets and liabilities validation excerpts: Key actions

The purpose of the exercise was to identify, verify, validate, and transfer the assets and liabilities of defunct local authorities to respective county governments. The following data collection strategies to collect both primary and secondary data were used:

Interviews. These were conducted with key informants and officers at the county headquarters and subcounties and others who had previously worked in the defunct local authorities including treasurers and clerks.

Document review. The team examined primary supporting documents like title deeds, logbooks, assets registers, valuation reports, certificates, and other related records. Secondary data was collected through valuation reports, auditor-general reports, handover and takeover reports, lands registry records, adjudication registers, preliminary index maps, registry index maps, bank statements, financial statements, and reviews of reports of the Local Authorities Integrated Financial Operations Management System [LAIFOMS].

Physical inspection [and/or] verification of assets through site visits.
Public participation. Additional data were collected from the public, members of which submitted written memoranda following public notices in both print and electronic media sent to churches and public gatherings requesting for information on assets and liabilities of defunct local authorities.

Data was analyzed using the narrative method and presented using thematic analysis and photographic evidence.

Source: Kakamega CALC 2017.

served as a starting point for validation. TA records show that Kakamega County inherited K Sh 431 million in current assets and K Sh 1,428 million in liabilities from the defunct local authorities.

Progress by 2019

The verification teams assigned by the Kakamega County CALC made site visits to physically identify, verify, and validate land parcels the county inherited from the defunct local authorities. The results presented below are from the Kakamega CALC report 2017 and cross-checked with the IGRTC 2018 summary report. Table 8.5 presents a summary of land and buildings Kakamega County inherited from the defunct local authorities. In the process of identifying and verifying land, the team found parcels that had been surveyed but not registered, so there were no records of users, and in other cases, some parcels did not have green cards that would have facilitated the identification of users and land size. Of a total of 6,138 plots, 352 (or 5 percent) were unsurveyed or unregistered.

Verification teams have identified and recorded numerous plots that had been illegally taken over by private or public third parties: that is, had been encroached. Shinyalu Subcounty had the highest number of encroachment cases, nearly half of total parcels. Of the total 717 parcels, 339 were found to have been encroached, 5 parcels were partially encroached, and 1 encroached parcel appeared in the Ndung'u Commission's land report. The most encroached areas were wells, cattle dips, markets, health centers, and market sites.

TABLE 8.5 **Kakamega County summary of inherited land and buildings**

ASSET	BLOCK OR SUBCOUNTY	NUMBER OF PLOTS
Land	Block I	905
	Block II	415
	Block III	386
	Block IV	745
	Lugari/Likuyani	975
	Navakholo	67
	Malava	371
	Ikolomani	306
	Shinyalu	717
	Mumias East	34
	Mumias West	158
	Matungu	79
	Khwisero	210
	Butere	191
	Lurambi	217
Subtotal		**5,776**
Unsurveyed or unregistered plots		352
Land total		**6,138**
Buildings		**347**

Source: Kakamega CALC 2017.

A total of 347 buildings were identified and verified. Of this total, 254 were residential units that were spread across the defunct local authorities, and the rest were offices, schools, or clinics, but the 19 hospitals, some with several buildings, have not been accounted as county owned.

The CALC team identified a total of 109 projects that were ongoing in March 2013. The projects were concentrated on building classrooms and dispensaries, rehabilitating roads, and protecting water sources. However, CALC teams failed to provide detailed information about the status of those projects as of 2017; experiences in other counties suggest that the bulk of those projects presumably were completed subsequently and became part of the asset inventory without notice or distinction. Likewise, part of these ongoing projects could have been left incomplete or even cancelled without commencing. The CALC team found no material evidence to authenticate the status of the list of ongoing projects.

The other immovable assets the Kakamega County CALC team identified were as follows:

- *Motor vehicles.* Sixty motor vehicles were identified and verified, but only 11 vehicles were operational. Furthermore, most of them did not have logbooks, which the CALC noted were lost during the transition to devolution to county government.
- *Furniture and fittings.* A total of 149 pieces of furniture and fittings were identified and verified. They were found to be in good condition and were in different offices in Butere, Kakamega, Lugari, Malava, Mumias, and Shinyalu.
- *Equipment.* There were 76 pieces of equipment in various locations of the county. The equipment identified and verified was in good condition. Some of the items identified under this category included medical equipment, office equipment, and telephone sets.
- *Computers.* One hundred forty-three sets of computers and 80 computer accessories were identified and found in working condition.
- *Biological assets.* A plantation of 0.5 acres of blue gum trees was verified by Malava Town Council.

Following national government guidance, the Kakamega County government prepared a fixed-asset register summary for the 2017/18 fiscal year (table 8.6). This is a step in a good direction. However, there are shortcomings: First, the financial report suggests a K Sh 17 billion asset acquisition since devolution (table 8.3). Against that, this summary reflects only K Sh 4 billion total gross value, and for fiscal year 2017/18 only K Sh 1 billion acquisition against the K Sh 3 billion in the financial report. Second, the report seems to reflect gross value, since no amortization is accounted despite rules set forth in PFM Act 2012. It is important to note that good asset registers should reflect book value and depreciation of assets regardless of whether the county follows cash-based accounting principles in bookkeeping and financial reports.

The Kakamega CALC team identified K Sh 580 million of inherited current assets, which is a much higher amount than the K Sh 431 million recorded in the TA report (table 8.7). The Kakamega and Lugari County Councils owned most of the current assets. A review of the current asset streams shows that compensation in lieu of rates (CILOR) by national government entities constituted 55 percent of the current assets, while uncollected rents from stalls, plots, or houses constituted 25 percent of the current assets. Uncollected property rates were also substantial and were particularly large in Kakamega and Mumias councils; late-payment penalties recorded in Kakamega County Council appeared to be greater than the principal value of the unpaid taxes. Kakamega County will have to develop a workout program to enforce collection of these inherited assets, at least a substantial portion of them with rebates if that helps. Meanwhile, the county should establish a reliable system for timely collection and enforcement of new tax payments.

Kakamega County CALC teams identified inherited liabilities worth more than twice as much as those indicated in the TA report (table 8.8). Teams identified a total of K Sh 3,070 million, while TA reported K Sh 1,429 million as of March 2013. The largest volume of inherited liabilities, nearly K Sh 3 billion, is listed as "other" without specifying, but those are supposedly claimed by contractors and suppliers. The CALC team left this single largest item uncommented and undetailed, except marking a small portion, K Sh 77 million, as the subject of court cases. Court-related creditors claim K Sh 56.6 million, the amount claimed by the plaintiff, while the associated legal fees amount to K Sh 21.1 million.

TABLE 8.6 Kakamega County fixed asset register summary, June 30, 2018

K Sh (millions)

	HISTORICAL COST JUNE 30, 2017	ADDITIONS IN FY 2017/18	HISTORICAL COST JUNE 30, 2018
Land	67	0	67
Buildings and structures	2,714	1,098	3,812
Transport equipment	211	27	238
Office equipment	27	16	43
ICT equipment and software	44	8	52
Other machinery	9	13	22
Heritage, cultural assets	—	—	—
Total in register	**3,071**	**1,162**	**4,233**
Total asset acquisition/development after devolution	n.a.	3,062	16,908

Source: OAG 2018.
Note: — = not available; n.a. = not applicable; FY = fiscal year; ICT = information and communication technology.

TABLE 8.7 Kakamega County summary of inherited current assets, by DLAs, 2013

K Sh (millions)

	CASH AND BANK DEPOSITS	PROPERTY RATES	HOUSE AND PLOT RENTS	OTHER CURRENT ASSETS	TOTAL
Butere-Mumias	14.8	0	13.6	1.7	30.1
Kakamega Municipal Council	0	14.9	96.6	3.6	115.0
Lugari County Council	0	0	11.3	211.3	222.6
Mumias Municipal	0	46.3	0.0	0	46.3
Malava Town Council	0	0	2.9	14.6	17.5
Kakamega County Council	0	30.8	17.0	101.4	149.1
Total	**14.8**	**92.1**	**141.4**	**332.5**	**580.9**

Source: Kakamega CALC 2017.
Note: DLAs = defunct local authorities.

TABLE 8.8 **Kakamega County summary of inherited liabilities, 2013 and 2017**
K Sh (millions)

	BANK LOANS	EMOLUMENTS	STATUTORY DEDUCTIONS	OTHER LIABILITIES	TOTAL
As of 2013, per TA report	0.0	18.6	99.0	1,311.0	1,428.6
As of 2017, per CALC report	0.0	18.6	99.0	2,953.2	3,070.8
Net value as of 2017 after settlements	0.0	2.8	64.5	2,953.2	3,020.5

Source: Kakamega CALC 2017.
Note: CALC = County Asset and Liability Committee; TA = Transition Authority.

Lack of specification or comments on the enormous other liabilities suggests that the team either had run out of time or lacked the professional capacity to verify these claims in any manner. Worth noting, however, is that the same team increased the volume of other overdue liabilities by a huge amount of K Sh 1.6 billion against TA estimates without making any comment on the claimants' names or statuses. Thus, the validity of this additional K Sh 1.6 billion needs verification. The team has implicitly approved validity by including this huge additional amount in the CALC list. Another important issue about the status of other liabilities is why and how the commercial creditors have remained silent and failed to take the cases to court. Hidden settlements and maybe land transactions or other compensation could be left to uncover.

There could be one more reason of such increase of identified liabilities, namely that debt repayments budgeted in 2013/14 for K Sh 1.7 billion might have happened before devolution or immediately after devolution (between March and June 2014), but the TA team did not perceive them or link them to inherited liabilities. Or the TA team noticed such settlements and reduced the volume of other liabilities accordingly (to K Sh 1.4 billion). Another reason could be that the CALC team misinterpreted these liabilities based on missing records and failed to find evidence of repayment of K Sh 1.6 billion liabilities. The amount seems to coincide with the difference estimated by TA and CALC on inherited liabilities vis-à-vis other creditors. The CALC or the Finance Department of Kakamega County should scrutinize the other liabilities closely because of their extremely large volume; workout of these liabilities requires specific information on creditors and proof of claims.

CALC teams verified the bulk of due emoluments and questioned or deemed unverified approximately K Sh 3 million unpaid emoluments, and then the county paid out all the verified emoluments (K Sh 15.8 million) to former staff of Kakamega, Mumias, and Mumias Butere councils. The CALC team did not question unpaid statutory deductions (K Sh 99 million), except a symbolic amount to National Social Security Fund, and then the county paid about a third of dues (K Sh 34.6 million), largely tax arrears, to Kenya Revenue Authority.

Challenges Kakamega CALC faced during verification and validation of inherited assets and liabilities in 2017

The CALC teams noted several challenges while undertaking asset verification and validation work. The main reported challenges include the following:

- Notice no. 2701 of March 24, 2017, required the respective CALCs to submit their reports by July 15, 2017, but the Kakamega CALC commenced the work quite late in May. The verification work was tedious because the huge number of assets required physical verification and validation and the geographic area to be covered was expansive.

- A lack of handover and takeover reports, the closure of defunct local authorities, and the closure of TA left CALC without guidance for undertaking the validation.
- Logistical constraints related to covering the vast county given limited time and shortage of transport or vehicles was another drawback. Only one vehicle was available for CALC teams, while at least three vehicles were needed.
- The county executive committee approved a budget of K Sh 9.8 million to facilitate the mandate of the committee. However, funds to cover both the logistical and living needs of the committee members were not released on time, forcing the committee to adjourn for weeks. Further, the funds were not consistent with the required workload and labor.
- There was a lot of hostility from some members of the community. Some may have encroached public county land. Pushback came especially from Elungito, Mautuma Scheme through Mukhuyu, Matunda, Nzoia Scheme, and Serekeya Scheme to Msalaba Yellow.

LESSONS LEARNED

Kakamega County acknowledges the importance of having an asset management unit within the Finance Department. The Finance Department has hired a consulting firm for asset tagging. This exercise is built on the CALC report. The county is in the process of updating the valuation roll, likely to take place in phases starting from urban areas and moving toward rural areas. The valuation roll will provide a reliable base for property taxation and in the meantime will provide Kakamega with a reliable inventory of county land assets and their corresponding market values. Kakamega County also plans to set up an Asset Management Directorate under the Finance Department soon. Asset management is getting on track in Kakamega County.

Through the Finance Department, Kakamega County can take several steps to effectively manage its assets. First, it could appoint an asset management team or set up an Asset Management Directorate, which should build close coordination with other sectors or departments in order to have an effective asset management framework. Then the development of an asset management policy, strategy, and annual plan is imperative to improve asset management and use assets strategically.

The verification of inherited assets and liabilities shows partial success, and the CALC is no longer functional. Thus, an asset management department should take the lead to complete asset takeover. This also should include protecting the interests of Kakamega County in taking over assets from national government entities, as national government programs will commence in coming years.

The total inherited current liabilities are almost four times greater than the total inherited current assets, which might have much lower present value than the reported K Sh 580 million estimated as of March 2013. The county has no financial capacities to work out the inherited liabilities and certainly requires guidance and support from the National Treasury (through its National Assets and Liabilities Management Department) and IGRTC for pragmatic workout.

The county will require collection of inherited current assets, largely uncollected taxes and fees, mostly from CILOR, and increased OSR. It also might need a bridge loan to work out all verified inherited liabilities in the medium term and stop fast accumulation of inherited liabilities by penalties or other charges. But the first and most important step should be verification and valuation of all land, especially the land parcels not related to key services, which can be sold to generate money for increasing key investments and settling inherited liabilities. The current land prices suggest that selling a small number of parcels can finance workout of inherited liabilities.

Kakamega County inherited a large volume of land (the total number of plots is twice as large as the number of plots Nairobi City County owns). One of the most urgent actions should be for the county to start a robust program to streamline management of land assets, work out disputed cases on encroached land, set market value for surplus land (land that does not serve specific services), and start using its land portfolio strategically to accelerate development and reduce inherited and new liabilities.

REFERENCES

CBK (Central Bank of Kenya). 2020. Inflation rates 2013-2019, https://www.centralbank.go.ke/inflation-rates/.

CGA. 2012. County Governments Act No. 17 of 2012. http://www.parliament.go.ke/sites/default/files/2017-05/CountyGovernmentsAct_No17of2012_1.pdf.

CRAB. 2015. County Revenue Allocation Bill 2015–2017. http://kenyalaw.org/kl/fileadmin/pdfdownloads/bills/2017 /CountyAllocationofRevenueBill_2017.pdf.

Farvacque-Vitkovic, C., and M. Kopanyi. 2019. *Better Cities Better World: A Handbook on Local Government Self-Assessments*. Washington, DC: World Bank. https://openknowledge.worldbank.org/handle/10986/32120.

IGRTC (Intergovernmental Relations Technical Committee). 2017. "Unaudited IGRTC Current Assets and Liability List as at 27 March 2013." Intergovernmental Relations Technical Committee from files of Transition Authority. Nairobi: IGRTC.

IGRTC (Intergovernmental Relations Technical Committee). 2018. *Report on the Identification, Verification, Validation, and Transfer of Assets and Liabilities of the Defunct Local Authorities as at 27th March 2013*. Nairobi: IGRTC. https://igrtc.go.ke/download/consolidated-report-on-assets-and-liabilities-of-the-defunct-local-authorities-2018/.

Kakamega CALC (County Asset and Liability Committee). 2017. *Kakamega CALC Report*. Kakamega County CALC.

Kakamega County. 2018a. *County Integrated Development Plan (CIDP) 2018–2022*. Kakamega, Kenya: County Government of Kakamega. https://kakamega.go.ke/download/kakamega-county-urban-institutional-development-strategy-2018-2022/.

Kakamega County. 2018b. "Kakamega County Budget Review and Outlook Paper (CBROP) 2018." Kakamega, Kenya: County Government of Kakamega. https://kakamega.go.ke/download/kakamega-county-budget-and-review-paper-cbrop-2018/.

Kenya Constitution. 2010. http://kenyalaw.org/kl/index.php?id=398.

KNBS (Kenya National Bureau of Statistics). 2018. *Basic Report on Well Being in Kenya* (based on Household Budget Survey 2015/16). Nairobi: KNBS. https://www.knbs.or.ke/download/basic-report-well-kenya-based-201516-kenya-integrated-household-budget-survey-kihbs/#.

KNBS (Kenya National Bureau of Statistics). 2019. "Kenya Population and Housing Census." Nairobi: KNBS. https://housingfinanceafrica.org/documents/2019-kenya-population-and-housing-census-reports/.

Ministry of Local Government (MLG) Circular, ref. no. MLG/1333/TY/ (52) of February 18, 2013.

Notice 858. 2017. Gazette Notice no. 858, January 8, 2017: Intergovernmental Relations Act no. 2 of 2012. https://gazettes.africa/gazettes/ke-government-gazette-dated-2017-01-27-no-13.

Notice 2701. 2017. Gazette Notice no. 2701, March 24, 2017: Intergovernmental Relations Act no. 2 of 2012. https://gazettes.africa/archive/ke/2017/ke-government-gazette-dated-2017-03-24-no-37.pdf.

OAG (Office of the Auditor General). 2013–19 (annually). *Report of the Auditor General on Financial Statement of Counties*. Nairobi: OAG. http://www.oagkenya.go.ke/index.php/reports/cat_view/2-reports/11-county-governments/203-county-government-reports.

OCB (Office of the Controller of Budget). 2014–18 (annually). *Annual County Government Budget Implementation Review Report*. Nairobi: https://cob.go.ke/reports/consolidated-county-budget-implementation-review-reports/.

PFM. 2012. Public Finance Management Act, no. 18 of 2012. https://www.pcf.go.ke/index.php/public-financial-management-act.

PPAD. 2015. Public Procurement and Asset Disposal Act, no. 33 of 2015, December 18, 2015. http://kenyalaw.org:8181/exist/kenyalex/actview.xql?actid =No.%2033%20of%202015.

TDG. 2012. Transition to Devolved Government Act, no. 1 of 2012, enacted March 9, 2012. http://www.parliament.go.ke/sites/default/files/2017-05/TransitiontoDevolvedGovernmentActNo1of2012.pdf.

UAC. 2011. Urban Areas and Cities Act, no. 13 of 2011. http://www.parliament.go.ke/sites/default/files/2017-05/UrbanAreasandCitiesAct_No13of2011.pdf.

UAC. 2019. Urban Areas and Cities (Amendment) Act 2019. http://kenyalaw.org/kl/fileadmin/pdfdownloads/AmendmentActs/2019/Urban AreasandCities_Amendment_Act_2019.pdf.

World Bank. 2018. *Kenya Economic Update*. 17th ed., April 2018. Washington, DC: World Bank. https://documents.worldbank.org/en/publication/documents-reports/documentdetail/327691523276540220/kenya-economic-update-policy-options-to-advance-the-big-4-unleashing-kenya-s-private-sector-to-drive-inclusive-growth-and-accelerate-poverty-reduction.

9 Kiambu County

INTRODUCTION

Kiambu County is in the central region of Kenya and borders Kajiado, Machakos, Murang'a, Nairobi, Nakuru, and Nyandarua counties. It covers approximately 2,544 square kilometers. The county has 10 administrative units (subcounties): Gatundu North, Gatundu South, Githunguri, Kiambu, Kikuyu, Lari, Limuru, Ruiru, Thika East, and Thika West. There are 12 political units (constituencies): Gatundu North, Gatundu South, Githunguri, Juja, Kabete, Kiambaa, Kiambu, Kikuyu, Lari, Limuru, Ruiru, and Thika Town (map 9.1). Unlike other counties, the political units do not match the administrative units; hence, there are 12 constituencies and 60 electoral wards with 60 elected members of the County Assembly.

Kiambu County had a population of 2.4 million and average population density of 952 people per square kilometer in 2019 (KNBS 2019). A review of population density by urban areas shows that Kabete constituency has the highest population density, with 2,534 people per square kilometer followed by Kiambaa constituency, which has 2,153 per square kilometer. These two constituencies are close to Nairobi City, which explains their high density. Kiambu County has a population dependency ratio of 59 percent as compared to the 78.3 percent national average; of a total population of 1,795,999 people, 666,446 were ages 0–14 or over 65 years in 2014 (KNBS 2018).

Out of its total land area of 2,544 square kilometers, 1,878 are arable (KNBS 2018). The main crops are maize and beans. A total of 11,323 hectares of land are under irrigation to produce fruits and vegetables (the top three products are kale, cabbage, and spinach). In the fishing sector, there are 1,379 ponds. The industrial sector is much more developed than the agriculture sector; there are 237 factories; of these, 152 are cottage factories that produce animal feeds (30), coffee (13), tea (13), milk (11), and other products. Most of the factories (113) are in Thika subcounty, followed by Limuru with 18.

There were 9,781 business licenses issued in 2017, the majority of which (6,230) were for trade activities (World Bank 2018). Kiambu County has 374 registered

MAP 9.1

Kiambu County

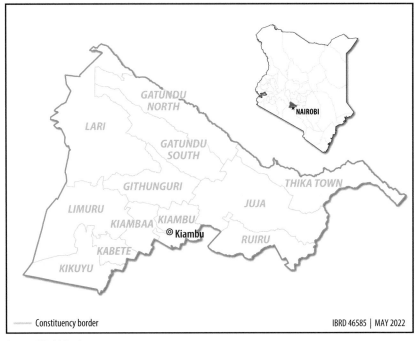

Source: World Bank.

cooperatives, of which 314 are active. The most common cooperatives are urban Sacco with over 82,000 members and an annual turnover of K Sh 1.2 billion. The Sacco dairy cooperative has approximately 60,000 members and an annual turnover of K Sh 7.2 billion. The Sacco coffee cooperative has 55,000 members with an annual turnover of K Sh 516 million.

There is one public university, four private universities, an institute of technology, and a technical training institute. The county has 1 county general hospital, 14 subcounty hospitals, 33 public health centers, and 72 public dispensaries. There are 26 private hospitals and 147 private clinics.

The decentralized functions (per Constitution 2010) of the county government include agriculture, health, control of pollution, cultural activities, transport, animal welfare, trade and development, county planning and development, preprimary education, village polytechnics, home craft centers and early childhood education, environmental conservation, public works, and local community public participation. The county is mandated per the Urban Areas and Cities Acts 2011 and 2019 (UAC 2011, 2019) and County Governments Act (CGA 2012) to provide the following services: solid waste disposal, street lighting, public housing, office and shop rental, hospitals, preschools, vocational schools, a sports stadium, a game park, markets, and constituency university campuses, among others.

The county has 3,954 kilometers of roads of which 2,034 kilometers are tarmac, 1,480 kilometers are gravel, and 430 kilometers are earth. There is a need to improve roads; many are impassable during the rainy season. The railway infrastructure includes a 13-kilometer line within the county with daily commuter trains, but the system remains underutilized even though there are four railway stations (in Kikuyu, Limuru, Ruiru, and Thika towns). Housing development remains a priority area in Kiambu County given its proximity to Nairobi (Kiambu County 2018a).

The county does not meet its water needs; of the total 469,244 households only 172,872 have access to piped water and 296,371 have access to potable or safe water, even though Kiambu County has 16 permanent rivers originating from Aberdare ranges. Solid waste service is underdeveloped in the county; only 2.6 percent of the urban population has facilities for waste disposal, of which less than 1 percent benefit from organized (private) waste collection: 29.1 percent use garbage pits, 29.6 percent dispose of waste in farm gardens, 12.1 use a public garbage heap, and 25.9 percent opt to burn the waste. The county plans to construct landfills and incineration facilities to handle this challenge (Kiambu County 2018b).

REVENUE AND EXPENDITURE ANALYSIS

Analysis of revenues and expenditures is an integral part of an assessment of asset management because it provides a solid background picture in which assets are positioned, developed, and managed. Revenues generate cash or cash-like instruments that are transient forms of assets, since land can be sold to generate cash revenue to develop schools, or cash can be saved for rainy days. Finally, the surplus remaining after current expenditures are covered with current revenues provides funds for development. Loans or other liabilities can also finance development. In short, revenue and expenditure analysis provides important insights and sheds light on the trends and capacities a county possesses in developing assets and expanding services.

Revenues

Kiambu County's revenues grew an average 13.8 percent per annum in the 2013/14–2017/18 fiscal period (table 9.1). The county relies strongly on national government transfers, which provide for around 80 percent of its revenues. Own-source revenue (OSR) provides for 20 percent of total revenues. This is a relatively high share compared to other Kenyan counties (except Nairobi), but the share of OSR shows a slightly declining trend. The national government has supported devolution by substantially and steadily increasing transfers to counties (CRAB 2015). Transfers from the national government grew on average 13.8 percent, while OSR grew only on average 9.3 percent per annum, which is moderately above inflation (CBK 2020). A closer look at OSR, however, shows a jump after devolution until the 2015/16 fiscal year and then a massive shrinking trend occurred (–17 percent per year) in the following years. One would expect the opposite, or at least a maintenance of the level of OSR in absolute terms; some may mistakenly read these figures that growing transfers crowding out OSR or reducing the willingness of local governments to seriously collect OSR. The equitable share from the national government grew by 15.4 percent per annum, twice as fast as inflation, providing a good cushion to cover growing expenditures and maintaining dynamic development.

TABLE 9.1 **Kiambu County revenues, fiscal years 2013/14–2017/18**

K Sh (millions)

	2013/14	2014/15	2015/16	2016/17	2017/18	AVERAGE GROWTH (%)
Transfers from national government	**6,264**	**6,660**	**8,247**	**9,142**	**10,501**	**13.79**
Equitable share	5,458	6,512	7,464	8,446	9,664	15.35
Conditional grants: National government	806	148	783	695.7	837	0.94
Own-source revenues	**1,246**	**2,107**	**2,446**	**2,217**	**1,778**	**9.30**
Taxes	—	486	298	566	587	6.50
Fees and charges	—	1,050	1,338	1,017	1,045	−0.17
Asset proceeds	—	447	710	491	54	−50.69
Other revenues	1,246	124	100	143	93	−9.14
Financing	**0**	**0**	**556**	**0**	**329**	**n.a.**
Cash reserve from previous year	0	0	0	0	0	n.a.
Loans and grants	0	0	556	0	329	n.a.
Total revenue	**7,510**	**8,767**	**11,249**	**11,359**	**12,608**	**13.80**
Share of OSR (%)	16.6	24.0	21.7	19.5	14.1	−3.98
OSR actual/planned (%)	49.0	65.0	75.0	66.0	88.0	15.76

Source: OAG 2014–18.

Note: — = not available; n.a. = not applicable; OSR = own-source revenue.

The conditional grants from the national government are small and show a flat trend (0.9 percent growth per annum), but they provide steady support to sustain health care services, including free maternal health care, provision of services for level-5 hospitals, leasing of medical equipment, road maintenance, and emergency funds. The conditional grants from development partners were from the Danish International Development Agency (DANIDA) and supported improvement of health facilities in projects in the 2015/16 and 2017/18 fiscal years.

Table 9.2 and figure 9.1 present details about OSR in Kiambu County based on audited accounts. The OSR actual/plan variations (table 9.1) are high above the (100 ±5 percent) international standards (Farvacque-Vitkovic and Kopanyi 2019), but they have steadily improved from 49 percent to 88 percent from the 2013/14 to 2017/18 fiscal year. Fee revenues generate steadily more than half of OSR, and interestingly, health service fees appear to be the largest fee-revenue source, quite an uncommon characteristic even in developed countries. The building permit fees also generate a high volume of revenues comparable to the health service fees.

Tax revenues are not only small, generating about 15–20 percent of OSR, they also show a slightly declining trend; and quite surprisingly the property tax revenues were reported (in audited statements) as decreased to zero in 2015/16. This issue deserves the attention of the county's highest executive bodies and should induce corrective measures. Asset proceeds generated a substantial volume of OSR and seem to have been used to counterbalance OSR volatility three years into transition with items such as "other property charges,"

TABLE 9.2 **Kiambu County OSR, fiscal years 2013/14–2017/18**
K Sh (millions)

	2013/14	2014/15	2015/16	2016/17	2017/18	AVERAGE GROWTH (%)
Taxes	—	**603**	**399**	**566**	**587**	**−0.89**
Property rates (property tax)	—	189	0	244	181	−1.48
Business permits (business tax)	—	297	299	202	182	−15.06
Other taxes and levies	—	117	101	121	224	24.24
Fees and charges	—	**900**	**1,458**	**1,017**	**1,045**	**5.11**
Parking fees	—	242	308	302	226	−2.31
Urban services	—	—	—	60	42	n.a.
Social services	—	535	511	433	494	−2.60
Licenses, permits, certificates	—	123	639	222	283	32.10
Asset proceeds	—	**232**	**448**	**491**	**54**	**−38.64**
Rents and leases	—	38	325	395	2	−62.39
Markets	—	194	123	96	52	−35.73
Other income	**1,246**	**373**	**141**	**143**	**93**	**−37.04**
Total OSR	**1,246**	**2,107**	**2,446**	**2,217**	**1,778**	**9.30**

Source: OAG 2014–18.
Note: — = not available; n.a. = not applicable; OSR = own-source revenue.

FIGURE 9.1

Kiambu County OSR, fiscal years 2014/15–2017/18

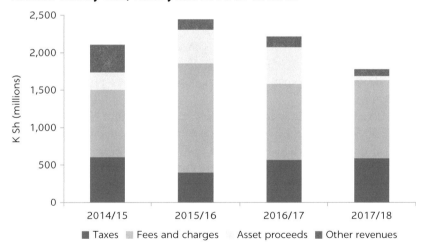

Source: OAG 2014–18.
Note: OSR = own-source revenues.

a one-time income that generated nearly half of asset proceeds in 2015/16. Revenues from taxes increased substantially, and in turn revenues from asset proceeds (presumably sales) dropped by the 2017/18 fiscal year. The reasonable volume of revenues from parking fees is a positive sign of good asset and revenue management.

TABLE 9.3 **Kiambu County expenditures, fiscal years 2013/14–2017/18**

K Sh (millions)

	2013/14	2014/15	2015/16	2016/17	2017/18	AVERAGE GROWTH (%)
Current expenditures	**5,066**	**6,256**	**8,162**	**9,247**	**10,286**	**19.4**
Personal emoluments	3,615	4,320	4,749	4,918	5,887	13.0
Operation and maintenance	1,451	1,936	3,413	1,954	1,449	0.0
Of which, repair and maintenance	—	147	436	384	195	n.a.
Transfers to other entities	—	—	—	2,375	2,950	n.a.
Noncurrent/development	**1,139**	**2,510**	**2,266**	**2,062**	**1,543**	**7.9**
Acquisition of assets	1,139	2,258	2,266	1,946	1,513	7.4
Debt repayment	0	0	0	0	0	n.a.
Other payments	0	252	0	115.7	29	n.a.
Total expenditures	**6,205**	**8,766**	**10,428**	**11,309**	**11,828**	**17.5**
Budget balance	1,305	1	821	50	780	−12.1

Source: OAG 2014–18.
Note: — = not available; n.a. = not applicable.

Expenditures

Kiambu County's total expenditures grew on average by 17.5 percent per annum (table 9.3), which is substantially above the 13.8 percent annual growth of total revenues (table 9.1). These signal an unsustainable trend, yet Kiambu managed to maintain a balanced budget in the surveyed fiscal period. The current expenditures grew remarkably faster than revenues (19.4 percent versus 13.8 percent per annum, respectively), which is a worrisome trend. Development expenditures rightly were spent to the extent the budget allowed to counterbalance the growing current expenditures; as a result, development spending shows high volatility, in part because of slow progress in some development projects.

Under current expenditures, operation and maintenance (O&M) expenses are extremely volatile, which could be a result of misclassification of expenditures. The main expenditures under O&M include domestic travel as the single largest item; the rest comprises maintenance, drugs and vaccines, advertising, printing, and publishing expenses.

The share of current expenditures in total remained high in international comparison (Farvacque-Vitkovic and Kopanyi 2019). It was also a volatile and increasing trend, moving from 82 percent to 87 percent share over the surveyed fiscal period (table 9.4). As a result, the share of development expenditures decreased from 18 percent to 13 percent from the 2013/14 to the 2017/18 fiscal years. Kiambu's development expenditures are somewhat better than most other counties in Kenya, but still are way below the 40 percent of international standards and the national policy target. The shares of personal emoluments show a reasonably declining trend (on average −5.4 percent per annum), but it remained high in international comparison, 57 percent compared to 35 percent, respectively.

The share of O&M in current expenditures grew dynamically from 29 percent in 2013/14 to 42 percent in the 2015/16 fiscal year, then dropped to 14 percent in

TABLE 9.4 **Kiambu County key financial ratios, fiscal years 2013/14–2017/18**

RATIOS (%)	2013/14	2014/15	2015/16	2016/17	2017/18	AVERAGE GROWTH
Operation and maintenance/current	28.6	30.9	41.8	21.1	14.1	−16.3
Personal emoluments/current	71.4	69.1	58.2	53.2	57.2	−5.4
Current/total	81.6	71.4	78.3	81.8	87.0	1.6
Development/total	18.4	28.6	21.7	18.2	13.0	−8.2
Repair and maintenance/current	—	2.3	5.3	4.2	1.9	−6.8

Source: Tables 9.1, 9.2, and 9.3.
Note: — = not available.

FIGURE 9.2

Kiambu County cumulative development expenditures, fiscal years 2013/14–2015/16

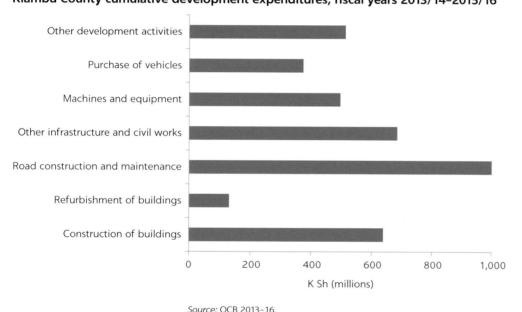

Source: OCB 2013–16.

2017/18, a low share. Kiambu is the best of the surveyed counties in terms of spending on repair and maintenance, but the shrinking share of expenditures on those tasks coincided with the declining O&M. The best share of repair and maintenance was 5.3 percent, still well below international benchmarks in 2015/16, but this share descended further, to 1.9 percent in the 2017/18 fiscal year. This is a very worrisome trend that undermines sustainability of assets and respective services. County government should scrutinize the underlying factors and implement corrective measures.

The share of development expenditures appears to be volatile; it was 29 percent of total expenditures in 2014/15 fiscal year (a good share in Kenya and developing countries) but decreased to 13 percent in 2017/18. Figure 9.2 offers a glimpse into the nature and composition of development expenditures in the first three years of devolution. Construction and refurbishment of roads and construction of buildings were the largest development programs. Oher construction and civil works and the spending development budget for other activities were also substantial. In 2016/17, the top development expenditures were on construction of roads, construction of Githunguri subcounty hospital, and installation of plant and machinery.

The absorption rates—the amount spent from the approved project budgets for the construction of roads and hospitals—were reported to be low (OCB 2017), about 55 percent and 25 percent, respectively. This poor rate of implementation could be attributed to either poor design or poor construction management, or most likely shortage of funds, since the budget surplus appeared to be miniscule (only K Sh 50 million) in 2016/17, and thus the county apparently lacked funds to complete substantially more development projects.

ASSET MANAGEMENT

The case studies of this book focus on the transition period, before which Kenyan local governments did not have asset management systems, frameworks, and policies except some sporadic practices to manage assets daily by officers of service units. Despite legislated mandates—Public Finance Management Act 2012 (PFM 2012), Kenya Constitution 2010, Public Procurement and Asset Disposal (PPAD) Act 2015 (PPAD 2015), County Governments Act (CGA 2012), and government circulars—local governments failed to establish asset registers, and even the accounting aspects of assets were poorly understood and obeyed before devolution. Local bodies failed to measure the wealth of public assets in the possession of local entities and did not aim for increasing it or manage the most important assets strategically. This case study illustrates both the enormous challenges the Kiambu government faced due to the inherited situation and the remarkable progress achieved after devolution. It also demonstrates that moving forward requires strong determination, vision, finances, and reformative actions toward modern and adequate management of assets that eventually determine the level and quality of local public services.

Asset ownership and transition to devolved government

Article 23 of Transition to Devolved Government Act (TDG 2012) regulated the takeover of the functions, assets, liabilities, and staff of the former local authorities—Karuri Town Council, Kiambu County Council, Kiambu Municipal Council, Kikuyu Town Council, Limuru Municipal Council, Ruiru Municipal Council, Thika Municipal Council, and Thika County Council—by the Kiambu County government. The Office of the Auditor General (OAG) further conducted a special audit for the period March 5 to June 30, 2013. The objective was to ensure a seamless transition process and proper systems for accountability on public resources before, during, and after transition to county governments (OAG 2013). The 2013 OAG report states that OAG faced delays in obtaining requisite information and supporting documentation required to complete the audit; documents were not secured, and key staff from the former local authorities were transferred to other positions and were not available to provide adequate information.

The OAG 2013 report also notes (box 9.1) that there was no procedure to prepare statements on inherited financial assets and liabilities as of February 2013. Furthermore, the Transition Authority (TA) did not prepare handover reports in 2013 that would account for what was transferred from the defunct local authorities to the county government.

BOX 9.1

Kiambu County audit report excerpts, 2013

Bank Accounts: Closure and Transfer of Bank Accounts

The defunct Local Authorities did not close their bank accounts as of 28 February 2013 as had been directed by the Transition Authority guidelines (TA 2013a). The defunct Local Authorities continued operating most of the accounts up to 2 July 2013 contrary to the directive by the Transition Authority. The total amount transferred from the eight (8) defunct Local Authorities to the County Government operations account was K Sh 281,567,386.

Assets Status

Debtors

Transition Authority Circular Ref. no. TA/2/5 dated 9 January 2013 (TA 2013b), required the Clerks of the Local Authorities to carry out an inventory of all assets, debts and liabilities including movable and immovable assets. All the eight (8) defunct Local Authorities did not maintain individual debtors' ledgers. It was therefore not possible to confirm the completeness and accuracy of the balances provided. Further, there was no evidence in the form of confirmations or correspondences to support the debtor's balance of K Sh 1,733,010,336 transferred from the defunct Local Authorities, out of which K Sh 1,463,562,822 (84.45 percent) relates to Thika Municipal Council. In addition, two (2) defunct Local Authorities had long outstanding Imprest totaling K Sh 3,276,109. Further, the debtors' balances were not

consolidated at the County Head Office. Individual debtors' ledgers should have been maintained and the long outstanding Imprest recovered from the staff through their payrolls. Debtors to be transferred to the County Government should be verified and consolidated in the County Government books after confirming their correctness.

Immovable Assets

A fixed asset register was not maintained and five hundred and ninety-three (593) parcels of land of undetermined value as shown below and within the jurisdiction of the County Government did not have title deeds.

Movable Assets

During the period under review, the County procured 9 motor vehicles for its County Executive Officers at K Sh 47,700,999. These vehicles were, however, fitted with private number plates instead of green number plates.

Creditors and Other Liabilities

The defunct Local Authorities did not maintain individual Creditors ledgers. Although balances of liabilities were given in respect of [Local Authorities Pension Trust of National Social Security Fund], payment in lieu of leave, suppliers and contractors and pending bills, it was not possible to confirm the completeness and accuracy of the same.

Source: OAG 2013.

There were several challenges associated with the move from defunct local authorities to the county governments. First, defunct local authorities did not have debtors' registers or updated debtors' records. Second, the creditors' ledgers lacked relevant supporting documents to authenticate the amounts that were claimed. Lastly, the defunct local authorities did not have fixed-asset registers, so there was no information to ascertain what assets the outgoing entities were supposed to hand over to the incoming county government in March 2013. Thus, it was an unfunded mandate for the incoming county government to establish a fixed-asset register during transition and in a few months' time between March 27 and June 30, 2013. They could have done more and followed due diligence regardless of difficulties and lack of information, especially in taking over current assets and liabilities, but instead the county government seems to have failed in reacting to the audit report, either in the 2014/15 fiscal year or later.

Informal takeover and use of assets, 2013–17

Kiambu County informally and pragmatically took over the defunct local authorities' assets that formed the material base of key local services; this is a major achievement, since the county managed to continue mandated services without interruption. The County Government of Kiambu has continued to manage, refurbish, and even expand some inherited assets through new acquisitions or development of assets. Various county departments continued managing and using the assets associated with their areas of local service mandates (table 9.5).

Sector departments were made responsible for managing assets whose possession was taken over and continued provision of respective services. Floor management of service assets had been established with clear responsibilities, but tasks did not include verification, validation, and establishment of asset registers, inventories, or proper maintenance of logbooks. In short, there was a low level of due diligence. There was some collaboration in managing assets and services; table 9.5 reflects only special arrangements. The Finance and Planning Department collects revenues on behalf of service departments; albeit not effectively.

TABLE 9.5 **Kiambu County asset management entities and their functions**

SERVICES OR FUNCTIONS THAT REQUIRE SPECIFIC ASSETS OWNED BY OR USED BY THE COUNTY	ASSET MANAGEMENT ENTITIES		
	COUNTY DEPARTMENT RESPONSIBLE FOR THE RESPECTIVE SERVICES	COMPANY OR OTHER INDEPENDENT ENTITY OWNED BY THE COUNTY	PRIVATE SERVICE PROVIDER OR PRIVATE MANAGING ENTITY UNDER A PPP
General administration			
Office buildings	Roads, Transport, Public Works, and Utilities	n.a.	Tendered out to private supply services
Urban services			
Roads and drainage	Roads, Transport, Public Works, and Utilities	n.a.	Tendered out to private supply services
Water and wastewater lines	Water, Environment, Energy, and Natural Resources	Kiambu Water Company	n.a.
Solid waste	Water, Environment, Energy, and Natural Resources	n.a.	Outsourced to private sector through competitive process
Social services			
Health	Health Services	Heads of health units	n.a.
Education	Education	Heads of schools	n.a.

Source: Kiambu County Government website and field survey.
Note: n.a. = not applicable; PPP = public-private partnership.

Asset takeover by the power of law, 2017

Legal Notice no. 858 (Notice 858, 2017) transferred the assets and liabilities of the defunct local authorities by the power of the law and set a framework for validation, verification, and valuation of the assets by the counties. Notice no. 858 stipulated establishment of the County Asset and Liability Committee (CALC), the function of which was the identification, verification, and validation of the assets and liabilities of the defunct local authorities as of March 27, 2013. The Intergovernmental Relations Technical Committee (IGRTC) provided policy, guidance, training, and leadership for completing the verification program. Legal Notice no. 2701 (Notice 2701, 2017) maintained the substance of Notice no. 858 but replaced it and extended the deadline for completion of the processes from March 31, 2017, to July 31, 2017.

The TA records that IGRTC handed over to counties in 2017 (IGRTC 2017) show that Kiambu County inherited over 2,000 pieces of fixed assets without value estimates, K Sh 2,011 million current assets, and K Sh 445 million current liabilities from the defunct local authorities. Verifying these and proposing workout was among the key tasks of CALC.

Progress by 2019

CALC teams made site visits to physically identify, verify, and validate parcels of land and buildings the county inherited from the defunct local authorities; results are summarized in table 9.6. Of the total 1,769 parcels of land, approximately 96 percent were surveyed. Land was used for various purposes such as bus parks, cattle dips, education or health facilities, rental housing estates, trading centers, water points/wells, social centers, dumpsites, cemeteries, markets, and administration purposes. CALC teams were unable to verify the size of land parcels and their respective values due to a shortage of time to complete the surveys. The CALC team reported no encroachments of land or buildings, a unique situation compared with other Kenyan counties. A total of 164 buildings were identified and verified; they were largely education facilities, health facilities, residential houses, and office blocks. Kiambu asset data are from Kiambu CALC report 2017 and cross-checked with the IGRTC 2018 report.

Inherited movable assets the Kiambu County CALC teams identified in 2017 were as follows:

- *Motor vehicles.* A total of 158 motor vehicles were identified and verified, but only 4 vehicles were operational or in good condition; 64 vehicles were serviceable, but not in use; and 58 vehicles were grounded and not in a state to move. The CALC team was unable to verify the existence of 32 vehicles that were either missing or had an unknown status.
- *Furniture and fittings.* A total of 2,022 pieces of furniture and fittings were identified and verified. They were in good condition and were located and in use in different county offices.
- *Equipment.* There were 127 pieces of equipment verified in various parts of the county. The equipment identified and verified was in good condition. Some of the items identified included printers, electric heaters, photocopiers, generators, and other electronic equipment.
- *Computers.* A total of 385 assorted computers and computer accessories were verified.

TABLE 9.6 **Kiambu County summary of land and buildings from the identification, verification, and validation process, 2013**

LOCAL AUTHORITY	TOTAL NUMBER OF PARCELS OR BUILDINGS	NUMBER OF PARCELS SURVEYED
Land		
Karuri Town Council	273	268
Kiambu County Council	193	189
Kiambu Municipal Council	100	98
Kikuyu Town Council	358	357
Limuru Municipal Council	212	195
Ruiru Municipal Council	314	314
Thika Municipal Council	131	115
Thika County Council	123	120
Outside the above DLAs' jurisdiction	65	35
Total	**1,769**	**1,691**
Buildings		
Karuri Town Council	10	n.a.
Kiambu County Council	2	n.a.
Kiambu Municipal Council	29	n.a.
Kikuyu Town Council	28	n.a.
Limuru Municipal Council	32	n.a.
Ruiru Municipal Council	4	n.a.
Thika Municipal Council	58	n.a.
Thika County Council	0	n.a.
Outside the above DLAs' jurisdiction	1	n.a.
Total	**164**	**n.a.**

Source: Kiambu CALC 2017.
Note: n.a. = not applicable.

The verification teams identified 246 projects valued at K Sh 697 million that were listed as ongoing in March 2013. The projects were aimed at building or renovation of classrooms and dispensaries, road rehabilitation, and protection of water sources. Most of these projects were completed after March 2013 and thus presumably were already included in the list of verified fixed assets, although some might have stalled, been left incomplete, or been canceled before construction commencement. The CALC team failed to find evidence of or information about the status of completed and incomplete or cancelled projects.

Kiambu County government has reported a summary of fixed assets acquired after the transition of March 27, 2013 (table 9.7). This is a move in a good direction. However, the reported numbers do not match the financial reports, in which the total value of investments into fixed assets is reported to be over K Sh 9 billion during the surveyed period as opposed to the register, which indicates only K Sh 5.5 billion value of new assets. Likewise, the reported annual investments in fixed assets were K Sh 1.5 billion, against the reported asset additions of K Sh 1.4 billion.

Finally, asset amortization apparently has not been accounted, or the asset register excludes such figures. Good asset registers should reflect both book value and depreciation of assets regardless of whether the county follows

TABLE 9.7 **Kiambu County fixed asset register summary, June 30, 2018**
K Sh (millions)

	HISTORICAL COST, JUNE 30, 2017	ADDITIONS IN FY 2017/18	HISTORICAL COST, JUNE 30, 2018
Land	15	13	28
Buildings and structures	1,180	376	1,556
Transport equipment	176	106	282
Office equipment	293	27	320
ICT equipment and software	396	0	396
Other machinery	1,051	79	1,131
Heritage, cultural assets	—	—	—
Projects	—	831	831
Biological assets	—	19	19
Total in register	**3,112**	**1,450**	**4,562**
Total asset acquisition/development after devolution	0	1,513	9,520

Source: OAG 2018.
Note: — = not available; FY = fiscal year; ICT = information and communication technology.

TABLE 9.8 **Kiambu County summary of inherited current assets, March 2013**
K Sh (millions)

CASH AND BANK BALANCES	PROPERTY RATE	PLOT AND HOUSE RENT	CILOR	OTHER	INVENTORY	TOTAL
529	1,616	129	121	59	16	2,469
21%	65%	5%	5%	2%	1%	100%

Source: Kiambu CALC 2017.
Note: CILOR = compensation in lieu of rates.

cash-based accounting principles in bookkeeping and financial reports. These discrepancies point to the need to improve consistency within and across financial reports and other statements, but more than that, a need to establish a reliable and up-to-date asset register, which should be a relatively easy task due to well-surveyed and well-identified land and buildings and a relatively small number of other fixed assets in Kiambu.

Kiambu County inherited K Sh 2,469 million current assets (table 9.8). Uncollected overdue property taxes represent about two-thirds of current assets, presumably with much lower present value, which was not estimated. The county inherited over half a billion K Sh in cash and bank balances, while uncollected plot and house rents and compensation in lieu of rates were also of significant value. Thika Municipal Council and Karuri Town Council used to own most of the inherited current assets. The historical face value of inherited current assets appears to be about four times greater than the face value of inherited liabilities, so it seems easy to settle liabilities from assets.

The value of inherited current assets estimated as of 2013 could have increased substantially with accrued interest by 2017. However, the CALC team did not explore, verify, or estimate the accrued value of inherited current assets in 2017. The CALC team has not flagged cases or found evidence of collection of portions of any of these collectibles between March 2013 and November 2017. Thus, these

TABLE 9.9 **Kiambu County summary of inherited liabilities, 2013 and 2017**
K Sh (millions)

	BANK LOANS	EMOLUMENTS	STATUTORY DEDUCTIONS	OTHER LIABILITIES	TOTAL
As of 2013, per TA report	—	—	—	—	444.8
As of 2013, per CALC report 2017	0.0	382.4	307.7	186.5	876.6
Net value, 2017	0.0	382.4	307.7	186.5	876.6

Source: Based on Kiambu CALC 2017.
Note: — = not available; CALC = County Asset and Liability Committee; TA = Transition Authority.

collectibles aged by an additional four years, making collection increasingly difficult. Furthermore, as previously mentioned, the present value of the inherited current assets is much lower, and collection of the present value is still to be tested and is likely to be extremely difficult, but a collection program should be commenced.

Kiambu County inherited K Sh 877 million in face value of liabilities valued as of March 2013, verified in the Kiambu CALC report in 2017 (table 9.9); this is twice as much as the K Sh 445 million value reflected in the unaudited TA report. However, the CALC team found insufficient supporting documentation for some of these liabilities, so they can be considered disputed and require further scrutiny to ensure accurate reflection of the status of liabilities as of 2017. The CALC team did not indicate the reason (for example, accrued interest) or classification of the liabilities identified above and beyond those included in the TA list of liabilities.

Furthermore, the CALC report does not make proposals for follow-up steps toward verification of disputed liabilities and actions toward workout of inherited current assets and current liabilities. This resolution also would include establishing the current value of these liabilities with interest and penalties accrued between March 2013 and the date of the resolution proposal. Table 9.9 suggests that the CALC team only wanted to flag the fact that no resolution or workout happened on any of these inherited liabilities between 2013 and 2017, which is why the team left the face values unchanged.

Challenges Kiambu CALC faced during verification and validation of inherited assets and liabilities

The CALC teams encountered several challenges while undertaking verifications. The main reported challenges included the following:

- Time constraints in obtaining required information for the assets, particularly the value of land and the title deeds for the land, were a major hindrance. Notice 2701 stipulated that CALC reports should have been submitted to IGRTC by July 15, 2017. However, the Kiambu CALC commenced the work quite late (only in May), the exercise was tedious because many assets required physical verification and validation, and the geographic areas to be covered were expansive.
- Inadequate information and lack of institutional memory also hampered efforts. These would have enabled better identification and verification of the assets.
- A limited number of skilled staff further hindered the asset identification process.
- The lack of handover and takeover reports and lack of a report from the TA, which would have guided the field verification work, made documentation difficult.

- Logistical constraints were a concrete challenge. For example, just one vehicle was made available for the field verification, while at least three vehicles were needed.
- There were limited financial resources to undertake the exercise.

LESSONS LEARNED

Kiambu County acknowledges the importance of having an asset management unit, but it is yet to establish one. Currently, the procurement team keeps and manages records of all assets purchased or disposed of since March 2013. There are plans to establish an Asset Management Directorate and develop a policy, but the transition to new leadership through the change of governor in 2017 also has delayed the process of setting up a framework and system.

The Kiambu County CALC team made tremendous efforts in verifying assets and liabilities. The identification and verification of county assets and liabilities requires further scrutiny, especially confirmation of supporting documents, to establish a reliable inventory of assets and liabilities. Even though most of the land is surveyed, there is a need to establish their respective values.

There is an urgent need to establish a reliable and up-to-date fixed asset register, which should be a relatively easy task due to well-surveyed and well-identified land and buildings and a relatively small number of other fixed assets.

Workout of inherited liabilities is very urgent; there is a need to appoint a team to conduct detailed scrutiny of inherited liabilities and seek workout options and modalities. The county may assign a small committee with high-ranking officers to initiate negotiations with creditors for workout of all inherited liabilities. Some of these may require the guidance and involvement of national government entities, especially the National Assets and Liabilities Management Department in the National Treasury and IGRTC.

Collection of inherited financial assets has not yet started. There is a need to set up a team with financial and legal expertise to analyze the portfolio of inherited financial assets, structure claims by age, and estimate present value and then explore options for collection of a fair share of these collectibles, aiming for full elimination of uncollected inherited assets.

There is an urgent need to set up a small and simple unit for asset management, as well as establish an asset management system, strategy, policy, and procedures and a simple initial asset management plan that summarizes the most critical first steps toward establishing a reliable asset management system. Initial actions should focus on strategically managing the high-value assets: land, buildings, and plants.

REFERENCES

CBK (Central Bank of Kenya). 2020. Inflation rates 2013-2019, https://www.centralbank.go.ke/inflation-rates/.

CGA. 2012. County Governments Act No. 17 of 2012. http://www.parliament.go.ke/sites/default/files/2017-05/CountyGovernmentsAct_No17of2012_1.pdf.

CRAB. 2015. County Revenue Allocation Bill 2015–2017. http://kenyalaw.org/kl/fileadmin/pdfdownloads/bills/2017/CountyAllocationofRevenueBill_2017.pdf.

Farvacque-Vitkovic, C., and M. Kopanyi. 2019. *Better Cities Better World: A Handbook on Local Government Self-Assessments.* Washington, DC: World Bank. https://openknowledge.worldbank.org/handle/10986/32120.

IGRTC (Intergovernmental Relations Technical Committee). 2017. "Unaudited IGRTC Current Assets and Liability List as at 27 March 2013." Intergovernmental Relations Technical Committee from files of Transition Authority. Nairobi: IGRTC.

IGRTC (Intergovernmental Relations Technical Committee). 2018. *Report on the Identification, Verification, Validation, and Transfer of Assets and Liabilities of the Defunct Local Authorities as at 27th March 2013*. Nairobi: IGRTC. https://igrtc.go.ke/download /consolidated-report-on-assets-and-liabilities-of-the-defunct-local-authorities-2018/.

Kenya Constitution. 2010. http://kenyalaw.org/kl/index.php?id=398.

Kiambu CALC (County Asset and Liability Committee). 2017. *Kiambu CALC Report*. Kiambu, Kenya: Kiambu County CALC.

Kiambu County. 2018a. "County Budget Review and Outlook Paper." Kiambu, Kenya: Kiambu County Government. https://repository.kippra.or.ke/handle/123456789/704.

Kiambu County. 2018b. *County Integrated Development Plan (CIDP) Covering the Period 2018–2022*. Kiambu, Kenya: Kiambu County Government. https://repository.kippra.or.ke /handle/123456789/709?show=full.

KNBS (Kenya National Bureau of Statistics). 2018. *Basic Report on Well Being in Kenya* (based on Household Budget Survey 2015/16). Nairobi: KNBS. https://www.knbs.or.ke/download /basic-report-well-kenya-based-201516-kenya-integrated-household-budget-survey -kihbs/#.

KNBS (Kenya National Bureau of Statistics). 2019. "Kenya Population and Housing Census." Nairobi. https://housingfinanceafrica.org/documents/2019-kenya-population -and-housing-census-reports/

Notice 858. 2017. Gazette Notice no. 858, January 8, 2017: Intergovernmental Relations Act no. 2 of 2012. https://gazettes.africa/gazettes/ke-government-gazette-dated-2017-01-27-no-13.

Notice 2701. 2017. Gazette Notice no. 2701, March 24, 2017: Intergovernmental Relations Act no. 2 of 2012. https://gazettes.africa/archive/ke/2017/ke-government-gazette-dated-2017-03 -24-no-37.pdf.

OAG (Office of the Auditor General). 2013–19 (annually). *Report of the Auditor General on Financial Statement of Counties*. Nairobi: OAG. http://www.oagkenya.go.ke/index.php /reports/cat_view/2-reports/11-county-governments/203-county-government-reports.

OCB (Office of the Controller of Budget). 2014–17 (annually). *Annual County Government Budget Implementation Review Report*. Nairobi: https://cob.go.ke/reports/consolidated -county-budget-implementation-review-reports/.

PFM. 2012. Public Finance Management Act, no. 18 of 2012. https://www.pcf.go.ke/index.php /public-financial-management-act.

PPAD. 2015. Public Procurement and Asset Disposal Act, no. 33 of 2015, December 18, 2015. http://kenyalaw.org:8181/exist/kenyalex/actview.xql?actid =No.%2033%20of%202015.

TA (Transition Authority). 2013a. "Transition Authority Guidelines," Ref. MOF/IFMIS/1/41 dated 7 March 2013.

TA (Transition Authority). 2013b. "Inventory of Assets and Liabilities Debts and Human Resource Profile in Public Organizations." Circular Ref. no. TA/2/5 dated 9 January 2013.

TDG. 2012. Transition to Devolved Government Act, no. 1 of 2012, enacted March 9, 2012. http:// www.parliament.go.ke/sites/default/files/2017-05/TransitiontoDevolvedGovernment ActNo1of2012.pdf.

UAC. 2011. Urban Areas and Cities Act, no. 13 of 2011. http://www.parliament.go.ke/sites /default/files/2017-05/UrbanAreasandCitiesAct_No13of2011.pdf.

UAC. 2019. Urban Areas and Cities (Amendment) Act 2019. http://kenyalaw.org/kl/fileadmin /pdfdownloads/AmendmentActs/2019/Urban AreasandCities_Amendment_Act_2019.pdf.

World Bank. 2018. *Kenya Economic Update*. 17th ed., April 2018. Washington, DC: World Bank. https://documents.worldbank.org/en/publication/documents-reports/documentdetail/32 7691523276540220/kenya-economic-update-policy-options-to-advance-the-big -4-unleashing-kenya-s-private-sector-to-drive-inclusive-growth-and-accelerate-poverty -reduction.

10 Machakos County

INTRODUCTION

Machakos County has a strategic location in the southern-central area of Kenya and borders seven counties: Embu, Kajiado, Kiambu, Kitui, Makueni, Murang'a, and Nairobi counties. Machakos County covers a total area of 6,208 square kilometers, mostly on hills and small plateaus, and lies at an altitude of 1,800–2,100 meters above sea level (KNBS 2017). Machakos County's administrative units include eight subcounties (Kangundo, Kathiani, Machakos, Masinga, Matungulu, Mavoko, Mwala, and Yatta), 22 divisions, 75 locations, and 239 sublocations. The county's political units include eight constituencies, which are also the sub-counties, and 40 wards. Machakos County was amalgamated in 2013 from two municipalities, Machakos and Mavoko, and three town councils, Kangundo, Masaku, and Matuu (map 10.1).

Machakos County had a population of 1.4 million in 2019, with an average population growth rate of 3.3 percent per annum and average population density of 235 people per square kilometer (KNBS 2019). Yatta subcounty had the highest density of 978 people per square kilometer while Kathiani had the lowest density of 116. The county also has a high population dependency ratio of 85 percent, which is above the national average (KNBS 2018).

Machakos County hosts Masinga Dam at the border of Machakos and Embu counties; it is a key national asset in the provision of water and electricity to Kenya. Masinga also hosts other downstream power plant turbines at Gitaru, Kamburu, Kiambere, and Kindaruma. Agricultural production and tourism are the main economic activities in Machakos County (World Bank 2018). Cash crops include maize, beans, and sorghum, while chicken, cattle, and goats are the most traded animals. Machakos County has 32 banks, mostly in Machakos and Athi River subcounties. The county has 5,614 wage employees, half of whom (2,800) are employed by the county government (Machakos County 2018b). The county has 16 primary schools, 7 high schools, 2 public universities (Machakos University College and South Eastern University), and 3 private universities.

The Constitution of 2010 sets decentralized functions of the counties, including agriculture, health, pollution control, cultural activities, transport, animal welfare, trade and development, county planning and development, preprimary education, village polytechnics, home craft centers and early childhood

MAP 10.1
Machakos County

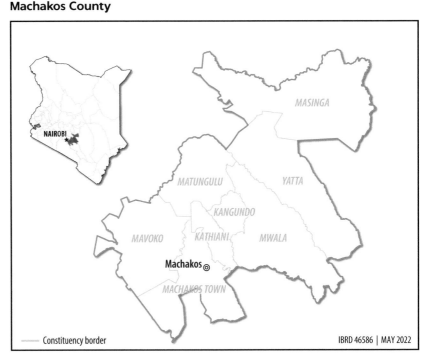

Source: World Bank.

education, environmental conservation, public works, and local community public participation. The services the county is mandated to provide per Urban Areas and Cities Acts 2011 and 2019 (UAC 2011, 2019) and actually provides include street lighting, public housing, office and shop rental, hospitals, preschools, vocational schools, a sports stadium, a game park, markets, and university campuses. Solid waste management remains an area that has not been fully exploited.

The main urban challenge is the inadequate supply of drinking water (Machakos County 2018a), but the county also needs to improve health care services to reduce mortality and morbidity rates, survey urban land, and enhance road infrastructure (of the total 12,152-kilometer road network, only 375 kilometers are tarmac, while 10,628 kilometers are gravel and 1,150 kilometers are earth). There are also needs for adequate marketplaces, street lighting, and sanitation facilities.

REVENUE AND EXPENDITURE ANALYSIS

Analysis of revenues and expenditures is an integral part of an assessment of asset management because it provides a solid background picture in which assets are positioned, developed, and managed. Revenues generate cash or cash-like instruments that are transient forms of assets, since land can be sold to generate cash revenue to develop schools, or cash can be saved for rainy days. Finally, the surplus remaining after current expenditures are covered with current revenues provides funds for development. Loans or other liabilities can also finance development. In short, revenue and expenditure analysis provides important insights and sheds light on the trends and capacities a county possesses in developing assets and expanding services.

Revenues

Machakos County's revenues grew steadily at an average rate of 8.7 percent per annum between the 2013/14 and 2017/18 fiscal years (table 10.1); this is a result of growth of transfers from the national government (10 percent per year) and shrinking own-source revenue (OSR). The national government has supported devolution by substantially and steadily increasing transfers to counties (CRAB 2015). The county is heavily and increasingly reliant on *equitable shares,* which grew by 10.6 percent per annum and provided the bulk of revenues (nearly 90 percent). The conditional grants appear to be small, volatile, and slightly decreasing as a share of total revenues and aim at supporting health and education. Grants were from the Danish International Development Agency, were of moderate size and supported health care service provision.

The county has flexibility in using revenues, because the share of conditional grants is less than 10 percent of total revenues. The County Governments Budget Implementation Review Reports (CBIRRs) (OCB 2014–18) refer to release of funds for "current operation and for development," usually 70 percent and 30 percent, respectively, but the county has disobeyed this rule since the share of development expenditures shrunk from 44 percent to 11 percent between 2013 and 2018 (table 10.1 and table 10.3). Funds used for development, however, do not appear to be conditional grants, since the bulk was from the unconditional equitable shares. Second, conditional grants are small and largely support operation of specific services such as the maternity center instead of development, except the road fund transfers that support road maintenance and development.

TABLE 10.1 **Machakos County revenues, fiscal years 2013/14–2017/18**
K Sh (millions)

	2013/14	2014/15	2015/16	2016/17	2017/18	AVERAGE GROWTH (%)
Transfers from national government	**5,583**	**6,063**	**6,973**	**8,057**	**8,162**	**9.96**
Equitable share	4,951	6,063	6,973	7,303	7,399	10.57
Conditional grants	632	0	0	754	763	4.81
Own-source revenues	**1,175**	**1,358**	**1,122**	**1,259**	**1,084**	**−1.99**
Taxes	—	230	208	178	189	−6.38
Fees and charges	—	416	261	239	189	−23.12
Asset proceeds	—	408	409	456	398	−0.78
Other revenues	1,175	304	244	386	308	0.49
Financing	**0**	**119.6**	**208**	**353.2**	**184.7**	**15.59**
Cash reserve from previous year	—	—	—	—	—	n.a.
Loans/grants	0	119.6	208	353.2	185	15.59
Total revenue	**6,758**	**7,540**	**8,303**	**9,670**	**9,431**	**8.69**
Share of OSR (%)	17.4	18.0	13.5	13.0	11.5	−9.82
OSR actual/planned (%)	48.0	48.0	47.0	44.0	47.0	−0.52

Source: OAG 2014–18.
Note: — = not available; n.a. = not applicable; OSR = own-source revenue.

The county's OSR was stable in size but shows a shrinking trend, declining by 2 percent per year between 2013 and 2018; as a result, the share of OSR shrunk from 17 percent to 11 percent by 2018; this is a very worrisome tendency. Besides, there is a revenue-classification issue, since "other revenues" are accounted steadily as the second largest source. Interviews suggest that transfers were largely released according to annual plans, albeit with fluctuation within the fiscal years. In contrast, the county repeatedly has collected less than half of the planned OSRs in each surveyed year (table 10.1), which signals the need for more accurate revenue forecasts and more effective and efficient revenue collection systems.

Proceeds from local assets, including rents and leases of land, shops, or housing units and loyalty from natural resources, provide for nearly half of OSR, which underlines the importance of good asset management and reliable asset records (figure 10.1). Figures show a downward trend of OSR and a steady decrease of tax and fee revenues both in absolute and relative terms. Furthermore, the OSR collection rates were low, around or below 50 percent in the surveyed period, and the county fails to improve collection although it repeatedly plans for and budgets a much higher volume of revenues from taxes, fees, and charges. Therefore, data do not support estimation of the real revenue potentials from OSRs.

The county presumably had strongly relied on asset proceeds to balance budgets; however, asset proceeds seem to have been collected from fees or sale or lease of assets, which were not yet taken over legally. Financial reports are not clear about whether Machakos County generated revenues by selling assets such as land or only collected fees from assets. Another challenge is that the large share of unspecified "other revenues" may cover sale of assets, which signals poor revenue management and misclassification of revenues. Office of the Auditor General (OAG) reports do not comment on possible misclassification of revenues.

FIGURE 10.1

Machakos County OSR, fiscal years 2014/15–2017/18

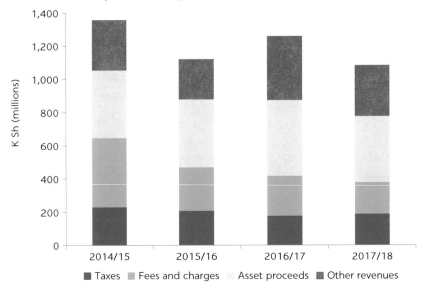

Source: OAG 2014–18.
Note: OSR = own-source revenue.

TABLE 10.2 **Machakos County OSR, fiscal years 2013/14–2017/18**
K Sh (millions)

	2013/14	2014/15	2015/16	2016/17	2017/18	AVERAGE GROWTH (%)
Taxes	—	**230**	**208**	**178**	**189**	**−6.4**
Property rates (property tax)	—	0	0	0	0	n.a.
Business permits (business tax)	—	199	198	171	183	−2.8
Other taxes and levies	—	31	10	7	6	−41.7
Fees and charges	—	**416**	**261**	**239**	**189**	**−23.1**
Parking fees	—	103	92	79	47	−23.2
Urban services	—	19	16	19	31	17.8
Social services	—	154	34	91	73	−22.1
Licenses, permits, certificates	—	140	119	50	38	−35.2
Asset proceeds	—	**408**	**409**	**456**	**398**	**−0.8**
Rents and leases	—	351	361	412	351	0.0
Markets	—	57	48	44	47	−6.3
Other income	**1,175**	**304**	**244**	**386**	**308**	**0.5**
Total OSR	**1,175**	**1,358**	**1,122**	**1,259**	**1,084**	**−7.2**

Source: OAG 2014–18.
Note: — = not available; n.a. = not applicable; OSR = own-source revenue.

The county did not report details of OSR for the 2013/14 fiscal year, instead reporting only a bulk number of total OSR (reflected in table 10.2 as other income). The county reported zero property tax revenues, which could be a classification error if they are accounted among other income. However, OAG audits did not comment on this, so likely they endorsed the zero property tax revenues. Machakos County stands out in uncollected property taxes among surveyed counties, and presumably also among all 47 Kenyan counties. The steadily declining revenues from parking fees and licenses and permits is also a worrisome tendency that eventually will undermine service sustainability and reflects poor asset management.

Expenditures

Machakos County's total expenditures show steady dynamic growth, on average 20.8 percent per annum, more than twice as fast as the growth of total revenues (8.7 percent per year) in the surveyed 2013/14–2017/18 fiscal period (table 10.1 and table 10.3). This is a worrisome tendency that will lead to financial distress in the short to medium term. There are many other worrying trends, too. First, the current expenditures grew much faster than the current revenues. Second, labor expenditures (personal emoluments) grew at an unprecedented pace, on average 24.7 percent per year in the surveyed period. The share of labor expenditures increased to 63 percent of current expenses in 2017/18 from the already high 56 percent share in 2013/14; this is not only an extraordinary movement, but also these shares are high above the 35 percent international benchmark (Farvacque-Vitkovic and Kopanyi 2019).

In sharp contrast, expenditures on operation and maintenance show a massive 9.8 percent contraction per year that will undermine the local services and indicates poor asset management, which is especially worrisome because the county subsequently completed a substantial volume of new investments (K Sh 8.5 billion) in the surveyed period.

Financial ratios show a mixed picture (table 10.3). Expenses on personal emoluments show a volatile but increasing trend, moving from 56 percent to 63 percent by 2018. In contrast to fast-growing current expenditures, actual expenses on asset acquisition show a steady and sharp decline from the peak of K Sh 2.7 billion in 2013/14 to K Sh 0.8 billion in 2017/18, and correspondingly from the share of 44 percent to 11 percent of total revenues. The share of operation and maintenance expenditures dropped to 11 percent in 2017/18 fiscal year. This is a very worrisome and unsustainable trend.

Machakos County mostly accounted positive closing balances and even carried forward some cash reserves over fiscal years, apparently from unspent development expenditures, especially in the 2017/18 fiscal year. Thus, the financial stability is weak and seems unsustainable, and revenue and expenditure trends undermine development capacity. Finally, the positive budget balance corresponds to the money unspent on development that indicates low capacities in managing and timely completion of development projects, which is a critical asset management issue.

The financial reports follow cash-based accounting and thus do not reflect the unpaid bills, neither those inherited from the amalgamated local entities nor those generated after devolution, that is, bills that may have remained unpaid at the end of each surveyed fiscal year. The CBIRR includes a sizable volume of

TABLE 10.3 **Machakos County expenditures, fiscal years 2013/14–2017/18**

K Sh (millions)

	2013/14	2014/15	2015/16	2016/17	2017/18	AVERAGE GROWTH (%)
Current expenditures	**3,401**	**5,105**	**6,400**	**7,682**	**7,239**	**20.8**
Personal emoluments	1,901	3,398	3,668	4,907	4,591	24.7
Operation and maintenance	1,500	1,313	1,321	1,083	993	−9.8
Of which, repair and maintenance	—	98	71	6	13	n.a.
Transfers to other entities	—	394	1,411	1,692	1,656	n.a.
Noncurrent/development	**2,700**	**1,926**	**2,101**	**1,797**	**851**	**−25.1**
Acquisition of assets	2,700	1,919	2,101	1,789	851	−25.1
Debt repayment	—	7.4	0	0	0	n.a.
Other payments	—	0	0	8.1	0	n.a.
Total expenditures	**6,101**	**7,031**	**8,501**	**9,479**	**8,090**	**7.3**
Budget balance	657	509	−198	191	1,341	19.5
Ratios (%)						
Operation and maintenance/current	44.1	25.7	20.6	14.1	13.7	44.1
Personal emoluments/current	55.9	66.6	57.3	63.9	63.4	55.9
Current/total	55.7	72.6	75.3	81.0	89.5	55.7
Development/total	44.3	27.4	24.7	19.0	10.5	44.3
Repair and maintenance/current	n.a.	1.9	1.1	0.1	0.2	n.a.

Source: OAG 2014–18.

Note: — = not available; n.a. = not applicable.

FIGURE 10.2
Machakos County cumulative development expenditures, fiscal years 2013/14–2016/17

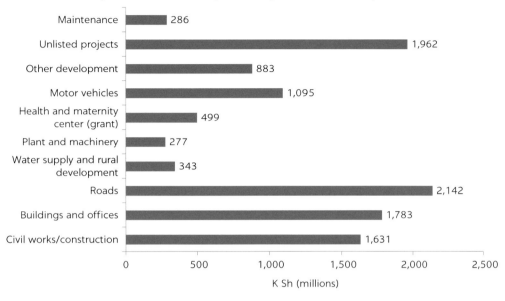

Source: OCB 2014–17.

pending bills for 2014/15 (over K Sh 900 million) and states other years that pending bills were not reported (although those may have existed). Thus, the stable closing balances are correct in cash accounting terms, but do not clearly reflect the financial position of the county unless pending bills were regular liabilities (not overdue) and paid out and accounted for in due time.

The county focused development on roads, buildings, civil works, construction, and acquisition of motor vehicles (figure 10.2). Routine maintenance of assets remained negligible (K Sh 286 million) during the entire five-year fiscal period; it represented about 1.9 percent of the total current expenditures in 2014/15 against the international benchmark of 15 percent (Farvacque-Vitkovic and Kopanyi 2019). The reasons may include either a general negligence of maintenance, a focus on development to the detriment of maintenance, the unclear classification of development and routine maintenance expenditures, or unclear legal status of assets. This is a major asset management challenge, since not only the old assets but also the newly acquired or built assets require routine maintenance. Thus, an increase of capital investments would entail a corresponding increase of maintenance expenditures; in contrast, Machakos County spent less and less on repair and maintenance, whose share in current expenditures dropped to 0.2 percent in 2017/18.

ASSET MANAGEMENT

The case studies of this book focus on the transition period, before which Kenyan local governments did not have asset management systems, frameworks, and policies except some sporadic practices to manage assets daily by officers of service units. Despite legislated mandates—Public Finance Management Act 2012 (PFM 2012), Public Procurement and Asset Disposal Act 2015 (PPAD 2015), Kenya Constitution 2010, County Governments Act

(CGA 2012), and government circulars—local governments failed to establish asset registers, and even the accounting aspects of assets were poorly understood and obeyed before devolution. Local bodies failed to measure the wealth of public assets in the possession of local entities and did not aim for increasing it or manage the most important assets strategically. This case study illustrates both the enormous challenges the Machakos County government faced due to the inherited situation and the remarkable progress achieved after devolution. It also demonstrates that moving forward requires strong determination, vision, finances, and reformative actions toward modern and adequate management of assets that eventually determine the level and quality of local public services.

Asset ownership and transition to devolved government

Article 23 of Transition Act 2012 (TDG 2012) regulated the takeover of the functions, assets, liabilities, and staff of the former local authorities of Machakos and Mavoko municipalities and Kangundo, Masaku, and Matuu Town Councils. Machakos County government considered that the TDG Act directed takeover of assets and liabilities *after validation and audit* by the Transition Authority (TA), and the operation of the TA underscored this approach. But before the devolution elections, a Ministry of Local Government Circular (MLG/1333/2013) directed the clerks as the chief executive officers of the outgoing local authorities to ensure proper handover of documents and accounts to the incoming county government, but this direction appeared to be powerless. This was a timely, sensible, and important directive, but it was in conflict with the interpretation of the TDG Act, which seemed to have paralyzed the local actions for years, since the counties were waiting for the TA to hand over its report to commence takeover accordingly while the TA did not direct or encourage takeover before its final assessments and reports.

The auditor general commenced a special audit in mid-2013 (OAG 2013) and raised several issues regarding lack of handover and takeover of assets and liabilities from the defunct Machakos County Council to Machakos County government (see box 10.1). The main findings include the following:

- There was no formal handover by the defunct local authority to the Machakos County government.
- The defunct local authorities did not close the bank accounts; hence, auditors were unable to establish the cash and bank balances as of March 2013, weeks after induction of the new county government.
- Even though the value of movable assets such as motor vehicles was estimated (K Sh 32.9 million), many vehicles were registered with private number plates, making OAG suspect private use.
- OAG found apparent land grabbing: some defunct entities subdivided land and allocated it to private individuals before transition without office documentation, and land was developed privately by the time of audit.

Informal takeover and use of assets

From its inauguration, Machakos County, without formal takeover, accounts, and valuation, started to use and develop assets, especially those that formed the basis of vital local services, to ensure uninterrupted provision of services.

BOX 10.1

Machakos County audit report excerpts, 2013

Failure to Hand Over by the Defunct Local Authorities to the County Government

Handing over was not done as instructed by the Ministry of Local Government Circular Ref. no. MLG/1333/TY/(52) dated 18 February 2013, which had directed the Clerks being the Chief Officers of the [outgoing] Local Authorities to ensure there was proper handing over to the incoming County Government and to ensure that they also prepared statements of Assets and Liabilities as at 20 February 2013.

Recommendation. Proper handing over should be done to ensure proper transfer of the assets and liabilities taken over by the County Governments.

Bank Accounts

The defunct Local Authorities/Councils did not close their accounts as at 28 February 2013 as had been directed by the Transition Authority guidelines given vide letter Ref. MOF/IFMIS/1/41 dated 7 March 2013. The defunct Local Authorities and Councils continued operating most of the accounts up to 2 July 2013.

Recommendation. The County should ensure in the future that instructions [and/or] guidelines given by relevant authorities are adhered to.

Bank Reconciliations

No bank reconciliations were done contrary to Financial Regulations [PFM Act] Chapter 5.9.2 that requires that bank reconciliations be done once a month and also there was no evidence of any cash survey done at the closure of the year contrary to Financial Regulations paragraph 5.9.9 that requires that a board of survey be constituted annually to examine and verify the cash on hand balances.

Recommendation. The County Government should ensure that financial regulations Chapters 5.9.2 and 5.9.9 that require bank reconciliations to be done once a month and that board of survey be constituted annually to examine and verify cash on hand balances respectively are adhered to. Bank reconciliation and bank certificates should be produced for audit review.

Debtors

Transition Authority Circular Ref. no. TA/2/5 dated 9 January 2013, "Inventory of Assets and Liabilities Debts and Human Resource Profile in Public Organizations," required the Clerks of the Local Authorities to carry out an inventory of all Assets, Debts, and Liabilities including movable and immovable assets. Most defunct Councils did not maintain individual debtors' ledgers, although they prepared a statement of assets and liabilities as at 28 February 2013 with a consolidated debtors' figure of K Sh 1,036,076,425. It was not possible to confirm the completeness and accuracy of the balances provided. Further, there was no evidence in the form of confirmations or correspondences to support the debtors. The County should maintain up-to-date debtor's ledgers and avail confirmations [and/or] correspondences to confirm the debtor's balances.

Immovable Assets

An undetermined number of land parcels and buildings belonging to the County valued at K Sh 961,451,472 did not have title deeds and were prone to grabbing or encroachment by unscrupulous individuals who might know this fact. There is need to move with speed to acquire titles to secure the parcels of land.

Public Utility Land

Records available show that 18 pieces of land of various sizes recognized by the then municipal council of Mavoko as public utilities in Syokimau and Numerical area of Mavoko Subcounty had been subdivided and allocated to individuals and institutions under unexplained circumstances; a physical check revealed that most of the land had been developed privately and others fenced off while a few were vacant. The County should avail documents for the subdivision of the 18 parcels of land allocated to the individuals [and/or] private developers if any, and also repossess the same since these parcels had been irregularly allocated.

Creditors and Other Liabilities

Individual Creditors ledgers and creditors analysis were not maintained by the defunct Councils and

continued

BOX 10.1, *continued*

Local Authorities. Although balances of liabilities were given in respect of LAPTRUST, Payment in lieu of leave, suppliers and Contractors, and some other pending bills, it was not possible to confirm the completeness and accuracy of the unconfirmed

consolidated Creditors figure of K Sh 280,734,871 as at June 2013. The County should maintain a complete individual creditor's ledger and the County Treasury to undertake an analysis of creditors and reconciliation in order to establish the true position of the Creditors.

Source: OAG 2013.

Some other assets unrelated to services (for example, land) remained unaccounted and mostly unattended, and hence, many had been lost, grabbed, or encroached (some of these were identified and discussed in the OAG 2013 report). OAG also recommended that Machakos County should coordinate with the TA on the asset and liability takeover; but no such coordination occurred. The TA did not act accordingly, and the county was not able to commence takeover by a unilateral action. However, nothing prevented it from starting accounting and registering new assets from day one.

The county has been using and developing most of the assets of the defunct local governments since March 2013. Despite the unresolved issues discussed, Machakos County government has taken a pragmatic approach in using and developing the assets. The magnitude of new investments is enormous; compared with the inherited K Sh 677 million current assets plus the unmeasured value of fixed assets, the county invested over K Sh 9 billion in new assets between 2013 and 2018 (table 10.3). Thus, the clear takeover and valuation of the inherited assets remain vital, but the asset management now is important for adequate protection and management of both the old inherited and the new assets, regardless of formal takeover procedures.

The possible magnitude of losses due to a lack of asset records and poor accounting could be shockingly high; the auditor's findings and comments (box 10.2) shed light on the main issues. However, financial records suggest that the county systematically divested large volumes of assets (presumably land) in the surveyed period and gained K Sh 1 billion to K Sh 2 billion in total income (figure 10.1). It is fair to assume that these asset proceeds were invested in new infrastructure as part of the K Sh 9 billion total investment of the 2013–18 fiscal period. Furthermore, the total income of K Sh 1.2 billion the county gained from divestitures (albeit possibly illegal due to the moratorium on divestitures by TDG Act 2012) far exceeded the estimated K Sh 961 million value of inherited total fixed assets mentioned in the 2016 OAG report. Also, the 2016 OAG report found no progress on or even initial steps to clarify the status of the grabbed land (box 10.2). In short, clear records on assets and especially divestitures are part of fundamental good governance practices, and hence should be institutionalized.

Given that Machakos County did not formally take over the assets from the defunct municipal and town councils, there were no formal procedures for undertaking asset inventories, nor have there been maintenance records of a

Machakos County losses due to lack of land records, audit report excerpts

As reported in fiscal year 2014/15, an undetermined number of land parcels and buildings belonging to the county government, valued at K Sh 961,451,472 did not have title deeds and were prone to grabbing or encroachment by unscrupulous individuals who might be privy to this fact.

Further, records available show that 18 parcels of various sizes recognized by the defunct Mavoko subcounty had been subdivided and allocated to individuals and institutions under unexplained circumstances. A physical check revealed that most of the county government has followed up on title deeds to secure ownership of these properties. In addition, no documents in support of subdivisions of the 18 parcels of land allocated to the individual and/or private developers have been made available for audit verification.

Source: OAG 2016.

complete stock of assets. However, conflicting regulations did not seem to have prevented the Machakos County administration (just like many other county administrations) from developing a systematic and reasonable asset inventory besides and before the TA actions. On the contrary, it would have been a very logical and pragmatic step to start unilaterally inventorying land and buildings immediately after devolution, because those strategic assets represent the major wealth of a county, and audit report clearly instructed inventorying all fixed assets (reference in audit report to TA 2013b).

The county also informally but still legally took over most staff from the defunct local entities in 2013 and then hired more staff to fill critical positions. These hires created substantial redundancies and contributed to the noted high growth and high share of labor expenditures. These actions raise concern over the employment policies and practices of the new county government.

The defunct authorities of Machakos County did not have a formal and comprehensive asset management framework, system, policies, or procedures (neither did the other counties). The counties simply were not equipped or prepared to establish asset management systems and procedures from scratch, since those had never existed under the defunct local governments and require clear vision and strategy. Establishing asset management also requires substantial investments of money and time. In short, establishing asset management systems overnight was an unfunded mandate of the new county governments and an unfunded expectation by the higher government bodies.

There was no dedicated team in the county administration to consolidate asset management issues and actions for strategy, planning, and development purposes. Despite national policies and legislation (TDG Act 2012, UAC Act 2011, PPAD Act 2015), the county did not formally take over the assets and liabilities inherited from the eight amalgamated and defunct entities at its inception, nor did it do so until mid-2017. However, various county entities continued performing key entity-level asset management functions and have maintained assets and ensured most service provision uninterrupted over the 2013–18 fiscal period. Table 10.4 suggests that there is a stable and reasonable

TABLE 10.4 **Machakos County asset management entities and their functions**

SERVICES OR FUNCTIONS THAT REQUIRE SPECIFIC ASSETS OWNED BY OR USED BY THE COUNTY	ASSET MANAGEMENT ENTITIES		
	COUNTY DEPARTMENTS RESPONSIBLE FOR THE RESPECTIVE SERVICES	COMPANY OR OTHER INDEPENDENT ENTITY OWNED BY THE COUNTY	PRIVATE SERVICE PROVIDER OR PRIVATE MANAGING ENTITY UNDER PPP
General administration			
Office buildings	Road Transport, Public Works, and Utilities	n.a.	n.a.
Urban services			
Roads and drainage	Road Transport, Public Works, and Utilities	n.a.	n.a.
Water and wastewater lines	Water, Environment, Energy, and Natural Resources	n.a.	n.a
Solid waste	Water, Environment, Energy, and Natural Resources	n.a.	n.a.
Social services			
Health	Health Services	Heads of health units	n.a.
Education	Education	Heads of schools	n.a.
Commercial services			
Livestock, saleyards, abattoirs, veterinary facilities	Agriculture, Livestock, and Fisheries	n.a.	n.a.
Museum, culture centers, sport, parks	Tourism, Sport, and Culture	n.a.	n.a.
Markets	Trade, Economic Planning, Investment, and Industrialization	n.a.	n.a.
Land, billboards, fire stations	Lands, Urban Development	n.a.	n.a.

Source: Machakos County Government website and field survey.
Note: n.a. = applicable; PPP = public-private partnership.

allocation of functions and responsibilities regarding daily operation and maintenance of assets.

Asset takeover by the power of law, 2017

Gazette Notice no. 858 (2017) transferred the assets and liabilities of the defunct local governments by the power of the law on January 27, 2017, and set a framework for validation, verification, and valuation of the assets by the counties through the County Asset and Liability Committees (CALCs) under guidance and control by the Intergovernmental Relations Technical Committee (IGRTC). Notice no. 2701 (2017) reconfirms and replaces Notice no. 858, extends the completion deadlines, and mandates that the unaudited inventories of assets and liabilities developed by the TA (IGRTC 2017) serve as bases and reference sources for the identification, verification, and validation of the assets in counties under CALC's management. Data presented below are from the Machakos CALC report 2017 and cross-checked with the IGRTC 2018 report.

Machakos inherited 2,284 parcels of land, of which 98 percent lacked a land registration (LR) number. In addition, two-thirds of parcels were surveyed, but the CALC team found no plan data for over 80 percent of parcels. Against the TA inventory of 858 parcels, the CALC team identified 2,284 parcels with no disputed land, a very remarkable achievement. The CALC team identified 250 buildings, with no disputed buildings, but 211 of the buildings have no land registration number. Thus, the most imminent tasks include establishing firm ownership of land in county possession by obtaining registration numbers. Furthermore, the number of parcels is 10 times greater than the number of buildings in county possession, and this suggests that the county presumably owns a large amount of, so to speak, surplus land that does not serve a direct purpose of providing local services. This enormous stock of land can and should be used strategically for accelerating infrastructure development and working out of inherited liabilities.

For the first time, the Machakos County government has reported a summary of fixed assets acquired after the transition of March 27, 2013 (table 10.5). This is a move in a good direction. However, the reported numbers are not in harmony with the financial reports in which the total value of investments into fixed assets appear to be over K Sh 9 billion as opposed to the register, which indicates only a K Sh 2 billion historical cost of fixed assets acquired after devolution. The reported annual investments in fixed assets in the 2017/18 fiscal year corresponds to the annual financial report (K Sh 851 million).

Finally, asset amortization has apparently not been accounted, or the asset register excludes such figures. But good asset registers should reflect both book value and depreciation of assets regardless of whether the county follows cash-based accounting principles in bookkeeping and financial reports. The shortcomings discussed indicate a need to improve consistency within and across financial reports and other statements. But more than that there is an urgent need for establishing a reliable and up-to-date asset register, which should be a relatively easy task due to well-identified and undisputed land and buildings and a relatively small number of other fixed assets.

With reference to Notice no. 858, IGRTC issued detailed guidelines and provided training on asset data collection for counties' staffs in May 2017. IGRTC also handed over to the county the unaudited preliminary list of assets and liabilities drafted by the TA (IGRTC 2017) to form the basis of the county-level

TABLE 10.5 **Machakos County fixed asset register summary, June 30, 2018**
K Sh (millions)

	HISTORICAL COST, JUNE 30, 2017	ADDITIONS IN FY 2017/18	HISTORICAL COST, JUNE 30, 2018
Land	18	0	18
Buildings and structures	170	706	876
Transport equipment	711	34	745
Office equipment	39	36	75
ICT equipment and software	57	0	57
Other machinery	110	57	168
Biological assets	4	12	17
Intangible assets	—	5	5
Total in register	**1,110**	**851**	**1,960**
Total fixed asset acquisition/development after devolution	n.a.	851	9,360

Source: OAG 2018.
Note: — = not available; n.a. = not applicable; FY = fiscal year; ICT = information and communication technology.

verification, validation, and valuation of assets and liabilities. TA records suggest that Machakos County inherited K Sh 677 million in current assets and K Sh 529 million in liabilities from the defunct local governments as estimated by the TA as of 2013. It is worth noting that the estimated values of inherited assets reflect the value of current assets as of 2013, since the files (IGRTC 2017) did not have value records for fixed assets such as land, buildings, and infrastructure networks. Thus, the verification and valuation of land remained among the most urgent tasks for the county.

The Machakos County CALC team identified K Sh 645 million in inherited current assets (table 10.6), somewhat less than the TA report (IGRTC 2017); three-quarters of these are uncollected property taxes, and most were overdue for more than five years already at the time of verification in 2017. Both compensation in lieu of rates (CILOR) and uncollected plot and house rents represented 11 percent of total inherited current assets. However, no action had been taken toward collection of either by 2017 or since then. These current assets were not included in the county's books apart from the CALC report. The present value of current assets could be higher than the 2013 face value due to interest accrued; this is largely true for house and plot rent and CILOR that should be collectible, but property taxes more than five years overdue are hard to collect, especially when lacking hard evidence of such claims.

Thus, although Machakos County (just like most counties) inherited more current assets than current liabilities on face value, it does not mean that the county would be able to settle inherited liabilities from inherited current assets easily. Collection of a fair share of inherited current assets remains a task that should be addressed urgently because of fast depreciation of net value.

The Machakos CALC team has identified K Sh 376 million in inherited liabilities (table 10.7), much less than the TA inventory. Unpaid statutory deductions represented more than half of total inherited liabilities. The CALC team did not make proposals for follow-up steps toward verification of disputed liabilities and actions toward workout of inherited current assets

TABLE 10.6 **Machakos County summary of inherited current assets, March 27, 2013**

K Sh (millions)

CASH AND BANK BALANCES	PROPERTY RATE	PLOT AND HOUSE RENT	STAFF DEBTORS	CILOR	OTHER	INVENTORY	TOTAL
0	481	71	12	70	11	0	645
0%	75%	11%	2%	11%	2%	0%	100%

Source: Machakos CALC 2017.
Note: CILOR = compensation in lieu of rates.

TABLE 10.7 **Machakos County summary of inherited liabilities, 2013 and 2017**

K Sh (millions)

	BANK LOANS	EMOLUMENTS	STATUTORY DEDUCTIONS	OTHER LIABILITIES	TOTAL
As of 2013, per TA report	—	—	—	—	529
As of 2013, per CALC report 2017	28	56	199	93	376
As % of total	7.4	14.9	52.9	24.8	100.0

Source: Machakos CALC 2017.
Note: — = not available; CALC = County Asset and Liability Committee; TA = Transition Authority.

and current liabilities. These steps and actions also would include establishing the current value of these liabilities with interest and penalties accrued between March 2013 and the time of valuation. Experiences in other counties suggest that the face value of statutory deductions has increased substantially and represented a much greater amount in 2017 and even greater in 2019. Inherited other liabilities come largely vis-à-vis commercial creditors; also, legal fees were found to be substantial in both volume and share of total and presumably have increased significantly. Unlike most other counties, Machakos County did not eliminate inherited overdue emoluments (inherited unpaid staff dues) until CALC verification.

LESSONS LEARNED

The pragmatic approach of taking over assets to support uninterrupted services has helped smooth transition of services. However, because of the lack of formal handover of assets (with a list of all assets, their locations, value, and purchase date), the assets are being managed by the respective departments without knowledge of the number, extent, or value of assets they operate. This missing information may result in the neglect of certain assets that require regular maintenance, substantial loss of revenue, and even loss of assets.

Lack of handover and takeover of assets and lack of action for immediate inventories, which auditors had recommended, apparently resulted in very substantial loss of strategic assets through taken or encroached land parcels and loss of other fixed assets (cars).

The lack of a confirmed list of liabilities may result in overpayment of debtors. One of the pending bills during the asset takeover was for remission of staff pension and benefits. The county took over liabilities such as overdue compensation of staff (salaries, severance payments, and other dues) and loans that lacked supporting evidence. This poses the risk of overcompensation due to inaccurate information and documentation.

OSR from rented assets is likely to be underestimated due to a lack of information on lease and rent agreements. The county Finance Department continued collecting rental fees from tenants of housing, shops, markets, and other rented facilities without establishing any evidence of rental agreements and terms and conditions. The use of an existing list of tenants without verification presents the challenge that the list could be incomplete or not updated with recent information, resulting in poor revenue performance.

A substantial volume of land can be considered surplus land that does not fulfill service functions, so it can be divested or used in other ways to accelerate development. Registration and strategic use of such land parcels is a bold opportunity for Machakos County.

REFERENCES

CGA. 2012. County Governments Act No. 17 of 2012. http://www.parliament.go.ke/sites/default/files/2017-05/CountyGovernmentsAct_No17of2012_1.pdf.

CRAB. 2015. County Revenue Allocation Bill 2015–2017. http://kenyalaw.org/kl/fileadmin/pdfdownloads/bills/2017/CountyAllocationofRevenueBill_2017.pdf.

Farvacque-Vitkovic, C., and M. Kopanyi. 2019. *Better Cities Better World: A Handbook on Local Government Self-Assessments*. Washington, DC: World Bank. https://openknowledge .worldbank.org/handle/10986/32120.

IGRTC (Intergovernmental Relations Technical Committee). 2017. "Unaudited IGRTC Current Assets and Liability List as at 27 March 2013." Intergovernmental Relations Technical Committee from files of Transition Authority. Nairobi: IGRTC.

IGRTC (Intergovernmental Relations Technical Committee). 2018. *Report on the Identification, Verification, Validation, and Transfer of Assets and Liabilities of the Defunct Local Authorities as at 27th March 2013*. Nairobi: IGRTC. https://igrtc.go.ke/download/consolidated-report -on-assets-and-liabilities-of-the-defunct-local-authorities-2018/.

Kenya Constitution. 2010. http://kenyalaw.org/kl/index.php?id=398.

KNBS (Kenya National Bureau of Statistics). 2017. *Machakos County Statistical Abstract*. Nairobi: KNBS. https://www.knbs.or.ke/download/machakos/#.

KNBS (Kenya National Bureau of Statistics). 2018. *Basic Report on Well Being in Kenya* (based on Household Budget Survey 2015/16). Nairobi: KNBS. https://www.knbs.or.ke/download /basic-report-well-kenya-based-201516-kenya-integrated-household-budget-survey -kihbs/#.

KNBS (Kenya National Bureau of Statistics). 2019. "Kenya Population and Housing Census." Nairobi: KNBS. https://housingfinanceafrica.org/documents/2019-kenya-population -and-housing-census-reports/.

Machakos CALC (County Asset and Liability Committee). 2017. *Machakos CALC Report*, Machakos County CALC.

Machakos County. 2018a. *County Integrated Development Plan (CIDP) covering the period 2018–22*. Machakos, Kenya: Machakos County Government. https://repository.kippra.or.ke /handle/123456789/611.

Machakos County. 2018b. "Machakos County Budget Review and Outlook Paper (CBROP)." Machakos, Kenya: Machakos County Government. https://repository.kippra.or.ke /handle/123456789/603.

Ministry of Local Government (MLG). 2013. Circular, ref. no. MLG/1333/TY/ (52) of February 18, 2013.

Notice 858. 2017. Gazette Notice no. 858, January 8, 2017: Intergovernmental Relations Act no. 2 of 2012. https://gazettes.africa/gazettes/ke-government-gazette-dated-2017-01-27-no-13.

Notice 2701. 2017. Gazette Notice no. 2701, March 24, 2017: Intergovernmental Relations Act no. 2 of 2012. https://gazettes.africa/archive/ke/2017/ke-government-gazette-dated-2017-03 -24-no-37.pdf.

OAG (Office of the Auditor General). 2013–19 (annually). *Report of the Auditor General on Financial Statement of Counties*. Nairobi: OAG. http://www.oagkenya.go.ke/index.php /reports/cat_view/2-reports/11-county-governments/203-county-government-reports.

OCB (Office of the Controller of Budget). 2014–18 (annually). *Annual County Government Budget Implementation Review Report*. Nairobi: https://cob.go.ke/reports/consolidated -county-budget-implementation-review-reports/.

PFM. 2012. Public Finance Management Act, no. 18 of 2012. https://www.pcf.go.ke/index.php /public-financial-management-act.

PPAD. 2015. Public Procurement and Asset Disposal Act, no. 33 of 2015, December 18, 2015. http://kenyalaw.org:8181/exist/kenyalex/actview.xql?actid =No.%2033%20of%202015.

TA (Transition Authority). 2013a. "Transition Authority Guidelines," Ref. MOF/IFMIS/1/41 dated 7 March 2013.

TA (Transition Authority). 2013b. "Inventory of Assets and Liabilities Debts and Human Resource Profile in Public Organizations." Circular Ref. no. TA/2/5 dated 9 January 2013.

TDG Act 2012. Transition to Devolved Government Act, no. 1 of 2012, enacted March 9, 2012. http://www.parliament.go.ke/sites/default/files/2017-05/TransitiontoDevolved GovernmentActNo1of2012.pdf.

UAC. 2011. Urban Areas and Cities Act, no. 13 of 2011. http://www.parliament.go.ke/sites /default/files/2017-05/UrbanAreasandCitiesAct_No13of2011.pdf.

UAC. 2019. Urban Areas and Cities (Amendment) Act 2019. http://kenyalaw.org/kl/fileadmin /pdfdownloads/AmendmentActs/2019/Urban AreasandCities_Amendment_Act_2019 .pdf.

World Bank. 2018. *Kenya Economic Update*. 17th ed., April 2018. Washington, DC: World Bank. https://documents.worldbank.org/en/publication/documents-reports/documentdetail /327691523276540220/kenya-economic-update-policy-options-to-advance-the-big-4 -unleashing-kenya-s-private-sector-to-drive-inclusive-growth-and-accelerate-poverty -reduction.

11 Makueni County

INTRODUCTION

Makueni County is in the eastern region of Kenya and borders Kajiado, Kitui, Machakos, and Taita-Taveta counties. It covers an 8,035–square kilometer area in a low-lying terrain from 600 meters above sea level at the southern area in the Tsavo region to 1,900 meters in Mbooni Hills in Mbooni Constituency (map 11.1). The county's political framework includes six constituencies—Kaiti, Kibwezi East, Kibwezi West, Kilome, Makueni, and Mbooni—and there are 30 County Assembly wards. The county's administrative framework includes nine subcounties: Kathonzweni, Kibwezi, Kilungu, Makindu, Makueni, Mbooni East, Mbooni West, Mukaa, and Nzaui; within these there are 32 divisions.

Makueni County's population was 987,653, and average population density was 121 per square kilometer in 2019 (KNBS 2019), with an average population growth rate of 0.96 percent. The county has a population dependency ratio of about 95 percent, much higher than the national average of 78.3.

Agricultural production is one of the main economic activities in Makueni County (Makueni County 2018a). The top three cash crops produced include tomatoes, assorted vegetables, and baby corn, while cattle and goats are the most traded livestock. In the trade and commerce sector, there are 17,390 registered businesses, of which 6,441 (or 37 percent) are canteen and retail shops. Other common business entities include hotels and butcheries (1,772); clothing, textiles, and cloth making (1,560); barbers and salons (1,213); restaurants (1,027); and mobile telephone service traders (882). There are six water service companies. Mining and quarrying are also important economic activities, with 24 sand-harvesting sites, two granite-quarrying sites, and four stone and aggregate quarrying sites (World Bank 2018). There are two game parks that not only serve the county but the country as a whole: Chyulu Game Reserve and the Tsavo West National Park. The two parks receive more than 50,000 tourists annually (KNBS 2017).

The Constitution 2010 sets decentralized functions of the county government: agriculture, health, control of pollution, cultural activities, transport, animal welfare, trade and development, county planning and development, preprimary education, village polytechnics, home craft centers and early childhood education, environmental conservation, public works, and local community public participation. The Urban Areas and Cities Acts—UAC Act

MAP 11.1

Makueni County

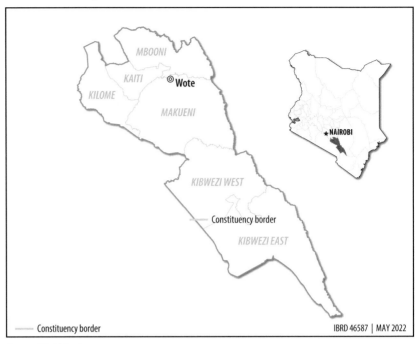

Source: World Bank.

2011 and its update Act 2019 (UAC 2011, 2019)—mandate the following services be provided in urban areas of Makueni County: garbage dumpsite, street lighting, public housing, office and shop rental, hospitals, preschools, vocational schools, markets, and Lukenya University, which is the only accredited university in the county.

The urbanization level is exceptionally low at 13 percent in Makueni County, with a 1 percent per annum growth rate (KNBS 2017). Still, there is growing pressure on the provision of urban services such as education and health (OCB 2017; Makueni County 2018b). Water supply remains a major challenge for Makueni, since only 36 percent of households have access to improved drinking water. Improved sources of water include protected spring, protected well, borehole, water piped into dwellings, and piped and rainwater collection. The total road network in the county is 3,203 kilometers, of which only 454 kilometers (14 percent) are asphalted. Part of the rest is gravel, but most is earth; hence, the county's road network is poorly developed.

REVENUE AND EXPENDITURE ANALYSIS

Analysis of revenues and expenditures is an integral part of an assessment of asset management because it provides a solid background picture in which assets are positioned, developed, and managed. Revenues generate cash or cash-like instruments that are transient forms of assets, since land can be sold to generate cash revenue to develop schools, or cash can be saved for rainy days. Finally, the surplus remaining after current expenditures are covered with current revenues provides funds for development. Loans or other liabilities can also finance development. In short, revenue and expenditure analysis provides important insights and sheds light on the trends and capacities a county possesses in developing assets and expanding services.

Revenues

Makueni County's revenues grew steadily at an average rate of 11.7 percent per annum between the 2013/14 and 2017/18 fiscal years (table 11.1). Equitable shares formed the bulk (over 95 percent) and a growing part of revenues; they grew on average by 11.8 percent per annum. The Government of Kenya has supported devolution by substantially and steadily increasing transfers to counties (CRAB 2015). Conditional grants were small and volatile and show a declining trend (–1.2 percent); thus, their share of total national government transfers in the surveyed fiscal period decreased. Conditional grants supported level-5 hospitals, free maternal health care, compensation of foregone user fees, leasing of medical equipment, and a road maintenance levy. Grants from development partners appeared to be small and volatile; a Danish International Development Agency grant supported specific health care service provision in the surveyed fiscal period.

Own-source revenues (OSRs) were extremely small with a low share of total revenues, 4 percent or less, but showed steady improvement (14 percent per annum) in the 2013/14 to 2017/18 fiscal years. Despite improvement, OSR remained small and the county is largely dependent on central government transfers. The county collected about half of planned OSR annually, albeit with a marginal average improvement of effective collection (OAG 2015–18), except in 2014/15 when OSR collected was 93.6 percent of the planned amount.

Fees were the main and expanding source of OSR and provided over a third of it by the 2017/18 fiscal year (figure 11.1). Fees were mainly collected from

TABLE 11.1 Makueni County revenues, fiscal years 2013/14–2017/18
K Sh (millions)

	2013/14	2014/15	2015/16	2016/17	2017/18	AVERAGE GROWTH (%)
Transfers from national government	**4,721**	**5,518**	**6,579**	**6,749**	**7,163**	**11.0**
Equitable share	4,366	5,209	5,970	6,441	6,825	11.8
Conditional grants	355	309	609	308	338	−1.2
Own-source revenues	**189**	**215**	**220**	**219**	**322**	**14.2**
Taxes	—	81	82	80	97	6.10
Fees and charges	—	59	72	72	119	26.53
Asset proceeds	—	49	51	40	42	−5.16
Other revenues	189	26	15	26	64	34.74
Financing	**0**	**0**	**244**	**12**	**157**	**n.a.**
Cash reserve from previous year	—	—	—	—	—	n.a.
Loans/grants	—	0	244	12	157	n.a.
Total revenue	**4,910**	**5,733**	**7,043**	**6,980**	**7,642**	**11.69**
Share of OSR (%)	3.8	3.8	3.1	3.1	4.2	2.25
OSR actual/planned (%)	54.0	94.0	53.0	66.0	42.0	−6.09

Source: OAG 2014–18.
Note: — = not available; n.a. = not applicable; OSR = own-source revenue.

liquor licenses, market and trade centers, and vehicle parking. Business permits provided the second largest OSR. However, the county reported no property tax revenues at all (table 11.2). Revenues from assets were quite moderate, including rent, incomes from plots, and charges on environment conservancy and administration. The small but increasing asset revenues suggest that Makueni County

FIGURE 11.1

Makueni County OSR, fiscal years 2014/15–2017/18

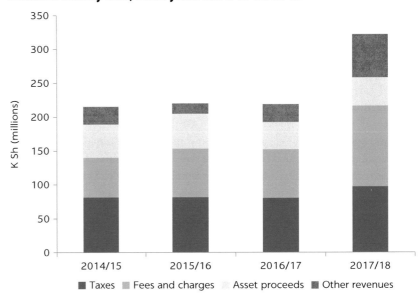

Source: OAG 2014–18.
Note: OSR = own-source revenues.

TABLE 11.2 **Makueni County OSR, fiscal years 2013/14–2017/18**

K Sh (millions)

	2013/14	2014/15	2015/16	2016/17	2017/18	AVERAGE GROWTH (%)
Taxes	—	**81**	**82**	**80**	**97**	**6.1**
Property rates (property tax)	—	—	—	—	—	n.a.
Business permits (business tax)	—	67	65	65	83	7.7
Other taxes and levies	—	15	17	15	14	−1.8
Fees and charges	—	**59**	**72**	**72**	**119**	**26.5**
Parking fees	—	23	26	26	29	7.6
Urban services	—	4	10	3	5	1.5
Social services	—	0	0	4	42	n.a.
Licenses, permits, certificates	—	32	36	39	44	12.0
Asset proceeds	—	**49**	**51**	**40**	**42**	**−5.2**
Rents and leases	—	12	16	7	8	−13.2
Markets	—	37	36	34	34	−2.8
Other income	189	**26**	**15**	**26**	**64**	**34.7**
Total OSR	189	**215**	**220**	**219**	**322**	**14.3**

Source: OAG 2014–18.
Note: — = not available; n.a. = not applicable; OSR = own-source revenue.

has the potential to further enhance its OSR collection if it installs effective asset management systems. This will enable accurate revenue targeting and collection as well as maintenance of the assets.

Expenditures

Makueni County's expenditures show very dynamic growth on average, about 25 percent per annum, twice as fast as total revenues over the 2013/14– 2017/18 fiscal period (table 11.3). This trend is unsustainable and requires scrutiny and corrective measures, because fast-growing current expenditures appear to have crowded out development expenditures, eaten up steady budget surpluses, and even resulted in a huge deficit in the 2016/17 fiscal year. The current expenditures grew by 23 percent per annum, a bit slower pace than growth of total expenditures; as a result, the share of current expenditures declined gradually to 76 percent but still remained much higher than best international practices (Farvacque-Vitkovic and Kopanyi 2019). Labor costs (wages and salaries) absorbed over half of current expenditures, high by international comparison. Operation and maintenance expenditures grew at a much slower pace than labor expenses (12.2 percent and 20.7 percent, respectively).

In 2016/17, the top three expenditures under operation and maintenance were specialized materials and drugs at K Sh 354.6 million (7.3 percent of current expenditures), domestic and foreign travel at about K Sh 277 million (5.7 percent),

TABLE 11.3 **Makueni County expenditures, fiscal years 2013/14–2017/18**
K Sh (millions)

	2013/14	2014/15	2015/16	2016/17	2017/18	AVERAGE GROWTH (%)
Current expenditures	**2,536**	**3,133**	**4,001**	**5,059**	**5,803**	**23.0**
Personal emoluments	1,433	1,946	2,184	2,425	3,039	20.7
Operation and maintenance	1,103	1,187	1,817	1,648	1,750	12.2
Of which, repair and maintenance	0	21	33	55	58	40.1
Transfers to other entities	0	0	0	987	1,015	n.a.
Noncurrent/development	**603**	**1,251**	**1,504**	**4,016**	**1,808**	**31.6**
Acquisition of assets	603	1,026	1,253	2,994	1,139	17.2
Debt repayment	0	0	0	0	0	n.a.
Other payments/investments	0	225	251	1,022	669	n.a.
Total expenditures	**3,139**	**4,384**	**5,505**	**9,075**	**7,612**	**24.8**
Budget balance	**1,771**	**1,349**	**1,538**	**–2,095**	**30**	**–63.8**
Ratios (%)						
Operation and maintenance/current	43.5	37.9	45.4	32.6	30.2	–8.7
Personal emoluments/current	56.5	62.1	54.6	47.9	52.4	–1.9
Current/total	80.8	71.5	72.7	55.7	76.2	–1.4
Development/total	19.2	28.5	27.3	44.3	23.8	5.5
Repair and maintenance/current	n.a.	0.7	0.8	1.1	1.0	n.a.

Source: OAG 2014–18.
Note: n.a. = not applicable.

and insurance at K Sh 214.2 million (4.4 percent). Expenditures on repair and maintenance grew extremely fast (40 percent per year) but remained extremely low (1 percent of current expenditures) in the surveyed fiscal period. Repair and maintenance are particularly important asset management actions to ensure that both inherited and the K Sh 7 billion in new assets acquired since devolution function well and effectively provide local services.

Spending on acquisition of assets increased dynamically (17 percent per year), grew to K Sh 3 billion in the 2016/17 fiscal year, and then went back to the regular range (table 11.3). As a result, the share of development expenditures within total expenditures increased slightly, from below 19 percent in 2013/14 to 24 percent in 2017/18. The 44 percent share of development expenditures in 2017/18 is high by international comparison (40 percent benchmark), and maybe it is a result of the delayed completion of construction projects in previous years. The county spent on infrastructure investments nearly K Sh 2 billion more than its revenues generated and accounted a huge K Sh 2 billion budget deficit in 2016/17. This could be an accounting or classification error, since the reserves from previous years generated by budget surpluses have not been reported.

Makueni County exemplifies a massive transformative program to enhance infrastructure and services; since devolution it has initiated 2,233 projects, of which 1,660 are completed, 346 are ongoing, and 33 are delayed, while 166 were in the procurement cycle in 2018. The county also made a big step toward improving project management and transparency by developing a platform-based Project Management System (Makueni PMS) with up-to-date reporting results in web postings. Makueni stands out among the 47 Kenyan counties with its transparent and well-performing PMS accessible to the public online (see the screenshot in figure 11.2).

Figure 11.3 summarizes the development results since the 2013 devolution that envisions a total of K Sh 12 billion in budgeted projects and about K Sh 6.5 billion completed over the five fiscal years. The main lessons include

FIGURE 11.2

Makueni County Project Management System dashboard, 2019

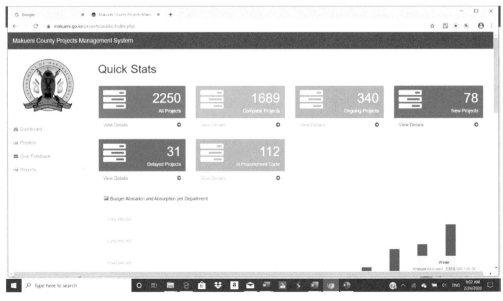

Source: © County Government of Makueni. Used with the permission of County Government of Makueni; further permission required for reuse. https://makueni.go.ke/projects/public/index.php.

FIGURE 11.3

Makueni County development expenditures, fiscal years 2013/14–2017/18

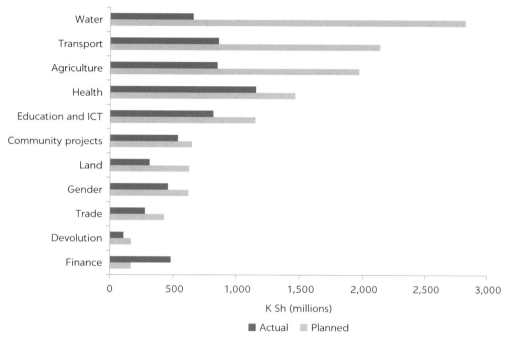

Source: Makueni County Project Management System.
Note: ICT = information and communication technology.

(1) project completion performance remained steadily low, 53 percent in a five-year average; (2) governor-initiated projects performed the best (actual/plan = 83 percent), and water-sector projects performed the worst (actual/plan = 23 percent), which suggests a great need to improve project programming, planning, and execution capacities; (3) highest emphases were put on health, transport, agriculture, and education; and (4) the water sector appears to be the most important area in terms of volume of money budgeted (nearly K Sh 3 billion in five years) but is only a fifth among completed projects. However, as indicated, fast-growing current expenditures and within them personal emoluments exhausted funds that would have been important for completing more investment projects.

ASSET MANAGEMENT

These case studies focus on the transition period before which Kenyan local governments did not have asset management systems, frameworks, and policies except some sporadic practices to manage assets daily by officers of service units. Despite legislated mandates—Public Finance Management Act 2012 (PFM 2012), Kenya Constitution 2010, Public Procurement and Asset Disposal Act 2015 (PPAD 2015), County Governments Act (CGA 2012), and circulars—local governments failed to establish asset registers, and even the accounting of assets was poorly understood and disobeyed before devolution. Local bodies failed to measure the wealth of the local public properties, increase it, or manage the most important assets strategically. This case study illustrates both the enormous challenges the incoming county governments faced due to the inherited situation and the remarkable progress achieved after devolution. It also demonstrates that moving forward requires strong determination, vision, finances, and reformative actions toward modern and adequate management of assets that eventually determine the level and quality of mandated services.

Asset ownership and transition to devolved government

Article 23 of Transition to Devolved Government Act (TDG 2012) regulated the takeover by the Makueni County government of the functions, assets, liabilities, and staff of the former local authorities of Makueni County Council, Mtito Andei Town Council, and Wote Town Council. Counties were largely assumed to take over assets and liabilities after validation and audit by the Transition Authority (TA). Although a Ministry of Local Government Circular (MLG/1333/TY), on February 18, 2013, days before the devolution elections, directed the clerks as the chief executive officers of the outgoing local authorities to ensure proper handover of documents and assets to the incoming county government, the clerks left offices without formal handover of documents and many were not even allowed to return to office a day after election.

The Office of the Auditor General (OAG) commenced a special audit after devolution elections and found that, by September 2013, the new Makueni County government had not taken over the assets and liabilities from the former local authorities (box 11.1). The county government did not revalue the assets taken over informally to reflect the market value. OAG found no handover memorandum or evidence about what had been taken over, and lastly, the accounts on cash in hand and bank balances were not established at the inauguration of the new county government a day after election.

While the MLG/1333/TY Circular's directives were timely, sensible, and important, neither it nor the TA guidance (TA 2013a and TA 2013b) triggered local policy and operations until the TA's closure in 2016. In its preliminary report on county assets and liabilities, the TA argued that inadequate budgetary allocation was among the key constraints that hindered timely asset identification and verification and the audit process. Likewise, the process required technical expertise, which the TA had a grave shortage of, such as forensic auditors, surveyors, engineers, lawyers, and actuaries.

It would have been ideal for county governments to assign staff for a few weeks to work together with TA staff and establish initial inventories together, especially on strategic assets such as land and buildings. But the TA hardly communicated about fieldwork with counties, and there were no established rules for joint work of county staff and TA consultants. In sum, the OAG audit report was accurate in exposing shortcomings from an audit perspective, but it did not take into account that verification and validation require much longer than a few weeks; in fact, it took three years for the TA to complete a preliminary, and incomplete, inventory of inherited assets and liabilities (IGRTC 2017).

Informal takeover and use of assets

From its inauguration, Makueni County government, without formal takeover, accounts, and valuation, started to use and develop assets, especially those that formed the basis of vital local services, to ensure uninterrupted provision of services. Other assets unrelated to services (for example, land) remained unaccounted, and some unattended to, and hence many may be lost or encroached.

BOX 11.1

Makueni County audit report excerpts, 2013

3.1 Failure to Take Over the Defunct Local Authorities

It was observed that the County Government of Makueni had not taken over the assets and liabilities of the former local authorities in Makueni County. The County Government did not provide handing-over memorandum to show what was taken over. The County Government did not revalue the Assets taken over to reflect the market value. No board of survey was constituted to come up with accurate balances of Cash on Hand as well as the bank balances.

Recommendation

The Government should ensure that accurate statement of assets and liabilities are prepared upon which the handing over taking over should be affected.

3.2 Current Assets and Liabilities

(i) Debtors

During the period ended 30 June 2013, the County Government of Makueni did not validate or consolidate its debtors, especially the debtors of the three defunct local authorities which totaled K Sh 121,572,468. However, appropriate systems for recording debtors by the County Government should be developed to ensure accuracy of records.

Source: OAG 2013.

Recommendation

Debt collection policy should be put in place to facilitate collection of County debts as and when they fall due.

(ii) Creditors

According to the statement of assets and liabilities as at 28 February 2013, the defunct local authorities had creditors totaling K Sh 70,819,700.

Recommendation

The creditors should be promptly recorded in a ledger indicating particulars of each creditor and the same updated on a regular basis.

3.3 Fixed Assets Records

There was no record provided to show the assets which were handed over to the County Government. During the period ended 30 June 2013, the County Government of Makueni did not validate or consolidate its Fixed Assets, especially those relating to the three defunct local authorities. The fixed Assets balances for the period ending 30 June 2012 totaled K Sh 30,472,084.

Recommendation

Appropriate systems for recording Fixed Assets by the County Government should be developed to ensure accuracy of records.

OAG (2013) repeated its former recommendation that the Makueni County government should coordinate with the TA on the asset and liability takeover; however, the county government could not commence takeover as a unilateral action. Further, there is no evidence that the TA had adopted procedures for assisting and guiding counties in a fast takeover, and especially not before the TA's completion of inventorying assets and liabilities in all 47 counties. The OAG reports and findings presumably had been shared with not only counties but also the TA and respective ministries in 2013 and after, but these messages had not induced policy dialogue or corrective measures from these higher governing bodies.

The Makueni County government took a pragmatic approach in using and developing most of the assets inherited from the defunct local governments after March 2013 despite the unresolved issues discussed above. The county departments are responsible for respective local services and in principle for managing assets, but the assets noted in table 11.4 have been identified as being managed by assigned entities in Makueni County.

TABLE 11.4 **Makueni County asset management entities and their functions**

SERVICES OR FUNCTIONS THAT REQUIRE SPECIFIC ASSETS OWNED BY OR USED BY THE COUNTY	ASSET MANAGEMENT ENTITIES		
	COUNTY DEPARTMENT RESPONSIBLE FOR THE RESPECTIVE SERVICES	COMPANY OR OTHER INDEPENDENT ENTITY OWNED BY THE COUNTY	PRIVATE SERVICE PROVIDER OR PRIVATE MANAGING ENTITY UNDER PPP
General administration			
Office buildings	Roads, Transport, and Infrastructure	n.a.	n.a.
Urban services			
Roads and drainage	Roads, Transport, and Infrastructure	n.a.	n.a.
Public transport	Roads, Transport, and Infrastructure	n.a.	County lorries offered to traders at discounted rate
Water and wastewater services	Water and Sanitation	Wote Water and Sewerage Services Company	n.a.
		Mbooni Water Services Company	
		Kibwezi-Makindu (KIMAWASCO) Kimwezi and Makundu Water and Sewerage Services Company	
		Noutresh (shared among Makueni, Kajiado, and Machakos)	
Solid waste	Water and Sanitation	n.a.	Local community-based collection
Social services			
Health	Health Services	Heads of health units	n.a.
Education	Education and ICT	Heads of schools	n.a.
Commercial services			
Local economic development	Devolution and Public Service	Fruit processing plant	n.a.

Source: Makueni County Government website and field visits.
Note: ICT = information communication technology; n.a. = not applicable; PPP = public-private partnership.

Asset takeover by the power of law, 2017

Gazette Notice no. 858 (2017) transferred the assets and liabilities of the defunct local governments by the power of the law on January 27, 2017, and set a framework for validation, verification, and valuation of the assets by the counties via County Asset and Liability Committees (CALCs) under guidance and control by the Intergovernmental Relations Technical Committee (IGRTC). IGRTC was established under the Intergovernmental Relations Act of 2012 and took over leadership on asset transition from the TA when it closed in March 2017. Further, Notice no. 2701 (2017) replaced Notice 858 and ruled that the unaudited inventories of assets and liabilities developed by the TA serve as a basis and reference for the verification, validation, and valuation of the assets under CALC's management.

According to IGRTC and TA files, Makueni County inherited K Sh 136 million in current assets and K Sh 81 million in liabilities from Makueni County Council, respectively, estimated on a 2013 basis. First, these figures differ from those of OAG, which estimated K Sh 122 million and

K Sh 71 million, respectively (box 11.1). Second, proper recordkeeping of assets and liabilities remained incomplete, since that was considered to be one of the duties of the CALC. Third, lack of verification of liabilities impacted human resource management: all employees were taken over informally without any approved establishment. The 2014 OAG audit report stated that the manual payroll that was used to pay employees' salaries (worth about K Sh 152 million annually) was not made available for audit verification, and there was payment of K Sh 295,540 to people without personnel files. Designated county officers were unable to establish the total number of employees inherited from the defunct local authorities in 2013 due to incomplete records and missing information in November 2017.

In order to ensure a smooth transition from the defunct local authorities, Makueni County government proceeded to classify its assets in three main categories: assets inherited from the defunct local authority, assets inherited from the national government due to devolved functions, and new assets acquired since March 2013. Notice no. 858 increased the impetus for asset transfers inherited from the defunct local authority; the IGRTC held trainings to build capacity of members of the CALCs on the procedures for asset and liability identification, verification, and validation. The Makueni CALC was able to identify, verify, and validate most of the assets with the help of technical experts from the county's lands and finance departments. The data presented in this section are from Makueni County CALC report cross-checked with the preliminary TA report managed by the IGRTC (IGRTC 2017).

The CALC team experienced several challenges while undertaking the exercise, including a short time frame for completing the exercise; the need for surveying services, confirmation of ownership, and valuation of land and buildings; and the need for an audit of current assets and liabilities (outstanding property rates and rents, cash and bank balances, unpaid legal fees, actuarial deficits, and unremitted statutory deductions). These challenges required the engagement of experts in each of the areas identified to establish closing balances of defunct local authorities retrospectively as of March 27, 2013, and to establish consolidated opening balances for the Makueni County government. Box 11.2 shows the terms of reference and timelines within which the exercise was planned to be completed.

Makueni CALC teams identified, verified, and validated (with land sizes) 520 parcels (against the TA inventory of 500 parcels) of inherited land with about 1,000 hectares of total area, excluding cemeteries and shrines for which the CALC team did not estimate land size (table 11.5). A good half of land parcels (342) were surveyed, and 285 parcels had registration numbers, while 90 parcels were identified as disputed, encroached, or taken over by private individuals without clear documentation. The bulk of the county public land (974 hectares, or 97 percent) hosts marketplaces and structures. The CALC team was unable to attach land values due to a lack of valuation and survey information; the CALC team also was unable to establish the value of 138 verified buildings. Most buildings were inherited from the defunct Makueni County Council but only one had an identification number. The inherited buildings included market sheds, public pit latrines, office blocks, and stockyards. Other assets that were identified, verified, and validated include 12 motor vehicles, 74 computers, 42 computer accessories, 155 pieces of equipment, and office furniture and fittings.

Makueni County Asset and Liability Committee terms of reference and timeline, CALC report excerpts

The Makueni County Asset and Liability Committee (CALC) draws its terms of reference from Gazette Notice no. 2701 in the Kenya Gazette vol. CXIX, no. 37, dated March 24, 2017, that revoked and replaced Notice no. 858. The CALC's mandates included:

1. Identify, verify, and validate all the assets and liabilities of the three defunct local authorities (Makueni County Council, Mtito-Andei Town Council, and Wote Town Council).
2. Identify, record, and secure all relevant documents in relation to the assets and liabilities of the defunct local authorities.
3. Corroborate the information collected in accordance with its function numbers (1) and (2) with the information contained in the unaudited inventory of assets and liabilities of the defunct local

authorities that was prepared by the Transition Authority (IGRTC 2017).

4. Identify and document the disputed assets or liabilities of the defunct local authorities.
5. Prepare a comprehensive register of assets and liabilities of the defunct local authorities as of March 27, 2013.
6. Submit a periodic report to the Intergovernmental Relations Technical Committee as may be required.

The committee was appointed on April 21, 2017, and carried out the exercise from April 24, 2017.

It undertook an induction workshop at Mombasa on guidelines and operationalization of the committee and was to finalize and hand over its report by June 30, 2017.

Source: Makueni CALC 2017.

For the first time, Makueni County government has reported a summary of fixed assets acquired after the transition of March 27, 2013 (table 11.6). This is a move in a good direction. However, the reported numbers are not in harmony with the financial reports (table 11.2), in which the total value of investments into fixed assets is reported to be K Sh 7.0 billion as opposed to the fixed-asset register, which indicates only a K Sh 3.4 billion historical cost of fixed assets acquired after 2013 devolution. The reported annual investments in fixed assets (additions) in the 2017/18 fiscal year correspond to the annual financial report's K Sh 1.1 billion. Finally, asset amortization has apparently not been accounted, or the asset register excludes such figures. Good asset registers should reflect both book values and depreciation of assets regardless of whether the county follows cash-based accounting principles in bookkeeping and financial reports.

The findings point to a need to improve consistency within and across financial reports and other statements, but more than that, there is an urgent need to establish a reliable and up-to-date asset register, which should be a relatively easy task due to well-identified land and buildings and the relatively small number of other fixed assets. Furthermore, valuation of assets to show the approximate market values as of 2019 is still incomplete and would presumably show manifold greater value of inherited assets than the TA estimates. Therefore, a pragmatic but reasonable valuation of all inherited assets, especially land, is an important next step moving forward. Given the limited amount of land and the well-identified locations, the valuation of these land parcels could be done relatively easily.

Makueni inherited only K Sh 137 million current assets (table 11.7), which is extremely small as compared with the other surveyed counties with budgets of

TABLE 11.5 **Makueni County land and buildings, March 2013**

USE	LAND (HECTARES)			
	MAKUENI	MTITO ANDEI	WOTE	TOTAL
Bus park	n.a	n.a	0.81	0.81
Cemetery	n.a.	n.a	n.a	n.a
Conservation area	0	0	18.90	18.9
Markets	704.02	1	268.51	973.53
Office building	1.21	0	0	1.21
Open spaces	0.42	0.2	0.40	1.02
Playground	1.64	0	0	1.64
Shrine	n.a	n.a	n.a	n.a
Social hall	0	0	1.68	1.68
Stockyard	2.23	0	0	2.23
Total	**709.52**	**1.2**	**290.31**	**1,001.03**

USE	NUMBER OF BUILDINGS			
	MAKUENI	MTITO ANDEI	WOTE	TOTAL
Bus park	2	2	0	4
Cattle dip	2	0	0	2
Chamber	1	0	0	1
Community library	4	0	0	4
Council offices (headquarters)	1	n.a.	n.a.	1
Incinerator	1	0	0	1
Market shade	24	n.a.	n.a.	24
Modern market	1	0	0	1
Office block	10	n.a.	n.a.	10
Pit latrine (not in use)	0	0	2	2
Plastic water tank and piping	2	0	0	2
Public latrine	4	3	0	7
Public pit latrine	52	12	0	64
Slaughterhouse	1	0	0	1
Stockyard	8	1	0	9
Stockyard office	2	0	0	2
Streetlights	2	0	0	2
Water kiosk/pumping machine	2	0	0	2
Water tank	5	0	0	5
Retailer	1	0	0	1
Total	**125**	**18**	**2**	**145**

Source: Makueni CALC 2017.
Note: CALC = County Asset and Liability Committee; n.a. = not applicable.

similar size (about K Sh 7–10 billion). Neither the CALC nor the TA has found uncollected staff debts, compensation in lieu of rates, or other current assets. Uncollected plot and house rent represent the bulk of inherited current assets (91 percent); in contrast, uncollected property rates are miniscule (K Sh 2.8 million, or 2 percent of total inherited current assets). Makueni County has not collected property taxes since devolution for reasons still to be explained, and OAG reports left this unnoticed.

The inherited current assets are very concentrated in Makueni subcounty and in rents. While the report was expected to verify the 2013 values, it was also expected to comment on the status and present value in 2017. The comparison of tables 11.7 and 11.8 suggests a convenient situation, since the inherited current assets appear to be about 40 percent greater than the inherited current liabilities, so the liabilities can be settled if the current collectibles are recovered.

TABLE 11.6 **Makueni County fixed asset register summary, June 30, 2018**

K Sh (millions)

	HISTORICAL COST, JUNE 30, 2017	ADDITIONS IN FY 2017/18	HISTORICAL COST, JUNE 30, 2018
Land	38	651	689
Buildings and structures	1,607	328	1,934
Transport equipment	164	49	212
Office equipment	279	7	286
ICT equipment and software	35	13	47
Other machinery	224	76	300
Biological assets	0	6	6
Intangible assets	0	9	9
Total in register	**2,345**	**1,139**	**3,484**
Total fixed asset acquisition/development after devolution	n.a.	1,139	7,016

Source: OAG 2018.
Note: FY = fiscal year; ICT = information and communication technology; n.a. = not applicable.

TABLE 11.7 **Makueni County summary of inherited current assets, March 2013**

K Sh (millions)

CASH AND BANK BALANCES	PROPERTY RATE	PLOT AND HOUSE RENT	STAFF DEBTORS	CILOR	OTHER	TOTAL
10	2.8	124.6	0	0	0	137.6
7%	2%	91%	0%	0%	0%	100%

Source: Makueni CALC 2017.
Note: CILOR = compensation in lieu of rates.

TABLE 11.8 **Makueni County summary of inherited liabilities, March 2013**

	BANK LOANS	EMOLUMENTS	STATUTORY DEDUCTIONS	OTHER LIABILITIES	TOTAL
As of March 2013, CALC 2017 (K Sh millions)	0	19.3	75.16	4.34	98.8
In % of total	0	20	76	4	100

Source: Makueni CALC 2017.
Note: CALC = County Asset and Liability Committee.

However, this is not an easy task. Collecting the long-overdue taxes and fees is a daunting project, but it should be commenced urgently, since these inherited claims have matured further during the nine years since devolution, and thus may represent only a symbolic size of present values. Nevertheless, working out and eliminating these claims would be a best practice public finance action.

The inherited liabilities identified by the CALC team (table 11.8) are substantially greater than the TA estimates (K Sh 99 million and K Sh 81 million, respectively). The bulk of the liabilities (76 percent) is due to statutory creditors; the next big item is unpaid emoluments (20 percent). The CALC report indicates the claims as of 2013 as being of nominal value without expected and mandatory statements about the status of these claims in 2017 (that is, whether verified, disputed, or settled). Experience in other counties (Nairobi City County, in particular) suggests that the present value of unpaid inherited statutory deduction claims has increased substantially since devolution.

Unpaid emoluments presumably have been verified and paid subsequently. But Makueni County government may be waiting for a resolution from national entities, particularly IGRTC and the Treasury National Assets and Liabilities Management Department, to issue rules or provide guidance for resolution of statutory deduction claims. However, it would be also wise to target creditors and settle these claims, which are comparable to a good 1 percent of the county's annual revenues. While the inherited liabilities are much smaller than the inherited current assets (K Sh 99 million and K Sh 138 million, respectively), the county needs to work hard to recover a good share of outstanding current assets from debtors (95 percent of total) in order to cover liabilities from gains of inherited current assets.

Challenges Makueni CALC faced during verification and validation of inherited assets and liabilities in 2017

The major challenges the CALC identification and verification teams reported include the following:

- Land disputes, grabbing, and/or encroachment of a total 90 parcels of disputed land, particularly in the following areas:
  - Resolution of land disputes in Kiaoni Market of the defunct Makueni County Council
  - Encroachment of public utilities at the Malili trading centers through reallocation by the Malili Ranch Ltd.
  - Encroachment of public utilities in various markets: Emali cemetery, public toilet at Emali, Ngosini rock catchment area, and Unoa Hill trust land
  - Grabbing of two-acre parcel no. 14 Kathekani area by an individual (land was purchased by the then Mtito Andei Town Council)
- It was not possible to determine the size and acquisition value of most lands and buildings because the defunct local authorities had not done surveys. Furthermore, public land records from both the county and national government offices that would have enabled verification information were missing.
- There was no inventory of land leases, especially leases done during the colonial period.
- Due to missing information, it was not possible to compute collectible property rates, lease premiums, or plot rents for the defunct local authority.

- Acquisition values for vehicles, computers, computer accessories, and furniture in all the defunct local authorities could not be established without purchase documents.
- Serial numbers, makes, models, and acquisition values of equipment in all the defunct local authorities required further investigations since documents were not available.

Progress after asset takeover

The Makueni CALC made several recommendations to the governor and County Assembly with regard to inherited assets and liabilities, including the following: establish an inventory of all the public assets in the county for safeguarding purposes; establish an inventory of land leases and verify their status; establish a system for effective levy and collection of property rates, land rates, and lease premiums; and finally, survey and register all land that is not yet surveyed and determine the size and acquisition values of all land, buildings, and all other assets.

Makueni County government commenced several measures and initiatives toward improving the management of its assets, including the following:

- The Finance Department assigned two officers to coordinate asset management. This is the first step toward establishing an asset management system as a follow-up regular business measure after the closure of the CALC.
- The government drafted a county fixed asset policy (Makueni County 2017) to establish procedures for acquisition, classification, valuation, recording, transfer, and disposal of fixed assets.
- The government planned to develop an asset inventory that would enable the county entities to continually improve their informed decision-making and risk mitigation capabilities on assets.
- The government planned to hire a professional who would guide developing and implementing the county asset management system, framework, and procedures. The activities include proposing an asset management system, tagging assets, and forming and maintaining an asset register, which has been a major audit query in audit reports since 2013.
- The county government introduced a project management system with a dashboard to publish all development projects, with technical and financial details and progress accessible to the citizens and other stakeholders.

LESSONS LEARNED

The institutionalization of county asset management is an important component of a good financial management system. The Makueni County government should no longer wait for the national government to set up a small, pragmatic asset management system, and also it should account, operate, maintain, and refurbish assets in a systematic manner.

The conflicting guidance between the Transition Act and the MLG/1333/TY Circular created a legal gridlock that seems to have paralyzed the counties on asset takeover. The lack of takeover of assets and liabilities has remained an audit query for all subsequent audit reports since fiscal year 2013/14. However, there have been no apparent county reactions to the audit reports.

The county pragmatically took over, maintained, and expanded the assets of key services without the formal accounts and formal takeover, and this helped uninterrupted provision of local services and fulfilling functions. But now the county needs to move to a higher class of action and institutionalize asset management.

Budgeting for asset maintenance and renovation or purchase of new assets under the development budget requires a comprehensive asset register, which provides estimates of depreciation and time for asset replacement or disposal. With this component missing, county budgeting for assets is more ad hoc than information based.

The list of assets produced by the Makueni County CALC is not sufficient to develop an asset register; it is, however, a good starting point to commence a comprehensive asset validation, tagging, and valuation process that can be used for an asset database.

The verification and valuation of assets are incomplete and need more time and concerted efforts. It is vital for the county government to understand the gravity of the next steps and assign adequate resources and human capacities. Adopting a short- to medium-term action plan to establish an asset management framework, work out disputed cases, and complete valuation is a logical and vital next step moving forward.

The CALC teams had no responsibility to identify assets, lands, and buildings or current assets that various national government entities are supposed to hand over based on the devolved functions (Constitution 2010). This is a substantial next step for full takeover of county assets and would move further toward a balanced devolution.

Inherited current assets and liabilities are small in Makueni County, yet they are toxic assets and liabilities, so concerted efforts are required to work them out. The county should increase emphasis on inventory and verification of revenue-generating assets, revise and update lease and rent contracts of land and buildings, and start collecting these asset revenues consistently and forcefully.

Finally, Makueni County's project management system and dashboard is an exemplary case of transparency to inform and convince current and future partners (banks, investors, and developers) and helps in the effort to develop assets strategically and expand assets faster. These have helped Makueni Government accomplish development projects; the county's development budget moved around or over 40 percent of total budget after devolution, an exceptional scale among the 47 Kenyan counties.

REFERENCES

CGA. 2012. County Governments Act No. 17 of 2012. http://www.parliament.go.ke/sites/default/files/2017-05/CountyGovernmentsAct_No17of2012_1.pdf.

CRAB. 2015. County Revenue Allocation Bill 2015–2017. http://kenyalaw.org/kl/fileadmin/pdfdownloads/bills/2017 /CountyAllocationofRevenueBill_2017.pdf.

Farvacque-Vitkovic, C., and M. Kopanyi. 2019. *Better Cities Better World: A Handbook on Local Government Self-Assessments*. Washington, DC: World Bank. https://openknowledge.worldbank.org/handle/10986/32120.

IGRTC (Intergovernmental Relations Technical Committee). 2017. "Unaudited IGRTC Current Assets and Liability List as at 27 March 2013." Intergovernmental Relations Technical Committee from files of Transition Authority. Nairobi: IGRTC.

IGRTC (Intergovernmental Relations Technical Committee). 2018. *Report on the Identification, Verification, Validation, and Transfer of Assets and Liabilities of the Defunct Local Authorities as at 27ᵗʰ March 2013.* Nairobi: IGRTC. https://igrtc.go.ke/download/consolidated-report-on-assets-and-liabilities-of-the-defunct-local-authorities-2018/.

Kenya Constitution. 2010. http://kenyalaw.org/kl/index.php?id=398.

KNBS (Kenya National Bureau of Statistics). 2017. *Makueni County Statistical Abstract.* Nairobi: https://www.knbs.or.ke/?wpdmpro=makueni-county-statistical-abstract.

KNBS (Kenya National Bureau of Statistics). 2019. "Kenya Population and Housing Census." Nairobi: KNBS. https://housingfinanceafrica.org/documents/2019-kenya-population-and-housing-census-reports/.

Makueni CALC (County Asset and Liability Committee). 2017. *Makueni CALC Report.* Wote, Kenya: Makueni CALC.

Makueni County. 2017. Proposed Fixed Asset Policy. Wote, Kenya: Makueni County Government.

Makueni County. 2018a. "County Budget Review and Outlook Paper." Wote, Kenya: Makueni County Government. https://academia-ke.org/library/ makueni-county-2/makueni-county-budget-review-and-outlook-paper-2018-2/.

Makueni County. 2018b. *County Integrated Development Plan (CIDP) 2018-2022.* Wote, Kenya: Makueni County Government. https://repository.kippra.or.ke/xmlui/handle/123456789/646#:~:text=The%20Makueni%20County%20Integrated%20Development,economic%20foundation%20in%20the%20county.

Makueni PMS. n.d. "Makueni Project Management System." Wote, Kenya: Makueni County Government. https://makueni.go.ke/projects/public/index.php.

MLG (Ministry of Local Government) Circular, ref. no. MLG/1333/TY/ (52) of February 18, 2013.

Notice 858. 2017. Gazette Notice no. 858, January 8, 2017: Intergovernmental Relations Act no. 2 of 2012. https://gazettes.africa/gazettes/ke-government-gazette-dated-2017-01-27-no-13.

Notice 2701. 2017. Gazette Notice no. 2701, March 24, 2017: Intergovernmental Relations Act no. 2 of 2012. https://gazettes.africa/archive/ke/2017/ke-government-gazette-dated-2017-03-24-no-37.pdf.

OAG (Office of the Auditor General). 2013–19 (annually). *Report of the Auditor General on Financial Statement of Counties.* Nairobi: OAG. http://www.oagkenya.go.ke/index.php/reports/cat_view/2-reports/11-county-governments/203-county-government-reports.

OCB (Office of the Controller of Budget). 2014–18 (annually). *Annual County Government Budget Implementation Review Report.* Nairobi: https://cob.go.ke/reports/consolidated-county-budget-implementation-review-reports.

PFM. 2012. Public Finance Management Act, no. 18 of 2012. https://www.pcf.go.ke/index.php/public-financial-management-act.

PPAD. 2015. Public Procurement and Asset Disposal Act, no. 33 of 2015, December 18, 2015. http://kenyalaw.org:8181/exist/kenyalex/actview.xql?actid =No.%2033%20of%202015.

TA (Transition Authority). 2013a. "Transition Authority Guidelines," Ref. MOF/IFMIS/1/41 dated 7 March 2013.

TA (Transition Authority). 2013b. "Inventory of Assets and Liabilities Debts and Human Resource Profile in Public Organizations." Circular Ref. no. TA/2/5 dated 9 January 2013.

TDG. 2012. Transition to Devolved Government Act, no. 1 of 2012, enacted March 9, 2012. http://www.parliament.go.ke/sites/default/files/2017-05/TransitiontoDevolvedGovernmentActNo1of2012.pdf.

UAC. 2011. Urban Areas and Cities Act, no. 13 of 2011. http://www.parliament.go.ke/sites/default/files/2017-05/UrbanAreasandCitiesAct_No13of2011.pdf.

UAC. 2019. Urban Areas and Cities (Amendment) Act 2019. http://kenyalaw.org/kl/fileadmin/pdfdownloads/AmendmentActs/2019/Urban AreasandCities_Amendment_Act_2019.pdf.

World Bank. 2018. *Kenya Economic Update.* 17th ed., April 2018. Washington, DC: World Bank. https://documents.worldbank.org/en/publication/documents-reports/documentdetail/327691523276540220/kenya-economic-update-policy-options-to-advance-the-big-4-unleashing-kenya-s-private-sector-to-drive-inclusive-growth-and-accelerate-poverty-reduction.

12 Nakuru County

INTRODUCTION

Nakuru County is in the Great Rift Valley and borders seven other counties: Baringo, Bomet, Kajiado, Kericho, Laikipia, Narok, and Nyandarua. Nakuru covers an area of 7,497 square kilometers (KNBS 2017). The name *Nakuru* has its origin in the Maasai language, meaning "a dusty place." This name is based on the frequent whirlwinds that engulf the area with clouds of dust. The county's political units include 11 constituencies (Bahati, Gilgil, Kuresoi North, Kuresoi South, Molo, Naivasha, Nakuru Town East, Nakuru Town West, Njoro, Rongai, and Subukia) and 55 wards (map 12.1). The county has nine administrative units (subcounties): Gilgil, Kuresoi, Molo, Naivasha, Nakuru, Nakuru North, Njoro, Rongai, and Subukia. The county has 31 administrative divisions and 124 locations.

Nakuru County had an estimated population of 2.2 million with an average population growth rate of 3.1 percent and an average population density of 290 persons per square kilometer in 2019 (KNBS 2019). The county has a low population dependency ratio of 44 percent as compared with the 78.3 percent national ratio.

Nineteen percent of the county's territory has high agricultural potential and 21 percent has medium potential (World Bank 2018). The main agricultural crops produced include Irish potatoes, wheat, and maize. Horticultural produce includes stevia, rose flowers, and arabicum. There are 4,326 hotels and restaurants that serve several tourist attractions: Kariandusi and Hyrax Hill museums, which receive over 35,000 visitors annually. There are three national parks: Hell's Gate, Lake Nakuru, and Mount Longonot, which together receive about 400,000 visitors a year (Nakuru County 2018b). There are 45 industries operating in Nakuru County, of which 16 produce animal feed, 5 process milk, 4 generate electricity, and the rest produce tea, timber, or clothes. In the education sector, there are two universities (one public and one private), 13 university campuses (six public and seven private), and 406 health facilities with a 2,375 total bed capacity.

The decentralized functions (Constitution 2010) of the county government include: agriculture, health, control of pollution, cultural activities,

MAP 12.1
Nakuru County

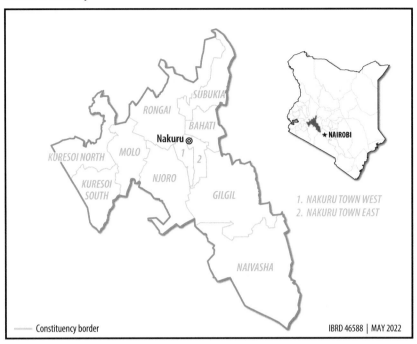

Source: World Bank.

transport, animal welfare, trade and development, county planning and development, pre-primary education, village polytechnics, home craft centers and early childhood education, environmental conservation, public works, and local community public participation. The county is mandated to provide the following services per the Urban Areas and Cities Act of 2011 and 2019 (UAC 2011, 2019): solid waste disposal, street lighting, public housing, office and shop rental, hospitals, preschools, vocational schools, a sports stadium, a game park, markets, and constituency university campuses, among others.

The county has 802 kilometers of paved roads and 8,851 kilometers of unpaved roads, a 193-kilometer railway line, and four airstrips (Nakuru County 2018a). The quality of infrastructure in the county is poor and dilapidated, largely because of low investment in the development of a road network, poor enforcement of axle load limits, and low diversification of transport. The county also experiences flooding due to poor drainage and stormwater management systems, which in turn affects the road quality. There is an inadequate quantity of drinking water. County citizens do not have full access to clean drinking or piped water, due to low investment in water development and unreliable rainfall. The county experiences a high level of environmental degradation caused by unplanned urban settlements, with poor solid waste management and high reliance on wood fuel, which results in widespread deforestation (OCB 2018). The high rate of urbanization due to natural growth and migration has resulted in encroachment on ecologically fragile riparian reserves and wetlands. With the inadequate land policy, laws, and regulations, there is poor land use practice in the county.

REVENUE AND EXPENDITURE ANALYSIS

Analysis of revenues and expenditures is an integral part of an assessment of asset management because it provides a solid background picture in which assets are positioned, developed, and managed. Revenues generate cash or cash-like instruments that are transient forms of assets, since land can be sold to generate cash revenue to develop schools, or cash can be saved for rainy days. Finally, the surplus remaining after current expenditures are covered with current revenues provides funds for development. Loans or other liabilities can also finance development. In short, revenue and expenditure analysis provides important insights and sheds light on the trends and capacities a county possesses in developing assets and expanding services.

Revenues

Nakuru County revenues grew steadily, on average 8.8 percent per annum in the 2013/14–2017/18 fiscal period (table 12.1); thus, revenues increased by 3 percent per annum in real terms above inflation. The Government of Kenya has supported devolution by substantially and steadily increasing transfers to counties after devolution (CRAB 2015). Like other counties, Nakuru County largely relies on national government transfers, which ranged from 78 percent to 85 percent of total revenues in the 2013/14–2017/18 fiscal period.

The county is heavily reliant on *equitable shares* that generated the bulk of total revenues (over 80 percent); they grew faster than other revenue components, on average 11.8 percent per annum. Conditional grants appeared to be very volatile and declining; they supported county functions and health facilities, free

TABLE 12.1 Nakuru County revenues, fiscal years 2013/14–2017/18
K Sh (millions)

	2013/14	2014/15	2015/16	2016/17	2017/18	AVERAGE GROWTH (%)
Transfers from national government	**6,962**	**7,423**	**8,818**	**9,733**	**10,030**	**9.6**
Equitable share	5,937	7,423	8,116	8,758	9,271	11.8
Conditional grants	1,025	0	702	975	759	–7.2
Own-source revenues	**1,373**	**2,109**	**2,295**	**1,961**	**2,280**	**13.5**
Taxes	611	654	795	522	574	–1.5
Fees and charges	388	1,389	1,162	976	1,264	34.3
Asset proceeds	102	30	218	106	241	24.0
Other revenues	272	35	119	357	202	–7.2
Financing	**600**	**116**	**129**	**15**	**214**	**–22.7**
Cash reserve from previous year	—	—	—	—	—	n.a.
Loans/grants	600	116	129	15	214	–22.7
Total revenue	**8,935**	**9,647**	**11,242**	**11,709**	**12,525**	**8.8**
Share of OSR/total revenues (%)	15.4	21.9	20.4	16.7	18.2	4.3
OSR actual/planned (%)	59.0	78.0	75.0	60.0	70.0	4.4

Source: OAG 2014–18.
Note: — = not available; n.a. = not applicable; OSR = own-source revenue.

maternal health care, compensation for foregone user fees, leasing of medical equipment, and the road maintenance levy. Transfers from the national government grew at an average rate of 9.6 percent, steadily but only slightly above the rate of inflation (CBK 2020).). The county also received a noticeable amount of grants from the Danish International Development Agency to support Nakuru Provincial General Hospital, especially at the beginning of the surveyed period. Donor grants, however, show a strong declining trend.

Nakuru's own-source revenues (OSRs) are of moderate size and grew by an average 13.5 percent per annum in the surveyed fiscal period. However, they remained flat (2.6 percent growth) after a jump in the 2014/15 fiscal year (table 12.2). The share of OSR varied between 15 percent and 22 percent in the 2013/14–2017/18 fiscal period; with that, Nakuru stays in the median among Kenyan counties. Nakuru County's OSR planning and collection efficiency is volatile and moderate (table 12.1); the highest actual/planned share was 78 percent in 2014/15, but it dropped to 60–70 percent in following years.

Taxes were the largest source (50 percent) of OSR in 2013/14. However, taxes show a downward trend, and their proportion declined to below 25 percent in 2017/18. Tax revenues declined an average 2.1 percent per annum in the surveyed period, due to a decline in all taxes (figure 12.1). Asset proceeds were volatile and small in the surveyed period.

Nakuru County made remarkable progress with a dynamic increase of fee revenues, with an average pace of 38 percent annual growth, albeit from a low level in the 2013/14 transition year. Royalties from the agriculture and mining sectors, liquor licensing, and advertising provided a large share of fee revenues. Advertising and billboard fees also grew fast (21 percent per annum) and became a substantial revenue source by 2017. Parking fees provide for stable albeit moderate volume and share of OSR (about 10 percent), but they grew at only a

TABLE 12.2 **Nakuru County OSR, fiscal years 2013/14–2017/18**

K Sh (millions)

	2013/14	2014/15	2015/16	2016/17	2017/18	AVERAGE GROWTH (%)
Taxes	**625**	**654**	**795**	**522**	**574**	**–2.1**
Property rates (property tax)	230	285	319	183	200	–3.5
Business permits (business tax)	345	327	430	314	347	0.2
Other taxes and levies	49	42	46	26	27	–13.9
Fees and charges	**349**	**1,389**	**1,162**	**976**	**1,264**	**38.0**
Parking fees	234	272	292	275	259	2.7
Urban services	73	105	187	204	131	15.7
Social services	0	64	608	497	154	n.a.
Licenses, permits, certificates	42	949	76	0	720	103.6
Asset proceeds	**102**	**30**	**218**	**106**	**241**	**24.1**
Rents and leases	32	30	151	47	151	47.1
Markets	69	0	67	59	90	6.8
Other income	**298**	**35**	**119**	**357**	**202**	**–9.3**
Total OSR	**1,372**	**2,109**	**2,295**	**1,961**	**2,280**	**13.5**

Source: OAG 2014–18.
Note: n.a. = not applicable; OSR = own-source revenue.

FIGURE 12.1
FIGURE 12.1

Nakuru County OSR, fiscal years 2013/14–2017/18

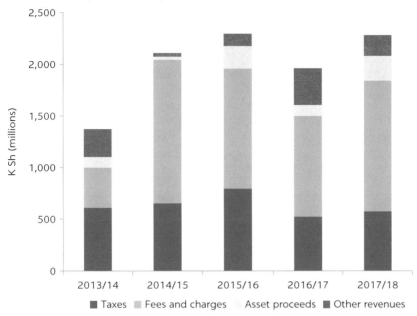

Sources: OAG 2014–18; Nakuru County 2018a.
Note: OSR = own-source revenues.

2.7 percent rate per annum, which is below inflation. Because of the coincidence of an increase in various fees that reflect improving fee policy and administration, fees and charges became the largest OSR source by 2017 (figure 12.1).

In contrast, the volatility and eventual decline of tax revenues (figure 12.1) is a warning signal that deserves the attention of the county's higher governing bodies, scrutiny, and corrective actions. Cess on agricultural produce declined by 26 percent per annum during the same period, possibly caused by a decline in agricultural production or trade, although there is no supporting evidence of real causes. The decline could be attributed rather to the changing of policy and collection practices. Asset proceeds were small and volatile but increased dynamically by 24 percent per annum, owing to the increasing collection of both market fees and house rents. Other incomes were substantial, signaling possible arbitrary misclassification of revenue items already discussed that may have caused volatility of some reported revenue streams.

Expenditures

Nakuru County's total expenditures grew at a remarkably high pace, on average 32 percent per annum against the very moderate 8.8 percent average annual increase of revenues (tables 12.1 and 12.3). This trend is undoubtedly unsustainable, even though the high average increase is partly attributed to the very low base expenditures on operation and development, and total expenditures in 2013/14 when the county seems to have been paralyzed by the transition from old to new local governments. The county realized a huge budget surplus apparently from unspent development expenditures and delayed payments for operation and maintenance in 2014.

TABLE 12.3 **Nakuru County expenditures, fiscal years 2013/14–2017/18**

K Sh (millions)

	2013/14	2014/15	2015/16	2016/17	2017/18	AVERAGE GROWTH (%)
Current expenditures	**3,194**	**6,958**	**7,884**	**8,166**	**9,508**	**31.4**
Personal emoluments	2,956	4,430	4,965	5,111	5,559	17.1
Operation and maintenance	238	2,412	2,266	2,362	1,474	57.8
Of which, repair and maintenance	0	17	36	70	19	3.0
Transfers to other entities	0	116	652	693	2,475	177.4
Development	**523**	**1,642**	**3,105**	**3,311**	**1,749**	**35.2**
Infrastructure investments	523	1,483	1,556	2,109	288	–13.9
Debt repayment	0	0	0	0	45	n.a.
Other payments	0	159	1,549	1,202	1,416	107.3
Total expenditures	**3,717**	**8,600**	**10,989**	**11,477**	**11,257**	**31.9**
Budget balance	*5,218*	*1,047*	*253*	*232*	*1,268*	*–29.8*
Ratios (%)						
Operation and maintenance/current	7.5	34.7	28.7	28.9	15.5	20.1
Personal emoluments/current	92.5	63.7	63.0	62.6	58.5	–10.8
Current/total	85.9	80.9	71.7	71.1	84.5	–0.4
Development/total	14.1	19.1	28.3	28.9	15.5	2.9
Repair and maintenance/current	0.0	0.2	0.5	0.9	0.2	n.a.

Source: OAG 2014–18.

Note: n.a. = not applicable.

The movements in the surveyed time period signal rational subsequent adjustments that include (1) an increase of development spending from a miniscule to a reasonable level and (2) a large increase of operation and maintenance (O&M), again from symbolic to a reasonably high level with a speed of 57 percent per annum, which resulted in a sixfold increase of O&M expenditures over five years.

Nakuru County's expenditure stream is very volatile in many line items: (1) transfers to other entities started with a small amount in 2014/15 but skyrocketed in 2017/18 (from K Sh 116 million to K Sh 2.4 billion), and (2) the high growth of development expenditures is only moderately attributed to infrastructure investment; instead, the county accounted for a steady stream of other payments, around K Sh 1.5 billion per year after 2014/15. This might be a result of spinoffs of service functions or supporting capital expenditures of semi-independent water companies. The big drop of infrastructure development expenditures (down from K Sh 2 billion to K Sh 300 million) is apparently a result of unfinished infrastructure projects with a corresponding realization of a huge budget surplus in the 2017/18 fiscal year.

Financial ratios show a mixed picture. Nakuru County government made a remarkable improvement by scaling down labor expenditures from the extremely high 93 percent to a reasonable 58 percent share in current expenditures (table 12.3). The share of current expenditures remained high, in part, because transfers to other entities counterbalanced the drop of labor expenditures and even pressed O&M expenditures down in 2017/18. These moves suggest that Nakuru County accumulated a substantial volume of unpaid bills (new overdue liabilities), because it is hard to believe that O&M costs can be cut by half from one year to another.

Despite the very volatile expenditure composition, the county managed to sustain a balanced budget by gradually absorbing the initial huge budget surplus into infrastructure investments. Nakuru stands out among the surveyed counties and most Kenyan counties with the extremely low level of repair and maintenance expenditures, the share of which often stayed below 0.5 percent of current expenditures against a 15.0 percent benchmark. This is a worrisome practice that eventually will undermine the functionality of assets and sustainability of services. One important action the county government may commence is a scrutiny of transfers to other entities and "other payments," which could be a simple misclassification of expenditures such as repair and maintenance. Should the county remain obliged to continue such high levels of subsidies to various service entities, introduction of performance-based subsidization would be a vital practice to commence.

Figure 12.2 further provides a glimpse into cumulative development spending from the beginning of devolution: construction of buildings, road construction and maintenance, and other infrastructure and civil works that largely include development of health, education, and housing facilities have received the most funds (Nakuru County 2018b). Development expenditures also included preparations for digital topographical mapping to support spatial planning and the preparation of a draft valuation roll that will not only improve the tax base and eventually increase OSR but also enable identification and valuation of county land and improve asset management.

FIGURE 12.2

Nakuru County cumulative development expenditures, fiscal years 2013/14–2015/16

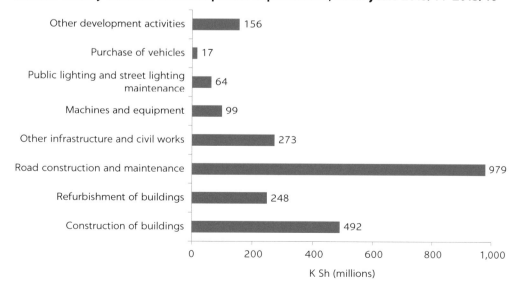

Source: OCB 2013–16.

ASSET MANAGEMENT

These case studies focus on the transition period before which Kenyan local governments did not have asset management systems, frameworks, and policies except some sporadic practices to manage assets daily by officers of service units. Despite legislated mandates—Public Finance Management Act 2012 (PFM 2012), Kenya Constitution 2010, Public Procurement and Asset Disposal Act 2015 (PPAD 2015), the County Governments Act (CGA 2012), and circulars—now defunct local governments failed to establish asset registers, and the accounting aspects of assets were poorly understood and disobeyed even before devolution. These local bodies failed to measure the wealth of the local government, aim for increasing it, or manage the most important assets strategically. This case study illustrates both the enormous challenges the incoming county governments faced due to the inherited situation and the remarkable progress achieved after devolution. It also demonstrates that moving forward requires strong determination, vision, finances, and reformative actions toward modern and adequate management of assets that eventually determine the level and quality of mandated services.

Asset ownership and transition to devolved government

Article 23 of the Transition to Devolved Government Act (TDG 2012) regulated the takeover of functions, assets, liabilities, and staff of the defunct local authorities in the Nakuru County jurisdiction, including Municipal Council of Nakuru and Naivasha, County Council of Nakuru, and Town Council of Molo. However, the 2013 Office of the Auditor General (OAG) report found that even though the Ministry of Local Government Circular no. MLG/1333/TY 2013 provided further instructions to outgoing entities for proper handover of assets and liabilities to the incoming county government, this was not done. The OAG audit team in July 2013 was unable to obtain supporting documents required for audit, mainly because documents were not secured and key staff from the former local bodies were transferred and were not available for the audit process. Furthermore, OAG found that the fixed-asset register was not updated, and records were made in pencil; the county government performed weak controls in maintaining an asset register (box 12.1). The main OAG findings include the following:

- It was not possible to establish cash-on-hand and bank balances because the defunct local authorities, particularly the outgoing officers of Nakuru County Council, did not provide the incoming officers with bank statements and bank certificates to confirm bank balances for the 10 bank accounts they operated.
- The bank accounts for Naivasha Municipal Council and Nakuru Municipal Council remained in operation after 28 February 2013, violating the rules the MLG/1333/TY Circular set to close all bank accounts by the end of February 2013. Naivasha Municipal Council operated eight bank accounts, which also continued operation after 28 February 2013, but the council did not maintain a register of the bank accounts.
- The revenues collected for the Nakuru County Council were not paid to main cashiers; furthermore, receipt books issued to the revenue collectors were not available for auditing. There was no evidence of collection of cess revenues worth K Sh 5.9 million in the Naivasha Municipal Council.

BOX 12.1

Nakuru County audit report excerpts, 2013

Failure to Take over the Defunct Local Authorities

The County Government of Nakuru had not officially taken over the assets and liabilities of the former municipal council of Nakuru, former county council of Nakuru and the former municipal council of Naivasha at the time of the audit, contrary to instructions issued by the Ministry of Local Government vide Circular No. MLG/1333/TY/52 of 18 February 2013. It was, therefore, not possible to establish the completeness of the assets and liabilities handed over to the County Government.

Utilization of Allocated Funds: K Sh 367,286,765

During the period under audit, the County Government of Nakuru was allocated K Sh 367,291,765.00 by the National Treasury for its operations. Out of this allocation, K Sh 102,126,434.00 was transferred to Nakuru County Assembly and K Sh 196,676,657.15 utilized by the County Executive for its operations, representing an absorption rate of 81 percent of the funding. The Balance of K Sh 68,483,673.85 was returned to the National Treasury. The County Government should endeavor to utilize all funds allocated as per the budget.

Failure to Maintain a Fixed Assets Register

The County Government did not maintain an asset register. There is risk of loss, misuse, pilferage, and misappropriation of the assets.

Source: OAG 2013.

Purchase of ICT Equipment: K Sh 8,662,964

The County Government purchased various ICT [information and communication technology] items at a cost of K Sh 8,662,964. However, they were not recorded in the stock control records contrary to Section 153(1) (b) of the Public Finance Management Act 2012.

Unaccounted-for Fuel: K Sh 5,062,973

The County Government purchased 34,399 liters of diesel and 14,660 liters of petrol at a total cost of K Sh 5,062,973. However, the County did not maintain a bulk fuel register, detailed fuels orders were not dated, and the relevant motor vehicle work tickets were not availed for audit verification. Therefore, the propriety of the expenditure could not be confirmed.

Unrecorded Purchase of Motor Vehicle Spare Parts: K Sh 2,343,292

The County Government purchased various motor vehicles spare parts and tires at a cost of K Sh 2,343,292 for repairs and maintenance. However, the items were not taken on charge in the stores and logbooks were not maintained to record repairs and maintenance works carried out on vehicles. Therefore, the propriety of the expenditure could not be confirmed.

- Nakuru County Council and Naivasha Municipal Council had no debtors' register as mandated by PFM Act 2012 which could be used to confirm the debtors' balances; they also did not have a creditors' ledger with records and supporting documents that could be used to confirm the creditors' balances.
- Nakuru County Council did not maintain an asset register as required by the PFM Act 2012.

Informal takeover and use of assets, 2013–17

The Nakuru County government informally took over the assets from the defunct local authorities (OAG 2013), especially those that formed the material base of local services and functions. OAG further recommended that the Transition

TABLE 12.4 **Nakuru County asset management entities and their functions**

SERVICES OR FUNCTIONS THAT REQUIRE SPECIFIC ASSETS OWNED BY OR USED BY THE COUNTY	ASSET MANAGEMENT ENTITIES		
	COUNTY DEPARTMENT RESPONSIBLE FOR THE RESPECTIVE SERVICES	COMPANY OR OTHER INDEPENDENT ENTITY OWNED BY THE COUNTY	PRIVATE SERVICE PROVIDER OR PRIVATE MANAGING ENTITY UNDER PPP
Urban services			
Roads and drainage	Public Works	n.a.	n.a.
Public transport	n.a.	n.a.	Private operators
Water and wastewater lines	Water, Environment, Energy, and Natural Resources	Nakuru Water and Sanitation Services Company	Naivasha Water, Sewerage and Sanitation Company Nakuru Rural Water and Sanitation Company
Solid waste	Water, Environment, Energy, and Natural Resources	n.a.	n.a.
Social services			
Health	Health Services	Heads of health units	n.a.
Education	n.a.	Heads of schools	n.a.

Source: Nakuru County Government website and field survey.
Note: n.a. = not applicable; PPP = public-private partnership.

Authority (TA) arrange formal handover of assets and liabilities of the former local authorities to the county government, but there is no evidence that the TA had ever either responded to or reacted positively to this OAG message during fiscal year 2013/14 or later. Instead, the TA handed over preliminary inventories only in March 2016, the day of its closure. Nakuru County has been developing most of the assets of the defunct local authorities since March 2013. Despite the unresolved issues mentioned earlier, Nakuru County has continued to manage, refurbish, or expand its inherited assets through various county departments or in partnership with independent service entities; table 12.4 summarizes the specific asset management arrangements without highlighting the general functions of various county departments.

Asset takeover by the power of law, 2017

Gazette Notice no. 858 (2017) transferred the assets and liabilities of the defunct local authorities by the power of the law and set a framework for validation, verification, and valuation of the assets by the counties. Nakuru County government established a County Asset and Liability Committee (CALC) based on Notice no. 2701 (2017) to lead, guide, and monitor identification, verification, and validation of the assets and liabilities inherited from the defunct local authorities, and verify inventory and values as of March 27, 2013. The Intergovernmental Relations Technical Committee (IGRTC) provided guidance, leadership, and training to facilitate the work of CALCs that were established mostly in May 2017.

Further, Notice no. 2701 reconfirmed Notice 858 on March 24, 2017, and extended the deadline for completion of the verification program from March 31, 2017, to July 31, 2017. IGRTC handed over the TA records to the county after establishment of CALC (IGRTC 2017). Box 12.2 explains the work methodology of Nakuru County CALC. TA records show that Nakuru County inherited from

BOX 12.2

Nakuru County Asset and Liability Committee work methodology

The process was guided by the guidelines and tools developed by the Interagency Technical Committee as per the classes of the assets and liabilities. The following data collection strategies to collect both primary and secondary data were also used:

Interviews. These were conducted with key informants and officers at the county headquarters and in subcounties and with those who previously had worked in the defunct local authorities, including treasurers and clerks.

Document review. The team examined primary supporting documents like title deeds, logbooks, asset registers, valuation reports, certificates, and other related records. Secondary data were collected through valuation reports, auditor-general reports, handover and takeover reports, land

registry records, adjudication registers, preliminary index maps, registry index maps, bank statements, financial statements, and review of Local Authorities Integrated Financial Operations Management System (LAIFOMS) reports.

Physical inspection and verifications of assets through site visits.

Public participation. Additional data were collected from the public, who submitted written memoranda following public notices in both print and electronic media and made available in churches and public gatherings requesting information on assets and liabilities of defunct local authorities.

Data were analyzed using the narrative method and presented using thematic analysis.

Source: Nakuru CALC 2017.

the defunct local governments K Sh 2,444 million in current assets and K Sh 1,332 million in current or overdue liabilities. The CALC teams established and verified different volumes of inherited assets. The numbers presented in this section are from the Nakuru CALC report and cross-checked with the IGRTC 2018 report.

Progress by 2019

The Nakuru County CALC was able to identify, verify, and validate 629 land parcels (table 12.5), nearly twice the 334 parcels of land listed in the TA report. Most of the land is located within the former Nakuru County Council jurisdiction (401 parcels), and of the total, 600 parcels are surveyed and have registration numbers. The former Nakuru Municipal Council had 29 parcels of unsurveyed land with no registration number; four parcels had multiple ownership, one was encroached, and six had illegal acquisition. The CALC team did not declare disputed land. However, encroached and illegally acquired land require follow-up action and settlement of these cases. The list of well-verified, surveyed, and registered land is a solid base for an initial land asset register that can be further enhanced with simple valuation, since most of the land is not marketable. Many parcels could be classified as surplus land, since the number of land parcels exceeds the number of buildings. Thus, Nakuru County should adopt an asset management policy that plans divestitures in order to generate development revenues but also create a rule that no land can be divested without individual market valuation, competitive bidding, and fair payment. Then the county could start using or divesting land assets strategically.

TABLE 12.5 **Nakuru County summary of verified land and buildings, by DLAs, 2017**

	NAKURU COUNTY COUNCIL	NAKURU MUNICIPAL COUNCIL	NAIVASHA MUNICIPAL COUNCIL	MOLO TOWN COUNCIL	TOTAL
Land					
Total parcels of land	401	161	36	31	629
Unsurveyed land	0	29	0	0	29
Multiple ownership	0	4	0	0	4
Encroached	0	1	2	0	3
Illegal alienation	0	6	0	0	6
Buildings					
Total number of buildings	210	153	23	96	482
Of which in use	153	210	23	23	409
Unprocedurally acquired	0	0	3	0	3

Source: Nakuru CALC 2017.

Note: DLAs = defunct local authorities.

The Nakuru CALC team verified 482 buildings, of which 409 were in use and three were disputed, since they had been illicitly divested in the Naivasha Municipal Council area (table 12.5). In contrast, the 2018 IGRTC report lists only 162 buildings without land registration (LR) numbers in Nakuru County, and this contradicts the CALC list of land that shows 95 percent of parcels with an LR number. The county government should revisit these records and clarify discrepancies. The main uses of the buildings include market stalls, office blocks, health facilities, housing estates, and primary schools. The Nakuru County CALC team further noted that some parcels of land hosted more than one building. Furthermore, the CALC team stated that it was not possible to identify, verify, and validate all the buildings due to the limited time that was allocated to this exercise. Nonetheless, the CALC inventory of buildings serves as a solid basis for an initial building asset register that should be further enhanced with precise technical details such as size, plinth area, age, technical conditions, and historic book value or assessed present value.

The movable assets the Nakuru County CALC team identified were as follows:

- *Motor vehicles.* One hundred sixty-seven motor vehicles were identified against 213 identified in the TA report. This discrepancy occurred because CALC found that the TA captured 20 vehicles twice, and 20 vehicles had been sold before 27 March 2013, but were still included in the TA report. Furthermore, the TA included 8 vehicles owned by the national government, and thus they were not part of the motor vehicle inventory of the defunct local authorities. Out of the 167 verified inherited vehicles, 11 vehicles are in the possession of Nakuru Water Service Company. Finally, of the 167 motor vehicles, only 85 were operational, 68 were grounded, and 14 vehicles need repair to resume operation.

- *Furniture.* Nakuru County inherited an assortment of furniture including office executive desks and chairs, a metal and steel cabinet, and visitors' chairs among other furniture items totaling 3,616. Of these, the Nakuru County Council had 216, Naivasha Municipal Council had 169, Molo Town Council had 213, and Nakuru Municipal Council owned the rest. Even though furniture existed at the point of verification, there were numerous movements and relocation to other offices within the county that were not properly documented during establishment of the new county government. Furthermore, most of the furniture was broken and verified as unusable.

- *Equipment.* This included items like medical equipment, office equipment, telephone sets and telephone headsets, among others.
- *Computers and accessories.* One hundred ninety-two items were recorded, comprising printers, photocopiers, scanners, network switches, shredders, uninterrupted power source, and projectors, among others.
- *Biological assets.* There were no inherited biological assets.

CALC teams identified a total of 196 projects that were ongoing at the time of devolution in March 2013. The total value of projects was K Sh 315 million in 2013. Of these, 113 projects were completed before CALC verification in 2017 and included in the inventory of buildings and structures, 70 were verified as incomplete without comments whether they were still ongoing or suspended, and 13 projects did not start, cancelled before construction commenced. Most of the projects (93) aimed to build classrooms, particularly in the jurisdiction of the Nakuru County Council. There were 20 road projects: 6 were in the jurisdiction of Nakuru Municipal Council and the other 14 were in the jurisdiction of Nakuru County Council. The other projects included: roofing of county houses, street lighting, public toilets and sanitation, and water provision. The CALC team lacked information to establish the values of completed, suspended, or cancelled projects.

Nakuru County inherited a substantial volume of investments due to outsourcing water and sanitation services, some in public-private-partnership modality. The defunct local authorities had invested K Sh 1,255 million in three water companies. Nakuru County Council held a 51 percent share in Nakuru Rural Water and Sanitation Company. The Nakuru Municipal Council held 100 percent of shares in Nakuru Water and Sanitation Services Company, and Naivasha Municipal Council held a 60 percent share in Naivasha Water, Sewerage, and Sanitation Company.

For the first time, Nakuru County government reported in 2018 a summary of fixed assets acquired after the transition (table 12.6). This is a move in a good direction. However, the reported numbers are not in harmony with the financial reports (table 12.3), in which the total value of investments into fixed assets is reported to be K Sh 6 billion as opposed to the fixed asset register, which indicates only a K Sh 1 billion historical cost of total fixed assets acquired after 2013 devolution. The fixed asset register also reports financial investments in 2018 with the value of K Sh 1.1 billion that are comparable, though not matched with, the "other development expenditures" in the financial report. The reported annual investments in fixed assets (additions) in the 2017/18 fiscal year corresponds to the annual financial report (K Sh 288 million). Finally, asset amortization has apparently not been accounted, or the asset register excludes such figures. Good asset registers should reflect gross value, depreciation, and net value of assets regardless of whether the county follows cash-based accounting principles in bookkeeping and financial reports.

Nakuru County inherited K Sh 4,026 million in current assets identified by the Nakuru CALC team (table 12.7). This value is nearly twice as much as the K Sh 2,444 million presented in the TA report. Uncollected property taxes constitute 80 percent of inherited current assets (over K Sh 3 billion), while

TABLE 12.6 **Nakuru County fixed asset register summary, June 30, 2018**

K Sh (millions)

	HISTORICAL COST, JUNE 30, 2017	ADDITIONS IN FY 2017/18	HISTORICAL COST, JUNE 30, 2018
Land	14	17	31
Buildings and structures	319	0	319
Transport equipment	99	49	148
Office equipment	35	8	43
ICT equipment and software	27	145	172
Other machinery	200	1	201
Intangible assets	91	69	160
Total in register	**785**	**288**	**1,074**
Financial investments	0	1,134	1,134
Total fixed asset acquisition/development after devolution	n.a.	288	5,959

Source: OAG 2018.

Note: FY = fiscal year; ICT = information and communication technology; n.a. = not applicable.

TABLE 12.7 **Nakuru County summary of inherited current assets, by DLAs, March 2013**

K Sh (millions)

	CASH AND BANK DEPOSITS	PROPERTY RATE	HOUSE AND PLOT RENTS	OTHER CURRENT ASSETS	TOTAL
County Council of Nakuru	7.9	832	329	0.2	1,170
Municipal Council of Naivasha	16.7	167	12	0	195
Municipal Council of Nakuru	0	2,181	422	11.2	2,614
Town Council of Molo	0.1	30	17	0	47
Total	**24.8**	**3,210**	**780**	**1.5**	**4,026**
Total in % of grand total	0.6	79.7	19.4	0.0	100.0

Source: Nakuru CALC 2017.

Note: DLAs = defunct local authorities.

uncollected fees make up 20 percent, with a negligible amount of bank deposits. Nakuru Municipal Council accumulated a particularly high volume of uncollected property taxes (K Sh 2 billion), while Nakuru County Council closed with K Sh 832 million in uncollected and overdue property tax revenues.

The same two councils failed to collect substantial rent payments from house and plots with the combined nominal (2013) value of K Sh 780 million. The CALC team made no comments on the possible present value of inherited current assets, which should have increased substantially because of due penalties and interests by 2017. Most of these arrears were already several years old in 2013, and were four years older in 2017, so they apparently represent a much smaller collectible value today. Establishing the present values and adopting a workout strategy for inherited current assets is among the most urgent tasks the Nakuru County government faces.

Nakuru County inherited K Sh 1,046 million in liabilities. This estimate is about 30 percent less than the K Sh 1,493 million listed in the unaudited TA report (table 12.8). The CALC team verified that the county had paid out immediately after inauguration all inherited due emoluments, reducing liabilities by K Sh 239 million; a further bank debt restructuring reduced the volume of total inherited liabilities to K Sh 785 million. The CALC report did not identify or

TABLE 12.8 **Nakuru County summary of inherited liabilities, 2013 and 2017**
K Sh (millions)

	BANK LOANS	EMOLUMENTS	STATUTORY DEDUCTIONS	OTHER LIABILITIES	TOTAL
As of 2013, per TA report	148	239	212	894	1,493
As of 2017, per CALC report	148	239	212	447	1,046
Net value as of 2017	92	0	212	480	785

Source: Nakuru CALC 2017.
Note: CALC = County Asset and Liability Committee; TA = Transition Authority.

comment on the issue of the huge difference between the TA report and the CALC report in identified other liabilities (dues to contractors and suppliers and legal fees). A precise comparison and explanation of such a big difference such as double-counted claims, unverified claims the creditors cancelled at verification, and so forth would have been a sign of due diligence. It could be the case, however, that unrecorded hidden settlements reduced the demand of the forced creditors, but the county government should presumably be aware of settlements with such a large magnitude.

Finally, a slight increase of value of other liabilities suggests that (1) the county did not recognize disputed claims or further work out claims verified in 2017, and (2) some creditors charged interest by 2017. Nakuru County has not addressed inherited statutory deductions; it did not estimate and present an increased present value in 2017 or signal negotiation with creditors toward workout of inherited statutory deductions, which apparently have increased quickly with penalties and interest, as other county experiences suggest.

The CALC verification revealed that the defunct Nakuru Municipal Council had taken four long-term loans from National and Family Bank with a combined value of principal and interest of K Sh 148 million. These loans were subsequently combined into one loan and rescheduled under a new agreement; some interest was paid, and bank debt was thus reduced to K Sh 92 million and became serviced debt by the time of CALC verification. During the same time, unremitted statutory deductions amounted to K Sh 212.4 million. The CALC team identified K Sh 212 million in unpaid statutory deductions but failed to qualify this amount by creditors or comment on the status: for example, if any of these had been disputed. Thus, the CALC report seems to have verified the county's statutory deduction liabilities without comments or workout plans.

Challenges Nakuru CALC faced during verification and validation of inherited assets and liabilities in 2017

The CALC teams reported several challenges while undertaking verification. The main challenges included the following:

- There was a lack of relevant documentation when it came to the verification of assets such as land and buildings in the defunct local authorities because most of them had LR numbers but did not have title deeds.
- There was a delay in obtaining documentation due to the unavailability of staff of the defunct local authorities. Furthermore, some of the records maintained by the defunct local authorities could not be traced, which caused delays.
- There was limited time to fully verify the assets and liabilities.

- There were insufficient financial resources to facilitate the verification exercise.
- The teams undertaking the exercise were not trained in good time; there was limited time for them to fully understand the process before commencing the exercise.

LESSONS LEARNED

The Nakuru County Finance Department has taken several steps toward improving asset management. First, a three-person asset management team was appointed within the Finance Department to manage the assets owned by the county. Second, the Finance Department procured an information technology system that would be used to capture all the information on the county assets. Third, the asset management team is in the process of capturing asset data in the field, including tagging of land and buildings. Once this process is complete and the data are entered in the asset management system, the county will have a working asset register. The most critical lessons include the following:

- Nakuru County has made good steps toward asset management by setting up an asset management unit in the Finance Department. This team is undertaking the verification of land and buildings, a key component of good asset management.
- Nakuru CALC did decent work, but verification and valuation of assets remained incomplete, and the process had been hampered by lack of time and resources. Since the CALC is no longer functional, the appointed asset management team and the Finance Department should take the lead to complete asset verification, validation, and eventually valuation of assets, especially land and buildings.
- County land and buildings have been well verified with a small number of disputed cases and with a high share of registered land. Thus, the CALC report and verified inventory serves as a solid base to establish a reliable fixed asset register.
- Finishing a comprehensive verification and valuation of inherited current assets and liabilities, closing disputes, and working out inherited current assets and liabilities is among the urgent tasks that may need guidance and support by national government entities, especially IGRTC and the National Treasury's National Assets and Liabilities Management Department.
- Nakuru County has no asset management system, framework, or procedures, nor does it have policy, strategy, or an asset management plan. Moving forward, it is important to establish a small, simple, reliable asset management system in the short to medium term.

REFERENCES

CBK (Central Bank of Kenya). 2020. "Inflation Rates 2013–2019.: Nairobi: CBK. https://www.centralbank.go.ke/inflation-rates/.

CGA. 2012. County Governments Act No. 17 of 2012. http://www.parliament.go.ke/sites/default/files/2017-05/CountyGovernmentsAct_No17of2012_1.pdf.

CRAB. 2015. County Revenue Allocation Bill 2015–2017. http://kenyalaw.org/kl/fileadmin/pdfdownloads/bills/2017 /CountyAllocationofRevenueBill_2017.pdf.

IGRTC (Intergovernmental Relations Technical Committee). 2017. "Unaudited IGRTC Current Assets and Liability List as at 27 March 2013." Intergovernmental Relations Technical Committee from files of Transition Authority. Nairobi: IGRTC.

IGRTC (Intergovernmental Relations Technical Committee). 2018. *Report on the Identification, Verification, Validation, and Transfer of Assets and Liabilities of the Defunct Local Authorities as at 27th March 2013.* Nairobi: IGRTC. https://igrtc.go.ke/download/consolidated-report -on-assets-and-liabilities-of-the-defunct-local-authorities-2018/.

Kenya Constitution. 2010. http://kenyalaw.org/kl/index.php?id=398.

KNBS (Kenya National Bureau of Statistics). 2017. *Nakuru County Statistical Abstract.* Nairobi: KNBS. https://www.knbs.or.ke/download/Nakuru/.

KNBS (Kenya National Bureau of Statistics). 2018. *Basic Report on Well Being in Kenya* (based on Household Budget Survey 2015/16). Nairobi: KNBS. https://www.knbs.or .ke/download/basic-report-well-kenya-based-201516-kenya-integrated-household -budget-survey-kihbs/#.

KNBS (Kenya National Bureau of Statistics). 2019. *"Kenya Population and Housing Census"* Nairobi: Kenya National Bureau of Statistics; https://housingfinanceafrica.org /documents/2019-kenya-population-and-housing-census-reports/.

Ministry of Local Government (MLG). 2013. Circular, ref. no. MLG/1333/TY/ (52) of February 18, 2013.

Nakuru CALC (County Asset and Liability Committee). 2017 *Nakuru CALC Report.* Nakuru, Kenya: Nakuru CALC.

Nakuru County. 2018a. "County Budget Review and Outlook Paper." Nakuru, Kenya: Nakuru County Government. https://nakuru.go.ke/download/county-budget-review-outlook -paper-2018/.

Nakuru County. 2018b. *County Integrated Development Plan (CIDP) 2018–2022.* Nakuru, Kenya: Nakuru County Government. https://repository.kippra.or.ke/bitstream/handle/123456789 /947/2018-2022%20%20Nakuru%20County%20CIDP.pdf?sequence=1&isAllowed=y.

Notice 858. 2017. Gazette Notice no. 858, January 8, 2017: Intergovernmental Relations Act no. 2 of 2012. https://gazettes.africa/gazettes/ke-government-gazette-dated-2017-01-27-no-13.

Notice 2701. 2017. Gazette Notice no. 2701, March 24, 2017: Intergovernmental Relations Act no. 2 of 2012. https://gazettes.africa/archive/ke/2017/ke-government-gazette-dated-2017-03 -24-no-37.pdf.

OAG (Office of the Auditor General). 2013–19 (annually). *Report of the Auditor General on Financial Statement of Counties.* Nairobi: OAG. http://www.oagkenya.go.ke/index.php /reports/cat_view/2-reports/11-county-governments/203-county-government-reports.

OCB (Office of the Controller of Budget). 2014–18 (annually). *Annual County Government Budget Implementation Review Report.* Nairobi: OCB. https://cob.go.ke/reports/consolidated -county-budget-implementation-review-reports/.

PFM. 2012. Public Finance Management Act, no. 18 of 2012. https://www.pcf.go.ke/index.php /public-financial-management-act.

PPAD. 2015. Public Procurement and Asset Disposal Act, no. 33 of 2015, December 18, 2015. http://kenyalaw.org:8181/exist/kenyalex/actview.xql?actid =No.%2033%20of%202015.

TDG. 2012. Transition to Devolved Government Act, no. 1 of 2012, enacted March 9, 2012. http:// www.parliament.go.ke/sites/default/files/2017-05/TransitiontoDevolvedGovernment ActNo1of2012.pdf.

UAC. 2011. Urban Areas and Cities Act, no. 13 of 2011. http://www.parliament.go.ke/sites /default/files/2017-05/UrbanAreasandCitiesAct_No13of2011.pdf.

UAC. 2019. Urban Areas and Cities (Amendment) Act 2019. http://kenyalaw.org/kl/fileadmin /pdfdownloads/AmendmentActs/2019/Urban AreasandCities_Amendment_Act_2019 .pdf.

World Bank. 2018. *Kenya Economic Update.* 17th ed., April 2018. Washington, DC: World Bank. https://documents.worldbank.org/en/publication/documents-reports/documentdetail /327691523276540220/kenya-economic-update-policy-options-to-advance-the-big -4-unleashing-kenya-s-private-sector-to-drive-inclusive-growth-and-accelerate-poverty -reduction.

County Asset Management Policy Model

DISCLAIMER

This asset management (AM) policy model presents one possible, detailed policy that utilizes lessons from a draft AM policy of Nairobi City County (NCC), a draft national asset and liability management policy and guideline, prepared under the National Assets and Liabilities Management (NALM) Department in the National Treasury (NALM 2020a, b, c), and international experiences (Cape Town 2012; Fiix 2019). Kenyan counties should tailor this model to local circumstances. There are two important clarifications worth mentioning.

First, this AM policy model has a broad scope and covers policy for all kinds of assets a county may own, use, and host without ownership and includes financial and nonfinancial assets in order to approach AM issues completely and consistently, because financial and nonfinancial assets are transient forms of each other. For instance, a county may sell a parcel of land or an office building and invest a part of the proceeds into treasury bills to save money for future investments. After one to two years, the county may sell a package of the treasury bills to obtain money to extend a water network. In short, a consistent and complete AM policy should cover all kinds of assets. However, this is not a regulation or prescription, so users have full liberty to draft a narrow-focus AM policy limited to only fixed assets or nonfinancial assets. It is easy to ignore sections of this model to narrow the focus.

Second, some policy documents mix policy and guidelines. This model policy focuses on county-specific policies, although the aim of the policies is to guide actions and behavior of regulated entities or persons. However, this policy assumes that detailed procedures should be included in a separate guideline the same way as NALM has issued separate AM guidelines for the national and subnational levels. This is indeed the case, since some fundamental guidance already exists, such as in the Public Finance Management Act (PFM 2012) or in the Public Procurement and Asset Disposal Act (PPAD 2015). In short, detailed procedures and actions should be and mostly are regulated in national legislation such as the two acts and NALM guidelines (NALM 2020b, c), but it is still useful to set applications with local specificities. In contrast, a county AM policy should focus on county-specific policy statements to regulate local circumstances with references to, but without repetition of, national guidelines and laws.

Subsections have been numbered in this appendix to enhance navigation and cross-referencing.

ACRONYMS USED IN MODEL AM POLICY

AM	asset management
AMCF	Asset Movement Capture Form
AMDR	Asset Management Directorate
CECM	county executive committee member
CFO	chief financial officer
CIP	capital improvement planning
DIR	departmental inventory register
IFRS	International Financial Reporting Standards
IPSAS	International Public Sector Accounting Standards
NALM	National Assets and Liabilities Management Department (in the National Treasury)
NCC	Nairobi City County
PFM	Public Finance Management Act 2012
PPAD	Public Procurement and Asset Disposal Act 2015
PPE	property, plant, and equipment
TA	Transition Authority

DEFINITION OF TERMS

For clarity and consistency in the use of terms, the following key definitions are presented.

asset. A resource that the county owns and controls or hosts or uses without ownership with current or expected future benefits that may include good service delivery, good public functions, or revenue generation.

asset management. A process of decision-making, planning, and control over the acquisition, use, safeguarding, and disposal of assets in order to maximize their service delivery potential and/or value and manage the related risks and costs over their entire life.

Asset Management Plan. An annual plan for managing the county's assets with the aim to deliver an agreed and accepted standard of services.

capitalization of assets. An action of recording of assets in the fixed asset register with their historical financial cost in accordance with IFRS (International Financial Reporting Standards) and IPSAS (International Public Sector Accounting Standards).

classification of assets. Assets can be classified from various perspectives. *Material form* (financial or nonfinancial assets) can include land, buildings, networks, infrastructure, equipment, and so forth. They can be classified per *use or service* (transport, health, water, housing, and similar assets) according to county departments or service entities. They can also be classified in terms of a county's *mandates and responsibilities*: core, (semi)marketable, or surplus assets.

contributed (or donated) assets. Assets received by the county in the form of in-kind donation.

cost. The amount of cash or cash equivalents paid or the fair value of or other consideration given to acquire an asset, at the time of its acquisition or construction.

departmental inventory register. A register for recording items with technical details according to department specificities.

depreciable amount. The cost of an asset less its anticipated residual value, or a regulated share of initial versus historical value that should be accounted as cost annually (for example, 2 percent of historical value of a building).

depreciation. The systematic allocation of cost of an asset over its useful life.

fair value. The amount for which an asset could be divested or a liability settled, between knowledgeable, willing parties in an arm's-length transaction.

fixed asset register. A register for recording all important characteristics of fixed assets.

general ledger. A register that contains all the financial accounts of a county.

impairment. Determined loss in future economic benefits or service potential of an asset, over and above the systematic recognition of the loss of the asset's future economic benefits or service potential through depreciation.

investment property. Land or buildings owned by a county and/or leased by way of a finance lease to earn rental income or for capital appreciation or both.

property, plant, and equipment (PPE). Tangible, identifiable assets that are held for (1) use in service delivery to county residents, (2) rental purposes, or (3) administrative purposes and are expected to be used for more than one year.

PPE should be classified according to the following definition groups:

- *Infrastructure assets.* They usually display some or all of the following characteristics:
  - They are part of a system or network.
  - They are specialized in nature and do not have alternative uses.
  - They are immovable.
  - They may not be subject to disposal by the county.

Examples are road networks, sewer systems, water, electricity networks, and so forth.

- *Community assets.* They contribute to the community's well-being: for example, social halls, libraries, recreational parks, and so forth.
- *Heritage assets.* They have culturally significant resources, such as heroes' statues, museums, and so forth.
- *Investment properties.* They are acquired for economic and capital gains, or are held by the county under finance lease to earn rentals, such as stalls, markets, and estates.
- *Other assets.* They are utilized in the normal operations: for example, furniture and fixtures.

- *Intangible assets.* They are without a physical substance: for example, granted right-of-way, special ownership rights in properties, software, or intellectual property.
- *Biological assets.* They are possessed for agricultural purposes: for example, any living animal or plant, forests.

repairs and maintenance. All actions and measures performed on existing tangible assets that are undertaken to prevent deterioration and failure and to restore the physical condition, quality of functionality, and operational performance of the asset.

residual value. The estimated amount that the county would obtain from disposal of an asset, after deducting the estimated costs of disposal, if the asset was already of the age and in the condition expected at the end of its useful life.

useful life. The period over which an asset is expected to be in use by an entity.

A COUNTY ASSET MANAGEMENT POLICY MODEL

This policy outlines the division of responsibilities in an integrated AM framework to guide practices that govern actions and decisions on AM at a county level to ensure the county accomplishes its mission of providing high-quality and expanded services to respond to the growing demands of citizens of the county's jurisdiction. This AM policy applies to all assets owned, used, or possessed by a county and all aspects of each asset, including planning, financing, project selection, design, construction, operation, maintenance, stewardship, and disposal. The policy aims to regulate actions of all employees, contractors, and consultants working on various aspects, functions, and areas of AM in a county. The aim is to ensure all entities, units, and employees are aligned with the goals and requirements related to AM and to ensure assets are managed in a manner that maximizes benefits, reduces risks, and provides satisfactory levels of service to customers in a safe and sustainable manner.

Objective and scope of this AM policy

The objective of this AM policy is to establish a framework for the accounting, treatment, utilization, and safeguarding of county assets including the proper selection, acquisition, construction or donation acceptance, recognition, operation, measurement, replacement, disposal, and retirement of fixed assets and adjacent financial assets and liabilities. This policy applies to all assets including, but not limited to, the following:

- *Nonfinancial assets*
These include tangible or fixed assets, intangible assets, and inventories, such as the following:
  - Land
  - Buildings
  - Infrastructure assets
  - Motor vehicles
  - Plants and machinery

- – Furniture, fittings, and fixtures
- – Equipment, computer accessories, electronic equipment, and projects
- – Community assets
- – Works in progress
- – Investment assets
- – Heritage assets
- – Biological assets
- – Intangible assets
- – Store inventories

- *Financial or current assets*
  - – Shareholdings, stocks, and bonds
  - – Bank deposits
  - – Receivables
  - – Loans to county entities and/or employees

This policy assumes parallel development and adoption of an AM strategy and an annual AM plan that correspond to and supplement the AM policy. The benefits of developing and implementing an AM policy, together with the AM strategy and Asset Management Plan, include the following:

- Better allocation of limited county resources
- Improved alignment of assets with services and county residents' expectations
- Reduced demand for new county assets through better integration of service planning and asset planning
- More effective use and maintenance of existing county assets
- Improved processes and accountability for capital and recurrent works
- Use of nonasset solutions to meet service demand
- Increased use of sustainable development solutions

This policy guides how stakeholders and the county shall interact with the county's high-level strategies formed in key documents such as the county strategic plan, the master plan, and the county development plan, which includes mission statements to commit to "delivering the services that fall under its mandate to residents and businesses in a cost effective and creative manner" as stipulated in the fourth schedule of the Constitution of Kenya on devolved functions (Constitution 2010).

Through the use of sound AM practices, the county and the community can be assured that the assets meet performance levels, are used to deliver the desired service in the long term, and are managed for present and future users. This policy also articulates the county's commitment to develop and implement an international standard system, framework, and procedures for AM in harmony with the respective national legislation and regulations summarized briefly in appendix F. This policy also outlines how AM should or will be integrated into the county's general business procedures, daily operation, and financial management system.

The policy recognizes that the takeover of assets from defunct entities and from national government entities in accordance with the allocation of functions (schedule 2 of Constitution 2010) is still incomplete because asset inventorying, verification, and valuation have not been completed, so reliable fixed asset registers are not yet developed. Nevertheless, this policy regulates actions in view of normal operation after expected timely correction of the gaps, that is, the required actions are or should be spelled out in both departmental and county Asset Management Plans assuming completed inventorying and established registers.

Legislative framework and legal base

In Kenya, laws have regulated AM at both national and subnational or county levels. Some regulations were in place decades before the devolution, but most of these regulations were ignored without penalty for decades. The devolution supported establishing larger local governments in the form of counties that now have (or should have) human, institutional, and financial capacities to comply with the legislation and establish reliable AM systems with international standard procedures. The most significant laws for AM include the following, which are the guiding rules for this AM policy:

The Kenya Ministry of Finance issued Circular no. 14 of 13 October 2000 (Circular no. 2000/14), which outlined the procedure for managing public assets. Based on the provisions of the circular, accounting officers were required to establish government AM registries and committees in their respective ministries or departments.

Circular no. 14/2000 was an important step in the creation of a central government asset register, although efforts to establish a central asset registry at the Ministry of Finance were later abandoned. Functions of the AM registries were spelled out and rightly applicable for county AM policy:

- Open files for each type of asset and record the history of the asset, including acquisition date, disposal date, survey plan, title, size, acreage, and instrument of transfer.
- Use appropriate forms to collect and collate asset data.
- Maintain accurate asset records that will provide pertinent information regarding assets, including both technical and financial details.
- Maintain details of the asset at historical cost and replacement value with depreciation.
- Regularly update records of all assets.
- Provide the requisite asset data to the AM registry at the Ministry of Finance for update of the central asset information database (if such exists).
- Carry out periodic inspection of assets wherever situated and seek authority for valuation where the property value cannot be ascertained or established.

Public Finance Management Act of 2012, (PFM 2012) Section 104(1) (g) outlines the responsibilities and powers of the County Treasury in regard to AM.

104. (1) Subject to the Constitution, the County Treasury shall monitor, evaluate and oversee the management of public finances and economic affairs of the county government including—

(g) Acting as custodian of the inventory of the county government's assets except where provided otherwise by other legislation or the Constitution . . .

Section 153(1) and (2) of PFM 2012 states the responsibilities of accounting officers in the county governments in regard to managing county assets and liabilities.

153. (1) The accounting officer for a county Government entity—

   a. Is responsible for the management of the entity's assets and liabilities; and
   b. Shall manage those assets in such a way as to ensure that the county government entity achieves value for money in acquiring, using or disposing of those assets.

(2) The accounting officer for a county government entity shall dispose of assets only in terms of an Act of Parliament pursuant to Article 227 of the Constitution and shall ensure that the proceeds from all asset disposals are credited into a bank account of the entity.

Public Procurement and Asset Disposal (PPAD) Act 2015 outlines how public institutions procure goods and services and how to dispose of assets in accordance to Article 227 of the constitution.

PFM 2012 Section 68(1) sets out the responsibilities of accounting officers designated for county government entities in regard to resource and asset management.

68. (1) An accounting officer for a national government entity, Parliamentary Service Commission and the Judiciary shall be accountable to the National Assembly for ensuring that the resources of the respective entity for which he or she is the accounting officer are used in a way that is—

   a. Lawful and authorized; and
   b. Effective, efficient, economical and transparent.

(2) In the performance of a function under subsection (1), an accounting officer shall—

   a. Ensure that all expenditure made by the entity complies with subsection (1);
   b. Ensure that the entity keeps financial and accounting records that comply with this Act;
   c. Ensure that all financial and accounting records the entity keeps in any form, including in electronic form are adequately protected and backed up . . .

This is the main legal instrument concerned with AM in the county. This policy shall therefore be implemented in tandem with other relevant legislations, which include but are not limited to the following:

- Constitution of Kenya 2010
- County Governments Act of 2012
- Public Procurement and Asset Disposal Act of 2015 and Regulations
- Land Act 2012 and 2016
- Public Finance Management Act 2012
- Transition to Devolved Government Act of 2012
- Urban Areas and Cities Act 2011 and 2019
- Public Audit Act 2015
- Public Sector Accounting Standard Board
- International Financial Reporting Standards
- International Public Sector Accounting Standards
- General recognized accounting practices
- Environmental Management and Coordination Act 1999 and supplement 2015

Key principles of asset management

The main principles of AM are to (1) support the county to make informed decisions, identify all revenues and costs (including operation, maintenance, replacement, and decommission) associated with fixed asset decisions, including additions and deletions; (2) support, articulate, and evaluate trade-offs, and serve as the basis to record decisions; (3) integrate corporate, financial, technical, and budgetary planning for fixed assets; (4) establish organizational accountability and responsibility for asset inventory and maintain technical condition, use, and performance; (5) define and articulate service, maintenance, and replacement levels and outcomes; (6) use available resources effectively; (7) manage assets to be sustainable; (8) minimize risks associated with service failure; and (9) pursue best practices where applicable.

The county will adhere to the following core principles in planning and decision-making relating to the selection, creation or acquisition, operation and maintenance, and renewal or disposal of all fixed assets, and require all our suppliers to adopt these principles:

- Service delivery drives AM practices and decisions.
- Asset planning and management have a direct link with the county's corporate and business plans, including the annual and long-term development plan and the long-term financial plan, annual budgets, and reporting process.
- The long-term financial plan (10 years) shall address the asset renewal gaps.
- Apply the "renewal before upgrade or new" philosophy for assets as appropriate.
- As a principle, asset depreciation is to be used to fund replacement, renewal, and/or rehabilitation of assets.
- AM decisions shall be based on service delivery needs and the benefits and risks of assets, with an evaluation of alternative options that take into account life-cycle costs.
- Use of a capital acquisition planning (also known as a capital improvement planning, or CIP) priority project evaluation process for new projects. Key questions to answer should be included in project proposal forms:
  - Is the project required to reduce or eliminate a hazard or address safety issues that may otherwise present legal implications to council?
  - Have there been changes in the law requiring changes to the council's service or asset?
  - Is the project needed to remedy the effects of accident, infrastructure failure, or natural disaster?
  - Has external funding become available with limited time for spending the funds or is the same likely to become available in the near term (that is, scope to seize the moment with limited impact on ratepayers)?
  - Is the project subject to carryover expenditure or existing contractual obligations or has there been a specific council resolution to fund within the appointed year?
  - Is the project a renewal of an existing asset?
  - Is the majority of funding for the project from sources other than the county's budget?

- Once the project is completed, will there be minimal or no ongoing maintenance cost?
- Is there a cost risk of not proceeding with this project?
- Will there be an impact on future budgets by completing this project?
- Does the project help the county government meet its vision of being a great place to live, work, and visit?
- Is the project specifically identified in the county strategic plan or other subordinate strategy objectives?
- Does the project improve the level of service provision?
- Does the project improve environmental outcomes such as reduced greenhouse emissions, energy consumption, water consumption, resource use, or waste generation?
- Have scheduled maintenance reports identified the need?
- Is the project listed in an approved Asset Management Plan?
- Will the project lead to improved public health and safety?
- Will the project result in reduced asset life-cycle costs?
- Does the county have the capacity (internal or external) to carry out the project?

- New or upgrade projects funded by grants should be assessed by including full life-cycle costs as part of the project evaluation.
- Asset Management Plans should be developed annually, should be integrated with a budget and financial reporting framework, and should be informed by community needs.
- Financial and AM reports should reflect operational, maintenance, renewal, upgrade, and new expenditure classification to enable sound AM decisions.
- Members of the County Assembly and staff with asset and financial responsibilities will be appropriately briefed in relevant asset and financial management principles, practices, and processes.
- After creation, the condition or structural integrity of assets will be managed by application of appropriate life-cycle management principles and practices throughout operations, maintenance, renewal and upgrade, and disposal.

AM policy, strategy, and plans

The county also will comply with required capital asset reporting requirements and integrate the AM program into operational plans throughout the county. An AM strategy should be developed and adopted for the county, and strategic Asset Maintenance Plans may be developed for a specific class of assets, or be generic for all assets, and should outline long-term goals, processes, and steps toward how they will be achieved. The annual Asset Maintenance Plans should be based on current inventories and condition (acquired or derived), projected performance, and remaining service life and consequences of losses (for example, vulnerability assessments). Operational plans should reflect these details. Replacement portfolios and associated financial plans should consider alternative scenarios and risks, but also take into account results of public consultation.

The context and integration of AM through the county's service delivery mandate is typically formalized through references and linkages between the county government's documents. Where possible and appropriate, this policy shall complement, communicate with, integrate with, and be in tandem with the current and future county government documents and existing systems, such as the following:

- County Integrated Development Plan
- County Strategic Plan
- County budget
- Sector plans
- Procurement plans
- Annual development plans
- Geographic information system
- Street address system
- Global positioning system–based information systems
- Any other system where necessary

Allocation of AM mandates, functions, and responsibilities across county departments and other units custodial of assets

Most of the county's departments and their subordinate entities have some responsibility for good AM, and many of them have been fulfilling some if not all AM functions, mostly in silos without proper integration and communication. The county is committed to taking steps to connect the appropriate departments, functions, and support activities to build effective working relationships and encourage information sharing. The AM governance framework aims to ensure that decisions are made collaboratively and consider and serve all life-cycle stages to drive optimum value for citizens. The policy promotes and guides interrelationships between asset, operational, and service performance and fosters decision-making that recognizes the interconnected nature of asset systems and shows how decisions about one set of assets may potentially interact with or affect assets controlled by other departments and functions.

Mandate of the Asset Management Directorate

The Asset Management Directorate (AMDR) was created to coordinate AM and to address challenges affecting AM in the county. The following are the key mandates of AMDR:

- Exercise high-level, central stewardship responsibilities over management of all assets.
- Take custody of and maintain the county AM system.
- Create and maintain the county master asset register.
- Develop, review, and implement AM policies and plans.
- Draft the annual county Asset Management Plan in cooperation with and with consolidating data from department plans of all other departments and entities.
- Draft the annual county repair and maintenance plan based on departmental repair and maintenance plans with a section that explains deferred maintenance of larger scale.
- Prepare annual financial statements on county assets, including a report on deferred maintenance with a section that explains deferred maintenance of larger scale.
- Draft proposal for higher governing bodies on strategic acquisition or divestiture actions in cooperation with respective departments.

- Complete analyses to support quality AM, including but not limited to demand assessment and preparation of a CIP in cooperation with and based on proposals submitted by service sectors or other departments.
- Advise the county secretary on matters related to prudent management of assets.
- Schedule and perform physical asset identification, verification, and validation of capital assets.
- Serve as custodian of county asset ownership documents.
- Approve and coordinate divestiture of surplus or final deposition of obsolete assets.
- Facilitate the insurance of county movable and immovable assets.
- Facilitate revaluation of assets.
- Measure and report the performance of AM programs to internal stakeholders.

Mandates, roles, and responsibilities of service sectors

The purpose of this section is to prescribe the responsibilities of various sectors and departments within the county regarding assets. The various service sectors and departments bear various AM mandates and responsibilities in various phases of the asset life cycle. This section explains the allocation of functions across sectors and functional departments in various phases of the life cycle of assets: planning, acquisition, operation and maintenance, and final disposal.

Planning and project selection phase

Planning for assets requires detailed contributions from sectors and departments in order to form medium-term CIPs and adopt an annual capital budget. Sectors and departments should analyze service-level needs annually in the development planning process to inform decisions on capital asset planning and development. An assessment of specific needs is particularly important for generating information to support proposals for significant or expensive projects.

Sectors and departments should contribute to the selection and prioritization of the medium-term CIP, which should have a five-year horizon and be revised annually on a rolling basis. Sectors and departments can initiate CIP by populating CIP templates to initiate priority projects for capital asset acquisition or development in their own specific service responsibility area. A CIP committee will screen proposals, coordinate proposals with sectors, prioritize projects, and submit the five-year rolling CIP for executive approval. Sectors and departments should consider and compare various alternatives for service possibilities in life-cycle costing, including acquisition of assets, leasing assets, selling and leasing back assets, and public-private partnerships. Likewise, the cost-effective scale, size, models, or technical specifications should be selected using life-cycle costing and net-present-value analysis.

The sectors and departments should form an annual sector capital development plan in harmony with the CIP, with necessary tailoring to changing financial or material circumstances. These plans will be coordinated by the Departments of Finance and Economic Planning and the supply chain management before final shortlisting and inclusion in the annual capital budget of the county. Specific analyses and approval requirements are spelled out in other parts of this policy.

Acquisition

Sectors and departments may commence asset acquisition in accordance with the approved budget and budgeted appropriation and necessary approval by the Supply Chain Management Department, or in specific large projects, approval by the county treasurer or the cabinet. A least-cost solution analysis should be completed on life-cycle modality in selection of the final specification and modality of the planned assets. Supporting documentation and arguments should be shared with the finance, planning, and supply chain management. Sectors and departments are responsible for timely and proper accounting of new assets as prescribed below.

Operation and maintenance

Sectors and departments should adopt an annual preventive maintenance plan for each fixed asset (except land) over and above individual value of (K Sh 10 million) and register these plans in the technical asset register (departmental inventory register, or DIR). These plans should be developed based on the technical characteristics of the assets, and also should take into account the maintenance schedules set by the producer of the specific assets (equipment, vehicle, or structure) and a risk-based assessment of due maintenance needs. Ideally, sectors can adopt a medium-term five-year preventive maintenance plan for each fixed asset on a rolling basis and include approved actions in the annual scheduled or preventive maintenance plan. These plans should be included in the annual budget, and an adequate volume of funds should be appropriated accordingly. Medium-term and annual maintenance plans also should include planned major repairs or refurbishments that are due or prioritized, but those should be accounted for among development plans and development expenditures following the rules explained in "The Supply Chain Management Department" section of this appendix.

The summary of the annual sector maintenance plan should include a section that explains any deferred maintenance of assets planned because of a shortage of funds and lower priority based on risk assessment. This is important to record, because deferred maintenance is often justified, but more often than not it induces higher maintenance costs or unplanned reactive maintenance to correct breakdowns of operating assets. In short, preventive maintenance is the preferred option against reactive maintenance, which happens inevitably but should be minimized in a cost-effective way by timely preventive maintenance.

Sectors and departments should fairly and in a timely manner record technical details and all actual costs of operation and maintenance during the fiscal year and include these respectively among expenditures and in logbooks and asset registers alike. Sectors and departments should complete in a timely manner an annual analysis of asset performance and report to AMDR.

Disposal of fixed assets

Sectors and departments are responsible for planning and proposing to the Supply Chain Management Department the disposition of assets they assume are no longer required or no longer able to serve the purpose for which the assets were acquired. The specific procedures to follow are spelled out in other sections of the AM policy. See the section "The Supply Chain Management Department," which follows.

The Finance and Economic Planning sector

The Asset Management Directorate

The AMDR director is designated to be the county AM coordinator and is responsible for ensuring the following:

- The general asset register is maintained.
- The general asset register is reconciled monthly with the general ledger.
- All departments are performing annual asset verification.
- The allocation of barcode ranges is coordinated.
- All asset audit queries are resolved effectively.
- The county's assets are valued in accordance with IFRS.
- Liabilities (for example, offtake guarantees and operating subsidies committed) that may be attached to some assets are properly valued, and cost-effectiveness is measured as part of asset performance and approved by the chief financial officer (CFO) and the county treasurer.
- The results of annual asset verification must be reported to the CFO, county executive committee member (CECM), and county manager.

The general asset register (also known as fixed asset register) may include a brief but meaningful description of each asset; the date on which the asset was acquired or brought into use; the purchase/original cost, the revalued amount, and/or the fair value if no costs are available; supplier details and payment voucher number; make or model of asset (equipment); serial number where applicable (for motor vehicles this should be the engine and chassis numbers); the location of the asset; host entity, department, and officer responsible; the tag number; repair and maintenance records (including scheduled preventive maintenance, reactive maintenance, renewal, or expansion, all of which should include date, costs, duration of inactivity, and closure); accumulated depreciation; the depreciation charge for the current financial year; the carrying value of the asset; the method and rate of depreciation; the title deed number, in the case of fixed property; the stand number, in the case of fixed property; the (last) revaluation date of the fixed assets subject to revaluation; the revalued value of such fixed assets; impairment losses incurred during the financial year (and the reversal of such losses, where applicable); the source of financing; whether the asset has been used to secure any debt, and, if so, the nature and duration of such security arrangements (contingent liabilities attached to an asset); the date on which the asset is disposed of; the disposal price; and the date on which the asset is retired from use, if not disposed of.

The Supply Chain Management Department

The Supply Chain Management Department shall adhere to the following rules and principles.

Acquisition and disposal of assets. Ensure that all assets are acquired in terms of the PPAD Act 2015, Section 26(1):

(1) For the purpose of ensuring that its decisions are made in a systematic and structured way, a public entity shall establish procedures to provide for the making of decisions, on behalf of the public entity,

(2) The procedures required under subsection (1) shall be consistent with this Act and the regulations.

(3) All procurement shall be—

    a. Within the approved budget of the procuring entity and shall be planned by the procuring entity concerned through an annual procurement plan;

    b. Undertaken by a procuring entity as per the threshold matrix as set out in the regulations; and

    c. Handled by different offices in respect of procurement initiation, processing and receipt of goods, works, and services.

Procurement

(1) Ensure that a completed Asset Movement Capture Form (AMCF) is presented with the assets before accepting an obsolete or damaged asset or asset inventory item;

(2) Ensure that a record is kept of all obsolete, damaged, and unused assets received from departments;

(3) Compile a list of the items to be auctioned in accordance with their guidelines . . .

Disposal

Ensure that all obsolete or damaged assets are disposed of according to the requirements of the PPAD Act 2015, Section 129(3):

(3) The disposal committee shall recommend to the accounting officer a method of disposing of the stores and equipment which may include any of the following—

    a. Transfer to another public entity or part of a public entity, with or without financial adjustment;

    b. Sale by public tender;

    c. Sale by public auction;

    d. Destruction, dumping, or burying; or

    e. Trade-in.

Transfers from one county department to another

(1) Transfer obsolete or unused assets to any department requiring such assets in consultations with the director of AMDR and respective chief officer;

(2) Notify the AMDR of such transfers within 10 working days of transfers taking place; and

(3) Ensure that a record is kept of all transfers from one department to another.

The Human Resources Department

The Human Resources Department shall ensure that no monies are paid to employees on termination of their service prior to receiving the relevant asset resignation form signed off by the relevant department.

All other departments

All the other departments within the county shall adhere to the following rules and principles:

- Ensure that employees in their departments adhere to the approved AM policy procedures, guidelines, and reflections.

- Ensure that all assets are procured in accordance with the PPAD Act 2015.
- Ensure that employees with delegated authority have been nominated to implement and maintain physical control over assets in their departments. Although authority has been delegated, responsibility remains with the respective chief officers of the sectors and overall accountability with the directors of relevant directorates.
- Ensure that the notice of termination of service clearance form for employees is duly completed and submitted to the human resource directorate.
- Ensure that assets are properly maintained in accordance with their respective asset operation and maintenance policy and plan.
- Ensure that adequate barcodes are always available to exercise management and control.
- Ensure that, where applicable, all their movable assets are reflected in the fixed asset register and are barcoded to exercise control.
- Ensure that the AMDR director is notified via the AMCF within 10 working days of any changes in the status of assets under the department's control.
- Ensure that transfers between departments within directorates are administered internally.
- Ensure that a complete asset verification of all inventory and asset items is performed annually.
- Ensure that all obsolete, damaged, and unused assets, supported by relevant asset and condemnation forms, are handed into the Supply Chain Management Department without delay and copied to the AMDR director.
- Be responsible for maintaining and managing own DIR.
- Ensure that all assets are safeguarded against loss and theft and that they are adequately insured.
- Ensure that location changes are made in a timely fashion and that all location information is updated regularly.

Regulation of asset management actions

Recognition of assets
An object shall be recognized as an asset as defined by the following:

- Land assets are recognized with estimated market value or acquisition value and are not subject of depreciation.
- PPE assets are recorded at cost, which shall include the purchase price and other acquisition costs directly attributable to bringing the asset to the location and condition necessary for its operation, such as installation costs, freight charges, transportation, taxes, legal costs, and duties.
- For a contributed capital asset, cost is deemed to be the fair value at the date the asset is contributed.
- Subsequent expenditures relating to PPE are capitalized if it is probable that future economic benefits or potential service delivery of the asset is enhanced in excess of the originally assessed standard of performance.
- Assets held under finance leases are capitalized and will be reflected in the fixed asset register.
- Major spare parts and standby equipment (strategic stock) qualify as PPE when they bear a significant cost in relation to the total cost of the item and will be used more than one year after installation.

Recording of assets

Acquisitions of items that do not meet the definition of tangible asset must be recorded in the DIR depending on the nature and aggregate value of the item. Maintaining the DIR is the responsibility of individual departments.

An acquired tangible asset will be barcoded and recorded within the fixed asset register. The following information must be captured when recording tangible assets:

- Date of acquisition
- Location
- Barcode allocated
- Asset class and type
- Asset master record number
- Measurement bases used
- Depreciation methods used
- Useful life or life expectancy
- Depreciation charges
- Gross carrying value
- Accumulated depreciation
- Valuation elements
- Ownership details
- Terms of tenancy, for example, leasehold, freehold, effective and expiration dates, and so forth
- Survey aspects, for example, deed plans, survey plans, acreage, global positioning system coordinates, and so forth
- Photos of assets

Investment property

An object shall be recognized as investment property if it meets such definition. Investment property is recorded at investment cost. But a disclosure value should be measured and recognized in the following ways:

- Measure initially at acquisition cost plus transaction cost, or nominal value.
- Where acquired at no cost or nominal value, fair value at acquisition is deemed to be cost for disclosure.
- If held under a lease and classified as investment property, use the lower of fair value and the present value estimated from minimum lease payments.
- Cost value is determined according to the requirements of the IFRS and IPSAS standard on investment property.
- Assets classified as investment property shall be redefined once such asset usage changes.

Financial assets

Financial assets are transient forms of tangible or fixed assets, and often they are attached to specific fixed assets. Financial assets include shareholdings, stocks, bonds, receivables, and bank deposits. The complete and comprehensive AM policy also should include rules for managing the financial assets. For instance, the county may decide to offer a piece of land or a building to a private partner and form a joint venture for certain services or purposes (for example, office, hotel, or housing). In such case, the respective fixed asset moves out from the fixed asset register and becomes a shareholding: a financial asset. This policy regulates two sets of financial assets: receivables and shareholdings (ownership shares, stocks, and bonds altogether).

Receivables

Receivables are current assets that may include uncollected taxes, service fees, and lease or rental fees. Fees are the primary results of using various assets that are vital for cost recovery of assets and services, and therefore should be properly measured. Running market spaces, parking sites, and rental offices and providing water and sanitation services are, on the one hand, important services for citizens; on the other hand, they should generate revenues for full cost recovery of services and assets. Receivables are forms of financial assets generated by the fact that billed or contracted fees or charges are partially collected. Uncollected fees and charges could be substantial. Sectors and departments that oversee assets used for providing fee-based services should carefully measure and report both collected and uncollected fees and charges and account them later as financial assets in the form of receivables or collectibles (also known as *arrears* when overdue).

Shareholdings

Managing shareholdings or other invested forms of assets (for example, stocks or bonds) is the domain of the Finance and Planning Department, which should maintain an itemized register of such assets with timely measurement and recording of financial performance. Shareholding may be attached to contingent liabilities the county had committed during formation of the joint ventures. The real values of such financial assets include not only the expected or realized revenues but also the net amount after deducting expenses on contingent liabilities. Proper AM should keep clear records and measure performance of each financial asset individually and as a portfolio alike.

Safeguarding tangible assets

Custody and security

- All barcoded assets shall be tracked by physical location through the fixed asset register.
- A physical asset verification process (stocktaking) shall be performed every year and be conducted simultaneously throughout the county.
- Overall coordination of the annual asset verification process shall rest with the chief officer of Finance and Economic Planning, but each department is responsible for the verification of assets in its custody.
- It is the responsibility of all the directors to report any grabbed, stolen, or damaged property to the chief officer of Finance and Economic Planning and the director of investigation and information analysis for investigations and resolution.

Communication of changes

All changes in asset status should be reported to the chief officer of Finance and Economic Planning and the AMDR director within 10 working days (or online real time as information and communication technology [ICT] enables doing so) to maintain accuracy of the fixed asset register. Accurate information in the system is dependent on the completion by departments of the appropriate AMCF for additions and transfers to other departments. Data updates are required for the following changes (the ICT system will include respective templates):

- Change in department ownership
- Change from location on record
- Change in usage of equipment
- Change in operating conditions (impairment)
- Change in property title
- Change in estimated useful life
- Disposal or retirement
- Replacement of damaged or lost barcodes

Departments must find and reconcile discrepancies between the fixed asset register and the physical inventory count results.

Annual verification process

The annual asset verification process shall be coordinated or/and determined by the AMDR director, who shall inform the CECM of Finance and Economic Planning and all the chief officers of the process and timelines at least two weeks before its commencement.

Assets not verified in the just-mentioned process (for example procured later) must be investigated and reported accordingly.

Hiring properties and equipment

A record of all hired (that is, rented) properties and equipment shall be maintained in a separate register by the chief officer of Finance and Economic Planning, giving particulars of each hiring and the amount paid as a refundable security deposit and hire fee.

Insurance

Identified insurable risks shall be covered with a policy of insurance issued by the insurer. The coverage shall be equivalent to its reinstatement as per the rule of indemnity.

Procedures

The county commits to adhere to the following principles and procedures:

- All assets shall be valued and assessed by professional valuers, loss adjustors, and assessors every two years.
- Professional risk managers shall advise the AMDR director on all insurable risks and their mitigation.

Maintenance of assets

Maintenance strategy

Each department must develop a maintenance strategy that will ensure that the county's assets are maintained at an adequate operational level or standard by ensuring that all statutory, technical, and operational objectives are achieved through the entire life cycle. This strategy must ensure that tangible assets under the custody and control of the relevant directors are properly maintained and repaired so that their possible maximum useful lives are realized.

Department's responsibilities

Each department shall be responsible for ensuring the following:

- All tangible assets under their control are maintained in good working condition. The departments must take adequate care that the working environments for the various assets are appropriate and suitable for such types of tangible asset.
- Assets under their custody are not misused or used for personal use or benefit.
- Repair and maintenance costs incurred are reviewed and properly controlled.
- Medium-term and annual maintenance plans for each tangible asset are developed and implemented and include financial plans according to the department's operating budget. The program must provide a schedule of the repairs and maintenance. The program and budgets also must consist of planned repairs and maintenance to be performed and contingencies for unplanned (emergency) maintenance.
- The departments should report all major deferred maintenance with plans for later performance of such due repairs and maintenances.

Retirement or disposal of assets

Governance

The disposal or retirement of assets are governed as follows:

- The county may only dispose of assets that do not provide minimum levels of basic services through a centralized open public tender or auction.
- Assets other than those utilized to provide minimum levels of basic services may be disposed of, subject to identification and recommendation by the asset disposal committee and approval by the executive committee or delegated authority.

Procedures and principles

- No disposal or retirement of any property can be conducted without the prior authorization of the chief officer of Finance and Economic Planning and the CECM of Finance and Economic Planning.
- Fixed assets are disposed of in accordance with PPAD and Public Procurement and Oversight Authority of Kenya regulations.
- The chief officer of Finance and Economic Planning shall appoint or nominate members of the Assets Management and Disposal Committee, which will be mandated to identify and recommend assets for disposal and retirement.
- Departments shall identify the mode of failure of their assets and communicate the same to the County Treasury for disposal of the asset.
- Any items declared obsolete or damaged must be accompanied by completed AMCF and condemnation forms, which must be countersigned by the respective chief officer and AMDR director before forwarding to the Supply Chain Management Department for safekeeping.

- Departments are responsible for submitting to the Supply Chain Management Department full documentation of all assets to be disposed and giving copies to the AMDR.
- All assets lost, stolen, or damaged must be reported to the AMDR director and the director of the Investigation Department for investigation and information analysis.

Prior approval is necessary for the following asset classes to be declared obsolete or damaged:

- *Vehicles and plant.* The fleet management department shall authorize the write-off based on the input of the relevant departments and the AMDR.
- *ICT equipment.* The chief ICT officer shall authorize the write-off.
- *Office furniture, fittings, and all other assets not already mentioned.* The respective chief officers shall authorize the write-off.

Procedure regarding donated assets

Governance

The authority to endorse and approve acceptance of assets contributed to NCC is vested in the executive committee as such assets have an impact on future operational costs. A report that includes the fair value or cost of the contributed assets and the financial implications of acceptance of the contributed asset must be submitted to the executive committee, so that acceptance of the asset can be confirmed. All ownership and transfer documents must be handed over to the county at the designated time.

Procedures

Once the executive committee has approved the donation, the departments must notify the chief officer of the Finance and Economic Planning sector of any assets contributed or donated by submitting to the county executive committee an approved report that includes the cost or fair value of the contributed asset, so that the asset can be recorded and capitalized at the appropriate value.

Budgeting

For effective implementation of the AM policy, the County Treasury shall ensure that there is an adequate budgetary allocation for AM activities. Operation and maintenance costs in the line sectors' budgets shall be utilized to operate and maintain county assets to avoid the risk of asset failures.

Reporting framework

The AMDR shall encourage networking and collaboration among departments, employees, and stakeholders on AM issues. These will include the National Treasury (via NALM), the County Treasury, sectors, subcounty offices, ward offices, development partners, and international organizations, among others.

Asset reports from departments shall be made on a quarterly basis and an inventory list shall be maintained by respective departments annually. The reporting structure for AM in the county is summarized in figure A.1, subject to further improvement as may be deemed necessary.

FIGURE A.1

Asset and liability management reporting framework in Nairobi City County

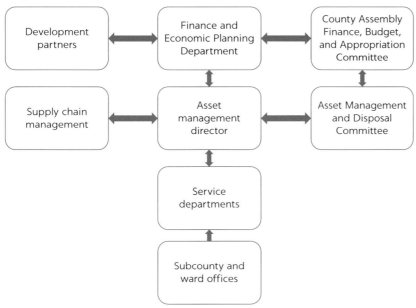

Source: Nairobi City County Government.

Policy review

This policy will be reviewed five years from the date of approval based on the long-term plan cycle. When considering changes to the policy, consultation will include the following as a minimum:

- The county governor
- The CECMs
- The CECM of the Finance and Economic Planning Department

Implementation framework

Employees will implement the policy through the development and use of AM guidelines and practices. Since the performance of AM in an organization is specific, reflective of knowledge, technologies, and available tools, and will evolve over time, the responsibility for obeying guidelines and practices is delegated to employees.

Capacity building on AM to the CECMs, chief officers, directors, and other key employees will be spearheaded by the AMDR director on an annual basis.

Asset codes

Organizations face a significant challenge in tracking the location, quantity, condition, maintenance, and depreciation status of their fixed assets. This challenge is met through asset identification and tagging.

Asset tracking

This is the method used to monitor and track an entity's physical assets. This is normally done using asset tags.

Asset tags

Asset tags identify equipment using a unique serial number or barcode. Asset tags are typically labels that have an adhesive backing. (Common asset tag materials are anodized aluminum or laminated polyester. Common designs include the company logo and a border that provides contrast to the equipment.) Asset tags have four basic functions:

(1) Tracking equipment: *Where is my asset?* Tags are used to track the asset's movement, for example, from room to room. Asset tags must stay with the asset over its lifetime.

(2) Inventory control: *What assets do we own?* Asset tags are the critical link for performing periodic audits of NCC asset and inventory control.

(3) Preventing theft: *Could you return the asset?* This makes it easy for anyone to return a valuable, for example, a laptop or equipment, to the proper owner. It prevents "accidental" misappropriation of an asset by another department.

(4) Maintenance, repair, and operations information: *What maintenance needs to be done?* Scanning a barcode can quickly bring the user to a database of repair instructions or maintenance schedule.

Main asset codes

The most modern and simple way of asset barcoding is to have a serialized barcoding process in which tags are sequentially generated for the approximate number of assets NCC possesses. For example, if NCC has an estimated 10,000 assets irrespective of class of assets, the asset tag numbers will be generated and appear as follows NCC00001 to NCC010000.

A tag is physically attached to the asset. The tag number then becomes the primary number identifier in the property record. If one wants to find out about a particular asset, for example, a laptop, entering the tag number (sometimes called the asset number) into the master property file brings up the complete record. This is essentially the only approach that will work when trying to find a specific asset in a file that may have thousands of items.

Templates

Policy administrator, owner, and approval form

The administration of this policy shall be spearheaded by the AMDR director (more templates can be attached by user counties).

The owner of this policy is the chief officer of finance and economic planning.

This policy was approved by the Nairobi City County Government on the.................................day of...in the year ....

Signed...Stamped.................................

By...

Designation..

Witnessed by ....

Signed...

REFERENCES

Cape Town. 2012. "Asset Management Policy." City of Cape Town, South Africa. https://apps .treasury.act.gov.au/__data/assets/pdf_file/0006/1069989/Budget-Paper-3.pdf.

Fiix. 2019. "Asset Management Policy Template." Toronto, Canada: Fiix Software, Information Technology and Services. https://www.fiixsoftware.com/blog/asset-management -policy-complete-guide.

Kenya Constitution. 2010. http://kenyalaw.org/kl/index.php?id=398.

NALM (National Assets and Liabilities Management Department). 2020a. "National Asset and Liability Management Policy, 2020." Nairobi: NALM. https://www.treasury.go.ke/wp -content/uploads/2021/03/Asset-Liability-Mgt-Policy.-doc-Final.pdf.

NALM (National Assets and Liabilities Management Department). 2020b. "General Guidelines on Asset and Liability Management in the Public Sector." Nairobi: NALM. https://www .treasury.go.ke/wp-content/uploads/2021/03/GeneralGuidelines-on-asset-and-liability -management-2020-Final.pdf.

NALM (National Assets and Liabilities Management Department). 2020c. "Guidelines for Management of Specific Categories of Assets and Liabilities, 2020." Nairobi: NALM. https:// www.treasury.go.ke/wp-content/uploads/2021/03/Specific-guidelines-2020-Final.pdf.

PFM. 2012. Public Finance Management Act, no. 18 of 2012. https://www.pcf.go.ke/index.php /public-financial-management-act.

PPAD. 2015. Public Procurement and Asset Disposal Act, no. 33 of 2015, December 18, 2015. http://kenyalaw.org:8181/exist/kenyalex/actview.xql?actid =No.%2033%20of%202015.

County Asset Management Strategy Model

INTRODUCTION

This template presents an asset management strategy (AMS) drafted for Nairobi City County (NCC). The NCC government (NCCG) has not approved it, but it represents a well-developed draft that could serve as a template for other counties. We present this because NCCG has been in the forefront in developing asset management (AM) frameworks, systems, and instruments, and this draft AMS is built on the approved and published strategy, and this strategy is cross-referenced to the noted documents. Other counties may lack some of these legislative documents, so they would need to tailor this NCC strategy to local circumstances.

The AMS is built on the NCCG's vision, mission statement, and the NCC Strategic Plan (SP) 2015–25 and covers 2016–25 (NCC 2014b). The SP puts high emphasis on developing AM policies, strategies, plans, and respective systems, procedures, databases, and capacities. The AMS also considers key strategic development objectives, the seven key performance areas (KPAs) of the SP, and other plans like the Nairobi County Integrated Development Plan 2013–17 (NCC 2014a), the Nairobi Integrated Urban Development Plan (NCC 2014c), and metropolitan vision 2030. A key mission statement from the SP includes the following:

> Asset management strategy allows us to make the right amount of investment in the right asset at the right location at the right time. It is through evidence-based decisions that NCC spends our financial resources to manage our physical assets for the best long-term benefit (NCC 2014b, 16).

The SP states that the mission of NCC is to "provide affordable, accessible and sustainable quality services, enhancing community participation and creating a secure climate for political, social, and economic development through the commitment of a motivated and dedicated team" (62).

The SP also states, "Nairobi City County as the Capital City, the seat of the National Government, the host to international and regional organizations, as well as the regional hub for international travel and economic activities [needs] to establish the necessary world class services within the City County" (16).

Against this strategic vision, the SP's situation analysis indicates a low level and poor quality of urban services, dilapidated assets due to deferred or poor maintenance, incomplete asset takeover from defunct local governments and state entities, and a lack of coordination across various NCC sectors and entities in developing and maintaining assets.

The SP aims to "translate the overall City County strategic objectives into sector-specific action plans, align existing sector plans and County Integrated Development Plan (CIDP) with the new Nairobi City County strategic objectives, and align sector and departmental budgets and resource implications" (25). The AMS and plans are coherent parts of the NCC strategic objectives and actions and eventually will be conduits in aligning strategies, objectives, and budgets across sectors.

The SP identifies seven KPAs, of which six include substantial and specific strategic programs or initiatives toward establishing an integrated asset management system, a key instrument in reducing the current silo-based planning and service approach.

> Based on the stakeholder engagement themes, seven thematic Key Performance Areas (KPAs) were identified. These cross-cutting KPAs form the basis of the strategic framework used to develop the strategic plan. This effectively addresses the silo planning approach previously followed by sectors and departments and will ensure that integrated planning is achieved (24).

COUNTY ASSET MANAGEMENT STRATEGY 2016–25

The AMS summarizes the most critical areas and actions required for establishing reliable AMSs, procedures, and capacities in the medium to long term in line with and to support the objectives of the NCC SP. The AMS aims to achieve an integrated asset management system that is also fully integrated into or interlinked with the integrated financial management information system (IFMIS), and other business processes, such as long-term planning, capital project prioritization (also known as capital improvement planning, or CIP), financing, and budget planning and implementation systems and procedures (many of which are still to be developed, too). NCC lacks an asset management policy, strategy, plan, systems and reliable databases, although some elements and procedures of a needed asset management system do exist in various service units of the sectors, and these can be useful parts of the planned new systems.

The AMS is the set of planned strategic actions that will enable the assets to provide the desired levels of service in a sustainable way, at the lowest life-cycle cost (for example, through preventive rather than reactive maintenance) and with measured and managed risks. AMS in cities with a long tradition of reasonable asset management addresses areas and actions to improve, via maintenance, renewal or rehabilitation, replacement, disposal, and expansion of assets in line with procurement, cost analysis, risk management, and integrated planning and financing. In contrast, the AMS for NCC requires putting emphasis first on establishing the core systems, procedures, and reliable databases before planning to use more sophisticated asset management tools and practices. However, full integration can reasonably be achieved by the end of the 10-year strategy cycle of the AMS.

Key strategic objectives of the AMS

The AMS is a set of asset-related actions that, taken together and in a coordinated manner, helps achieve the lowest overall cost of operation as opposed to the lowest cost for each individual action or asset. The AMS aims to coordinate capital spending across sectors and multiple assets and optimize life-cycle costs (for example, to replace water or sewer mains in coordination with major rehabilitation of a city road section, rather than doing them in separate actions).

The SP summarizes the "desired future" of the AM that can be considered key strategic objectives of the AMS (NCC 2014b, 73):

- A functional central asset register, management system, and procedures
- All county property secured and in full possession of NCC
- Controlled acquisition, management, and disposal of all assets
- Well-maintained assets that support cost-effective and quality services

Key actions and areas

The SP highlights key actions and areas, but the AMS needs to include more. These actions need careful planning, timing, and sequencing since completing these altogether requires a decade or more of work:

- Positioning AM in the NCC organization, systems, and procedures
- Establishing the core AM system
- Adopting AM strategy, policy, and short- to medium-term plan
- Developing and maintaining asset registers
- Verifying all assets taken over (or to be taken over) from defunct local entities and central government bodies
- Reaching settlements on disputed assets and liabilities
- Completing and maintaining needs assessments by sectors
- Completing assessments of asset condition, replacement value, risk, and life-cycle cost
- Introducing an information technology system for the integrated asset management system
- Institutionalizing preventive asset maintenance and reducing the role of reactive maintenance
- Institutionalizing integrated capital improvement planning led by the Asset Management Directorate (AMDR) and coordinated with engineering units, directorates, and sectors
- Fostering collaboration among engineering, operations, planning, and finance/AMDR departments
- Integrating AM systems with IFMIS, capital planning, engineering, and service operations
- Developing adequate human capacities for AM

POSITIONING ASSET MANAGEMENT IN COUNTY ORGANIZATION AND SYSTEMS

From an organizational perspective, AM has been structured to be a key element that fosters collaboration with multiple business units. In this sense, AM will be a conduit of communication and coordination between traditional organizational silos (for example, sectors). To achieve this vision and objective, NCCG needs to develop several key systems and adopt policies and procedures in various areas of operation (IFMIS, CIP, repair and maintenance plan, advanced budgeting, and so forth).

The asset management positioning summarized in figure B.1 is a possibility in the distant future; it can be achieved by the end of this AMS cycle. During this time, the adopted systems and framework may change substantially to tailor the systems to the emerging reality of the NCC organization and subsystems. Figure B.1 is a schematic interpretation of positioning asset management and does not represent a specific information and communication technology (ICT) realization.

In the short and medium terms, the AMDR will be positioned gradually into the current set of NCC organizations. Figure B.2 summarizes the framework into which the AM will be developed gradually. Establishing adequate AM systems will start with a small, pragmatic framework that can be expanded into a more developed integrated AM framework toward the one depicted in figure B.1.

The initial framework forms the basis of a future reliable AM system in harmony with the NCC's AM policy. The AMDR was established under the chief financial officer, but NCCG also will establish an asset and liability management committee (ALC) to review and forward for the governor's or the County Assembly's approval of AM plans and proposals of strategic importance. The ALC will form from its members a temporary asset transfer subcommittee to represent NCC in discussions and settlement of disputed assets due to be transferred to NCC. AMDR also assigns an asset verification and audit team to lead or commence verification and audit of assets and liabilities and provide analysis and options for AMDR and the asset transfer subcommittee.

FIGURE B.1

Integrated asset management as a conduit across sectors and functions: Vision for the future

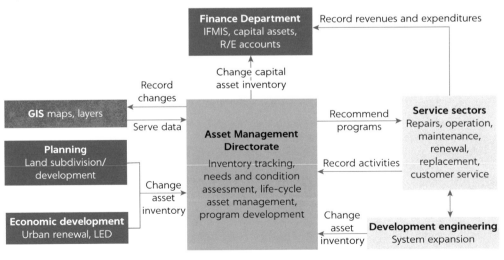

Source: World Bank based on Cambridge 2013.
Note: GIS = geographic information system; IFMIS = integrated financial management information system; LED = local economic development; R/E = revenue and expenditure.

FIGURE B.2

Initial asset management framework in Nairobi City County

Source: Nairobi City County Government.
Note: AM = asset management; AMDR = Asset Management Directorate.

The AM framework (figure B.2) indicates that strategic AM issues are the domain of the chief officers (county executive committee member, chief financial officer, and the chief officers of sectors), and the planning and system issues are the domain of the AMDR director. Finally, AM officers will be assigned to the sectors to be the conduits of the operational-level issues to ensure communication, information sharing, and data collection to feed AM and support operations in parallel.

TIME FRAME FOR STRATEGIC ACTIONS IN DEVELOPING AND IMPLEMENTING RELIABLE ASSET MANAGEMENT

The implementation of the AMS requires a decade of work, so actions are scheduled for short-, medium-, and longer-term accomplishments without specific dates. The AMS is a living document; actions may need to be added, modified, moved to a later time, or annulled as the AM systems and other operation systems (IFMIS, planning, ICT) are developed gradually. Table B.1 summarizes the most critical actions in short-, medium-, and long-term clusters.

STRATEGIC DEVELOPMENT OF ASSETS

The NCC has ambitious development plans for the next 10 years as set out in the SP and in this AMS. An about K Sh 200 billion development expenditure budget plan for the 10-year period from fiscal years 2015/16 to 2024/25 has been developed to support these plans. The development (capital) budget is allocated across 10 sectors.

Grouping the sectors enabled consideration of broader development priorities and the relative weight of each sector's role in achieving the development

TABLE B.1 Strategic actions and responsibilities in developing the asset management system for Nairobi City County

ACTIONS	PERFORMANCE INDICATOR	RESPONSIBLE UNITS
Short term (1–2 years)		
Establishing and positioning AM in the NCC organization	AM framework adopted, operational	AMDR and county executive committee
Adopting AM policy, strategy, and short-term plan	AMS, policy, and plan approved	AMDR and AM committee
Establishing the core AM system and initial procedures	Initial AM systems and initial procedures operational	AMDR
Developing and maintaining asset registers	Initial asset inventories complete	AMDR
Developing human capacities	Key staff related to AM assigned and trained	AMDR
Consolidating development plans and actual performance at NCC level	Structured consolidated development plans and results are complete and shared with NCC top management	AMDR
Medium term (5–6 years)		
Developing and maintaining full asset registers	Registers complete, reliable, operational	AMDR and sectors
Verifying assets taken over (or to be taken over) from defunct local entities and central government bodies	90% of assets verified and audited	AMDR, verification team, and sectors
Settlement of disputed assets and liabilities	95% of assets settled and in full possession by NCC	AM subcommittee, AMDR
Developing human capacities	Advance training for key staff related to AM	AMDR
Adequately connecting supply chain management and asset management functions, roles, and responsibilities	AM and supply chain management are adequately linked	AMDR, sectors, and supply chain management
Adopting SOPs for key AM activities and functions	SOPs adopted and operational	AMDR and sectors
Completing and maintaining needs assessments by sectors	Complete, baselines established	AMDR and sectors
Completing assessment: asset condition, value, risk, and life-cycle cost	80% of each sector's assessment complete	Sectors
Introducing information technology system for the integrated asset management system	Installed and operational	AMDR and ICT
Institutionalizing preventive asset maintenance and reducing the role of reactive maintenance	Preventive AM institutionalized	AMDR, sectors, and CFO
Increasing funding for development, repair, and maintenance	Development budget > 40% of total budget Budget for repair and maintenance > 4% of current expenditures	AMDR, sectors, CFO, and CO budget
Adopting rules and procedures for how to integrate decisions, plans, and finances on assets managed by external entities (water companies, ministries, agencies) but vital for citizens and quality of life	Rules and procedures adopted and operational	AMDR and CO finance and planning
Long term (7–10 years)		
Institutionalizing integrated asset management to optimize life-cycle costs	Integrated AM system is in operation	AMDR and sectors
Fostering collaboration among engineering, operations, planning, finance, and AMDR	Work procedures adopted and operational	AMDR, CO finance and planning, and sectors
Integrating AM systems with IFMIS, capital planning, engineering, and service operations	Integrated AM is operational	AMDR, ICT, and respective CO finance and planning
Developing adequate human capacities for AM	Staff for new systems trained	AMDR and ICT
Increasing funding for development, repair, and maintenance	Development budget > 40% of total expenditure Repair and maintenance > 10% of current expenditure	AMDR, sectors, CFO, and CO budget

Source: Nairobi City County Government.
Note: AM = asset management; AMDR = Asset Management Directorate; AMS = asset management strategy; CFO = chief financial officer; CO = chief officer; ICT = information and communication technology; IFMIS = integrated financial management information system; NCC = Nairobi City County; SOPs = standard operating procedures.

TABLE B.2 **Development and rehabilitation plans by sectors: Long-term preliminary list form**
K Sh (billions)

SECTORS AND GROUPS	DEVELOPMENT	REHABILITATION
Physical infrastructure and productive sectors (40% of development budget)		
Transport, roads, and public works		
Water, energy, forestry, environment, and natural resources		
Agriculture, livestock, development, and fisheries		
Information, communication, and e-governance		
Governance, social, and service sectors (30% of total development budget)		
Public service management		
County health services		
Education, children, youth affairs, sports, culture, and social services		
Economic sectors (30% of total development budget)		
Finance and economic planning		
Trade, industrialization, cooperative development, and tourism		
Lands, housing, and urban planning		
Total		

Source: Nairobi City County Government.

objectives set out in the CIDP 2014–17 and 2018–22 (NCC 2014a, 2018) and the SP 2015–25 (table B.2). The projects were identified in various forums, including Kenya Vision 2030; the first medium-term plan dissemination forums; medium-term expenditure framework consultative forums; and the second medium-term plan consultations and other development consultations at devolved levels. The AMS incorporates these project plans from the noted sources without modification.

WARDS DEVELOPMENT FUND

To address existing disparities and promote equitable distribution of resources in NCC, the Wards Development Fund (WDF) was established under the WDF Act 2014, section 4 (NCC 2014d). This fund will be set aside to provide financing of community-based projects for an amount of not less than 5 percent of all the ordinary revenue of NCC in each financial year. The fund also can receive donations or loans from other authorized organizations.

Eligible community-based projects are identified annually by the Ward Development Committee established under section 19(11) of WDF Act 2014 and included in the annual budget. On an annual basis, a minimum of five projects and a maximum of 25 projects will be submitted per ward under the fund. During the period 2015–25, an estimated K Sh 24 billion will be appropriated to various capital programs across NCC over the 10-year SP period. The projects for FY 2015/16 have been identified for all 85 wards for a total of K Sh 1.7 billion.

DEVELOPMENT FINANCING

Developments will be funded from savings in the recurrent budget, through incurring debt, or by engaging in public-private partnerships. Large infrastructure projects will be financed through external borrowing, as this effort is concessional and requires longer periods of time than commercial banks normally offer. NCC will look into money and capital markets through bond issues by the end of this SP period.

Long-term borrowing will be used only to finance development projects as approved in the CIDP (with an annual limit of debt service as 5 percent of total revenues in recently audited financial statements), and projects funded by debt will be funded only for their expected useful life. Operation and maintenance expenditures will not be funded through debt. To maintain debt at sustainable levels, NCC's annual borrowing per the debt management strategy will be capped at 15 percent of total revenues.

REFERENCES

Cambridge (City of). 2013. *Asset Management Plan—Core Service Sustainability.* Ontario, Canada: City of Cambridge. https://www.cambridge.ca/en/learn-about/resources/Asset -Management-Plan---City-of-Cambridge---AODA.pdf.

NCC (Nairobi City County). 2014a. *Nairobi County Integrated Development Plan (CIDP) Covering the Period 2013–17.* Nairobi City County Government. https://www.cog.go.ke /downloads/category/82-county-integrated-development-plans-2013-2017.

NCC (Nairobi City County). 2014b. *Nairobi County Strategic Plan 2015–2025.* Nairobi City County Government.

NCC (Nairobi City County) 2014c. *Nairobi County Urban Development Master Plan.* Nairobi City County Government. https://www.kpda.or.ke/documents/Nairobi%20Integarted%20 Urban%20Development%20Master%20Plan.pdf.

NCC (Nairobi City County). 2014d. Nairobi City County Wards Development Fund Act. Nairobi City County Gazette Supplement no. 4, February 11, 2014. http://kenyalaw.org/kl/fileadmin /pdfdownloads/Acts/NairobiCityCountyWardsDevelopmentFundAct2014.pdf.

NCC (Nairobi City County). 2018. *Nairobi County Integrated Development Plan (CIDP) Covering the Period 2018–22.* Nairobi City County Government. https://repository.kippra.or.ke /handle/123456789/2019.

County Asset Management Plan Model

INTRODUCTION

This asset management (AM) plan is built on the county asset management strategy, the county strategic plan, and the county integrated development plan drafted for Nairobi City County (NCC). This AM plan is an interim plan as opposed to the commonly understood AM plans, because the county has just started to develop an AM system, strategies, plans, and procedures. Therefore, this AM plan covers the first one- or two-year period and is focused on establishing the initial AM framework, systems, plans, and databases.

Figure C.1 provides a comprehensive schematic picture of the AM plan sequences, with sophistication deepening from top to bottom. More detailed AM plans will be developed, adopted, and implemented. Basic AM plans can be developed gradually in the short to medium term, while the county can adopt advanced AM plans in the medium to long term (5 to 10 years' time). The asset management plan of the City of Cambridge, Ontario, Canada, offers glimpses into the nature of an advance stage AM Plan (Cambridge 2013).

INTERIM ASSET MANAGEMENT PLAN

Establishing the Asset Management Directorate (AMDR) or appointing a dedicated team is strong evidence of the common understanding that the county government's goals and strategic priorities strongly depend on the size, scope, and quality of infrastructure. However, utilization of assets depends on the capacity, quality, and reliability of asset management systems and practices. This plan is the first asset management plan in the county's history, and it is interim, since it focuses exclusively on establishing the initial framework, adopting an initial strategy of sector AM plans, collecting basic information, and developing asset inventories. The county has a development plan and program, but those were developed before and outside of this AM plan. That is why this interim AM plan focuses on establishing systems and excludes specific asset development plans that would discuss investment, refurbishment, replacement, or maintenance plans, which can be incorporated in this AM plan or a revised version of it in one to two years.

FIGURE C.1

Asset management plans with growing scope and deepening sophistication

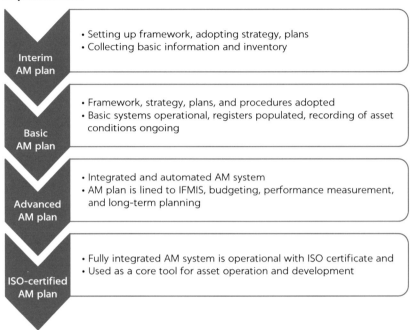

Source: Nairobi City County Government.
Note: AM = asset management; IFMIS = integrated financial management information system; ISO = International Organization for Standardization.

Critical actions in the interim AM plan and during the first one or two years of asset management include the following: establishing and positioning AM in the county organization; adopting an AM policy, strategy, and short-term plan; establishing the core AM system and initial procedures; inventorying assets, developing and maintaining asset registers; developing human capacities; and gradually establishing baseline information for measuring progress and performance.

Establishing and positioning AM in the county organization

The AMDR or AM team is a new entity in the county organization, but various functions and fragments of AM have been built into the county organization, and several required procedures have been performed under the various sectors, by different service directorates, and/or by managers of various facilities (for example, markets or sport or cultural facilities). The aim of the AM strategy and this plan is to institutionalize a coordinated professional AM system and build the foundation of future integrated AM in harmony with the county AM policy.

Figure C.2 exhibits the current players in the Nairobi City County (NCC) AM who will undoubtedly remain key parts and members of the new AM system and community but repositioned in the new framework. Sectors and the units under them today tend to act in silos and perform AM by implementing their unit budgets, which are somewhat coordinated by the budgeting procedures largely in financial terms but remain detached during budget implementation. The AM system and AM policy aim to shift AM to the highest county strategy and budget

FIGURE C.2
Old asset management framework or practices in Nairobi City County

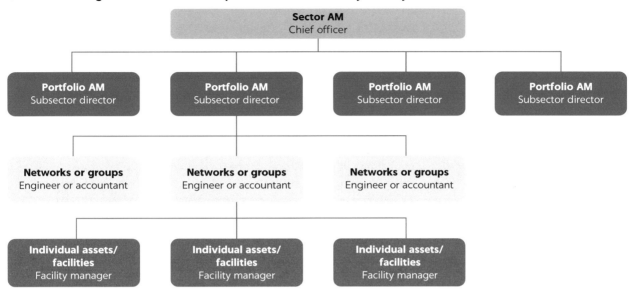

Source: Nairobi City County Government.
Note: AM = asset management.

FIGURE C.3
New asset management framework option in Nairobi City County

Source: Nairobi City County Government.
Note: AM = asset management; AMDR = Asset Management Directorate.

level with adequate coordination across sectors and units and a high level of professionalism based on systematically collected and maintained asset information.

Figure C.3 summarizes the framework, in which AM will be developed gradually. Establishing adequate AM systems will start with a small, pragmatic framework that can be expanded and turned into a more developed, integrated AM framework in which the AMDR will be the conduit across the various sectors, units, and functions.

Entities with specific responsibilities on asset and liability management

The AMDR will be the focal point of the AM system, but appointed entities or teams will be responsible to fulfill specific functions under the general guidance and control of AMDR and higher governing bodies of the county.

AMDR (or AM team in small counties). The AMDR is established under the Finance and Economic Planning sector with a small core team of professional AM officers and led by the director or team leader, and it reports directly to the chief financial officer.

Asset and Liability Management Committee. The county will form an asset and liability management advisory committee (ALC) empowered to discuss, filter, and guide strategic decisions and documents in AM and submit them to the governor or county executive committee for approval, as necessary.

County Asset and Liability Committee (CALC). The CALC has been established under the rules of Gazette Notice no. 2701 to guide an initial inventory of assets taken over by law without handover by the defunct local governments. The CALC or a successor Asset and Liability Workout Committee (ALWC) should deal particularly with issues of disputed assets and liabilities and represents the county in high-level discussions with external partners, including ministries, other central government entities, or counties. This committee will disband after completing the asset transfers and settling the disputed asset cases.

Asset and Liability Workout Committee. Unless the CALC continues working after full takeover of assets and liabilities, the county may establish an ALWC with a mandate to manage and approve takeover of assets and liabilities to be taken over from national government entities (ministries, deconcentrated entities, or state corporations). The ALWC will be supported by AMDR and the asset verification team.

Asset verification team. The AMDR will form an asset verification team with legal, engineering, finance, and planning capacities and responsibility for completing verification and audit of assets and asset-related liabilities. It also will explore and propose settlement options for disputed assets and liabilities under ALWC guidance and control.

Debt Management Office. The chief financial officer will appoint a debt management team or office to deal with planning, incurring, servicing, and reporting debts, including direct debts and contingent liabilities.

AM officers in sectors. The AMDR will assign AM officers to other sectors to establish a direct link to sectors and sector entities and ensure information flows across the AM system to support data collection and dissemination. The AM officers will have no decision power; they have only reporting and guiding power.

ADOPTING AM POLICY, STRATEGY, AND SHORT-TERM PLAN

The county's existing strategic plan includes actions for adopting a policy, strategy, and plan for asset management. The AMDR will draft the core policy, strategy, and short-term AM plan documents, and then will submit them for review by sectors. The AMDR will finalize the documents based on feedback and submit them for approval by the ALC. The AM strategy and policy may require approval by higher bodies after screening and approval by the AM committee. The AM policy, strategy, and plan should be used as binding documents after county approval.

Adopting the AM action plan

Adopting an AM action plan could be an effective tool for facilitating the most urgent actions with indicative sequences (perhaps with specific timing and an estimated time for completion). But also the action plan can include the estimated expenditures needed to complete specific actions. AMDR may seek approval of the AM action plan and respective budget allocations for the first year. Table C.1 is a template of a possible action plan. Figure C.4 illustrates how the IFMIS and financial reporting system relate to the asset management information systems and the NCC departments, sectors, and key asset management functions.

TABLE C.1 **Asset management action plan indicative template**

ACTIONS	PERFORMANCE INDICATOR	RESPONSIBLE
Establish AMDR	Established and functions	CFO
Draft terms of reference for AM committee	Approved ToR	AMDR
Propose initial AM framework	Approved and effective	AMDR, CFO
Establish asset verification team	Established and functions	AMDR
Establish asset management committee	Established and functions	CFO, executive committee
Draft AM policy	Approved	AMDR
Draft AM strategy	Approved	AMDR
Draft AM plan	Approved	AMDR
Draft job descriptions for key AM staff	Approved and effective	AMDR
Draft terms of reference for hiring an AM inventorying firm	ToR approved	AMDR
Commence procurement of consulting firm	Firm mobilized and operating	AMDR, procurement
Develop initial asset inventory and gradually populate it	Inventory complete, approved, and operational	AMDR
Draft capacity-building plans with budgets	Plans approved	AMDR, CFO
Commence capacity-building programs	Workshop for elected officers completed Training for directors and managers completed Training field staff on AM completed	AMDR
Analyze required capacities and in-sourcing staff or firms for the most critical functions (an ongoing task)	In-sourcing approved and implemented	AMDR
Consolidate development plans and actual performance at the county level	Structured consolidated development plans and results are complete and shared with county top management	AMDR

Source: Nairobi City County Government.
Note: AM = asset management; AMDR = Asset Management Directorate; CFO = chief financial officer; ToR = terms of reference.

FIGURE C.4
Asset management information system option

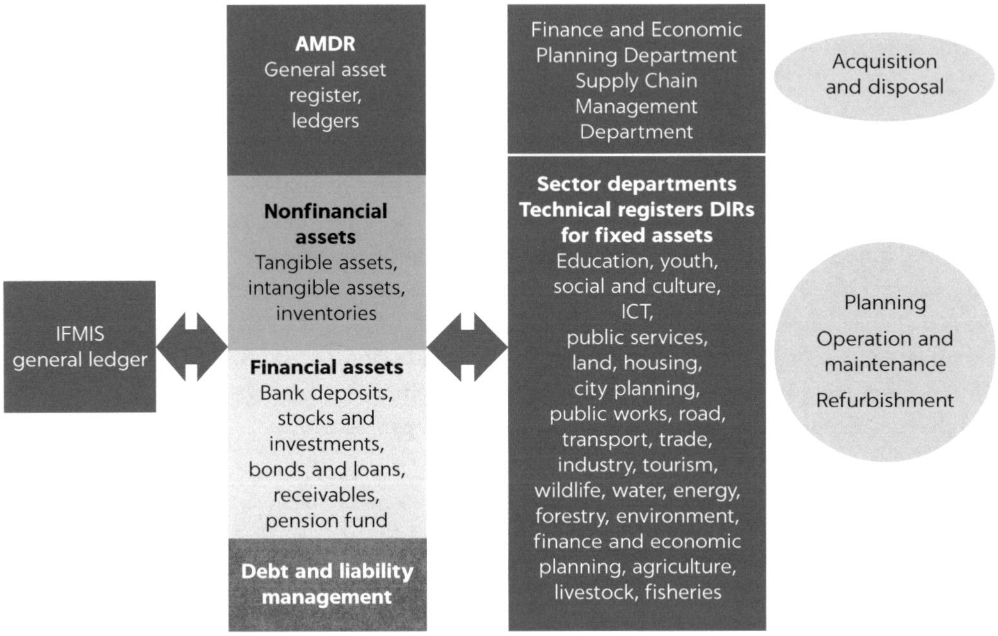

Source: World Bank.
Note: AMDR = Asset Management Directorate; DIRs = departmental inventory registers; ICT = information and communication technology; IFMIS = integrated financial management information system.

Establishing the core AM system and initial procedures

Based on the approval of the AM policy, strategy, and plan, the AMDR will set up the core initial AM system and draft initial procedures for the established bodies and to ensure coordination across various sectors, entities, and functions. AMDR will then draft job descriptions for the key AM functions, positions, and staff.

Developing and maintaining asset registers

Reliable information and asset inventories and registers are the most critical pillars of a solid AM system. The AMDR will commence a program for developing asset registers in a sequenced and gradual way in several phases. The first phase includes defining the asset hierarchy and framework for asset inventorying and starting extensive data collection to form the initial asset inventory during the first year. The data collection and inventorying require close cooperation of sectors and entities under them, like directors of asset groups or networks (for example, roads or drainage) and managers of large individual facilities (for example, city hall or stadium). Developing the initial asset inventories with good or partial data is the most substantial development action of the interim asset management plan.

This data collection requires substantial professional capacity, expertise, and experience in asset inventories and registers, so ideally it would be supported by a consulting firm specializing in asset registers and inventorying, because county officers in sectors will not have enough time for extensive data collection in addition to their daily tasks. Counties with a small number of fixed assets may be able to develop an initial asset inventory with in-house staff and capacities and may obtain only supporting data management software from the market. AMDR should develop terms of reference and obtain funds to hire a firm for asset verification and tagging. The inventory will form the basis for more advanced asset registers; the inventorying should be considered a continual exercise and the inventory and the subsequent registers as living, emerging documents.

Establishing the initial asset inventories by sectors and then consolidating them at the county or AMDR level to an integrated central asset register will be a learning process for the staff of the sectors, directorates, or facilities. They will work together and then take over the information results or actual inventories from the consulting firm, and they will then need to populate them with subsequent collection of information (for example, filling information gaps and verifying or valuating assets). The AMDR will coordinate the process by hiring a consulting firm; but asset inventorying will require very substantive involvement and work by the sectors and other units responsible for groups of assets or levels and functions of asset management. Sectors and the directorates of asset networks or groups will need to take full ownership of the asset inventories; they will be responsible for gradually populating the inventories and ensuring reliable information is recorded, errors corrected, and registers updated until a high level of accuracy is achieved.

The Department of Land in cooperation with the chief valuer will take over the records of land with county ownership from the mass valuation project that has identified not only private land but land owned by NCC and attached updated market values to the land parcels based on land transaction data from the national land registry. The results of mass valuation will be the basis of the land asset register that will also inform the building register.

Developing human capacities

Adequate human capacities and mixes of skills are vital pillars of a well-functioning AM system. It is assumed that the respective sectors and units of the county have most of the required capacities; in contrast, they may face shortages in adequate skill mixes, knowledge, and experience in advanced asset management. Further development of the AM system and capacities may require insourcing several skilled specialists in temporary or permanent positions and also hiring specialized firms to complete specific development actions at required timelines and quality levels. Decisions on required insourcing capacities will be made based on a brief capacity and skill assessment.

The AMDR will design and begin various capacity-building programs for targeted groups of county staff to support implementation of the new elements, plans, rules, and procedures in the new AM system. The AMDR will need to bring in external training capacities to provide training in best international practices tailored to Kenya's situations and the emerging asset management framework unless national entities (the National Treasury's National Assets and Liabilities Management Department, Intergovernmental Relations Technical Committee, or the Office of the Auditor General) organize such trainings for some or all counties. AMDR will seek international donors' support in capacity building. The county results, procedures, and documents will be offered to other counties for training purposes; likewise, representatives of selected counties may be invited for capacity-building events. Possible capacity-building actions include the following:

- AM workshop for elected officers and high-level officers (chief officers of sectors):
  - Aims to explain the AM policy, strategy, and plan, and some specific critical actions tailored to the county strategic management level (half to one day)
- AM training for directors and network or asset group, facility managers, and AMDR staff:
  - Aims to explain AM fundamentals, key systems and subsystems, rules, and procedures with templates, tailored to the specific responsibilities and work requirements of the trainees (4 days)
- AM training for field staff of sectors responsible for various operation aspects of the asset management:
  - Aims to explain AM fundamentals, key systems and subsystems, rules, and procedures with templates, tailored to the specific responsibilities and work requirements of the trainees (2 days)

CONSOLIDATING DEVELOPMENT PLANS AND ACTUAL PERFORMANCE AT THE COUNTY LEVEL

The AMDR will start collecting some AM information in structured forms to support monitoring the strategic objectives spelled out in the county strategic plan and the AM strategy. The key objectives include gradually increasing development spending to 40 percent of the total budget year by year, increasing spending on repair and maintenance, and increasing funds for and expanding preventive maintenance.

AMDR will start establishing the baseline data for measuring progress on the noted strategic performance areas and consolidate results at the county level in the first year. Then AMDR will continue collecting the respective data to measure, exhibit, and share with higher-level county management the progress toward fulfilling these critical strategic objectives. Collecting these baseline data requires good cooperation among the AMDR and the service sectors, networks or asset group directors, and facility managers. The sectors and managers also will benefit from these benchmarks and performance measurement indicators; such indicators also can be included in the AM Action Plan.

REFERENCE

Cambridge (City of). 2013. *Asset Management Plan—Core Service Sustainability.* Ontario, Canada: City of Cambridge. https://www.cambridge.ca/en/learn-about/resources/Asset -Management-Plan---City-of-Cambridge---AODA.pdf.

County Asset and Liability Management Committee

INTRODUCTION

Asset management (AM) is a process of making and implementing decisions about operating, maintaining, refurbishing, acquiring, disposing of, or developing assets cost-effectively, with the ultimate objective of providing the best possible services to local citizens. AM is a complex and permanent process. It includes three different and interrelated functions: *strategic asset management*, *life cycle-technical* asset management, and *accounting-financial* asset management. All three functions include financial aspects and need to be linked to county financial management and budgeting.

Good AM is important for several reasons. First, fixed assets are used to deliver local services, so the range and quality of public services often depend on the existence and condition of the related fixed assets. In general, the availability of fixed assets and the quality of their management define both the quality of life and the power of the local economy. Second, land owned by local governments is a crucial resource for providing space and resources for further urban development. Third, immovable property (land, buildings, infrastructure facilities, and networks) is typically the most valuable component of all the fixed assets owned by urban local governments. Fourth, the quality of AM can have a strong impact on the local budget. Accordingly, prudent asset management can reduce budget expenses on operation and maintenance of assets without jeopardizing their condition or the quality of related services; likewise, good asset policies and practices can increase budget revenues substantially.

Strategic AM is a higher-level management function for all types of assets; it consists of high-level decisions on the overall asset portfolio of fixed, financial, or intangible assets and decisions about transforming the wealth of the county from one of these forms to another: for example, spending money to build infrastructure or buy land, or selling land to generate money to fund construction of public facilities like schools, roads, and so forth. Strategic AM is therefore a domain of the highest decision bodies of the county that should discuss and approve asset decisions of a strategic nature, or of a large value or volume.

GOVERNANCE FRAMEWORK FOR ASSET MANAGEMENT

Three specific bodies play important roles in strategic AM: the County Assembly, the Asset and Liability Management Committee (ALC), and the Asset Management Directorate (AMDR). The chain of command regarding strategic asset management is reflected in figure D.1. In harmony with the Urban Areas and Cities Act, Nairobi City County sets up an ALC in accordance with terms of reference that summarize the composition of the proposed committee, its mandates, scope of work, priorities, and initial steps. Figure D.1 illustrates the governance framework for strategic-level AM.

The Asset and Liability Management Committee

The ALC is a permanent committee under the County Assembly, and it is the highest body for policy development and strategy; it works for decisions and agreements among members about implementing strategic changes regarding county assets. It also acts as an advisory body to the County Assembly on strategic decisions that require assembly resolutions. The ALC is chaired by the deputy governor, who represents the governor and the County Assembly. Permanent ALC members include the chief financial officer; the chair of the Finance, Budget, and Appropriation Committee; the chair of the County Public Service Board; a member of the Urban Board; the director of AM; department heads (of the departments that deal with management, operation, and maintenance of high-value county assets); and subcounty administrators. (Should the county or governor prefer a smaller committee, then the subcounty

FIGURE D.1

Governance framework for asset management

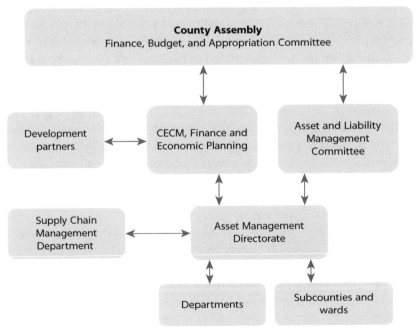

Source: Nairobi City County Government.
Note: CECM = County Executive Committee.

administrators can be excluded from the permanent ALC and called in for meetings as deemed necessary.) The Asset and Liability Management Committee may invite other county officers for specific meetings as necessary for supporting informed decisions and their prompt implementation.

ALC scope of work

The ALC should discuss and approve all kinds of asset and liability management decisions and actions that have strategic impact on how AM is conducted and on assets themselves. For decisions about asset values above a certain threshold or with exceptionally high strategic importance, the ALC needs to get approval from the County Assembly and, as a rule, present alternatives to the Assembly.

The ALC meets quarterly or holds extraordinary meetings if necessary, to support and approve timebound actions. The AMDR should serve as a permanent secretariat and as a technical department for the ALC. Under its mandate, the AMDR should provide information, draft all kinds of documents (proposals, policies, procedures, and so forth), and maintain daily communication on behalf of the ALC and between it and other county stakeholders. AMDR should monitor implementation of various actions and plans and assist other departments to implement asset management.

The ALC will form, from its members, an Asset and Liability Workout Committee (ALWC) to represent the county in dialogue with national or peer-county governments, state entities, or state corporations on disputed assets. The ALWC should include finance, engineering, and legal specialists and should be authorized for dialogue and to reach agreements on disputed assets, conditioned on final approval by the ALC or County Assembly, as deemed necessary. The ALWC will start with a temporary mandate (three years initially) and will operate until the completion of asset transfers and conclusion of resolutions on disputed assets. But the ALWC can later receive a permanent mandate, since workout issues will result from regular operation of the county over time, albeit in a smaller number of cases.

ALC competencies

The specific areas of ALC competencies include but are not limited to the following:

- Adopt initial priorities and an initial action plan for AM (which is of crucial importance for the first years due to the large number of actions and incomplete transfer/takeover of assets).
- Approve annual asset management plans and advise on budgeting of the respective actions.
- Approve a draft AM strategic plan and submit it for the County Assembly's approval.
- Approve five-year capital improvement plans on a rolling basis.
- Approve an AM policy and submit it for the County Assembly's approval.
- Approve or advise the County Assembly on high-value divestitures.
- Approve or advise the County Assembly on high-value acquisitions and investments.

- Appoint, guide, and monitor an asset transfer committee.
- Approve proposals from the ALWC on disputed assets and conclude agreements with respective partners on behalf of the county.
- Discuss and approve annual asset management performance reports by entities under the ALC, including the AMDR and sectors.
- Conduct directly or appoint a specialized auditor for targeted investigation, as it may deem necessary, to analyze suspected ineffective, irresponsible, or fraudulent actions.
- Issue guidelines, orders, or resolutions regarding AM policies, systems, or procedures.
- Approve asset management registers and templates drafted and proposed by the AMDR.
- Approve information and communication technology (ICT) realization of the AM systems, registers, and reporting formats and rules.

Member entities of the ALC can delegate technical experts or officials to support AMDR's elaborations when it drafts proposals important for a particular member entity.

Chain of command

The AMDR should serve as a permanent secretary of the ALC and as a technical department, and hence acts daily. The AMDR is responsible for preparing documents and proposals for regular ALC meetings, proposing extraordinary ALC meetings as necessary, and maintaining communication between the ALC and other entities responsible for some areas or actions on AM. Should an entity aim to approach the ALC, it should do so via the AMDR, which will review a request, return it if needed for clarification and revision, and then submit the request to the ALC chair with a proposal for discussion at the next ALC meeting. The AMDR should represent the ALC and serve the other stakeholders with guidelines, orders, policies, and resolutions. The AMDR should also monitor implementation of asset management plans and activities throughout the county.

The decisions of the ALC are deemed to be final and complete. Stakeholders may appeal to the County Assembly via the governor's office.

PRIORITY ISSUES TO BE ADDRESSED IN THE SHORT TERM BY HIGH-LEVEL DECISION-MAKING BODIES: GOVERNOR, COUNTY ASSEMBLY, ALC

- Finalize a composition of the ALC according to the list just noted, including designation of individual officials or staff.
- Establish ALC.
- Adopt an initial asset management action plan for the first one to two years and start implementing it. Incorporate in this plan the following: (1) issues of completing asset transfer from the central government, (2) entities responsible for operating and maintaining the fixed assets received, and (3) sources of budgeting operation and maintenance of these assets.
- Establish and start a process of systematically populating a temporary fixed asset inventory as an instrument for identifying assets that are already the

property of the county or should become the county's property as a result of asset transfer from the central government. Use a simple Excel spreadsheet and agree on the content of the temporary fixed asset register, if no more advanced ICT realization is available.

- Appoint an initial asset verification and audit team under the AMDR with legal, financial, and technical specialists to lead asset verification and audit of asset use.
- Revise and finalize the initial AM policy as a guiding document based on the draft prepared by AMDR.
- Appoint the ALWC.

Checklist for Public Water Supply System Operation and Maintenance and Examples of Operation and Maintenance Tasks

INTRODUCTION

The following checklist, from the United States Environmental Protection Agency (EPA), provides a glimpse into the rigor and complexity of the intertwined operation and maintenance of water supply systems (EPA 2015). The EPA aims to guide owners and operators to reduce possible negative environmental effects of substandard operation and maintenance (O&M) of water supply systems. The checklist and list of tasks are derived from a workbook, *Getting Started with CUPSS: A Workbook for Users* (EPA 2012). The vast majority of these actions are directly and immediately applicable in Kenya or other developing countries because the water service system and subsystems are quite similar and deserve similar rigor and due diligence in operation and maintenance.

CHECKLIST

These key documents are to be verified and kept in the files of the asset management entity:

- Map of all source/intakes and raw water transmission lines to plant(s)
- Map of current finished water distribution system
- Inventory list of property, service lines, equipment, tools, and instruments; include manufacturer, model, serial number, and condition
- Locations of spare parts (including pumps and backup power source) and vendor contact information or repair service used
- O&M technical manuals for equipment and water system facilities (for example, treatment plant, distribution system)
- Lists of daily, weekly, monthly, quarterly, and/or annual maintenance tasks to be performed; log sheets for recording maintenance performed
- Location of first-aid instructions and supplies
- Contact names, telephone/fax numbers, and email addresses for:
  - System operators, including contract support
  - System owners or local government officials
  - EPA-equivalent agency in Kenya

- State/county public health organization
- Certified laboratories used, with identification for each type of sample analyzed
- Local responders (law enforcement, fire, hazmat)
- Experienced operators at nearby systems who can serve as backup or provide help in an emergency

- Monitoring plan: Current-year EPA monitoring requirements, location of sampling or monitoring sites, sampling/reporting forms, and instructions for reporting and recordkeeping
- Location of sampling and monitoring records
- Location of other formal communications from/to EPA regional office and others on the contact list above
- Locations of spare sample bottles, sampling technique information, and monitoring plans
- Instructions when notified by lab of regional health office on fecal positive sample
- Location of public notice forms and instructions
- Instructions for pressure loss in system (flow chart)
- Instructions for flushing and shock chlorinating tanks, wells, distribution system mains, etc.
- Location of secured instructions for maintaining security in your system
- Takeaway emergency response plan:

  - Flow charts for operators to handle specific problems (main breaks, chlorine leaks, chemical spills);
  - Names and phone/fax numbers of state and local responders (police, fire, hazmat, county, etc.); and
  - Names/numbers of county and state agencies to call in case of waterborne disease outbreak or other health emergency.

EXAMPLES OF OPERATION AND MAINTENANCE TASKS

Listed below are examples of tasks that might be included in your O&M manual and instructions to personnel involved in servicing your public water supply system. Use these lists only as examples for creating your own lists appropriate to your system.

Daily tasks

Tasks derived from the CUPSS workbook (EPA 2012, 14):

- Check water meter readings and record water production.
- Check chemical solution tanks and record amounts used.
- Check and record water levels in storage tanks.
- Inspect chemical feed pumps.
- Check and record chlorine residual at the point of application.
- Check and record chlorine residual in the distribution system.
- Inspect booster pump stations.
- Check and record fluoride concentration in the distribution system.
- Record well pump running times and pump cycle starts.

- Check instrumentation for proper signal input/output.
- Investigate customer complaints.
- Record threats or suspicious activity.
- Complete a daily security check.
- Inspect heater operation during winter months.
- Inspect well pumps, motors, and controls.

Weekly tasks

Tasks derived from EPA (2012, 18):

- Inspect chlorine and fluoride testing equipment.
- Clean pump house and grounds. Make sure fire hydrants (if any) are accessible.
- Record pumping rate for each well or source water pump.
- Conduct weekly security check.

Monthly tasks

Tasks derived from EPA (2012, 21):

- Read electric meter at pump house and record.
- Take appropriate monthly water quality samples.
- Check and record static and pumping levels of each well.
- Read all customer meters and compare against total water produced for the month.
- Inspect well heads.
- Lubricate locks.
- Check onsite readings against lab results.
- Confirm submittal of monthly reports.

Annual tasks

Tasks derived from EPA (2012, 24): The possible time of year for each task is provided in parentheses.

- Overhaul chemical feed pumps, such as O-rings, check valves, and diaphragms (first Monday in January).
- Inspect and clean chemical feed lines and solution tanks (first Monday in January).
- Calibrate chemical feed pumps after overhaul (first Monday in January).
- Begin safety equipment repair log. Maintain log continuously throughout the year (first Monday in January).
- Operate all valves inside the treatment plant and pump house. Maintain log continuously throughout the year (first Monday in January).
- Review emergency response plans (first Monday in January).
- Inspect chemical safety equipment and repair or replace as needed (first Monday in February).
- Operate all valves inside the treatment plant and pump house (first Monday in February).
- Inspect, clean, and repair control panels in pump house and treatment plant (first Monday in March).

- Exercise half of all mainline valves (first Monday in March).
- Inspect and clean chemical feed lines and solution tanks (first Monday in April).
- Calibrate chemical feed pumps (first Monday in April).
- Inspect storage tanks for defects and sanitary deficiencies (first Monday in May).
- Clean storage tanks if necessary (first Monday in May).
- Flush the distribution system and exercise/check all fire hydrant valves (first Monday in June).
- Perform preventive maintenance on treatment plant and pump house buildings (first Monday in June).
- Inspect and clean chemical feed lines and solution tanks (first Monday in July).
- Calibrate chemical feed pumps (first Monday in July).
- Prepare a demand forecast. Identify and evaluate energy conservation measures (for your utility).
- Identify and evaluate distribution system leaks. Establish/update water loss mitigation program.
- Establish/update customer incentive program for water-efficient home devices (first Monday in July).
- Operate all valves inside the treatment plant and pump house (first Monday in August).
- Exercise mainline valves that were not exercised in March (first Monday in September).
- Prepare system for winter operation. This task may be postponed until October or November, depending on local conditions (first Monday in September).
- Make sure unnecessary equipment is properly decommissioned (first Monday in September).
- Inspect and clean chemical feed lines and solution tanks (first Monday in October).
- Calibrate chemical feed pumps (first Monday in October).
- Prepare system for winter operation if not completed in September or October (first Monday in November).
- Contact an electrician to check running amps on well pumps (first Monday in December).

REFERENCES

EPA (US Environmental Protection Agency). 2012. *Getting Started with CUPSS: A Workbook for Users.* Washington, DC: US EPA. https://www.epa.gov/sites/production/files/2015-10/documents/gettingstartedworkbook.pdf.

EPA (US Environmental Protection Agency). 2015. "Suggested Checklist for Public Water Supply System Operation and Maintenance Manual." Washington, DC: US EPA. https://www.epa.gov/sites/production/files/documents/om_checklisttasks.pdf.

Key Legislation

Cabinet Secretary to the Treasury (Incorporation) Act (TA), Revised Edition of 1982 Act.

Constitution of Kenya 2010.

County Governments Act (CGA), no. 17 of 2012.

Draft Regulation to the Public Procurement and Asset Disposal (PPAD) Act, no. 33 of 2015.

Environmental Management and Coordination (EMC) Act 2012, Revised Edition 2012 of 1999 Act.

General Guidelines on Asset and Liability Management, National Assets and Liabilities Management Department (NALM) 2020.

Guidelines for Management of Specific Categories of Assets and Liabilities, National Assets and Liabilities Management Department (NALM) 2020.

Intergovernmental Relations (ITGR) Act, no. 2 of 2012.

Land Act (LA) 2012.

Land Laws (Amendment) Act, no. 28 of 2016.

Legal Notice (LN) no. 34: Legislative Supplement, no. 17 March 20, 2015, to the Public Finance Management Act, no. 18 of 2012.

Legal Notice (LN) no. 44: Regulation on Transition to Devolved Government (Mechanism for Closure and Transfer of Public Records and Information), Legislative Supplement no. 23, March 11, 2016.

Ministry of Finance (MoF) Circular no. 14 of 2000, October 13.

Ministry of Local Government (MLG) Circular ref. no. MLG/1333/TY/ (52), February 18, 2013.

Nairobi City County Gazette Notice no. 2101: Committee on the Nairobi City County Government Pending Bills, Appointment 2018.

Nairobi City County Strategic Plan (SP) 2015–2025.

Nairobi City County Wards Development Fund (WDF) Act 2014.

National Assets and Liabilities Management Policy. National Assets and Liabilities Management Department (NALM) 2020.

National Government Constituencies Development Fund Act 2015.

Notice 858. "Gazette Notice no. 858, January 8, 2017: Intergovernmental Relations Act no. 2 of 2012."

Notice 2701. "Gazette Notice no. 2701, March 24, 2017: Intergovernmental Relations Act no. 2 of 2012."

Notice 4370. "Gazette Notice no. 4370, May 11, 2018: Intergovernmental Relations Act no. 2 of 2012."

Physical Planning Act (PPA), Cap 286, 2012.

Public Audit Act (PAA), no. 34. of 2015.

Public Finance Management (PFM) Act, no. 18 of 2012. (Amended in 2015 by Legal Notice no. 34. Legislative Supplement no. 17, County PFM Act, March 20, 2015.)

Public Finance Management (PFM) Transition Act, no. 8 of 2013.

Public Procurement and Asset Disposal (PPAD) Act, no. 33 of 2015.

Transition Authority Circular "Inventory of Assets and Liabilities Debts and Human Resource Profile in Public Organizations." Circular Ref. no. TA/2/5 dated January 9, 2013.

Transition Authority guidelines "Handover and Takeover of Documents" Ref. MOF/IFMIS/1/41.7 March 2013.

Transition to Devolved Government (TDG) Act, no. 1 of 2012. www.kenyalaw.org.

Urban Areas and Cities (UAC) Act, no. 13 of 2011.

Urban Areas and Cities (Amendment) Act, 2019.